Delicate Subjects

DELICATE SUBJECTS

Romanticism, Gender, and the Ethics of Understanding

Julie Ellison

Cornell University Press

ITHACA AND LONDON

First published 1990 by Cornell University Press.

International Standard Book Number 0-8014-2378-3
Library of Congress Catalog Card Number 45979
Printed in the United States of America
Librarians: Library of Congress cataloging information
appears on the last page of the book.

⊛ The paper used in this publication meets the minimum requirements of the American National Standard for Permanence of Paper for Printed Library Materials Z39.48-1984.

For Mark

Contents

The fairest part of the most beautiful body will appear deformed and monstrous, if dissevered from its place in the organic Whole. Nay, on delicate subjects, where a seemingly trifling difference of more or less may constitute a difference in *kind,* even a *faithful* display of the main and supporting ideas, if yet they are separated from the forms by which they are at once clothed and modified, may perchance present a skeleton indeed; but a skeleton to alarm and deter.

—Coleridge, *Biographia Literaria*

Preface

Although I have never thought of "romanticism" as more than a confession of critical temper and an occasion for historical questions, in the course of writing this book I have come to rely on it with increased ambivalence. My faith in romanticism has diminished, for obvious reasons. First, literary historians continue to push back the heyday of romantic subjects, subject matters, and forms to a far earlier date than "the romantic period" can accommodate, leaving us with the problem of discerning what, if anything, is particular to it. Second, writers (especially women writers) and kinds of writing are being brought to the fore in numbers that explode received romantic canons.

But I have retained the term "romanticism," nonetheless, as particularized but more inclusive scholarship has brought us to the point where Arthur O. Lovejoy's notion of "romanticisms" ("On the Discrimination of Romanticisms," 1924) can be revived in an altered context. The plurality of romanticisms derives not only from the dissolving of chronological barriers and reintroduction of certain eighteenth- and nineteenth-century texts, but also from the way that romantic philosophy was disseminated throughout Europe and the United States. The texts that we call romantic invoke philosophical generality on their own behalf—usually as "Reason"—and consequently acquire an analogical resemblance to one another. This habit of reference to forms of post-Kantian idealism, in quite different local circumstances, generates sufficient textual linkages to justify retaining the rubric of romanticism. The history of criticism subsequently reproduces the contextual differences of romantic literatures. For if there are many romanticisms in the eighteenth and nineteenth centuries, the strategies for remembering or even antagonizing these romanticisms are equally variable, equally specific. Interpretive genealogies operate through the critical styles of the present: an ongoing, if modified, deconstructive practice; the agon of critical personality; surprisingly affect-laden postmodernisms; feminist theories with their skeptical resistance to sublimity and revaluing of sentiment; antitranscendental historicism. Although it proved impossible both to work closely with eighteenth- and nineteenth-century writings and to trace in a detailed way the history of the reception accorded to these manifold approaches, I have tried to make selectively apparent the key differences and redundancies of several strains of critical response.

The shift to more diverse views of romanticism puts us in a position to be more precise about the relationship between the two other key terms in my title, "gender" and "understanding." The specific interaction of these two terms, in the end, defines what I mean by romanticism in this book. A linked set of three premises organizes the work: that gender is the site of self-consciousness about understanding, that theories of understanding are the site for reflection on interpretive ethics, and that ethical discourse is the site of gender awareness. For the romantic subject of either gender, the feminine stereotype (not surprisingly) is associated with the receptive attitude in which understanding is accomplished. Narratives of social and domestic life become utopias of comprehension. At the same time, analysis, method, logic, and system-formation take on a mixed ethical character. These modes of thought are felt both to produce the "beautiful body" of the "Whole" (to refer to my epigraph from Samuel Taylor Coleridge's *Biographia Literaria*) and to do violence to it. Analysis and its associated procedures carry out a gothic transformation of the feminine body of understanding that leaves it "deformed and monstrous," "a skeleton to alarm and deter." The "delicate subject," then, is a conflation of subject matter that requires precise intuition and the womanly organism or system of such divinatory judgments once completed. In Coleridge's typically drastic but nonetheless representative version of ethical anxiety, idealism strives to become feminine. But in the process, it encounters the grotesque image of reason inherent in feminine understanding and exposed by analytical excess. Classifications according to "kind," therefore, cause intuition to be ambivalently regarded.

My choice of writers was the result, as must usually be the case, of critical positions operating on personal tastes and exposures, including my previous work on Ralph Waldo Emerson. Emerson, with his tolerance for antagonism, was a productive foil to my present subjects—Friedrich Daniel Ernst Schleiermacher, Coleridge, and Margaret Fuller—chosen because of their demonstrable unease in the face of intellectual aggression. The selection of Schleiermacher, Coleridge, and Fuller has in fact provided the combination of situational differences and common obsessions which I was seeking. Though relatively unfamiliar to Anglo-American literary scholars, Schleiermacher, the "founder," as he is always called, of hermeneutic philosophy, is of particular interest because his hermeneutic innovations followed his participation in the literary and erotic discourses of late eighteenth-century Berlin. The self-consciously "romantic" and subjective style of his early writings exposes the gendered structure of understanding which is mostly suppressed in the later hermeneutic manuscripts.

In Schleiermacher's lecture notes and academic lectures on hermeneutics, system comes to the fore. The artistic and feminine qualities of understanding are restricted to one quadrant of the diagram of hermeneutic strategies. And the term "divination," with which these qualities are linked, is sufficiently doubted to make necessary an alternate route to understanding. A peculiar redundancy is brought about by the fact that spontaneous divination needs to be verified by the labor of comparison. My readings of the texts of recent hermeneutic philosophy open up the paradoxical situation of a theoretical enterprise in which the feminine is repressed and divination renovated.

Coleridge was a virtually inevitable choice in this book, mostly because he takes interpretive anxieties to a point of almost pathological expression. In the process, misgivings that are widespread but often tacit in critical culture attain a useful degree of overtness. Like Schleiermacher's friendships with Henriette Herz, a prominent Jewish salonière, and Friedrich Schlegel, Coleridge's relationships with the women in Wordsworth's domestic circle and with Wordsworth himself exhibit fluctuations in pathos, competitiveness, and dependency which are written into his theoretical allegories of understanding. Coleridge compulsively attaches the question of understanding to techniques of classification. He identifies aspects of understanding with particular genres and then proceeds to dramatize ethical and political tendencies in terms of these generic relations. This habit of mind accounts for the methodological asymmetry of the middle section of this book, where my study of understanding becomes, for a time, the study of critical prose itself as an element in Coleridge's code of literary ethics.

Coleridge's poetry of the mid-1790s is organized by the mutual dependence of fantasies of rural domesticity and national prospect. During this period, his polemical prose veers between tones of assault and good will. After this early phase the relationships among content, voice, and genre alter. Coleridge's subsequent prose texts cast out the feminine in an effort to construct the discourse of "Method." His poetry loses its political orientation but remains the place where speakers long for familial nurture and imagine its vicarious fulfillment or demonic inversion. The wish for vicarious gratification, in poems written throughout Coleridge's career, produces stories of self-exclusion. And these lead, in his critical writings, to distinctions and oppositions that serve retaliatory aggression.

Coleridge increasingly merges Jacobin journalism, anonymous reviewers, and novel-reading into the figure of the saboteur of the family sanctuary. *Biographia Literaria,* as a memoir and defense of Wordsworth and as an *ars poetica,* develops an ambivalent view of understanding under these perceived conditions of cultural siege. Coleridge describes his first readings of Wordsworth's poetry as proceeding from a moment of intuition followed by the activity of critical distinction. This sequence is duplicated in his attraction to the women of Wordsworth's writerly household, a temptation countered by a determined effort to repel Wordsworth from the domain of criticism. In *The Friend* Coleridge's critical prose is constituted even more overtly through gendered allegories of exclusion. He expels the feminine, often with considerable violence, as part of the series of negative metonyms which includes radical politics and loose talk. The feminine is still invoked in *The Friend* as the form of spontaneous receptivity, but more characteristic are the episodes in which the excluded feminine returns in troublesome and guilt-inducing ways. Coleridge's "Essays on the Principles of Method" points toward the displacement of feminine understanding by a philosophy of fraternal forgiveness. By the time he writes *Confessions of an Inquiring Spirit* in the mid-1820s, a hypothetical church has become the agency of inclusion and wholeness. As the object of the unqualified mercy bestowed by this spiritual community, Coleridge can feel almost wholly unambivalent.

Margaret Fuller took on an inevitability of her own in this project. Like many nineteenth-century American intellectuals, she encountered German romanticism as a potential identity or vocation—as the career of "Critic." She works within romantic hopes even as she frames them with an ironic mastery of social realism worthy of Jane Austen; she articulates romantic values while she bestows on aggression an honorific status. More crucially, she introduces self-consciousness about gender into the project of understanding, where the feminine had resided mostly unchallenged and apparently naturalized.

To describe the structure of Fuller's ironic social *reportage* and its usefulness as a frame for her romantic vocation as critic and scholar, I begin with a reading of her remarkable early letters. The letters introduce us to the emerging figure of the "Interpreter," the embodied voice of silent participants in the drama of expression. The "Interpreter" becomes feminine in the sentimental economy of the Conversations for women held by Fuller in the early 1840s. Accounts of the Conversations reveal the extent to which Fuller both feminizes intuition and insists on her right to abstract logic and rational aggression. Completed shortly after the Conversations, *Woman in the Nineteenth Century* argues for a complex view of feminist understanding which demands both a divinatory mystique and the full repertoire of analytical distinction. Fuller's drama of feminist ethics is played out largely through allusive structures that transform literary history into a serial reflection of feminist desire. But the content of Fuller's catalog of "signs of the times" suggests that restraining aggression within inherited literary culture and within socially acceptable behavior exacts a price. The cost of such inhibition surfaces in themes of self-discipline, refuge, and victimage.

Some recent readers of Fuller have maintained that romantic subjectivity yields, once she leaves Boston for New York and then Europe, to a more politicized perspective in which socioeconomic categories displace individuals. This is a view I dispute in my readings of Fuller's letters to the New York *Tribune* during the Roman Revolution of 1848–49. In these essays and in her private correspondence the feminine alliance of Fuller with the city of Rome itself leads to the identification of mourning with history writing. But the radicalism made possible by this series of associations operates wholly *within* romanticism, within the habit of referring political sensation to the interpretive theater of the observing mind.

Appropriately enough, for a book about several romantic traditions, this project was carried out with the support of many and varied professional friendships. The early interest of my colleagues at the University of Michigan, Ingo Seidler and Terrence Tice, was encouraging at a time when my ideas were hazy and tentative; the latter continued to assist in revisions of the Schleiermacher chapters until the very last minute. The help of Anne Herrmann and her work in feminist theory made a significant difference at several junctures, as did the conversation of Susan Carlton and the responses of Joel Weinsheimer. Tobin Siebers became an even closer friend while acting as one of this project's ongoing consultants. Tilottama Rajan and Lawrence Buell offered cogent suggestions for revision.

I am indebted to the National Endowment for the Humanities for a fellowship in 1987; to the University of Michigan College of Literature, Science, and the Arts for additional support during the same period; and to my own department for a term off in the early phases of the book. Versions of two sections of the manuscript have appeared elsewhere: parts of Chapter 6 as "Rousseau in the Text of Coleridge: The Ghost-Dance of History," in *Studies in Romanticism* 28 (1989) and, also from Chapter 6, "The Daughter of Logic: Coleridge's 'Essays on the Principles of Method,'" in *Prose Studies* 12 (1989), which is reprinted by permission from and published by Frank Cass & Co. Ltd, 11 Gainsborough Road, London E11 1RS. I thank the editors for permission to reprint these essays in revised versions here.

Grateful acknowledgment is extended to Little, Brown, and Company, Inc., for permission to reprint passages from Ellen Conford, *Felicia the Critic* (1973) and to Harper & Row, Publishers, Inc., for permission to reprint passages from Louise Fitzhugh, *Harriet the Spy* (1964), copyright © 1964 by Louise Fitzhugh. I also thank Scholars' Press for permission to reprint excerpts from Schleiermacher's *Hermeneutics: The Handwritten Manuscripts,* ed. Heinz Kimmerle, trans. James Duke and Jack Forstman (1977); Edwin Mellen Press for permission to cite the forthcoming translation of Schleiermacher's *Monologen* by Terrence Tice; and Princeton University Press and Routledge & Kegan Paul Ltd. for permission to reprint excerpts from the following publications: *The Collected Works of Samuel Taylor Coleridge,* ed. Kathleen Coburn and Bart Winer, Bollingen Series 75, Volume 1, *Lectures 1795: On Politics and Religion,* ed. Lewis Patton and Peter Mann (1970), copyright © 1971 by Princeton University Press; Volume 4, *The Friend,* ed. Barbara E. Rooke (1969), copyright © 1969 by Princeton University Press; and Volume 7, *Biographia Literaria* (Vols. I and II), ed. James Engell and W. Jackson Bate (1983), copyright © 1983 by Princeton University Press. I am grateful to the Chicago Historical Society for permission to quote Margaret Fuller's letter of 30 March 1830 to Amelia Greenwood, now in the society's collection. It is a pleasure to thank Joanne Leonard for permission to reprint the cover photo, "Romanticism Is Ultimately Fatal."

Bernhard Kendler and Kay Scheuer of Cornell University Press and

copy editor Kim Vivier handled the manuscript with gratifying atten-
tiveness.

Finally, I thank my husband, Mark Creekmore, the connoisseur of
the domestic sublime to whom this book is dedicated, and also my
son, Peter Ellison Creekmore. In the course of this project both of
them became expert enough in the familial possibilities of understanding to raid my office often, shouting, "Can you read me?"

JULIE ELLISON

Ann Arbor, Michigan

Translations and Abbreviations

Where a reliable English translation exists, I have used it, in some cases with supplementary references to original texts. The translations of Schleiermacher's letters and the *Confidential Letters on Lucinde* are mine; those of the *Soliloquies* are from the manuscript of Terrence Tice's forthcoming translation of that work to be published by Edwin Mellen Press. When Schleiermacher's letters appear in both the old and new editions of his correspondence, to the extent that the latter is available, I have cited both sources.

PART I. SCHLEIERMACHER

BO   *Brief Outline of the Study of Theology*. Trans. Terrence Tice. Richmond: John Knox Press, 1966.

BR   *Aus Schleiermachers Leben in Briefen*. 4 vols. Ed. Ludwig Jonas and Wilhelm Dilthey. Berlin, 1858–63.

BW   *Briefwechsel 1775–1796*. 2 vols. Ed. Andreas Arndt and Wolfgang Virmond. KGA V.1, V.2. 1985, 1988.

BZ   *Schriften aus der Berliner Zeit 1796–1799*. Ed. Gunter Meckenstock. KGA I.2. 1984.

H   *Hermeneutik: Nach den Handschriften*. Ed. Hans Kimmerle. Heidelberg: Carl Winter, Universität-verlag, 1974.

HM   *Hermeneutics: The Handwritten Manuscripts*. Ed. Heinz Kimmerle. Trans. James Duke and Jack Forstman. Missoula, Mont.: Scholars Press for The American Academy of Religion, 1977.

KD   *Kurze Darstellung des theologischen Studiums zum Behuf einleitender Vorlesungen entworfen*. SW I.1. 1843.

KGA   *Kritische Gesamtausgabe.* 7 vols. to date. Berlin, New York: de Gruyter, 1980–.

L   Schlegel, Friedrich. *Lucinde* in *Dichtungen.* Ed. Hans Eichner. Munich: Schöningh, 1962.

LF   ———. *Friedrich Schlegel's Lucinde and the Fragments.* Trans. Peter Firchow. Minneapolis: University of Minnesota Press, 1971.

M   *Monologen: Eine Neujahrsgabe [Soliloquies].* Kritische Ausgabe. Ed. Friedrich M. Schiele. Leipzig: A. von Hermann Mulert, 1914.

OR   *On Religion: Addresses in Response to Its Cultured Critics.* Trans. Terrence Tice. Richmond: John Knox Press, 1969.

SW   *Schleiermachers Sämmtliche Werke.* 31 vols. Berlin: G. Reimer, 1834–64.

UR   *Über die Religion: Reden an die Gebildeten unter ihren Verächtern.* Ed. Georg C. B. Punyer. Braunschweig: E. U. Schwetschke, 1879.

VB   *Vertraute Briefe über Friedrich Schlegels Lucinde [Confidential Letters on . . . Lucinde].* SW III.1. 1846.

PART II. COLERIDGE

BL   *Biographia Literaria.* 1 vol., 2 parts. Ed. James Engell and Walter Jackson Bate. CC VII. 1983.

CC   *The Collected Works of Samuel Taylor Coleridge.* Bollingen Series 75. 16 vols. London: Routledge & Kegan Paul; Princeton: Princeton University Press, 1969–.

CIS   *Confessions of an Inquiring Spirit.* Ed. H. StJ. Hart. Stanford, Calif.: Stanford University Press, 1956.

F   *The Friend.* 2 vols. Ed. Barbara E. Rooke. CC IV. 1969.

LPR   *Lectures 1795: On Politics and Religion.* Ed. Lewis Patton and Peter Mann. CC I. 1971.

LS   *Lay Sermons.* Ed. R. J. White. CC VI. 1972.

N   *The Notebooks of Samuel Taylor Coleridge.* 3 vols. Ed. Kathleen Coburn. Vols. 1 and 2, New York: Pantheon, 1957, 1961; Vol. 3, Princeton: Princeton University Press, 1973.

PW   *Poetical Works.* Ed. Ernest Hartley Coleridge. New York: Oxford University Press, 1912.

W   *The Watchman.* Ed. Lewis Patton. CC II. 1970.

PART III. FULLER

CHD   (Healey) Dall, Caroline Wells. *Margaret and Her Friends.* Boston: Roberts Brothers, 1895.

EAL   *Essays on American Life and Letters.* Ed. Joel Myerson. Schenectady, N.Y.: College & University Press, 1978.

LMF   *The Letters of Margaret Fuller.* 5 vols. Ed. Robert N. Hudspeth. Ithaca: Cornell University Press, 1983–.

MMF   *Memoirs of Margaret Fuller Ossoli.* 2 vols. Ed. R. W. Emerson, W. H. Channing, and J. F. Clarke. Boston: Phillips, Sampson, and Co., 1852.

NYT   New York *Tribune* 1846–50 [microfilm].

SEC   "A Short Essay on Critics." EAL 51–57.

WNC   *Woman in the Nineteenth Century.* EAL 82–239.

Delicate Subjects

Introduction:
Constructive Criticism

In two contemporary books for preteen girls, *Harriet the Spy* by Louise Fitzhugh and *Felicia the Critic* by Ellen Conford, we find succinct narratives of critical aggression.[1] If one requires evidence that romantic anxieties about writing, ethics, and gender still actively enter into the most broadly shared views of literary culture, one may find it in the common plot of these stories.

The protagonist is a critical girl of ten or eleven who devotes herself energetically to the project of writing. Through this identity she negotiates the protocol of antagonism in the world of junior high, where popularity is the most acceptable form of dominance. Felicia's writing begins at the suggestion of her mother, who proposes that she turn her gift for negativity to good use by becoming a "constructive critic." Maternal anxiety about the hurtful character of "destructive" criticism is palpable, a version of the discomfort expressed so often in undergraduate classrooms over the "dissection" of poetry ("you just tear something apart"):

---

[1] A memorable excursion into the children's section of an Ann Arbor bookstore provoked my then-colleague Margot Norris to introduce me to *Harriet the Spy*. *Felicia the Critic* appeared in my Christmas stocking with an inscription from my spouse: "To Julie, a Constructive Critic." Louise Fitzhugh, *Harriet the Spy* (New York: Dell, 1964); Ellen Conford, *Felicia the Critic* (New York: Pocket Books, 1973).

"Constructive criticism?"

"Instead of saying, 'This is lousy, this is lousy and this is lousy,' you point out how it could be better. See, constructive criticism is helpful. If you just tear something apart, you're being *de*structive. But if you show how it could be made better or done better, you're being *con*structive. And that's a very valuable talent to have, to be able to be a constructive critic."[2]

The documents of aggression inevitably fall into the wrong hands— that is to say, the hands of those criticized. Harriet tries to keep her notebook secret; Felicia delivers her notes to her victims in person. Both girls are confronted with the social and psychological price exacted by the pleasures of critical violence. The plot summary on the back cover of *Harriet the Spy* captures the crisis atmosphere of these moments:

Harriet the Spy has a secret notebook that she fills with utterly honest jottings about her parents, her classmates, and her neighbors. Every day on her spy route she "observes" and notes down anything of interest to her:

I BET THAT LADY WITH THE CROSS-EYE LOOKS IN THE MIRROR AND JUST FEELS TERRIBLE.

PINKY WHITEHEAD WILL NEVER CHANGE. DOES HIS MOTHER HATE HIM? IF I HAD HIM I'D HATE HIM.

IF MARION HAWTHORNE DOESN'T WATCH OUT SHE'S GOING TO GROW UP INTO A LADY HITLER.

But when Harriet's notebook is found by her schoolmates, their anger and retaliation and Harriet's unexpected responses explode in a hilarious way.

The theme of ostracism is worked out in both stories in the classic manner: the protagonist's friends form a club from which she is excluded or one for which the price of admission is censorship. Felicia is forbidden to indulge in criticism, constructive or otherwise, a ploy that backfires to her advantage:

"Why didn't someone *think?*" Phyllis cried dramatically. . . .

[2]Conford, *Felicia the Critic*, 20.

Suddenly their heads turned toward Felicia. She was startled as she saw the accusing looks on their faces. She cast her eyes downward into her cocoa cup.

"Felicia," Phyllis began slowly, "you're always criticizing everything. Why didn't you think up all the things that could go wrong *this* time?" . . . .

"I was going to tell you," she began slowly, "but I promised not to say anything. Cheryl told me I had to not criticize anything if I wanted to be in the club."

Truth-telling has its rewards, although here they are not very convincing. Felicia's status in the group rises as she is defended by her one ally. When the book ends a few pages later, she is offering "a couple of suggestions" to the president of the United States "to help you run the country a little better."[3]

It is hard to imagine confronting the dilemmas of critical ethics with less equivocation. These books make explicit the anxiety about cruelty to human beings which produces the concern, among critics and writers, about "doing violence to the text." Writing is painful in both stories. Although Felicia is already notorious for her verbal criticisms, the missives composed after she enters on her vocation as "constructive critic" are far more hurtful. And Harriet's notebook exists almost exclusively to receive the invective she censures in her speech. "Ole Golly," Harriet's former nurse, writes her a letter in the midst of the hypochondria and dread induced by the exposure of her notebook. Like the scene in which Felicia's mother presents her with the idea of a vocation, this is a moment of election in which the difference between love and truth, and the priority of the former, are delivered to the aspirant as the conditions of authorship:

Naturally, you put down the truth in your notebooks. What would be the point if you didn't? And naturally those notebooks should not be read by anyone else, *but if they are,* then, Harriet, you are going to have to do two things, and you don't like either one of them:
1) You have to apologize
2) You have to lie.
Otherwise you are going to lose a friend. Little lies that make people feel better are not bad, like thanking someone for a meal they made even if you hated it, or telling a sick person they look better when they

[3]Ibid., 146–47, 150.

don't. . . . Remember that writing is to put love in the world, not to use against your friends. But to yourself you must always tell the truth.

You're eleven years old which is old enough to get busy at growing up to be the person you want to be.[4]

Harriet neither lies nor apologizes, although she does refrain from notebook entries that degrade her friends. Instead, she goes public, drawing on the collective fascination of her classmates with each other's dirty secrets and with moral evaluation. Harriet's parents, teachers, and psychologist conspire to appoint her editor of the sixth-grade paper. She composes items like the following:

JANIE GIBBS HAS WON HER BATTLE. THIS SHOULD BE A LESSON TO ALL OF YOU IN COURAGE AND DETERMINATION. IF YOU DON'T KNOW WHAT I'M TALKING ABOUT, THEN ASK HER.

JACK PETERS (LAURA PETERS' FATHER) WAS STONED OUT OF HIS MIND AT THE PETERS' PARTY LAST SATURDAY NIGHT. MILLY ANDREWS (CARRIE ANDREWS' MOTHER) JUST SMILED AT HIM LIKE AN IDIOT.

"During the ensuing weeks" new entries along the same lines "held the class enthralled." If journalism sanctions critical aggression, so does fiction. Outside of school Harriet turns "spying" into the raw material of narrative. She appropriates her father's typewriter and begins to compose a story for the *New Yorker*. The next entry in her notebook reads, "I AM GOING TO WRITE A STORY ABOUT THESE PEOPLE. THEY ARE JUST BATS. HALF OF THEM DON'T EVEN HAVE A PROFESSION."[5]

The late-twentieth-century "profession" imagined by Harriet and Felicia (compounded of the gossip columnist, the book reviewer, the political reformer, and the novelist) is a far cry from the professions available to Margaret Fuller in the 1830s and is even more remote from the vocational environments of Coleridge or Schleiermacher. These three writers, my principal subjects, attempt to describe the ethical qualities of criticism during the early institutionalization of the modern critical profession in the university, the periodical, and the newspaper.

---

[4]Fitzhugh, *Harriet the Spy*, 275–76.

[5]Ibid., 288, 278. The one professional novelist Harriet knows, the suddenly successful father of her friend Sport, is sometimes gloomy but never aggressive. On the whole, he is "a nice-looking man with laughing eyes like Sport and funny hair that fell over his eyes" (261).

They do not illuminate the far earlier moments when criticism was first defined as transgression but mark a later point at which the perpetuation of this notion becomes nervously explicit. The stories of Harriet and Felicia, therefore, capture a remarkably persistent set of beliefs about criticism with all the clarity bestowed by preadolescent stereotypes.

According to these convictions, which express both popular misgivings and the critical profession's own crises of conscience, the critic is one who states painful truths, provoking anxiety and retaliation. In *Harriet the Spy* and *Felicia the Critic* the anxiety is expressed most of all by maternal figures whose task it is to explain that criticism hurts. Ambivalence about the ethics of logical truth-telling is dramatized through representations of gender, while gender is exposed through the double binds of criticism. The girl who wants to criticize violates the morality of her mother, whose expertise in the realm of manners and domestic relations makes her sensitive to all such transgressions. Even more painful is the fact that criticism costs the critic her girlfriends. The tension between the "profession" of critic and the ethic of sensibility culturally bound to the feminine is played out with gratifying, if bleak, economy.

Margaret Fuller is the first American theorist of the predicament in which Harriet and Felicia find themselves. She reflects on feminine subjectivity as the experience of conflict between the critical passion and the passion for intimacy. In the writings of Coleridge and Schleiermacher, we encounter the configurations Fuller apprehended and changed, but ones that have nonetheless persisted in the chronicles of literary criticism and philosophy.

For Coleridge and Schleiermacher criticism and the related acts of understanding and interpretation are associated, as they will be for the next two hundred years, with the risk of violence, pain, discord, and reduction. In England, by the late eighteenth century, a vernacular literature of secular opinion and the means for its distribution were well developed—developed to the point where theories of understanding need to be approached through the specific economy of critical texts, that is, through the question of genre. It is going too far to say that, by 1800, debates over the proper conduct of criticism and discourses on the place of critical prose in relation to popular genres are identical, but the two enterprises—theorizing interpretation while giving it a precise cultural position in a specific kind of text—are inseparable. The negativity of prose was firmly established in the essay, the review, the pamphlet, the editorial, the lecture series, and the literary life. The genres of criticism were by no means the only cultural symptom of concerns about analytical violence, but they formed a setting in which the awareness of such violence became particularly acute. In the years of and after the French Revolution the political subject was caught between spectacles of inspiration and the material threat of official violence; caught also between the quasi-feminine hysteria of Rousseau and its analytical correction. At the same time that the feminine was linked with political instability, it was becoming psychologically and morally idealized. Religion and nature, the emerging domains of interiority, were increasingly feminized as ethical sanctuaries. Coleridge's prose and poetry construct the theorist of this uncomfortable milieu.

The configuration of critical thought in Germany in the 1790s was thematically similar if institutionally different. In the German Protestant tradition the risks of criticism had been felt first in the arena of the higher criticism and contiguous philological and theological disciplines. Like all European interpretive environments in the eighteenth century, this one wavered among the temptations of historical demystification; the defensive clustering of faith, peace, and community; and the literary empowerment of the reader, who becomes the text's unifying agent. As in England, romantic subjectivity was theorized through the idea of the text as both whole and fragment—ample evidence that there never was a time when the subject was available as a category and not in a state of crisis. The structural and thematic analogies between representations of the self and representations of texts should not, therefore, surprise us. Anxiety about the self-conscious individual, about the texts written by such individuals, and about understanding, in which text and subject meet, makes the hypersystematic constructions of romantic philosophy both desirable and suspect. Kant's massive delineations, the structural ambitions of Jacobi and Schelling, and the crucial figure of the romantic Spinoza were perceived by the early German romantics as dubiously heroic manifestations of the rational will. For Schleiermacher's generation, system formation itself was an ethical issue. Romantic criticism and interpretation theory were partly constituted in resistance to methodological excess or in the interests of systems modeled on the mind or body of the living subject. Hence Schleiermacher's investment in the phenomenology of mood, the erotics of fragmentation and heterogeneity, and the circular intuitions of hermeneutics. The discourse of the Berlin romantics descends from the male characters of Goethe, who conflate their own capacity for pathos with the feminine in both woman and nature. This tendency, mediated by the Berlin salons, produced femininity as a social tone in the "dialogue of love" (OR 211).

Common to all of these settings, then, are theories of understanding in which gender and ethics impinge on one another in variable resistance to "the rhetoric of violence." Reviewing the way in which this notion has developed over the last decade, Teresa de Lauretis enumerates the steps by which we have come to debate whether language itself is a violent category:

> The very notion of a "rhetoric of violence" . . . presupposes that some order of language, some kind of discursive representation is at work not only in the concept "violence" but in the social practices of violence as well. The (semiotic) relation of the social to the discursive is thus posed from the start. But once that relation is instated, once a connection is assumed between violence and rhetoric, the two terms begin to slide, and, soon enough, the connection will appear to be reversible. From the Foucauldian notion of a rhetoric of violence, an order of language which speaks violence—names certain behaviors and events as violent, but not others, and constructs objects and subjects of violence, and hence violence as a social fact—it is easy to slide into the reverse notion of a language which, itself, produces violence.

The association of language with violence has been theorized concurrently with the critique by feminists and others of the particular qualities of scientific and philosophical languages—languages that are abstract, systematic, and methodologically reflexive. In both projects the unequivocal assertion of de Lauretis holds true: "the representation of violence is inseparable from the notion of gender," or, even more succinctly, "violence is engendered in representation."[6] Inevitably, the construction of nonviolence likewise occurs within and through the history of gender. Indeed, the tendency of our present theoretical moment to reexperience philosophical language as both violent and masculine is one of its more romantic attributes.

Because so many of the metaphors in these traditions emerge in binary formulations, it is important to grasp the ways in which the feminine doubles, repeats, and parallels what appears to be opposed to it. The divinatory alternative to effortful analysis, for example, has to be read as a supplement to as well as an attack on method. The privacy of

[6]Teresa de Lauretis, *Technologies of Gender* (Bloomington: Indiana University Press, 1987), 32–33.

the home, drawing room, or personal letter supports the scholar's labors and helps him recover from their alienating effects but also forms part of labor's compensation. Feminine understanding frequently leads to the same conclusion as analysis or forms the context in which logic is nurtured. The virtues of the feminine community are sanctified within and by philosophy. Indeed, it is because metaphors of gender are historically attached to philosophical idealism that a comparative study of this kind is possible, for the romantic redefinition of reason and understanding has a peculiar historical status. Ideas of philosophical transcendence functioned in local situations—such as the Wordsworth circle or the Boston Transcendentalists—for local cultural ends. Romantic philosophical criticism was a unifying discourse introjected by different historical environments. As though the very exteriority or abstractness of philosophical idealism fitted it for conflict, the transcendental impulse was repeatedly perceived by advocates and skeptics alike as a vehicle for antagonism. This typology fueled the need for nonviolent conceptual styles.

Perhaps the crux of our unresolved ambivalence about romanticism is the ethical problem of how aggressive or receptive to be toward romanticism itself. In Part I, after exploring Schleiermacher's restructuring and renaming of the feminine in his hermeneutic theory, I turn to the treatment of Schleiermacher by twentieth-century hermeneutic philosophers. The process, apparent in Schleiermacher's manuscripts, of suppressing the feminine aspect of understanding is carried to its logical conclusions in the works of Gadamer and Ricoeur, where Schleiermacher's analysis of language is embraced, his divinatory tendencies are rejected, and the link between divination and the feminine is forgotten. When I bring to bear on philosophical hermeneutics feminist theorists of a similar ethics of speech communities among women, this gesture in turn raises the question of the romantic provenance of this feminist metaphor.

In the context of Coleridge studies, debate about ethics, politics, and even (lately) gender is so abundant as to make these issues both more accessible and more perplexed. It draws us down a speculative path shaped by the history of responses to Coleridge played out in terms of love, guilt, and political apostasy. It carries us, therefore, into the field of inquiry defined most recently by the term "romantic ideology," that is, into the most recent episode of the academy's love-hate relationship with romantic texts. Polemicized by Jerome McGann, the critique of Anglo-American "romantic ideology," aimed especially at the theoretical defense of romanticism since the 1960s, updates the charge of romantic apostasy or the betrayal of an avowed social vision. I am clearly much in sympathy with the historicizing energy that places romantic texts within the dense textures of social life. But in spite of the excellence of work done in this regard, some of which I rely on heavily, I have misgivings about its theoretical basis.

McGann wants the contemporary reader of romantic texts to put the past firmly in its place, regardless of the history of subsequent critical identifications with it. In order to free oneself from romantic ideology, according to his program, one would have to practice criticism from a position of "alienated vantage." Recognizing our difference from romanticism has the therapeutic effect, argues McGann, of preserving us from transcendental contagion while allowing us to "observe as well our own ways of thinking and feeling from an alien point of view."[7] By so fully renouncing curiosity about the periodic impulse to identify with romanticism, McGann loses patience with the recurring confusions of language, ethics, and feeling which the contemporary study of romanticism has sanctioned. In the context of the ethical concerns of recent criticism and the theoretical revival of subjectivity, we need to tolerate romanticism long enough to think about philosophical criticism as more than the simple repression of sociohistorical specificity.[8] Romantic critical texts promote, supplement, and chastise perceived ideologies, and our response to them has to reflect our own similarly mixed motives.

Insofar as Fuller herself seeks to describe the relationships among gender, ethics, and the subject, the task of mediating between romanticism and feminism is far easier in the final portion of this book. In a field where much of the significant recent work is feminist, we can

[7]Jerome J. McGann, *The Romantic Ideology: A Critical Investigation* (Chicago: University of Chicago Press, 1983), 66. Marjorie Levinson operates energetically if cantankerously within McGann's program in *Wordsworth's Great Period Poems* (Cambridge: Cambridge University Press, 1986), as does Jon Klancher in a book from which I have learned a great deal, *The Making of English Reading Audiences (1790–1832)* (Madison: University of Wisconsin Press, 1987). Eric Cheyfitz, although writing in advance of McGann, argues from a similar position in *The Trans-Parent: Sexual Politics in the Language of Emerson* (Baltimore: Johns Hopkins University Press, 1981). Frances Ferguson wittily evaluates McGann's tendency to hypostasize the human in "Historicism, Deconstruction, and Wordsworth," *Diacritics* 17 (Winter 1987): 32–43.

[8]The return of the subject to theoretical legitimacy can be seen, for example, in Frederic Jameson, "Postmodernism, or the Cultural Logic of Late Capitalism," *New Left Review* no. 146 (July/August 1984): 63, 90–92; in Julia Kristeva, *Revolution in Poetic Language,* trans. Margaret Waller, intro. Leon S. Roudiez (New York: Columbia University Press, 1984); and in Paul Smith, *Discerning the Subject* (Minneapolis: University of Minnesota Press, 1988).

engage the question of Fuller's romanticism from a position already within the critique of gender. The most influential feminist readings of Fuller's authorial career equate her relation to Transcendentalism with the romanticism that, it is believed, she outgrew when she left Boston for New York, the *Dial* for the New York *Tribune,* and philosophical criticism for politics. The resonant coincidence in Italy of her involvement in the Roman Revolution and the birth of her son provides an inviting image of radical maternity which has seemed to confirm Fuller's healthy turn from romanticism to leftist activism.

It is precisely the disjunction between feminism and romanticism assumed by this view of Fuller's work which I argue against in Chapters 7 and 8. Whatever changes from one phase of her life to another, it is not the romantic. The conceptual imperative of spiritual laws, the value of subjective impressions, the idealistic analysis of history, and the belief in the social value of myth persist from the letters of her late teens to descriptions of the Italian Revolution written shortly before her death.

Within Fuller's aspiring arguments, a more particular concern with the ethics of the feminine is no less bound up with romantic genealogies. As Fuller measures the degree of aggressiveness appropriate to the feminist critic, we can see her surprisingly explicit need for social integration and her acceptance of middle-class manners. Her firm grasp of the material context of the romantic individual produces a powerful realism that sees in fantasy no contradiction to itself. Within this frame of social necessity, Fuller presents her aggrandizing theory of sexual difference, in which a binary view of gender becomes the logical basis for her "both . . . and" demands. She claims for women not only the sublime gratifications of masculine reflection but also their projected other, the divinatory sympathy of the romantic feminine; and she claims, furthermore, the social autonomy of nineteenth-century middle-class males as well as the domestic expertise of middle-class women. It is certainly Fuller's realistic strain that has lent support to the view that at some point she went beyond romanticism. But insofar as her realism supplements or enlarges her notion of desirable subjectivity without undercutting it, pragmatism arises within the ethics of idealism, or vice versa.

What is the place of gender, then, within a theory of romanticism? What is the place of romanticism within a theory of gender? In romantic texts gender ideology becomes apparent in the theme of love and in the importance of affect or mood. For it is the language of mood—to speak from within the wishful thinking of romantic poetry, poetics, and hermeneutics—that is interpreted by love's cognitive faculty, divination. The key terms of romantic poetics—the sublime, the haunted, the grotesque, the sentimental, the ironic, memory, desire, imagination—are accompanied by the demand to be understood intuitively.

Intuition is marked as a feminine quality, just as most objects of romantic longing are, including childhood, nature, and the demonic. The invention of the romantic subject as the hero of desire is therefore wholly bound up with the feminine. At the same time, romantic writers suspect that desire may be a form of power, understanding a form of science, and woman a form of sabotage. Objects of desire are lost or violated in ambivalent allegories of the domestic and the maternal. Ultimately, the feminine becomes, first, wholly figurative or non-referential and then invisible. When a feminist critique is brought to bear on the languages of such longing, as it is in much of this book, romanticism is exposed as a partial or false account of the periods it claims to dominate.

But what of the place of romanticism in a theory of gender? Feminist theory has exhibited sustained dislike for the romantic. Nonetheless, feminism and romanticism share an anxiety about aggression and violence; a critique of authority; a commitment to the cognitive validity of feeling and atmosphere; an identification with the victim; an intrigue with the construction and deconstruction of subjectivity. Both psychoanalysis and Marxism, the most prestigious influences within feminist theory, have a romantic prehistory that is powerfully revised but not negated by feminist thinkers. Given this large and endlessly disputable common ground, can one say that feminism is not romantic? Or that a feminist ethics is not descended from the gendered figurations of romantic criticism?

Cora Kaplan has summarized with energetic concision the way in which literary romanticism, Anglo-American political radicalism, the critique of sexual difference, and the psychological subject emerge in related configurations during the 1790s, only to be divided during the nineteenth century as socialism turned against romantic psycho-poetics.[9] As Kaplan argues (in the company of many other feminist writers), the current task of feminist criticism is to reimagine the relationship between subjectivity and social economies. Since the late 1970s, the feminist awareness of romanticism both recognized and "unrecognized" has grown to the point of constituting, as the romantics would say, a bona fide "tendency."[10] This recognition, I should quickly add, is largely of a negative kind. In *The Madwoman in the Attic,* Sandra

[9]Cora Kaplan, *Sea Changes: Culture and Feminism* (London: Verso, 1986), 150–52.
[10]"Unrecognized Romanticism" is Jan Montefiore's term in *Feminism and Poetry* (London: Pandora, 1987), 8.

Gilbert and Susan Gubar, who are capable of a certain romantic swash-buckling themselves when it comes to plotting cultural history, map the permutations of feminine romanticism as it modifies Miltonic heroics over the course of the nineteenth century.[11] Working within the problems of tradition, but to some extent against Gilbert and Gubar, Margaret Homans and Jan Montefiore have since written finely articulated studies of the persistent difficulties of romanticism for women poets. The books of Homans and Montefiore have a bearing on the investigation of romantic criticism. First, in theorizing the relationship of the woman poet to romanticism, Homans reveals the gender-specific qualities of Wordsworthian poetics. She regards romantic philosophy as ambivalently constructed by male writers in order to transcend and return to the feminine. In her analysis of contemporary feminist poetics she resists the call for the unmediated communication of women's truth and urges poets to "embrace and exploit language's inherent fictiveness," the literary equivalent of the reality principle. This is the only way, Homans suggests, for women poets to avoid identifying the feminine with the literal, which merely reenacts the myth of nature developed by canonical romanticism.[12]

Montefiore wants to discriminate the romantic impulses of modern feminist poetry more fully from eighteenth- and nineteenth-century poetics, again, seeking to distance feminism from romanticism: "The Romantic myth of the great poet with his universal sympathies is replaced by a vision of multiple-authored poetry as a highly charged collective respository of female experience. Or to put it more concisely, the poet as 'man speaking to men' is transformed into a poetry of 'women speaking to each other.'" In fact, however, what Montefiore identifies as a tropological change in the history of romanticism is one of the most striking instances of its metaphoric continuity. The metaphor of a feminine speech community, "women speaking to each other," which has now been appropriated by some feminists, was indispensable for both male and female romantic writers. Montefiore resists this ideal on the basis of its "political evasions," not its view of language: "the tendency to privilege the notion of female experience, and to think of women's poetry as a magically powerful collective consciousness, can make for a too easy and uncritical assumption of

[11]Sandra M. Gilbert and Susan Gubar, *The Madwoman in the Attic* (New Haven: Yale University Press, 1979), 201–12, 219.

[12]Margaret Homans, *Women Writers and Poetic Identity* (Princeton: Princeton University Press, 1980), 13–14, 217.

identity between all women."[13] If readings of women poets and their compositional practice are grounded in historical and textual circumstance, Montefiore hopes, then romantic generalities—romanticism being a discourse in which masculine desire generalizes—will be unable to get off the ground. For Homans, nonliteral discourse presents the proper swerve away from romantic determinism in women's poetry; for Montefiore, extreme particularity leads to a notion of plural traditions which accomplishes the same thing.

All the critics I am characterizing here resist the tendency to confuse history with nature in celebrating an essential feminine difference. Because the glorification of a naturally feminine experience depends on metaphors with a long romantic past—speech, nurture, or community—feminist critics who resist this logic find it especially urgent to call attention to their theoretical procedures. Theory, which identifies itself as historically self-conscious, marks the resistance to wish fulfillment. It is precisely as a way of avoiding these somewhat predictable encounters between the feminist reader and the romantic text, I think, that Mary Jacobus describes her critical style with a greater emphasis on obliquity: "the buried letter of Romanticism and the phantom [again] of feminism both owe their uncanny power to their subterranean and unacknowledged presence—to repression itself." In Jacobus's formulation romanticism and feminism are structurally similar (or 'correspondential') by virtue of their repression in literary and psychoanalytic texts.[14] Linked by a shared ontology to the romantic, feminism cannot condescend to it.

With the exception of portions of Jacobus's *Reading Woman*, these feminist mediations of romanticism are oriented entirely to fiction and poetry. The question of gender needs to be introduced into the history of criticism in order for the ethical stresses of the tradition to become more fully apparent. Tobin Siebers's view of the "ethics of sexual difference" emphasizes the function of suffering in romantic criticism in a way useful for this book.[15] For pain, the link between power and

[13]Montefiore, *Feminism and Poetry,* 11–12.

[14]Mary Jacobus, *Reading Woman* (New York: Columbia University Press, 1986), 61, 285–92.

[15]Siebers probes the extent to which worrying about the violence of criticism has displayed romantic qualities since the eighteenth century. The sharp lines drawn between literature and contiguous practices—replicated in the nervous delineations of genre, discipline, and vocation which I describe in this book—are motivated, he argues, by claims of disinterestedness: "'Literature' is an ethical category, an invention of Romantic ideals used to protect the integrity . . . of authors and works against colonization by politics, mores, and alien ideologies in general." Siebers traces the persistent

the body, is always gendered. Romantic protagonists suffer as woman; their suffering is assuaged by woman; it is perceived to be caused by the lack of woman and also by her disturbing presence. Raising questions about the ethical uses of feminine victimage clarifies the role of suffering in romantic understanding as more differential than substantive. If we think of understanding as interpretation that wants to avoid the guilt of inflicting pain, suffering will always enter into the critical equation as what is to be avoided. But if understanding did not habitually repeat in an altered tone the classificatory achievements of logic (did not, in other words, participate in the trajectories of power), it would not need to call attention to its difference from critical aggression.

In the immediate future, theoretical work and historical work on the relationship of feminism and romanticism ought to be indistinguishable. The rereading of women poets, contemporaries or predecessors of the canonical romantics, is broadly reorganizing our sense of the significance of gender in the lyric and in the dynamics of literary influence. The complicated relationships between sentiment and sublimity, which appear to be collapsing into one another, will cause us, as they are unfolded in detail, to revise our views about how subjectivity has been rhetorically empowered in literary and political domains. Attention to the economies of romanticism—its notions of labor, relaxation, and expenditure—is growing and will alter our sense of romantic ambitions.[16] Literary history is currently being approached with vigorous theoretical intentions that need only see themselves as such to be productively revisionary.

---

metaphoric conflation of aggression, systematic thought, and literary criticism, focusing on its continued force in current theoretical debate, where the aversion to violence generates the preference for the margin. *The Ethics of Criticism* (Ithaca: Cornell University Press, 1988), 66, 106–7n, 114, 194.

[16]These scholarly tendencies became apparent with the publication of Anne K. Mellor, ed., *Romanticism and Feminism* (Bloomington: Indiana University Press, 1988), and with subsequent studies now in print or in progress. These include Marlon Ross, *The Contours of Masculine Desire: Romanticism and the Rise of Woman's Poetry* (New York: Oxford University Press, 1989); Kurt Heinzelman's study of the tradition of the georgic, which will extend his earlier reading of eighteenth-century economic discourse in *The Economics of the Imagination* (Amherst: University of Massachusetts Press, 1980); and Susan Wolfson's work on gender in romantic poetry.

PART I

SCHLEIERMACHER

CHAPTER I

The Terms of Address

Family, Salon, and the Labor of Understanding

In *Soliloquies (Monologen,* 1800), as Schleiermacher reflects on the direction of his career, he composes a parable of his hermeneutic ethics which accurately describes the way he encloses conflict within a community of understanding. This sense of community is later translated into the tolerant systems of his academic works, a series of shapely outlines in which all views have their place, as he predicts here. Taken in such a figurative—or prefigurative—way, this passage (to which we shall, at length, return) sets forth Schleiermacher's "terms of address," the terms in which he addresses hermeneutic opportunities:

> My late-awakened spirit, remembering how long it bore an alien yoke, ever fears to be dominated again by an alien opinion, and whenever a mode of life as yet unexplored is disclosed to it in new objects, it at first prepares, weapon in hand, to struggle for its freedom, in order not to begin enslavement to foreign influence in this case as before. However, as soon as I have gained my own point of view the time for strife is past; I gladly let each of the other views stand beside my own, and my sensibility peacefully completes the task of interpreting each one and of searching into its standpoint. (M 40)[1]

---

[1] "Terms of address" is Tice's phrase, OR 47.

Schleiermacher (1768–1834) asserts that his struggles for freedom and antithetical self-definition are restrained through the work of interpretation, which acknowledges the equal legitimacy of other perspectives. Understanding is the peaceful negotiation that brings conflict [*Streit*] to an end. But comprehension nevertheless requires antagonism, because the interpreter's self-respect is forged through resistance. The tendency to seek understanding by tempering the claims of the self is still a self-avowed characteristic, though a frequently qualified one, of the strain of hermeneutics that acknowledges Schleiermacher as its founder. Criticism with this generous ethos emerged with and in response to a strong sense of the potential violence of analysis and a consciousness of the will to power in interpretation.

I am not writing an account of the origins, in Western European culture, of the sense that interpretation, or even knowledge itself, is transgressive—a form of intellectual mastery or aggression for which the medical-scientific procedure of dissection is persistently the most negative metaphor. To narrate the provenance of these complex ethical misgivings, one would have to work through the history of Jewish and Christian biblical interpretation, then through the discourses in which philosophy lays claim to analytical rigor and purity, and finally, and perhaps most crucially for the late eighteenth century, through the figurative connections between the classificatory operations of science and the social effects of technological change. Like the persistent relationships between poststructuralist absorption in the ethics of criticism and earlier romantic versions of understanding, the links between these romantic theories and their cultural pasts are overdetermined and redundant. To write their history would require a more complicated (and even longer) book than this. The investigation of late-eighteenth-century constructions of understanding is an episode in a broader history that is open at both ends, with no discernible moment at which reading and interpretation are *not* bound up with questions of love, aggression, and morality. The issue is not, as the Nietzschean title of a well-known photograph by Joanne Leonard warns, that "Romanticism is ultimately fatal" but, less apocalyptically, that "the most definite characteristic of romanticism is the obstinate questioning of its own ambiguous status: its lineage, inheritance, privileges, and powers," in Jerome Christensen's words.[2]

The question with which we might begin, if we are to understand

---

[2]Jerome Christensen, *Coleridge's Blessed Machine of Language* (Ithaca: Cornell University Press, 1981), 23.

the ambivalent dynamics of romantic hermeneutics, is, What does the hermeneutic theorist desire? For hermeneutics is above all a mode of desire.[3] Its wish is for relationship, even for love, as the condition that guards against committing rational violence through reflective excess. Understanding, the avowed goal of hermeneutics, was and still is imagined as making possible communion and community. If we are to pursue the argument that hermeneutics itself is properly understood as a system of desire, the proximate questions become, Under what conditions does this desire emerge? Through what metaphors is it expressed? And these last two questions lead directly to the subject of gender.

The metaphors used by romantic theorists of interpretation to describe the ethical tenor of understanding—friendship, conversation, religious community, intuitive or divinatory insight—are associated by them with woman. In its most reductive form the antidote to science is femininity. Feminine qualities represent not only the antithesis of science, but also an alternative style of mental power, since the desire to be ethical is not inconsistent with the exercise of authority. Recent literary criticism, in its encounters with romanticism, has moved openly and often brilliantly to articulate the dynamics of gender in the ethics and politics of interpretation. Male fantasies of androgyny are by now recognized as strategies of totalization and ethical compensation.[4] Hermeneutic philosophy in the line of Schleiermacher has re-

[3]Jacques Derrida, "Violence and Metaphysics," *Writing and Difference*, trans. Alan Bass (Chicago: University of Chicago Press, 1978), 92–109. Derrida discusses ways in which "metaphysical transcendence is *desire*," linking desire, the drive to create totalizing schemes, and the relationship of the theorist to the other and to the dream of community. See also Julia Kristeva on the relation of science to writing in *Desire in Language: A Semiotic Approach to Literature and Art*, ed. Leon S. Roudiez, trans. Thomas Gora, Alice Jardine, Leon S. Roudiez (New York: Columbia University Press, 1980), 94.

[4]In 1980 Carolyn G. Heilbrun commented on the changing implications of the word "androgyny" since the publication of her *Toward a Recognition of Androgyny* in 1973. She rightly pinpoints the basis for the widespread feminist suspicion toward the term as lying chiefly in the fact "that in the history of the androgyne, it has been the male who assumes female aspects, leaving the female to keep all the inconvenient female duties." "Androgyny and the Psychology of Sex Differences," in *The Future of Difference*, ed. Hester Eisenstein and Alice Jardine (New Brunswick, N.J.: Rutgers University Press, 1987), 260–66. One of the articles to which Heilbrun replies is Barbara C. Gelpi, "The Politics of Androgyny," *Women's Studies* 2 (1974): 151–60. For discussions of androgyny in specific romantic contexts, see Alan Richardson, "Romanticism and the Colonization of the Feminine," in *Romanticism and Feminism*, ed. Anne K. Mellor (Bloomington: Indiana University Press, 1988), 19–22; see also Sara Friedrichsmeyer, *The Androgyne in Early German Romanticism* (Bern: Peter Lang, 1983).

pressed the fact that it once almost knew this about itself; it has re-pressed the link between figurations of the feminine and the desire for an ethical community.

My interest in hermeneutic philosophy arises, then, not from any philosophical loyalties to it, but from the ironies generated by the peculiar status of twentieth-century hermeneutics as a discourse grounded in the desire for an ethics of the feminine. It is so dedicated to rejecting its own romanticism that the feminine has been wholly forgotten. As such, the discourse of hermeneutics is doomed to the nostalgia for the feminine other, the longing based on forgetting of which Luce Irigaray, in *Ethique de la différence sexuelle,* has captured the specific tonality. The irony of some feminist discourse, including that of Irigaray, is that the collectively projected morality of the speech community is available as a feminist ideal arising in part from a forgotten masculine romanticism.[5]

Until the 1980s, the ethical was not singled out as a crucial term, either within poststructuralist discussions of cultural and literary theory generally or in relation to romantic texts. But viewed in the light of renewed interest in both ethics and gender, the encounter between Schleiermacher and Schlegel becomes one in which theoretical reflection mediates differing styles of masculinity which also represent modes of interpretive power. For Schleiermacher's deliberately marginal place in relation to the *Athenaeum* group, marginal by virtue of its religious and ethical resistance, expresses the competition for the ethical which is played out in terms of the feminine. When one approaches this encounter with an awareness of the distance between the hermeneutics of suspicion, in which I would include most poststructuralist and feminist theories, and the discourse of philosophical hermeneutics, the significance of the way interpretive community is constructed around the desire for the feminine in the latter tradition is even more apparent.

The key metaphor of the language of hermeneutics, the circle that describes the reader's mental spiral between anticipated and proven coherence, referred initially and perhaps most powerfully to social experience: the idealized experience of a group created by intimate self-revelation and the reciprocal activity of understanding. The circle had "a material basis" in the communal life of the early German romantics in the Berlin salons of the 1790s, presided over by wealthy Jewish

[5]Luce Irigaray, *Ethique de la différence sexuelle* (Paris: Les Editions de Minuit, 1984), 64–70, 94–99.

women.[6] Schleiermacher used the figure of feminine intimacy to describe his strategies of comprehension in this context; ultimately, he employed it to differentiate his own vocation from the aesthetic and philosophical commitments of the other members of the *Athenaeum* group, and from those of Friedrich Schlegel in particular. The connections between strife and interpretation in this milieu yielded Schleiermacher's increasingly distinct notions of the structure of understanding. Despite the fact that, by the time he became involved with the Berlin romantics, Schleiermacher was already substantively engaged in what might be described as professional philosophical work, his theories of hermeneutics first emerged in this highly charged psychological, erotic, and social domain.

The familial and institutional cultures of Schleiermacher's first thirty years provide the idioms and structures of desire which pervade his texts. The first thing we discover from Schleiermacher's meditations on his own life is the constitutive role of conflictual difference in inventing, against romantic literature, secular hermeneutics and romantic religion. My approach to Schleiermacher operates within fuller accounts of the changing cultural conditions negotiated by university-educated German males in the last two decades of the eighteenth century.[7] In the decade between the French Revolution and the turn of the century, vocational agons were common among the population to which Schleiermacher belonged, that is to say, among upwardly mobile male intellectuals oriented to urban centers, particularly Berlin. During the reign of Friedrich Wilhelm II (1786–97) and the first decade of the rule of Friedrich Wilhelm III (1797–1840), Prussian society was organized not by modern class relations, but by the sociology of es-

[6]Tzvetan Todorov, *Theories of the Symbol,* trans. Catherine Porter (Ithaca: Cornell University Press, 1982), 165.

[7]The most pertinent historical studies include Deborah Hertz, *Jewish High Society in Old Regime Berlin* (New Haven: Yale University Press, 1988), an investigation of the socioeconomic and cultural factors that gave rise to the influential Berlin salons of the 1790s; and Albert Blackwell, *Schleiermacher's Early Philosophy of Life: Determinism, Freedom, and Phantasy,* Harvard Theological Studies 32 (Greenville: Scholar's Press, 1982), the only twentieth-century discussion of Schleiermacher's development which displays a sophisticated grasp of the relationships between philosophical and material conditions. The social and cultural dynamics of early German romanticism are described in Roger Ayrault, *La Genèse du romantisme allemand,* 4 vols. (Paris: Aubier-Montaigne, 1961–76), and Henri Brunschwig, *Société et romantisme en Prusse au xviiie siècle: La crise de l'Etat prussien à la fin du xviiie siècle et la genèse de la mentalité romantique* (Paris: Flammarion, 1973).

tates. The government's effort to promote economic growth while inhibiting social change resulted in the peculiarly improvised careers of Prussian intellectuals during this period. Schleiermacher's persistent concern with the phenomenology of intellectual labor and its dependent but antithetical relationship to social sympathy reflects the unsteady mix of attitudes toward work in such an environment. Laboriousness is a form of alienation but also of self-creation.

Despite the fact that Berlin did not have its own university until 1809–10, it offered a variety of intellectual employment for tutors, professors at gymnasia and knightly academies, private lecturers, state officials, and, for the small proportion of non-noble salon participants who were ordained ministers, as preachers, chaplains, and instructors in church institutions. Consequently, as "many noble fortunes sank and some commoner fortunes rose," some individuals from each estate found themselves with shared intellectual commitments.[8]

The intersection between noble and commoner interests, the necessary precondition for the flourishing of the salons, occurred, in Schleiermacher's case, as a result of the influence of familial and ecclesiastical networks. Descended from a long line of clerics, he numbered among his mentors the influential court chaplain Friedrich Samuel Gottfried Sack, who acted as both his patron and his censor. It was Sack who introduced Schleiermacher to the aristocratic Dohna family, whom he served as tutor between 1790 and 1793. And it was the grown son of that family, Alexander Dohna, who introduced Schleiermacher into the salon of Henriette Herz during his first brief residence in Berlin in 1793–94.

In spite of the difference made by the functioning of pastoral contacts within the Reformed (German Calvinist) Church, which had a distinct estate of its own, the improvisational quality of his career until his early forties typifies the vocational transience of early German ro-

---

[8]"A specific pattern of downward and upward mobility made salons possible by creating a new sort of person whose needs could be met in salons. Social classes based on common economic and professional achievements had hardly begun to form by the close of the century. Rising land prices, high fertility, urbanization, and inadequate education polarized the Prussian nobility; as a result, some nobles came to be rich in status but poor in cash. Meanwhile, the monarchy adhered to a rigid mercantilism, was unwilling to sell bureaucratic offices, and tried to promote industry without making any gentile commoners rich. These policies all hindered the formation of a gentile bourgeoisie able to compete for social dominance even with a wounded nobility. The large elite of the tiny Jewish community, instead, increasingly came to play the role of a surrogate bourgeoisie during the eighteenth century." Hertz, *Jewish High Society in Old Regime Berlin*, 20–21.

mantics. He lived and studied with an uncle, a professor of theology, both during and after his studies at the University of Halle. His residence with the Dohnas was followed by a year and a half in Berlin, where, while studying for the theological examinations that qualified him for ordination, he was employed in an orphanage and as an instructor for teachers. These two compensatory periods of theological study, as a postgraduate in Halle and again in Berlin, indicate Schleiermacher's more thorough involvement with philological and philosophical subjects while at the university but also suggest a pervasive ambivalence during these years toward theology itself.[9]

Schleiermacher's definitive act of self-creation belonged to the order of strife, not that of interpretation. Son of an army chaplain, with generations of clerics on both his mother's and his father's sides, he rejected intellectual constraints that operated more strongly in his educational environment than in his family. In 1787, at nineteen, he left the Bohemian Brethren, or Herrnhuter, seminary at Barby, where he had resided for two years following two years at a similar community in Niesky. These pietistic establishments were strongly associated with his mother's religious style, not his father's; the link between piety and the feminine continued when his sister, Charlotte, herself became a resident member of a Herrnhuter community. His somewhat precocious skepticism, which, as he declared it at this time, extended to rejecting the divinity of Jesus, was an adventure in doubt, a move toward philosophy and the classics. He placed himself henceforth in a vicarious relation to pietism, largely through his relationship with his sister.

Schleiermacher's letters to his father directly address the recurring dilemma of the educated Protestant divine between 1750 and 1850: the peculiarly hermeneutic predicament of how to reconcile the scholar's awareness of the demystifying effects of the higher criticism with the

---

[9]Schleiermacher worked in Landsberg, near Drossen, as assistant minister to another uncle until 1796, when he returned to Berlin as chaplain at the Charité Hospital, a post he held for six years. Exiled from Berlin as a result of pressure from the Church Directorate, which disapproved of his involvement with Eleanore Grunow (a minister's wife) and the publication of *Confidential Letters on Lucinde,* he was posted to a pulpit in Stolpe, near the Baltic, from 1802 until 1804. In that year he was appointed preacher and professor at the University of Halle. From then on, the disruptions in his life came more from the armies of Napoleon, which occupied Halle in 1806, than from his own fascinated tendency to hover in the discursive and erotic terrain that lay in the area bounded by pastoral, academic, and literary careers. For Schleiermacher's reaction to the French occupation, see Jerry F. Dawson, *Friedrich Schleiermacher: The Evolution of a Nationalist* (Austin: University of Texas Press, 1966).

need—perceived always as inhering in the less educated—to have a collective faith supported.[10] Schleiermacher did not deny his "natural inclination toward whatever is openly suppressed." In response, the elder Schleiermacher gave vent to epistolary *cris du coeur* that fret over the two dangers of "oversensitized sentimentalism" and the "mania for system and system-making" [*Systemsucht und Systemmacherei*]. "What will finally become of . . . our Bible," he warned, when "teachers and commentaries" have alienated it from the people? (BR I 50–51, 74–75, 83; BW I 57, 180, 198).

Gottlieb Schleiermacher nonetheless had a realistic view of his son's position. He himself had espoused rationalistic theology in response to the risky extremism of a pietistic father.[11] His warnings, therefore, came out of a long experience with the emotional and moral costs of critical detachment. Later he admitted that he "once preached for at least twelve years as an actual unbeliever," but one convinced that Christian doctrine could be applied with "comfort and improvement . . . even though I was not myself convinced of its truth." Schleiermacher's attraction to the tree of knowledge repeated his father's own defensive distance from pietism, despite the latter's protective decision to educate his son among the Bohemian Brethren. In some sense, perhaps, this background of oscillation between skepticism and belief was already habitual to Schleiermacher, to the point where his doubt was as firmly directed against theological rationalism as against the pietistic resistance to critical exegesis (BR I 65–66, 83–84; BW I 88–90, 198–99).[12]

Reflecting on the moment at which he decided to leave Barby for the secular milieu of Halle, Schleiermacher wrote, "I began to think by doubting." Schleiermacher's first advocacy of the sophisticated hermeneutics of his time took the form of generational conflict precipitated by his resistance in the name of free inquiry to attitudes of both pietistic and rationalistic submissiveness. The hermeneutic critique of interpretive aggression developed out of his celebration of the pleasurable autonomy of skeptical reading, a freedom that was never dis-

---

[10]In an American context one can point to a generation of young men trained as Unitarian ministers who suffered the same conflict. Emerson's brother William abandoned his pastoral vocation after studying at Göttingen and deciding, finally, that he could not practice the necessarily schizophrenic ministry that his newfound skepticism would require.

[11]Wilhelm Dilthey, *Leben Schleiermachers* (Berlin: G. Reimer, 1870), 5–9.

[12]Blackwell, *Schleiermacher's Early Philosophy of Life,* 209 and Part I, "Determinism (1789–1795)," esp. chaps. 2–5.

sociated from, but always dependent on, the dream of familial unity. After he had found a way of describing understanding which cleansed persuasiveness of its associations with mastery, he could say, in 1802, "I have become a Herrnhuter in the end, only of a higher order" (BR I 78, 295; BW I 183).

Despite Schleiermacher's excited entry into his brief university career, he quickly came to look back on the mood of his two years at Halle (1787–89) and the following year of independent study (1789–90) as signifying isolation and confusion. In the aftermath of this period he began to address the relationship among love, work, and ethics in a model of mental economy which is fundamental to his sense of intellectual labor. "With me, study is too passionate . . . to keep to certain hours," he wrote his father, who had urged better time management. He read with impetuosity [*Vehemenz*], his studies advancing "not by a daily routine, but by fits and starts" [*nicht tageweise, sondern stossweise, periodenweise*], according to his interests of the moment. He worked "*con amore,*" not "for the sake of adhering to . . . rules." This ad hoc autodidacticism, instigated by the clarifying motives of love and need, would, he hoped, keep him "from becoming scattered and confused [*zerstreut und verwirrt*] by the quantity of quite different subjects." Later, he regretfully described the lack of harmony [*Einheit*] in his "fragmentary study" in a way that reveals his emerging desire for a harmony of disciplines reflected in a pleasurable ordering of his time (BR I 78–80; "Selbstbiographie," BR I 12; BW I 183–84). What he learned at Halle was that the unity of intellectual endeavor is dependent on affect; what he learned from the Dohnas was that affect is dependent on domesticity.

Schleiermacher responded gratefully to the warmth extended him, particularly by the Countess Dohna and her daughters. His attachment to one of the daughters was imbued with the sensibility of the family's collective life. Affection for the circle of Dohna women represents the first of Schleiermacher's vicarious marriages—as Albert Blackwell notes, "a veritable *leitmotif* throughout the early romantic movement."[13] He was drawn to married women or, in his friendship with Schlegel, to friendship as metaphoric marriage (however ironically this

---

[13]Ibid., 18. See also Dilthey, *Leben Schleiermachers,* chap. 1, "Der religiose Familiengeist," and Schleiermacher's sermon series of 1820, *Predigten über den christlichen Hausstand;* and Robert M. Bigler, *The Politics of German Protestantism: The Rise of the Protestant Church Elite in Prussia, 1815–1846* (Berkeley: University of California Press, 1972), 12. Schleiermacher also became emotionally involved with his married cousin during his tenure as assistant minister in Landsberg.

was meant). He himself married, in 1809, the young widow of an intimate friend. "My heart is properly cultivated here [*ordentlich gepflegt*]," he wrote his father from the Dohnas' estate, reflecting on the neglect of the heart at Halle. It "is not required to fade under the weeds of cold erudition, and my religious sentiments are not buried in gloomy theological speculations" [*unter theologischen Grübeleien*] (BR I 94; BW I 221). The rationality of scholarship, which will reach theoretical designation as the labor-intensive "grammatical" method of the hermeneutic manuscripts, finds its early experiential analogue in barely tolerable solitude. Schleiermacher was certain, according to this logic, that he could undertake critical investigations only when the antidote of family or friendship was available.

On taking his place as a private tutor, he was convinced that congeniality enables the mind to intuit relationships between pieces of learning as the heart does between persons. This social mediation of intellectual labor points toward and helps explain the form of his later works. Almost all of them follow the logical outlines of his university courses but are imbued with the conviction that this form reflects an ideal community of *Geisteswissenschaften,* the human sciences.

With these predispositions, Schleiermacher's experience of the salon or of more intimate relationships in the home of the salonière not surprisingly enters into his allegories of work and desire. The Berlin salons were "the meeting places of those who had learned to represent themselves through conversation," as Hannah Arendt observes.[14] The salon "demanded subjectivity—as intersubjectivity—on everyone's part" and dramatized an illusory dialogical equality between author and reader.[15] This fantasy of classless immediacy was absorbed structurally and thematically into Schleiermacher's writings as a set of topoi manifest in dialogue, dialectic, system-formation, and understanding.

Deborah Hertz seeks to demonstrate a specific socioeconomic rationale for the combination of men and women congregating in the salons; that, in other words, the economic circumstances of certain (male) nobles, Jews, and commoner intellectuals set in motion the development of institutions of leisure and cultural innovation which matched the aspirations of the cultivated daughters of Jewish intellectuals. Hertz gives a careful account both of the fluidity of Jewish identity, particularly that of salon women, and of the persistent anti-Semitism of the gentile

---

[14]Hannah Arendt, *Rahel Varnhagen: The Life of a Jewess,* Publications of the Leo Baeck Institute (London: East & West Library, 1957), 29.

[15]Helen Fehervary, "Christa Wolf's Prose: A Landscape of Masks," *New German Critique* 27 (Fall 1982): 79.

men who were socially and emotionally involved in friendships with intellectual Jews.[16]

But Arendt has a more dynamic view of Jewish society as deriving its cultural value precisely from its marginal status. She is able to link the erotic and psychological intensity of salon friendships to the atmosphere of transience and alienation within which they developed. And she is able to connect the disintegration of the salons more clearly to the hegemony of the middle class, making this process less dependent on the increasing conservatism of Berlin society in the aftermath of the Napoleonic invasion. Not the least of Arendt's contributions is her emphasis on the self-consciousness, among salon participants, of their peculiarly signifying, representational, or, as she says, theatrical meanings.[17] In Schleiermacher's intimacy with Henriette Herz, what is enacted or represented is understanding, and talk about intimacy is the discursive proof of intimacy itself.

The salon of Henriette Herz, oriented to "women, emotion, and belles-lettres," was expressive of the later phase of the salon culture which lasted from 1780 to 1806. Markus and Henriette Herz established a "double salon" that evolved from his lectures in their home on natural science. The salon was "double in ideological style as well as in leadership," Hertz remarks, for "Henriette discussed poetry and novels with the young romantics in one room while her husband lectured on reason, science, and enlightenment in the other."[18]

Schleiermacher's somewhat anomalous inclusion in this milieu, as a young minister, suggests an unusual need to carry on a romance with the feminine and the literary while pursuing a career in the church and in philosophy.[19] He virtually lived at the house of Henriette Herz, as he wrote his sister in 1798, and spent his afternoons alone with her. Herz's knowledge of numerous languages made possible the linguistic sophistication of her friendship with Schleiermacher. Shared reading

[16]Hertz, *Jewish High Society in Old Regime Berlin*, 252–59.

[17]Arendt, *Rahel Varnhagen*, 46–47.

[18]Hertz, *Jewish High Society in Old Regime Berlin*, 96–97, 99–100. For the development, in 1787, of the Tugendbund ("League of Virtue") out of Henriette Herz's Tuesday evening reading society, a group devoted to acting out heterosexual intimacy within a collective celebration of "moral perfection," see 92. On the end of Herz's salon, out of economic necessity, with the death of Markus Herz in 1803 see 100.

[19]Ibid., 72, 117. The romance, as I have noted above, was pushed to the point of scandal. In addition to his banishment to Stolpe, which resulted from his association with Schlegel and Herz and from his writings, Schleiermacher was caricatured in an anti-Semitic cartoon of 1800 showing him with Herz and Schlegel. Blackwell, *Schleiermacher's Early Philosophy of Life*, Fig. D.

and translation projects—parallel endeavors to his vexed collaboration on a translation of Plato with Schlegel—were extensions of exercises in interpersonal hermeneutics. Schleiermacher's more problematic relationships, to Schlegel and to Eleanore Grunow, a married woman, were mediated by his conversations about them with Henriette Herz. The fact that, despite the attraction between the two, Schleiermacher regarded Herz as emotionally committed to Alexander von Dohna (for himself, Schleiermacher hoped to persuade Grunow to divorce her husband and marry him) makes it clear that *interpreting* love, not love itself, was the basis for their closeness.

Schleiermacher grew to be "a virtuoso in friendship" because it could heal the effects of intellectual isolation—or, put another way, he became an intellectual isolato as a way of eliciting the care of others. In a letter to his sister written after their father's death, Schleiermacher describes how writing that inspires or is inspired by a fantasy of communion with family members becomes blocked by the reality of their absence:

> At this time, I had been writing on much that is immediately from the heart, on religion, and I heartily wished that I could have shown it to him and have conversed with him about it; in short, I was full of intensely felt [*inniger*] yearning. I firmly resolved to write you at least a couple of words that evening. But afterwards the time passed again in the dullness of mind which happens in me when I am isolated. I cannot surmount this: to be without friends, without heartfelt conversation, without alternation between work and social intercourse, is no kind of life for me.

The reiterated theme of compensatory communication pervades the correspondence through which intimacy is sustained. He defends his own "multifarious connections to people," his "manifold and complex activity," his "multiple life" and "divided interest" on the grounds of the need to "make known his innermost being" (BR I 224, 209; see also 331).

By the end of the decade, this credo has become a conscious program. The activity of friendship, manifest in the movement of feeling, fuels the individual's activity in work. To Henriette Herz, who, like his sister, is one of the frequent recipients of these urgent equations, Schleiermacher writes in 1802, "Does it not lie in my nature, that I have no independent existence? that all my activity is the product of communication? And that the former only persists in relation to the latter? For all that I should do depends on that fact that I am quickened and affected; and your letters, therefore, not only help my being [*Sein*] but also, more than anything, my doing [*Wirken*]" (BR I 320). Intersubjectivity provides the structural model for his relationship to philosophical material, and friendship provides the emotional energy to keep this model "working," or "quickened." The middle term between communication and work is "being," the process that gathers emotion and then productively applies it.

Schleiermacher's evident worry during the later 1790s about sustaining the activities of reading and writing suggests that these occupations present some unusual resistance or difficulty for which friendship must compensate. Reading and writing in his professional disciplines prejudice Schleiermacher against isolation partly because they are bound to logic and partly because they involve large quantities of merely dutiful work. He repeatedly distinguishes systematic writing, "the dead thoughts which one computes in one's head," from "ideas that really live" and come productively "into conflict"—into conversation— "with the influences and remains of earlier ones" (BR I 401, 277–78). The problem with undertakings such as his exhaustive *Groundwork to a Critique of Previous Ethical Theory* (1803) lies in the preparatory reading, a stumbling block he confesses in the *Confidential Letters on Lucinde:* "You know how difficult it is for me to find the end of reading and the beginning of writing" (VB 429).

For someone who felt himself to be a "virtuoso" reader of persons, Schleiermacher has a surprising sense of laborious progress in the study of texts. "You cannot believe how slowly my reading must proceed as soon as it has to do with something critical," he tells Eleanor Grunow in 1802. This tediousness is due partly to "unbelief in myself," insecurity before the weight of philosophical tradition aroused by Schleiermacher's awareness of his own strongly negative evaluations of earlier theories. He offers as an example of his slowness the following agonistic description of his research, in which understanding Plato is the model for the labor of love, understanding ethics the model for reading in a mood of contempt and disgust:

> To understand a dialogue of Plato . . . costs me easily again as much time as it takes me to bring the translation to fruition. And yet Plato is inarguably the writer whom I know best, and with whom I have almost merged into one. Now consider all I have to read for the purpose of the Critique, how much more difficult it all is to understand the more confused and defective it is; how almost all of it will be disgusting to me because of its miserable state and doubly disgusting because of the height

to which the world has raised it; consider further that everything of antiquity which I shall have to read in this connection will, at the same time, be a philological study, in pursuing which I cannot possibly restrain myself from devoting many a half-hour (often in vain; often, perhaps, not) to a corrupt passage. (BR I 326–27)

In the process of understanding, he must either become one with the author/text (Plato) or overcome it by completing and correcting all "confused" or "defective" passages. Schleiermacher is frustrated not only by the unappealing character of the material itself, but by his own polemical relation to it. Not surprisingly, this account of "disciplining" the text is followed by a paragraph devoted to the troublesome need to make "the gentle approach [*die Milde*] prevail in this book which is so fitting a companion for profound rigor." Distaste may be his motive, but he must produce a forgiving tone, the feminine rhetorical "companion" of masculine aggression transposed into methodological rigor. As a reward for restraining his aggressive impulses, he allows himself "the prospect of feeling his heart open," when he turns to the dialogues, in the "mental play [*Gedankenspiel*] of Platonic irony."

Reading is made difficult precisely by its ethical requirements. Mastering the works of others in "this disagreeable reading and studying, gives me unspeakable trouble," particularly when the author in question is an opponent or competitor: "If it were only the ancients I had to deal with, I should be safe. . . . But the moderns . . . particularly the philosophers, must have been created by God for my torment. You would not believe the unspeakable trouble it costs me to grasp such a book." He concludes humorously, "That is precisely the reason why I believe I have a rightful calling to administer criticism. For when one takes so much trouble with reading, and takes it so thoroughly, one really has a right to comment on the worth of books." Schleiermacher's reading is a struggle with other writers in which the animus thus aroused becomes channeled into hermeneutic superiority, into the goal of "understanding the author better than he understands himself," to echo the Kantian tag appropriated by both Schlegel and Schleiermacher but most closely identified with the latter (BR I 278–80; HM 242–43 n. 48).[20] The texts of philosophical hermeneutics are laden with arguments seeking to convince us that "better," in this dictum,

[20]Hermann Patsch, "Friedrich Schlegels 'Philosophie der Philologie' und Schleiermachers frühe Entwürfe zur Hermeneutik: Zur Frühgeschichte der romantischen Hermeneutik," *Zeitschrift für Theologie und Kirche* 63 (1966): 456–57.

does not signify the dynamics of power relations or a personal desire for mastery. With this I agree—insofar as I read it as a move that translates into ethically acceptable terms the feeling of competitive aggression which Schleiermacher cannot confront directly.

The difference between intimate and alienated reading frequently comes down to the difference between voice and text, with the former typically privileged by Schleiermacher and by the hermeneutic tradition generally. Since the voice is metaphorically the medium of the "revelation of love" or personal being, his own preaching, "the only means of personal influence on the communal sensibility of people *en masse*," causes him "deep emotion." He immediately likens this pleasure to that of reading his own most romantic text aloud to Herz: "The reading of the *Monologen* was actually a sermon from me to you." Afterward, paradoxically, both were silent, evidence of the "peculiar effect" of the rendition (BR I 338).

The voice, as Derrida has argued, is a figure for presence, especially for the presence of an ideal of love.[21] Coming from within the body, the voice signifies feelings of love bordering on the erotic, as well as feelings of power. Speech issues metaphorically from the site of desire, bypassing the mind's mediation and producing rapid, accurate comprehension. The erotic qualities of the voice are reinforced by Schleiermacher's belief that understanding among friends is peculiarly a woman's gift and that his own feminine side emerges in his need for it: "I constantly reveal myself more accurately to women than to men, for there is so much in my soul that the latter rarely understand" (BR I 207). As we shall see in his "marriage" to Schlegel, understanding is the means of wifely superiority. In Schleiermacher's remarks on feminine sensibility (including his own), one senses the tentative but nonetheless utterly stereotypical contrast between the feminine voice as the agent of understanding and masculine reading-for-writing as the occasion of conflict.

Conversation and its historical correlative, the letter, permeated the romantic writings by men for which women provided models, audiences, and metaphors. Anne Herrmann, in her study of the dialogic, describes the late-eighteenth-century salons as a cultural outgrowth of the more thoroughly private epistolary sphere. As Herrmann points out, female subjectivity was idealized by male salon participants "as

---

[21]Jacques Derrida, *Speech and Phenomenon*, trans. David B. Allison (Evanston, Ill.: Northwestern University Press, 1973), chap. 6, "The Voice That Keeps Silence," esp. 77–79.

more authentic because it expresses itself in speech or its written equivalent, the epistle." This idealization recurs in feminist accounts, in which the salons provide a model of specifically feminine communicative ethics.[22] Christa Wolf and some of her commentators, for example, have recognized the salon and its epistolary correlatives as a mode "based on the social relations of affective perception and communication between Others, on the pattern of . . . friendship." The ethical import of such language in its twentieth-century context lies in the way it "effects the relinquishment of the authorial ego in favor of reciprocal involvement." "Friendship," or the discourse in which it is represented, "is synonymous with the politics of peace." These feminist responses to early German romanticism clarify the persistent association of interpretive nonviolence with the speech of woman. But they also make necessary, within feminist discourse, the critique provided by Herrmann's insistence that the dialogic "does not refer to a harmonious dialogue based on amiable disagreement; rather it refers to the struggle between antagonistic discourses."[23]

"I must write, too": Schleiermacher and Schlegel

The complicated ethical relations between speaking and hearing, writing and reading in Schleiermacher's developing hermeneutics are

[22]Anne Herrmann, "'Intimate, Irreticent and Indiscreet in the Extreme': Epistolary Essays by Virginia Woolf and Christa Wolf," *New German Critique* 38 (Spring–Summer 1986): 166. See also Herrmann's *The Dialogic and Difference: "An/Other Woman" in Virginia Woolf and Christa Wolf* (New York: Columbia University Press, 1989), 38–39. Kay Goodman, "Poesis and Praxis in Rahel Varnhagen's Letters," *New German Critique* 27 (1982): 132–34. Fehervary, "Christa Wolf's Prose," 79–80. See also Marianne Thalmann on the effect of the romantics' urban context on their awareness of conversation and discourse, in *The Literary Sign Language of German Romanticism,* trans. Harold A. Basilius (Detroit: Wayne State University Press, 1972), 13.

[23]Fehervary, "Christa Wolf's Prose," 79–80. If Wolf's prose style embodies an ethic of friendship, her view of the romantics is nevertheless an agonistic one, focusing on romantic discourse as an early experience of subjectivity: "They were probably one of the first generations to feel torn inside by their inability to realize in action the possibilities which they sensed were there, inside them, very much alive and alert; which they rehearsed in debates and literary experiments." "Culture Is What You Experience—An Interview with Christa Wolf," trans. Jeanette Clausen, *New German Critique* 27 (1982): 91–92, 96. See also François Rigolet, "Montaigne's Purloined Letters," *Yale French Studies* 64 (1983), on the connection among the spoken word, the letters, and the essay; also Mikhail Bakhtin, *The Dialogic Imagination,* trans. Caryl L. Emerson and ed. Michael Holquist (Austin: University of Texas Press, 1981), 143, on the emergence of a drawing-room style and the familiar letter. Herrmann, *The Dialogic and Difference,* 148; see also 6, 12, 14.

dramatized in his friendship with Schlegel. The more amity is strained, the more pronounced the theme of understanding becomes in Schleiermacher's evaluations of his former roommate. Ultimately, Schleiermacher's superior gift of understanding claims a moral victory over Schlegel. If the quasi-marital harmony that at first prevailed between the two played out the ideal of intimacy toward which hermeneutics strives, their subsequent tensions are constituted by the misunderstanding in which interpretation occurs.

It was Schlegel who caused Schleiermacher to think of himself (however ambivalently) as an author. Without Schlegel, we would have the early philosophical manuscripts, the *Critique of Previous Ethical Theory,* and the later works that originated in Schleiermacher's teaching, but we almost certainly would not have *On Religion,* the *Soliloquies,* or the *Confidential Letters on Lucinde,* the texts that generate and are glossed by Schleiermacher's self-revising hermeneutics. Schlegel made it clear that in the romantic circle, if feminine prestige was attached to talk, masculine prestige was attached to writing—writing of a novelistic and subjective kind that nonetheless takes its particular significance from the philological and critical investigations pursued separately by Schlegel and Schleiermacher but providing the subject matter of their conversation.

In a letter of October 1797 to his sister, Schleiermacher announced that "a new epoch . . . for my existence in the philosophical and literary world has begun." Through Schlegel's "inexhaustible stream of new views and ideas . . . much that has been dormant in me has been set in motion." And Schleiermacher adds, "He constantly plucks at me: I must write, too. . . . he leaves me no day of rest." A month later, at the famous surprise birthday party for Schleiermacher given by Schlegel, Herz, and others, the demand was reiterated:

> Schlegel played me a little trick, inciting [the others] to join *in choro* in his old wish, namely, that I should be diligent, that is, should write books. Nine-and-twenty years, and nothing done yet. He went on and on, and I had to give him my hand on it, really solemnly, that I would write something original this year—a promise that presses heavily on me, as I have no inclination to be an author.

Schleiermacher was delighted by the "compensation" [*Ersatz*] of "exchanging my empty solitude for such society" as would be provided by Schlegel, who had on the same occasion promised to move in with him (BR I 161–62, 165–66; BW II 177–78, 212–14). Schlegel must have seemed to offer an ideal synthesis of speech and writing. He uttered his demand for literary production in the context of a ritual celebration of friendship. He offered his personal presence in return for Schleiermacher's future text. Nonetheless, Schleiermacher's account of Schlegel's "little trick," or birthday contract, reveals the triple burden of labor ("be diligent"), textual production ("write books"), and originality ("write something original this year"). Schlegel, the theorist of play in his fragments on romantic irony, puts Schleiermacher to work. But as the outcome shows *(On Religion* and *Soliloquies),* the therapeutic intimacy of Schlegel's imperative lets Schleiermacher "work" in the genres of playful subjectivity.

From the auspicious start of Schleiermacher's involvement with Schlegel to his more skeptical retrospective evaluations of it, Schlegel comes to stand for the idea and the problems of influence itself:

> he has caused me joys and sorrows which no one else could produce, and should it ever happen that the differences in our mentalities, which lie deep within us, develop more and become clearer to us than our equally . . . remarkable agreement on many other points—should this ever happen (as is indeed likely, given Schlegel's innate vehemence) so that our mutual understanding be, for a while, interrupted and disturbed, I would still continue heartily to love him and thankfully to recognize the great influence which he has had on me. (BR I 240)

The breakdown of closeness was brought about not only by Schlegel's vehement temper, but also by Schleiermacher's relentless understanding. His ongoing analysis of Schlegel suggests that understanding is not innocent, though it may involve a quest for innocence. Over time, the question of understanding became bound up with the dynamics of power. The tendency among hermeneutic philosophers to deny to the interpreter an active interest in exercising authority is belied by this very early stage of hermeneutic theory. Schleiermacher claimed that his understanding was a manifestation of love and tolerance superior to Schlegel's truculence, but his letters indicate that interpretation is only a subtler form of defense and aggression than outright bad temper.

Schleiermacher was exquisitely aware of the fact that intimacy involved not only the will to understand, but also the willingness to be understood. As tensions accumulated, he concealed part of himself from view in anticipation of the other's misunderstanding. Schlegel's "hasty, violent temper, his infinite irritability, and his devouring tendency to suspicion," Schleiermacher wrote to Ehrenfried von Willich, "these make me unable to treat him with the perfect sincerity for which

I yearn; I must express everything to him other than I express it to myself lest he misinterpret it. Within me, there are still secrets for him, or some which will be imagined by him." Schleiermacher prefers the defensive tactic of being unknown or cryptic to unequivocal misunderstanding. But even earlier, at the outset of his close relationship to Schlegel, he contrasts Schlegel's failures of perception or paranoid resentment to his own hermeneutic strength or "grasp": Schlegel "will always be more than I am, but I shall grasp and know him more completely than he me" (BR I 277, 170; BW II 219–20).

Significantly, the aspects of himself that Schleiermacher feels it necessary to conceal are his feminine qualities, scorned by Schlegel, whom he always characterizes as hypermasculine. Schleiermacher refers to their living together [*unser Zusammenleben*] as "a marriage, in which all our friends . . . agree . . . that I must be the wife." Schlegel, he observes, lacks

> the tender feeling and the fine sense for the delightful trifles of life and for the refined expression of beautiful sentiments which in small things often involuntarily reveal the soul entire. . . . Just as he prefers books with large print, so he likes men with large, bold features. That which is simply gentle and beautiful has no great attraction for him, because, to carry out the analogy, it does not seem ardent and strong.[24]

Manipulating the dynamics of understanding so that one comprehends more than one is comprehended is a strategy long defined as feminine. Behind this maneuver lie the unarticulated associations between understanding as possession or control and between being understood as submission, even violation. Only in ideal (or idealized) marriages does love make each person equally transparent to the other. Where the balance of power and trust is not maintained, understanding may well turn into a competition to see who knows most but reveals least. "Before me the great and truly sublime image of his tranquil perfection is always suspended," Schleiermacher admits, but he allows Schlegel only "sometimes . . . to see himself reflected in the image of himself which is sketched in me" (BR I 169–70, 332–33; BW II 219–20). In this parable of unequal transitivity Schleiermacher concedes force to Schlegel, keeping knowledge to himself. Understanding compensates for

---

[24]The homosexual suggestions contained in the joke about marital roles are significant, less for the possibility that they convey suppressed erotic desire than for the facility with which they communicate stereotypes of character, particularly stereotypes of power and receptivity.

the absence of sublimity on Schleiermacher's part but offers its own gratifications as a figure for masculinity asserted as the empowered feminine.

Schlegel appears to feel more wounded by Schleiermacher's subtle determination to understand him than Schleiermacher is by Schlegel's *"Vehemenz."* In June 1799 Schlegel rejects Schleiermacher's cool response to his *Ideen,* the collection of fragments inspired by but significantly diverging from *On Religion.* Their unsettled and short-lived collaboration on the Plato edition, furthermore, was the occasion of "pique and even provocation on both sides." Outright discord is less hateful to him, Schlegel writes, than "the whole nature and nuisance of understanding and misunderstanding" [*dieses ganzen Verstandes und Misverstandes Wesen und Unwesen*]. He accuses Schleiermacher of interpretation devoid of feeling: "My writings give you only the opportunity to grapple with a hollow ghost of understanding or of understanding nothing" [*Nichtverstehen*]. In Schleiermacher's letters to Schlegel "a taunting irony plays between [the lines]," Blackwell observes. "Was Schlegel, the connoisseur of romantic irony, to take them as conciliation or rebuke?"[25] Schlegel's pained sarcasm on the subject of understanding makes it clear that being the object of hermeneutic expertise was tantamount to victimization:

> It would be good if you felt something about it [the farewell Schlegel has just uttered] since it could cause you to make an exception of your exegesis at least once, and possibly, if your understanding admits it, to think, as hypothesis, that you have not understood me from the beginning to the end. And so at least the hope remains that we will learn to understand each other in times to come.[26]

The fact that the word "to understand" [*verstehen*] and its variants are used to caricature Schleiermacher suggests that the latter's protective strategy of understanding was to a degree correctly understood by Schlegel as a form of critical intrusion. From both perspectives, then, efforts at understanding are viewed as conflictual moves and as symptoms of embarrassed estrangement. In a passage from *On Religion* which points us toward the binarisms of the masculine domain dramatized in that text, Schleiermacher allegorizes the unease and instability

---

[25]Blackwell, *Schleiermacher's Early Philosophy of Life,* 130.

[26]This letter appears in Walter Benjamin's little collection of German letters, *Deutsche Menschen* (Frankfurt am Main: Suhrkamp, 1972), 123–24.

of this situation, casting himself and Schlegel as "Religion" and "Art," respectively:

> Religion and art stand beside each other like two kindred beings. . . . Friendly words and outpourings of the heart are ever on the tips of their tongues. But art and religion always hold back, unable to re-cover . . . the right manner of yearning and sensitivity in these incipient utterances. . . . Straining and sighing under a similar oppression, they look upon each other's difficulties with profound affection and sympathy perhaps but without a truly uniting love. (OR 200)

In his contribution to Novalis's *Blütenstaub* Schlegel wrote, "If in com-municating a thought, one fluctuates between absolute comprehension and absolute incomprehension, then this process might already be termed a philosophical friendship" (LF 160). The relations between Schleiermacher and Schlegel show that an ironic perspective develops in the mind of the one who understands but feels he is not reciprocally comprehended. Schlegelian irony and hermeneutic understanding, de-veloped by these two friends against each other, are structurally alike in being grounded in the subject's experience of epistemological dis-junction.[27]

Schlegel's successor (and foil) in Schleiermacher's affections was Ehrenfried von Willich, whose widow Schleiermacher married in 1809. In Willich, significantly drawn to him by the rhapsodic *Solilo-quies,* Schleiermacher found a nonthreatening male friend from whom he need not protectively withhold himself. As he had "married" Schlegel, he now married through Willich. He participated vicariously in the other man's betrothal and came to be addressed passionately by Henriette von Willich as "Father." He entered into their marriage as an androgynous third person, sharing Willich's love for Henriette and hers for him. A passage in a letter from the bride describing Schleier-macher's "presence" at their wedding in 1804 confirms this: "How entirely you were with us the day before yesterday! At the moment that we were blessed, and fell into each other's arms, in the greatest emotion and joy, we called out to each other "Schleiermacher and

[27]Jack Forstman links Schlegelian irony to Schleiermacher's hermeneutics in a struc-tural way, comparing the mental oscillations of hermeneutic understanding to the alter-nations of irony. *A Romantic Triangle: Schleiermacher and Early German Romanticism* (Mis-soula, Mont.: Scholars Press for The American Academy of Religion, 1977), 102–3.

Jette" [Henriette Herz]; then our brother gave us your letter, and we really felt how you love us, how we belong to you" (BR I 405).

This triangle is the benign opposite of Schleiermacher's difficult love for Eleanore Grunow, who would not, in the end, divorce her husband; the marriage of Henriette and Ehrenfried also knowingly takes as its model the friendship of Schleiermacher and Herz. Schleiermacher was in love with marriage as the home of understanding free from concealment and resentment. "I love your marriage," he wrote the newlyweds, "as something outside of yourselves, as if it were a distinct being" (BR II 7). This, perhaps, is the ideal stance for the hermeneutic philosopher: to enter into marriage, or into interpretation, not as husband or wife, but as the self-consciousness of understanding itself. The longing for such a marriage is a personal expression of what is also a philosophical desire, the desire for understanding sequestered from power.

Confidential Letters on Lucinde

The negotiations between analysis and intimacy are played out in their most overtly gendered form in Friedrich Schlegel's *Lucinde* (1799) and Schleiermacher's *Confidential Letters on Friedrich Schlegel's Lucinde (Vertraute Briefe,* 1800).[28] In them we can discern the same anxieties about the ethics of interpretation—and the significance of gender in structuring understanding—which surface in the correspondence. The link between hermeneutics and psychology (always a vexed issue in the literature on hermeneutics, where the charge of "psychologism" is rampant) is never more evident than in writings like *Confidential Letters* and the novel it defends. Both works depend on fictions of dialogue or correspondence. Writing is meant to evoke speech and, through that, subjectivity; in these texts, where interpretive and erotic roles are fully intertwined, it is meant to evoke the social problems of the sexual body as well. These two works remind us once again that the double role of misunderstanding, its function both as the catalyst of and the obstacle

---

[28]Although the *Confidential Letters* was written in the very short period between the composition of *On Religion* and the *Soliloquies,* I take it up here in order to pursue more lucidly the dynamics of the Schlegel-Schleiermacher relationship. For commentary on the connections between the two works, see Paul Kluckhohn, *Die Auffassung der Liebe in der Literatur des 18. Jahrhunderts und in der deutschen Romantik* (Tübingen: Max Niemeyer, 1966), 435–50, and Blackwell, *Schleiermacher's Early Philosophy of Life,* 256–58.

to understanding, is the theme of self-conscious reflection for German romantics long before its academic formulation by Schleiermacher.

Lucinde is a series of love letters, prose poems, fantasies, confessions, and character sketches. Most of them are sent from the protagonist and occasional narrator, Julius, to his mistress, Lucinde, but a few are directed elsewhere, notably the letter from Julius (Schlegel) to Antonio (Schleiermacher). Schleiermacher's "confidential" letters on *Lucinde* are exchanged among "Friedrich" and the members of a predominantly female circle of fictive friends; they likewise exploit the erotic potential of the epistolary form. The love affair of Julius and Lucinde is re-enacted (more discreetly) by "Friedrich," the ostensible author of Schleiermacher's letters, and his "Eleanore."

Schleiermacher, as "Friedrich," insists that *Lucinde* represents the multiple harmonies of sexuality and spirit united in the individual, in the love affair itself, and in its social milieu. The novel, he argues, celebrates these harmonies not only narratively but also linguistically in the co-presence of sexual explicitness and philosophical abstraction. But *Lucinde* and the *Confidential Letters* are also riddled with threats to sustained communion or community of any kind, a thematic that is addressed more obliquely. Most significant for our purposes are the pointed, at times hostile, references aimed by Schlegel and Schleiermacher at each other.

These are most overt in *Lucinde* in the letter from Julius to Antonio containing accusations of misunderstanding and speculations about the nature of intimate speech, monogamy in friendship, and the violence of analytical observation. Schleiermacher's response in the *Confidential Letters* is more enigmatic. Schlegel enters Schleiermacher's text as its occasion but is never himself directly invoked or addressed. *Confidential Letters* stages a defense of *Lucinde* in the form of a hermeneutic contest among readers, which Schleiermacher ("Friedrich") wins on Schlegel's behalf by answering their objections or explaining their enthusiasms. He dwells on the interpretive delicacy required of lovers, friends, and readers and, in the "Essay on the Sense of Shame" ["Versuch über Schaamhaftigkeit"], discourses at length on the violations of mental privacy which are society's mode of interpretive abuse. In defending the book from its strongly negative reception, he refrains from attacking Schlegel and applies his hermeneutic expertise instead.

It is precisely Schleiermacher's excessive cultivation of tact that Julius protests in his letter to Antonio in *Lucinde*. A superfluity of intellectual "delicacy and refinement" [*Zartheit und Feinheit*], Julius warns, will weaken "heart and feeling," depriving one of "manhood and practical power." Antonio's "sense for everything beautiful," for intellectual exquisiteness, is not accompanied by a sense for friendship. Julius charges Antonio with presuming "morally [to] criticize" his friend: "do you seek virtue in those cool subtleties of feeling, in those gymnastics [*Kunstübungen*] of the spirit that hollow out a man and gnaw the healthy marrow of his life?" (LF 121–22; L 74–75). Schleiermacher is taunted in his own terms, as in Schlegel's actual letters. Julius equates reflective understanding with criticism, criticism with emotional distance and negative moral judgments. He operates according to the inherited cultural division of thought from feeling and its corollary, the association between thought and aggression.

In the "Letter to Antonio" this binary metaphor of ethical expression is linked to the difference between linguistic exposure and protective silence. The text hints at a triangular relationship among Julius, Antonio, and a third friend, Edward. Julius contrasts Antonio's persistent questions to the silence that shields "the invisible communion" between himself and Edward. "You who know so much, would also know the reasons why our friendship has died," Julius charges. But perhaps "I've been wrong in this assumption," he goes on, "since you've shown yourself to be so surprised that I want wholly to open myself to Edward . . . you seemed to ask almost without comprehending how you had offended me" (LF 122).

Julius feels that it is "a desecration to tell you everything about Edward." To speak of a friend to an analyst like Antonio/Schleiermacher is to betray him to injury. "You've done nothing against him," Julius concedes, "or even said anything out loud; but I know and see very well how you do think about him." To think critically about someone is as much a violation as to speak critically. Antonio's "mere finesse" and his "spectatorial personality" [*beschauende Natur*] "close [him] off" from feeling, Julius charges. Julius mocks Schleiermacher's "vaunted tolerance" in the dictum "Each one is misunderstood in his own way." This inverts a passage earlier in the novel, in the section that provided Schleiermacher with the plot of the *Confidential Letters*. Julius speculates on *Lucinde's* effect on female readers and, in the process of celebrating the innate and superior apprehension of women, parodies what would become the catch phrase of Schleiermacher's hermeneutics: "Many would understand me better than I do myself, but only one would understand me completely, and that is you" (Lucinde herself) (LF 122–23, 62). Faith or belief in the other, not reflective judgment, is the ethical stance appropriate to friendship, according to Julius. He casts off Antonio's refinement in favor of the manly heroism of Edward and the accessible interiority of Lucinde herself, to whom he writes, "Misunderstandings are good, too, in that they provide a chance to put what is holiest into words [*zur Sprache*]. The differences [*Das Fremde*] that now and then seem to come between aren't in us. . . . They are only between us and on the surface" (LF 109; L 64). Julius suddenly sounds like Schleiermacher, who situates misunderstanding "between" intimates and understanding "in" them.

In a swerve typical of the mood swings of Schlegelian *Witz,* the second part of the letter describes a tentative reconciliation based on a shift of focus from thought to language and, within language, to the relative merits of speech and writing. The change derives from Julius's sudden tolerance for mediation. In the gap between the two parts of the letter Julius and Antonio have talked about talk. "It's all right with me that you prefer not to write but to scold the poor innocent alphabet," Julius begins. He himself now elects writing as slightly "more delicately veiled" than conversation, which is "too loud and too close and too individual." He has accepted the linguistic condition as appropriate to modern friendship, to the "mutual stimulation and development" of the companionable "mysticism" between himself and Antonio, if not to the heroic brotherhood of former ages represented by Edward.

As one might predict, Schleiermacher's response to *Lucinde* in *Confidential Letters* is far less antagonistic than the fictive text directed by Schlegel at him. *Confidential Letters* interpreted the novel (despite Schleiermacher's misgivings about it) to the public and to Schlegel's intimates, audiences that were equally appalled by *Lucinde* for different reasons.[29] *Confidential Letters* offers a model of reception much in the spirit of portions of *Lucinde* itself, not a critique of the book or its author. But since the letters operate according to the fiction of an exchange of views among readers, views that reveal the entire culture of the correspondent, the collection is of considerable interest as a document in the argumentative invention of hermeneutic understanding.

The epigraph to the *Confidential Letters* might well be the statement addressed with a sigh of ironic pessimism by "Friedrich" to his correspondent in the sixth letter: "The talent for misunderstanding is infinite, and it is really not possible to overcome it." For the most part, the letters to Friedrich are analyzed by him in the return post as exemplars

---

[29]Dilthey, *Leben Schleiermachers,* 494–96.

of various kinds of misreading. Karoline's indignant outburst in the fourth letter on behalf of "Mädchen" elicits a stern response for its partiality (in both senses of the word). The sixth letter, expressing Edward's moral squeamishness, which uses the classics to justify itself, provokes an equally forceful correction in defense of the moderns. And in the ninth and final letter Friedrich reprimands Ernestine's apparent preference for more conventional novels by prodding her to develop an artistic kind of reading that will illuminate the authorial motives of Julius, of Schlegel, and of Lucinde herself: "without grasping something artfully . . . you will not understand much" (VB 480, 504).

The most interesting portions of the letters, however, in view of the aesthetic and ethical concerns of Schleiermacher's hermeneutic manuscripts, are the more meditative reflections by Friedrich, Ernestine, and Eleanore on the problems of discourse about love. They continue the investigation into the language appropriate to intimacy begun in *Lucinde* itself. The hermeneutic themes of the letters remind us that the collective embarrassment of the Schlegel circle brought the *Confidential Letters* into being. Schleiermacher studies the self-consciousness that *Lucinde* arouses in those who read it and the limited possibilities of vindicating the text in analytical language. To Ernestine, for example, Friedrich questions the efficacy of abstract language in literary works or in responses to them. He raises an analogous issue when, in the "Versuch über die Schaamhaftigkeit" ["Essay on the Sense of Shame"], he explores the fine line between shame as marking societal violations of mental privacy and modesty as the liberating condition of love. In both cases Schleiermacher focuses on the potential conflict between love and reflection on it. This has its literary equivalent in the experience of *Lucinde* and reflection on it.

The second letter, in which he chastises Ernestine for her reluctance to speak about *Lucinde* in the sexually mixed company of the salon, describes the kind of social discourse such a book should produce. It is a discourse, ultimately, that mirrors the structural integrations accomplished in the text itself between predictable binarisms: masculine and feminine qualities, intellect and feeling, mind and body. As a happily married woman ("one of the chosen few who dwell in a true marriage"), Ernestine is uniquely qualified to speak productively and authentically on books about love: "And in this perplexity, to whom should one pay attention but to an honorable woman whose vocation is love. . . ?" Such understanding must be shared in a "circle" of friends, the salon that instructs young men and women, through conversation, in the art of love. The experience of love is the prerequisite for understanding and for the crucial ability to communicate understanding: "Love is an infinite object of reflection, and so should reflect endlessly on itself, and reflection does not find its place without communication, particularly among those who, according to their natures, see various aspects of it" (VB 436–37, 440).

The circle of readers, animated by Ernestine's sympathetic position, her place "in love," as it were, and by her verbal art (her correspondent tells her, "You are a champion of speech" [*Meisterin des . . . Gespräches*]), will come to imitate the topic of conversation, the book of love. The desire for "discourse" about readerly "impressions" is fulfilled by the literally impressionable cognition of women:

> You know that in general we do not credit the talent of abstraction to your sex. Thus, if you discourse with or before men on impressions occasioned by a book in which love is sought out in its innermost mysteries, you must believe accordingly that we would necessarily think that your imagination is busily retracing these impressions at the same time, in the view that you could not speak from experiences without inwardly repeating them. (VB 438–40)

Because women do not argue abstractly, their remarks *about* love draw men, the "slaves of abstraction," *into* love, which is what they wanted all along.

The same conviction that understanding can arise only from identities of action, speech, and feeling emerges in the interpolated "Versuch über die Schaamhaftigkeit" ("Essay on . . . Shame"). Here Schleiermacher resists attempts to segregate animality and idealism, which lead to the ever more energetic repression of sensuality. In this portion of the *Confidential Letters* the hermeneutic web of relationships binding together apparently opposite qualities corrects the conceptual and moral violence of prudery's oversimplified distinctions. Schleiermacher justifies reading works on love by arguing that one can innocently reflect on forms of sensuality one would not engage in and can navigate the fine line between the permissible and the forbidden without severing the healthy relationship between sex and spirit.

In this context sexual decency depends on understanding that, if talking about love makes love possible, love becomes ethical as the subject of conversation. Ultimately, Schleiermacher defines the state of "shame," connoting a sense of sexual decency, as intimacy that is individually negotiated without coercion. Among consenting lovers shame is a condition of "free play," which is also the condition of art:

"The shame of lovers toward each other" inheres in their ability to fend off any "encroachment" on their mutual involvement. Schleiermacher writes: "Each charming hint, each ironic play [*witzige Spiel*], which fantasy produces, has its place in the order [of love], in which, because of modesty, there is no [question of] excess or limitation" (VB 457, 460). A refined sense of shame makes possible the tact that desires to talk about *Lucinde,* not censor it.

The peculiarly feminine mediations of inner feeling and social expression are a step on the way to Schleiermacher's late theology, in which the feeling of dependency is so important. There, too, he seems to be trying to achieve a universally androgynous outlook by subjecting masculine critical habits to feminizing influences. In the sixth of the *Confidential Letters* he urges this kind of spontaneity on Edward, who is too conventional to open himself up to the theory intrinsic to the work of art itself and keeps trying to establish his theoretical perspective in advance of reading. How should one prepare to read, Friedrich demands in return, "through theory? how, then, should one prepare for theory, and where will this course of precautions end?" (VB 481). The gesture of starting to theorize in the midst of reading is motivated by the wish to avoid the style of mastery.

CHAPTER 2

Understanding and Defense

Against Art, *On Religion*

The connections among antagonism, love, and understanding are unfolded with increasing complexity in the successive editions of *Über die Religion* (1799, 1806, 1821). *On Religion: Addresses in Response to Its Cultured Critics,* the book demanded by Schlegel at Schleiermacher's surprise birthday party, is a text predicated on the author's argument with his audience. "This book bears the marks of controversy [*Oppositionscharakter*] throughout," he remarks. The dual character of the addresses is reflected in the dual function of the term "religion," which refers throughout to what divides the speaker from his auditors as well as to the mutual communication of pious feeling to which he would convert them. In "the struggle of the learned and cultured against the pious," he announces, "faith is the object of our controversy." "Religion" designates both the erroneous perceptions of the secular humanist and the corrective psychology of Schleiermacher, which finds its pleasure in the need to transform difference into community (OR 73–74, 93).

Controversy, therefore, is taken up on behalf of a theory of sympathetic absorption mirrored in a mode of argument that repeatedly brings external realms of difference within the circle of subjectivity (OR 327). Despite the theme of receptivity, habitually associated by Schleiermacher with the feminine, the subject in question is certainly masculine, as the argument is one between men, between religion (Schleiermacher) and art (Schlegel). Religious feeling operates as a kind of allusion to feminine understanding as represented in the *Confidential Letters on Lucinde*. But metaphors of gender are absent throughout most of the book and surface only in a few telling episodes.

The silence of the feminine and its structural efficacy are conveyed through an allegory of understanding, language, and gender, one of Schleiermacher's rare fables, rare even in his rhapsodic prose of the late 1790s. Adam, the hero of the allegorical narrative, presides over acts of comprehension and communication; he operates through language and *as* language but only after Eve's speechless otherness situates him in a dialogue with a differentiated world.

> As long as the first man was alone with himself and with nature, the deity held sway over him and addressed him in various ways, but that first man neither understood nor answered him. His paradise was beautiful, the heavens shone with all the splendor of the stars, but no real awareness of the world had yet developed within him, not even from within the depths of his soul. Yet his spirit was moved by longing for a world, and so he took charge of the animals to see whether he could make a world of them. Recognizing then that the world would be nothing as long as man was alone, the deity created a helpmate for him, and now for the first time there arose in him the sounds of wit and quickening [*lebende und geistvolle Töne*], and there before his very eyes the world was formed. In flesh of his flesh, bone of his bone, he discovered humanity, catching already in this primitive love, the dim presentiment of all the forms and tendencies of love. And in humanity he found his world. From this moment on, he was capable both of hearing the voice of the deity and of giving response. No more would even the most wanton transgression of the divine laws serve to cut him off from all contact with the sacred being. (OR 120–21)

In this parable comprehension and speech come into existence simultaneously, mediated by the feminine figure through whom the world of discourse and difference comes into being despite her wordlessness. Prior to this moment, neither God nor the world enters into human awareness; the man is not only unself-conscious but almost devoid of perception. His only sensation is the primordial "longing for a world," longing correctly interpreted by God as desire for the feminine. Love originates with its object and calls forth language, "the sounds of wit and quickening." The first man is able to converse (with everyone except Eve, apparently), to hear and answer God. Schleiermacher's favorite metaphors—marriage, speech, world—coalesce here as he dramatizes the centrality of the linguistic occasion. In this version of Genesis neither God's word nor Adam's brings the cosmos into being. Rather, it is the silent but language-provoking presence of Eve, crystallized in response to (or as the manifest form of) man's desire, which initiates conversation. Adam's "helpmate" offers the self-alienation necessary for language, but she also represents the mediated entry of the divine into the human sphere, in the guise of divination. God and woman, in other words, are two versions of the otherness that makes possible the "shuttling pulse of address and hearing" in both religion and hermeneutics (OR 120–21, 210).

The tension between the book's antagonistic and conciliatory gestures demonstrates its intentional production of conflict in the interests of ethical accomplishment. The hermeneutic tasks generated by the ethical will are manifold: to show religion's cultured despisers that Schleiermacher understands them better than they understand themselves and then to instruct them in a proper reading of the word "religion"; to develop models, therefore, of understanding itself as a religious activity and of religion as an interpretive activity; at the same time to evolve a conception of the subject as it engages in such transformative mediations and to provide that subject with a personal and cultural history. The vision that results, of a universe constituted in its minute and grandiose features by the synthesis of religious feeling— that is, by communicated understanding—dramatizes the unity made possible by Schleiermacher's limitless tolerance. He possesses a power of incorporation barely distinguishable from the prideful ambition of the systematic scientific knowledge he chastises elsewhere.

Schleiermacher wishes not to do away with conflict but to draw it inside the empire of understanding. In a wonderfully unexpected moment in the fifth address, for example, he defines Christianity as *essentially* divisive, discontented, and argumentative. "Because it expects to find godlessness everywhere," he writes, "Christianity is polemical through and through" and remains in "the most vehement inner turmoil." He applauds the antithesis between the Protestant and Roman Catholic churches, but the antithesis loses its sting once he characterizes their interaction as dialectical "interchange" and mutual "influence," as *a friendly rivalry, stimulated by calm reflection, in which each church seeks to appropriate whatever special values it recognizes in the other for itself*" (emphasis added; OR 310, 342). Rivalry grows out of and merges back into reflection. By transforming every opposition into conversation, into "friendly rivalry," he retains the privilege of passionate denunciation without incurring the guilt of perpetrating mental violence on the other side.

Fundamental to the hermeneutic morality emerging in Schleiermacher's writings of the 1790s is his preoccupation with questions of method. In many moments in *On Religion* irritation at the trappings of rationalism suggests that he is going to defend the logically inaccessible processes of religious feeling against systematic thinking. The definitional section in the first address mockingly concedes the methodological expectations of secular intellectuals. Since "without [the] separation of [religion into] a 'theoretical' and a 'practical' side you could hardly think at all," he charges, he can dramatize the errors of such definitions only by reenacting them (OR 69, 74). He follows the conventional division of knowledge into practical and theoretical realms, then subdivides practical activity into life and art, each of which in turn yields further distinctions.

Since religion has no clear place in this scheme, Schleiermacher's cultured audience can define it only as a methodological error, a "clouded . . . mixture of life and art." On the epistemological plane, where a similar division occurs between "'physics' or 'metaphysics'" on the one hand and "'ethics' or 'theory of obligation'" on the other, cultivated skeptics repeat the error of fancying that, as a mode of perception, religion is again "a mixture of theoretical and practical knowledge." Schleiermacher's correction in both instances is the same. Piety "cannot arise as a result of life and art conjoining; it must be an original unity of the two"; "the two factors which you are used to separating [that is, metaphysics and ethics]" join in a "higher unity of knowledge." Schleiermacher ends up advocating the negative value of systematic definition as the only tactic that can divorce religion from what it is not. He argues ironically for definitions that divide mental life into piety, morality, and science, and then he maintains that piety is unavailable to such definitional thinking. Philosophy, he grants, legitimately seeks "to know things in their distinctive essence; to display the particular relations through which each thing is what it is; to determine the place of each thing within the whole and to distinguish it correctly from all else; finally to present all the aspects of reality in their necessary interconnections and to demonstrate the correspondence of all phenomena, with the eternal laws that lie behind them." But "I would . . . contend that religion has nothing to do . . . with this knowledge," he concludes (OR 71–78, 80–82). In the course of this demonstration, he has set up another pair of terms, this one not ironically intended: the perspective from within piety and the perspective from without.

Schleiermacher thus uses but also denounces attitudes associated with systematizing disciplines. Without the difference made by piety in the operation of cultural classification, both ethics and philosophy would be destroyed, victims of analytical excess. Without piety, morality would "encapsulate . . . human life within a solitary and dead formula," a "lifeless bandying about of concepts" which cannot admit the feeling for the infinite. One would be left in the wasteland with other men (although it is I, not Schleiermacher, who introduces gender at this point), exiled to "the dominion of the bare concept," "mechanical devices," and "the vain juggling of analytical formulas." Schleiermacher reveals the chain of analogies by which scientific method, abstract ideas, spiritual pride, and masculinity belong together; they are grouped over against the feminine implied in the trope of fluid, unified experience, with its temporal priority as origin and its therapeutic "realism"—perhaps the literal impressionism of the woman destined to save the "slaves of abstraction" in the *Confidential Letters:*

> What, then, shall become of full-blown idealism—that most elevated speculative utterance of our day—if it does not submerge itself in this unity once again? How else may the humility that belongs to religion offer prideful idealism [*Stolz*] an intimation of another kind of realism, another kind than that idealism so boldly—and rightly— subordinates to itself? Contemporary idealism is in process of annihilating the universe while seeming to aim at forming it. It is degrading the universe to a sheer analogy, to a nonexistent phantom of the warped prepossessions of its own empty consciousness. (OR 83–84)

Schleiermacher himself aptly sums up his double conclusion on the virtues of systems: "From all this you can readily see how the question of whether religion is a system or not is to be handled: with both a hearty 'no' and 'yes.'" He stipulates that if "some inward and necessary cohesion of factors determines the formation of religion, so that every different way in which the religious sensitivity of people is activated makes up a discrete whole but so that their being differently aroused by the same object is definitely purposeful. . . . then religion is certainly a system." Experience that has this systematic character, however, is betrayed by language, which reveals the split between the quality of ethical cohesion and the quality of generality. Persons must not be thought of as "at set distances from each other," because such lack of differentiation leads to each "being determined, explained, and quantified in terms of all the rest . . . so that anything characteristic can be precisely defined by referring to a general concept" (OR 95–96).

Conceptual definition is associated with "external compulsion and bondage" by virtue of the link between system and uniformity (OR 95–97). The redemption of the system, then, largely depends on re-nouncing the discourse of concepts or—a crucial alternative—on the development of a way of reading philosophical discourse in the light of what it necessarily fails to articulate, in the light of an experienced coherence that cannot be captured in language, particularly written language. The ongoing debate among Kimmerle, Gadamer, and others about the extent, at different periods, of Schleiermacher's hermeneutic focus on mind as opposed to language only makes explicit the problem of mediating between the two which comes to the fore in his earliest works. The highly figurative style of *On Religion* and the *Soliloquies* partly reflects his interest in rhetoric that points beyond or behind itself. These experiments are succeeded by the theory of hermeneutic understanding, in which it becomes the reader's task to supply the word's silent context. The nonlinguistic supplement of religious feeling occupies the position of Adam's voiceless helpmate, producing dialogue but unheard in it.

The association between cohesiveness and piety rests on the non-violent ethos they have in common. There is almost no difference between the pacific temper of brotherly love and the method of re-flective integration that transforms spatial and temporal isolation into self-reliant timelessness. The religious individual is summoned "to ap-propriate [worldly activity] within the innermost depths of his spirit, to amalgamate it with the rest. In this way," Schleiermacher con-cludes, "he may divest it of its mere temporality, so that it no longer exists as an isolated particle within him, so that it is no longer a distur-bance but is sustained within him as something eternal, tranquil, and uncorrupt" (OR 105).

Despite the evident distaste for classification in *On Religion,* the best evidence of the conflation of hermeneutic procedure and religious feel-ing lies in Schleiermacher's description of religion as (*pace* Lacan) struc-tured like a language. "And you may therefore ask," he tells his read-ers, "what language is appropriate to the mysterious reality of religion: that of speaking? writing? action? the mind's silent pantomime [*die stille Mimik des Geistes*]? I answer: all ways!" All forms of expression can be religious, as long as the catalog ends with the shift away from text-like codifications to the quiet, gestural language used internally by the subject. Language is the "shell" that "profane men gnaw at." It protects the "secret, mysterious, hidden" inner self and, when its de-fensive services are not required, becomes transparent to other members of the "indivisible communion of saints," malleable to "emerging" piety. Understanding entails the reader/hearer's passage from outside to inside, a rite of initiation (like the indoctrination of men into the feminine knowledge of love in the *Confidential Letters*) into the "sanctuary which cannot be entered by force" (OR 322, 180). The interior life of all subjects is feminine in relation to external process, and the community similarly generates itself as an interior vis-à-vis less organized populaces.

The "city" of God is the setting for a fantasy of individual eloquence in which Schleiermacher carefully divorces rhetoric from "pride and self-conceit." Under the "free impulse" of a "heartfelt sense of unity and fullest equality" ("the communal abolition of all 'first and last'"), the priest "comes forward . . . to lead [the others] into the province of religion where he is at home so as to inject them with his own sacred feelings." The ministerial figure is a linguistic mediator who disciplines his superiority in order to lead the people "home." The priestly capacity belongs to "whoever has fully and distinctively developed his feeling to the point of gaining facility in some form of religious communication."

Schleiermacher's hero ranges through the cosmos in order to articulate it: "he unveils a hidden wonder, or with prophetic confidence links the present to the future. . . . Or his fiery imagination takes him through sublime visions . . . into another order of things." There is certainly pride, if not conceit, in the aspiration to "prophetic confidence," but (like Wordsworth, Coleridge, and Emerson) Schleiermacher quickly binds this self-indulgence to the general good: "when [the priest] returns from his journeys . . . his heart and the hearts of all have become the communal dwelling of a feeling they all share," a feeling they express collectively, like "some antiphonal choir" (OR 224, 212).[1]

The nostalgia still evident in modern hermeneutic theory, which often appears to stem from a dislike of twentieth-century technological culture, organizes such passages, where the spatial logic of analogy is transposed into the narrative logic of desire. "Longing" or "yearning" is a fundamental constituent of the hermeneutic tradition, in which understanding is a mode of desire arising from a sense of loss and in which loss itself is a belated figure for reflective violence. The violence of theory, which English romantics (after Burke) located in the French

---

[1]For a discussion of a similar passage in Emerson's early journals, see my *Emerson's Romantic Style* (Princeton: Princeton University Press, 1984), 22–23.

Revolution, is worked out through the tensions between religious ideology and aesthetics by clerical Germans.

"This business of extending religion," Schleiermacher writes, "is
simply the pious longing of the traveler for his home." But his vision
of return centers not only on the nostalgia produced by religious striving, but also on the moment. The *Soliloquies* contains Schleiermacher's
testimony to the revelatory effect of his decision to leave the Herrnhuter college; the fifth address of *On Religion* bears witness to it in more
impersonal terms. The "birthday of [my] spiritual life," as he calls it,
unified the divided self and altered the temporal structure of its subsequent existence (OR 217, 293).

Experience underwent a temporal restructuring that left the self in the
middle of a circle of time, where each point lies at a finite and precisely
comprehended distance. This event makes phenomena historical, determinate—the temporal symptoms of achieved understanding. And yet,
as I have said all along, the energy of Schleiermacher's hermeneutics
seems to arise from an unassuaged craving for love, community, and
wholeness. Given the co-presence in Schleiermacher's writings (early
and late) of both optimism and skepticism about the possible fulfillment
of desire, it is difficult to know how to evaluate the force of longing in
his work. The presence of determinate meaning begets the desire to
dissolve meaning, and so the absorptive energy of the mind's circle still
draws in or reaches toward what lies outside it. The mind absorbs
otherness not in order to erase its difference, but in order to care for it.
Difference can be protected from uniformity, according to Schleiermacher's paradox, only on the *inside* of the self, marriage, church, or
system.

The conception of the self implied by this expansive process has a
significant bearing on Schleiermacher's view of the ethical relations
between author and reader, or speaker and hearer. For although the
individual at any single instant occupies a circle clearly set off from the
world and from other persons, over time she or he tends to dissolve
into the social atmosphere; in the process, personality as the locus of
aggression and possession also fades. The self's circumference becomes
malleable as personality ceases to be defensive. When individuals are
afloat in the cultural fluid as Schleiermacher imagines it, the processes
of understanding or being understood come close to implying a temporary softening of the subject's distinctness: "those boundaries of
personality that you think are so settled are seen to dissolve away. The
magic circle of prevailing opinions and epidemic feelings surrounds
everything human, plays in and about everything, like an atmosphere

electric with all that is human. By the most volatile diffusion it stirs even the most remote elements of humanity into active contact with the rest" (OR 127–28). The particularity of opinion and temperament generates a "magic circle" of (perhaps) telekinetic maternity, where difference itself undoes individuality.

Throughout most of *On Religion,* however, difference is manifest as "the struggle of the learned against the pious," the duel between art and religion which does not vanish into "volatile diffusion." The 1799 text bluntly confesses that Schleiermacher is constitutionally incapable of understanding artists, a remarkable admission, given his milieu during the 1790s. "I should like to be able to gain a clear perspective on how artistic sensibility passes over into religion," he begins wistfully. "Why are those who have taken this [artistic] way such reserved natures? I do not understand them, and that is my sharpest limitation, the lacuna which I feel deep within my being. . . . the possibility of the matter now stands clearly before my eyes, only as something which is to remain a mystery for me" (OR 363–64).

In the revisions of 1806 the mystery has not diminished. Art remains the one area of experience Schleiermacher feels is closed even to his omnivorous comprehension. He formulates his query about the connection between art and piety in such a way as almost to answer it with his conviction that the artist's "spirit is gratified by immersing itself in each individual pleasure" (OR 198).

His own rhetorical strategies, commented on throughout the notes to *On Religion,* are distinct in Schleiermacher's mind from art. Rhetoric is pragmatic and communal: preaching, persuasion, self-dramatization, verbal adventure, and social experiment. Rhetoric cannot produce the *Kunstwerke,* the perfected verbal artifact. Numerous remarks added to clarify passages in the first and second editions of the addresses indicate that Schleiermacher regards rhetoric as characterized by formal looseness, a series of expendable approximations. Schleiermacher's easy detachment from his own statements, his willingness to rephrase, modify, and explain them in new contexts, is symptomatic of a loose connection between text and intention. He treats "rhetorical discourse" as a style in which "strict definitions are dispensed with and descriptions take their place, mixed with criticism of other positions I consider false" (OR 158n2).

The essentially descriptive or evocative function of rhetoric has its corollary in the reader's increased tolerance for inaccuracy. Since mood matters more than definitional precision, audiences are less judgmental. In a note devoted to the term *"Mythologie,"* Schleiermacher connects the mythological or nonliteral view of history with the generosity of an audience unified by its understanding of this historical perspective:

> There is no particular danger in using mythological language in scientific discourse about religion, since . . . the standard procedure there is to move away from the form of temporality and the specific contents of history anyway. Mythological language is clearly indispensable in poetic and rhetorical discourse [*der religiosen Dichtkunst und Redekunst*], however. With such discourse one generally has to do with audiences whose members have similar experience. The chief value of these notions for such audiences consists in their usefulness for expressing and eliciting awareness of the particular religious moods and attitudes of their members. In such persons the tendency to make allowances for defective expressions is already built in continuous revision. (OR 163n6)

Given the cultural atmosphere in which Friedrich Schlegel and Novalis, in particular, were defining art as the heterogeneous and fragmentary form of aspiration, Schleiermacher's notion of "rhetoric" seems to concur in their view. We may apply to him what he says of Plato: "one can only marvel at the awesome self-forgetfulness of Plato's speaking, in a moment of intense solemnity, against art—like a just king who will not spare judgment even of his too soft-hearted mother!" (OR 200). As in Plato's judgment, there is something willful about Schleiermacher's effort to define art so as to devalue it, all the while appropriating to himself the characteristics of the romantic imagination. The moral of the story purports to be that, as kings must demonstrate that they will sacrifice family for state, Schleiermacher, an aspiring "prince of the church," must reject his romantic influences by expelling them under the rubric of art.[2]

Art—the mother—seems to be the victim of the philosopher. But since the real issue is the tension in this parable between justice and leniency, the sovereign must really decide not only whether or not to sacrifice his mother, but whether or not to take on her merciful qualities himself. The cryptic otherness of art, its ability to "[take] its satisfaction in particulars" without the process of elevation which makes them "disappear" (OR 198), bears some resemblance to the immediate mimetic receptivity of the feminine mind praised by "Friedrich" in the *Confidential Letters*. Schleiermacher invests art with the softheartedness

---

[2]For the definition of the *Kirchenfürst,* or "prince of the church," see below, Chapter 3, the section entitled "The System-Subject."

he feels toward particularity, then throws in his lot with the drive toward totality, here cast as the superego that presides over systematic justice.

Soliloquies

Insofar as *Soliloquies: A New Year's Gift (Monologen: Eine Neujahrs-gabe)* is about art (and the work is about much else besides), it rejects art in favor of the subject as the chief result of imaginative creation.[3] Schleiermacher defines conventional aesthetic performances as bound by extreme formal and psychological limitations; he is then free to pursue, anywhere but in art, the pleasures of growth, synthesis, vision, and inspiration. *Soliloquies,* even more than *On Religion,* constitutes both an expression and a critique of German romantic literary culture. The soliloquist believes his text is revisionary insofar as it carries spiritual values away from the aesthetic realm and restores them to their rightful place in a modernized or romanticized religion. Individuals, Schleiermacher claims, are more important and more hermeneutically interesting than art; the highest kind of understanding, consequently, is elicited by persons, not by writing.

The economy of understanding gives the reflective self greater conceptual power than the artist, and power of a more moral kind. According to Schleiermacher's critique of the ethical limitations of the aesthetic, art is insufficiently human. *Soliloquies* opens with a discourse on "Reflexion," whose complexities end up revealing "the human being" to be the "artful voice" from which "the harmony between the temporal and the eternal proceeds." If humanity is such an "artful voice" and at the same time an "object of . . . reflection," the activity that links these two states is interpretive. The person who attains "freedom and infinity" is the one who "has clearly solved the great puzzle" of how self and nonself both differ from and operate on each other. The self is constituted as a whole by virtue of its power to rise to a total understanding of its own difference: "The distinction between inner and outer standing clearly before me, I know who I am." Comprehension turns the inner domain of the spirit into an integrated, though

---

[3]*Soliloquies* was begun before *On Religion* although completed several months later, after *Confidential Letters on Lucinde.* It draws heavily though not directly from thoughts dating from 1792 which, contained in sermons and essayistic experiments, made the works of 1799–1800 possible. The publication of *On Religion* released the bolder expressive indulgences of *Soliloquies,* the "New Year's gift" of 1800.

finite, system "viewed as in a distinct order and within fixed limits."
Schleiermacher continues triumphantly, "Whenever I turn my gaze
back into my inner self, however, I am at once within the domain of
eternity. There I can behold the life of the spirit, which no world can
change and no time destroy, which itself creates both world and time"
(M 14, 15, 20–22). Hermeneutic philosophy is typically hard put to
find a legitimate place for narcissism, but Schleiermacher's self-sys-
tematizing regard is unmistakable. Even more than *On Religion, Soliloquies* is most visibly organized by the contests and pleasures of subjectivity, including the fantasy of autogenesis.

The insistent way in which Schleiermacher brings together what
artists and philosophers had divided is typical of the way romantic
writers of all sorts try to join sublimity and analysis.[4] "Do not divide
what is eternally united, your nature, that cannot forbear either action
or *knowledge of its action* without destroying itself!" he exhorts (emphasis added). Although typifying the desire to unite reflection and originality expressed by almost all late-eighteenth- and early-nineteenth-
century writers, Schleiermacher's definition of art deprives the literary
artist of this synthetic program. In the second soliloquy, after he has
gleefully summarized his own development, Schleiermacher stresses
the difference between self-creation and artistic creation. The fact that
he regards the split between these two vocations as the "most striking"
that can be made, vocations only consummately united and then but
rarely, strengthens the logic of his defense of the naturally human and
the ethical against the merely literary.[5]

Schleiermacher offers himself as an embodiment of the mutually
exclusive character of art and reflection. The pathos with which he
regards the unavailable mystery of art in *On Religion,* in this (mostly
earlier) text, fixes on a wholly available object, his own subjectivity.
He has always "emphatically avoided" embroiling himself in "whatever makes one an artist" and has instead "longingly seized upon everything that serves self-development." In the lengthy exposition of
what this definitive difference implies, the cultivation of the self becomes associated with energy that flows into the enjoyment of shared
leisure and community and with the freedom granted by such out-
goingness. Artists, in contrast, are doomed to seek perfect execution
attained by dint of repetitive labor carried out in solitude. Bound to the

[4]Ellison, *Emerson's Romantic Style,* 3, 103–4.
[5]Tobin Siebers, *The Mirror of Medusa* (Berkeley: University of California Press,
1983), 22–29.

work ethic familiar to us from Schleiermacher's own laments about analytical reading in his early letters, artists tend in every project to "thoroughly work at the effect all its parts, the law and structure of the whole, will produce. . . . Their diligence knows no rest, as they move back and forth between design and execution. Gradually, through un-flagging effort, their practice improves, riper judgment serves to rein in and check fantasy. Thus does their creative nature advance toward the goal of perfection" (M 34–35). This ironic portrait of the artist at certain points resembles romantic caricatures of neoclassical practi-tioners of aesthetic correctness. Conversely, attributes usually associ-ated with the romantic artist are instead made to serve a countering, nonartistic vocation:

> If I must offer some presentation, it is never my concern to smooth away every last trace of refractory material so as to make the work consum-mate, as the artist strives to do. Moreover once I have expressed in action something that resides within, I do not trouble myself further about whether the act is repeatedly renewed in ever fairer and clearer fashion. The free use of leisure is my beloved goddess. Therein does a person learn in quieted sensibility to grasp and define oneself. Therein does thought establish its power, so that it can readily manage all, when the world summons that person to act as well. On that account, I cannot develop in isolation like the artist; in solitude, the very sap of my mind and heart dries up, the current of my thought comes to a standstill. I must move out into various sorts of communion with other spirits, this not only in order to see how varied humanity is, what aspects of it long remain alien to me or constantly so, and what, in contrast, can be appro-priated, no, through giving and receiving also in order to define my own being ever more firmly. The unquenched thirst for ever-expanding de-velopment of my own being does not permit me to give this act, this communication of what is within, external completeness as well. I place my action and my discourse out in the world, not troubled as to whether those who watch and listen will penetrate the rough exterior, given their sensibility, whether they will happily find my innermost thoughts, my singular spirit, even in a presentation lacking completeness. I have neither time nor inclination to ask about this; I must be moving on from where I stood, bringing my own being to completion, so far as may be possible in this short life, through fresh activity and thinking. An inartistic spirit, I hate to repeat myself even once. (M 35–36)

As though he had never been exposed to the *Athenaeum*'s aesthetics of the fragment, he claims that his elected imperfection in stylistic matters is unartistic. As though he had never heard Schlegel discourse on irony, Schleiermacher claims that his defiance of readerly opinion is unlike that of the literary writer. He indulges in a leisure denied to artists as though he had forgotten the prose poem on idleness [*Müssiggang*] in *Lucinde* and consigns them to solitude in a way that would have seemed peculiar to the eminently sociable Berlin "symphilosophers." Finally, he takes to his own hermeneutic vocation (and denies to the artist) a poetics of expressive energy which celebrates the word as deed, the word continually thrown off by the momentum of expansive self-development. Schleiermacher ends the paragraph with what must be his most Whitmanian trope, a song of the self that "must be moving on."

These canny contradictions show how persistently Schleiermacher claims for hermeneutics the powers of art. By "hermeneutics," here, I mean the project of defining the self in terms of its desire for a passionate analysis of experience, Wordsworth's "Knowledge not purchased by the loss of power" in which the gratifications of philosophy and poetry are conflated.[6] The soul's motives are transparent: "Gladly I renounce everything with which they [artists] credit me, if only I may find myself less imperfect in the area where I have positioned myself." Schleiermacher does not, finally, "exclude [himself] from the sacred territory of the artist" at all (M 36). Rather he takes his stand on precisely that ground.

Having done so, he proceeds to discuss the self as though it were an art object of the perfected variety. He applies to it the criteria of unity and clarity of outline, coherent form sharply distinguished from its surroundings. Although he again disavows the desire to create a lasting work, he critiques himself like a painting: "Here I will see whether a place of my own is fitting for me or not, whether there is some accord within me or whether some inner contradiction keeps my profile from being filled in so that soon, like a miscarried sketch, my own being is dissolved into an empty nothingness instead of reaching completion." "Only through contrast does the individual come to be recognized," he asserts, certainly a true statement of the irritable dividing lines that, paradoxically, underlie Schleiermacher's loyalty to dialectic in *Soliloquies*. He then moves on to the relationships that allow contrast to become conscious. He wants to maintain the distinction between difference and conflict, even though the *difference* between personality and artifact is generated by his own *conflict* with romantic aesthetics. "The

[6]William Wordsworth, *The Prelude 1799, 1805, 1850,* eds. Jonathan Wordsworth, M. H. Abrams, and Stephen Gill (New York: Norton, 1979) V, line 425, p. 175.

first condition for individual completion within a distinct circle is general sensibility," which cannot exist "without love." Love operates as the energy of self-consolidation. Social relationships prevent even one's "first attempt to form oneself" from being a shattering encounter with the external world (M 37, 39, 38). It is both ethically and psychologically desirable, therefore, for the soul to objectify itself as a perfected, distinct, and internally organized artwork over against the "homogeneous mass" of human experience. It is desirable in a way that the finished poem, sonata, or still life is not, for the independent status of artworks pretends to an ontological meaning that only persons can legitimately possess.[7]

Schleiermacher's curious resentment of art leads us at last, and in the proper context, to the passage on strife and interpretation with which the first chapter of this study began. We are now in a position to appreciate more fully the way in which understanding governs the relationship between love and autonomy. Love emerges as the prerequisite for understanding, but here understanding is also the prerequisite for love. This significantly qualifies the hermeneutic desire for community. The unnamed provocateur behind (or in) this passage is Friedrich Schlegel, personifying the element of conflict in the dynamics of friendship. Schleiermacher's emotional and philosophical maneuvering in response to Schlegel brings the subject of antagonism to the forefront of his thinking.

The pages to which I refer follow the long discourse in the second monologue, entitled "Trials" (or "Testings" or "Soundings") [*Prüfungen*], on how Schleiermacher's temperament differs from that of artists. This discourse concludes in praise of love as the power that enables the individual to stand apart from others as a coherent whole.

---

[7]According to Schleiermacher in *Soliloquies,* the precisely delimited meanings of language that truly serves sensory experience are exactly commensurate with the cultural assumptions of artists and art critics. These aesthetic presuppositions, in turn, are linked by implication to the ideology of an age in which "all things stand under the rule and command of thought," an age in which "in the feeling of such mastery over its body humanity takes pleasure in a power and fullness of sensuous life otherwise unknown." Against the forces of language, Schleiermacher arrays the soldiers of subjectivity, looking for a reliable sign "in order to dispatch . . . innermost thought under its protection." Since there are no reliable signs for inwardness, however, the individual must use language cautiously, as an imperfect, perhaps traitorous, messenger who carries love letters, in code, from one loyalist to another. In "the great battle around the hallowed banners of humanity," language offers "exact signs" and "the clearest mirror of the times" for the worldly party, but for the army of the spirit it "is still crude and undeveloped, a difficult medium for community" (M 50–51, 63–64).

The discussion of love then takes an even more defensive tack. After responding to observers who criticize his lack of specialization ("I need not cultivate science, because my disposition is to cultivate myself!"), Schleiermacher turns to "others who complain about me" for the opposite reason, his allies "who also strive to penetrate into the core of all things human." These intimate friends charge "that I am capable of indifferently passing over much that is sacred while spoiling a deep impartial view through mere contrariness [*Streitsucht*]," the same accusation made by Schlegel in *Lucinde*.

Then follows an explanation of Schleiermacher's habitual alternation between reticence and argumentativeness. "Yes, I do pass over many things," he admits, "but not indifferently; I dispute [*streite*], yes, but only to keep my viewing impartial." His defense of the necessary connection between conflict and understanding takes the form of an autobiographical narrative in which strife and interpretation are successive phases in the process of self-creation. Schleiermacher encapsulates the story of his conversion to self-determining freedom and uses this moment as the paradigm for all later encounters with otherness. Clearly, "alien opinion" means alien masculinity here, since his approaches to feminine difference nearly always assuage rather than stimulate antagonism.

> My late-awakened spirit, remembering how long it bore an alien yoke, ever fears to be dominated again by an alien opinion, and whenever a mode of life as yet unexplored is disclosed to it in new objects, it at first prepares, weapon in hand, to struggle for its freedom, in order not to begin enslavement to foreign influence in this case as before. However, as soon as I have gained my own point of view the time for strife is past; I gladly let each of the other views stand beside my own, and my sensibility peacefully completes the task of interpreting each one and of searching into its standpoint. (M 40)

The protective function of dispute emerges in this account of the self's ongoing discovery and defense of its point of view. Argument is a response to the power struggle between the subject and experience, which repeatedly threatens to dominate it from without. The ethical justification of conflict resides in its enabling contribution to the morally self-determined spirit. Disputes and quarrels characterize the process by which the mind places new perceptions in an intricate system of relationships. Argument belongs to the processes of knowledge which have as their reward the condition of sociable understanding. In this latter stage, when one's internal hermeneutic labor has been completed, it is safe to open oneself to the interpretive scrutiny of others. The peace of mutual understanding depends on the security of each party—security initially established by mutual suspicion.[8]

Schleiermacher's soliloquist proceeds to apply this model to the history of his relationships with the romantics. The initial striving of his sensibility "has had to strike those who were sources of new insights for me as antagonistic," he admits then with some complacency: "I have observed this calmly, trusting that they too would understand it once their sensibility will have searched more deeply into me." Despite the tone of self-satisfaction that pervades *Soliloquies*, Schleiermacher still sounds victimized when his calm contrariness and reserve are resented. "Even my friends have often misunderstood me thus," he laments, "if I passed without quarreling quietly by whatever they had seized upon with warmth and new zeal" (M 41).

Although he may rebuff those whom he is endeavoring to know, he wants ultimately to be transparent to them. "Is the distinct character of my being so hard to discern, then?" he complains. "Shall this difficulty always deny me the dearest wish of my heart, more and more to reveal myself to all worthy persons?" The pathos of this lament is self-inflicted, for Schleiermacher wishes to be understood without communicating, in the faith that communication will be forthcoming. To the degree that he will articulate only what he himself has first understood, sharing must wait on such possession. "Nor do I tend to speak of what still lies within me obscure and unformed, lacking the clarity which would make it mine," he insists in language that reveals the connection between clarity and appropriation. In such states of mind he will not permit himself to be understood by others more fully than he understands himself.

> How am I to convey to my friend what does not yet belong to me, why thereby hide from my friend what I really am already? What hope have I of communicating, without misunderstanding what I do not yet understand myself? . . . As soon as I have appropriated something new, gaining in culture or personal distinctiveness from whatever source, do I not hasten to announce it in word and deed to my friend so that this friend may share my joy and profit from perceiving the growth of my inner life? (M 43)

[8]Marshall Brown discusses the relationship between bias and tolerance in early romantic thought and connects it to the ideal of dialogue, which, in turn, he links to notions of the hermeneutic circle. *The Shape of German Romanticism* (Ithaca: Cornell University Press, 1979), 57–63.

Despite his view that misunderstanding is the normal condition of human relationships, nowhere does Schleiermacher deviate more from Schlegel's thinking of 1798 and 1799, as expressed in the fragments and in "On Incomprehensibility" ["Über die Unverständlichkeit"], than in his refusal to take pleasure in his own "incomprehensibility" (LF 259–71). Self-understanding is so closely bound up with Scheiermacher's individual well-being that it sometimes strikes him as simply illogical that his friends would expect him to share inchoate thoughts. His self-protective strategies lead him into arguments that reveal the potential for inequality in his vision of friendship. To the degree that he has appropriated the unfamiliar aspects of a new friend, he will allow his mind to be observed in turn. But, though he claims the right to sympathetic patience from his friends, he offers them something chillier—an apparent indifference to certain features of their experience, based on the just king's rigorous comprehension. A friend's "outward behavior leaves me calm and unconcerned, if I already understand the interior from which it flows and know that it must be thus because this is the way my friend is." Schleiermacher goes on to boast that his friendship has so "noble" an origin in a pure appreciation of his own and the other's "distinct innermost being" that "other things do not disturb me, and I calmly look upon my friend's fate as I do my own. Who will regard this as cold indifference?" (M 43–44).

The difference between what Schleiermacher may ask of others in *Soliloquies* and what he may offer them suggests not that he is cruel, illogical, or neurotic, but that relations of power and conflict enter into the construction of the philosophy of understanding. When the first-person voice ceases, as it does in Schleiermacher's subsequent writings, conflict persists as the condition hermeneutics wants to overcome. As we turn to Schleiermacher's theoretical works to describe the structural and rhetorical transformations of desire, then, it is all the more crucial to keep fresh in our minds his early defense of strife. The representations of misunderstanding in the works of the 1790s form the ground against which the compensatory strategies of hermeneutic understanding must be viewed.

CHAPTER 3

Hermeneutics as Desire

The "System-Subject"

After the publication in 1806 of his dialogue *Christmas Eve,* his last work in an early romantic mode, Schleiermacher's engagement with readers outside academic circles took the form of sermons and statements on public affairs.[1] During the uncertain years of the French invasion and occupation of Prussia (1806–14), Schleiermacher was first appointed lecturer at the University of Halle and preacher at the University Church; after his move to Berlin in 1807, he became preacher at Trinity Church in 1809 and professor at the newly formed University of Berlin, inaugurated in the same year. From his Berlin pulpit and chair, he urged a vehement but increasingly critical nationalism and set forth a pragmatic theology of feeling.[2] Except in his immense private correspondence, he never again invoked in secular rhetoric an intimate circle of friends, the stage for dramas of self-revelation and antagonism.

The confessional, polemical voices of *On Religion, Soliloquies,* and *Confidential Letters on Lucinde* seem at first to be lost or repressed in the

---

[1]*Die Weihnachtsfeier: Ein Gespräch* (Halle, 1806). Trans. Terrence Tice, *Christmas Eve: Dialogue on the Incarnation* (Richmond: John Knox Press, 1967).

[2]Jerry F. Dawson, *Friedrich Schleiermacher: The Evolution of a Nationalist* (Austin: University of Texas Press, 1966), 43–121.

academic treatises that form the core of Schleiermacher's publications after the turn of the century. A reader encountering the hermeneutic manuscripts after the works of the 1790s might well agree with McGann's ironic accusation that these texts have been "marked by that sign of Cain, a passion for systematic knowledge."[3] The logic is there, indeed, but the rhetoric of the system turns out to be remarkably continuous with the concerns of the romantic salonier.[4] The language of method, labor, and systematic analysis confines and disciplines the impulses of erotic receptivity. But the integrated, flexible totality of the system itself also arises from a desire for the feminine, for divination. Even though divination is isolated within the system as its most extreme mood, this position expresses the ambivalent tendencies of romantic system-formation as a whole.[5]

Schleiermacher generalizes his hermeneutic experiments of the 1790s into a method of compensatory understanding in the face of inevitable misunderstanding. The "art of hermeneutics" substitutes the interpreter's comprehension for immediate access to others (to authors). Community is taken up into the circling mind that insists on totality. Schleiermacher does not oscillate, as Coleridge does, between critical aggression and the desire for ethical sanctuary in feminine domains. Instead, he argues from the start that classificatory energy and receptive intuition complement each other, imitating the wholeness of the phenomena they seek to understand. The only sign that the two exist in some kind of ambivalent tension is the peculiar redundancy by which each forms an independent path to the same end of understanding.

[3]Jerome J. McGann, *The Romantic Ideology: A Critical Investigation* (Chicago: University of Chicago Press, 1983), 41.

[4]As Albert Blackwell and the recent edition of Schleiermacher's *Jugendschriften* remind us, Schleiermacher had been engaged in writing philosophical analyses ("Philosophische Versuchen") in tandem with more popular treatments of philosophy and ethics ("Kritische Briefe") since 1787. Before 1800, he wrote simultaneously but in separate productions for academic and nonacademic audiences. The change apparent after 1800, when he began serious work on *Groundwork to a Critique of Previous Ethical Theory* (1804), marks only the intensification of an already fairly expert 'scientific' idiom. See Schleiermacher, *Jugendschriften 1787–1796,* ed. Günter Meckenstock (1984), KGA I.1 xviii, and Blackwell, *Schleiermacher's Early Philosophy of Life: Determinism, Freedom, and Phantasy,* Harvard Theological Studies 32 (Greenville: Scholar's Press, 1982), 9–10.

[5]I share Robin May Schott's interest in the structural absence of the erotic in German idealism, although her treatment of this in *Cognition and Eros: A Critique of the Kantian Paradigm* (Boston: Beacon, 1988) is too remote from the specific dynamics of philosophy and philosophical texts to be useful except as an introduction to the issues.

The tradition of philosophical hermeneutics still regards itself as a search for moral ways to mitigate interpretive aggression. It is not surprising, therefore, that the ethical desires of Schleiermacher's theory of understanding are perpetuated today in writings on hermeneutics through metaphors of intuition, speech, and mutuality. The trope of the feminine, however, has vanished into the suppressed romantic past of contemporary hermeneutic theory. This collective evasion becomes visible when we focus on the unintentional resemblance of the language of the hermeneutic tradition to the language of feminists. At the end of this chapter, therefore, I turn to a comparison of these two discourses, each drawing on the same inheritance of gendered metaphors, which reveals the failure of hermeneutic philosophers to reflect on the implications of their own desirous configurations.

The challenge to Schleiermacher's readers is to follow the thematic patterns of the 1790s through later works in which they are not directly represented. As a preliminary exercise to such a study of the hermeneutic writings, it is useful to look at Schleiermacher's *Brief Outline of the Study of Theology* (1811, 1830). Although the *Brief Outline* presents itself as a theological curriculum, the preface suggests that Schleiermacher is strongly motivated by the need to imagine the proper relationship among his own multifarious endeavors. The textbooks available to him, he observes, organize theological instruction according to their authors' viewpoints. It is "necessary for me to draw up my own" scheme because, he implies, such topographies are the formal manifestation of personal perspectives (BO 17).

The strictly methodical arrangements through which he distinguishes the three main branches of theology—philosophical, historical, and practical—and their numerous sub- and sub-sub-headings arise from a commitment to the subject's totality. This perfected diagrammatic condition, like Coleridge's "Noetic Pentad," inherits the privileges of the circle Schleiermacher had defined in the 1790s as an interior domain. Then the craving for personal wholeness stemmed from the conviction that individual happiness and unity of intellectual endeavor depend on each other and on an "internal connection" among one's studies. This link between knowledge and feeling receives its scholastic representation in the outline form of Schleiermacher's handbook.

Perhaps the most telling evidence of the extent to which systems of knowledge are modeled on subjectivity in the *Brief Outline* comes in the figure of "the prince of the church" [*Kirchenfürst*]. This religious hero, the romantic "system-subject" or embodiment of *"the will to system,"* presides over the argument that the integrity of theology depends on the ability of individuals to understand the claims of all three theological modes.[6] The structure of the discipline must be represented in the consciousness of its practitioners in order not to disintegrate into competing or simply unrelated specialties. For "if everyone should decide . . . to confine himself wholly to some one part of theology, the whole of theology would exist neither in one person nor in all together." The problem is both social and linguistic, as threats to community always are in Schleiermacher's imagination: "with such a division of labor there would be no way for experts from different fields to cooperate. In fact, strictly speaking, they would not be able to communicate at all" (BO 21).

The solution to such alienation is an inward one. The structure of the profession must arise from the minds of its members. "If one should imagine both a religious interest and a scientific spirit conjoined in the highest degree and with the finest balance for the purpose of theoretical and practical activity alike, that would be the idea of a 'prince of the Church.'" In the absence of this mental image of the place of one's work in relation to undertakings motivated by the same spirit, labor loses its meaning in a "muddle" of atomistic enterprises, each carried out "in the spirit of whatever particular science is proper to them" (BO 21–22).

The fascination with method comes from the same impulse that generates the notion of a hermeneutic circle, method as the mental activity of subjective comprehension in ordering diversity. In the eighteenth century, the renaissance of Western European imperialism, the proliferation of available mythologies, cultures, and languages gave rise to the strategies of the comparative disciplines. These disciplines have their analogue in the way that the mind of the scholar guarantees spiritual or psychological connections among his or her objects of study. For some authors, like Emerson, Carlyle, and Fuller, the capacity to play with the cultural matter of diverse histories is a sign of power. For others, including Schleiermacher and Coleridge, heterogeneity carries with it a more intense anxiety about the potential dangers of a fragmented self or environment. Consequently, their statements on method tend to emphasize—under the sign of the feminine—

---

[6]Philippe Lacoue-Labarthe and Jean-Luc Nancy, *The Literary Absolute*, trans. Philip Barnard and Cheryl Lester (Albany: State University of New York Press, 1988), 33 (authors' emphasis).

healing, integration, and mutuality. Insofar as the hermeneutic circle embodies the strategy by which a disunified culture is reorganized in the individual mind, hermeneutic understanding is almost by definition an allegory of community.

Schleiermacher, like Coleridge, thinks of method as an image of community existing within the mind, where a variety of subjects—in both senses of the word—are held meaningfully together by the scholar's higher comprehension. Since this kind of method is ultimately grounded in the conviction that all subjects and all subject matters peacefully coexist in the mind of God, the romantic concern with method is inseparable from religious preoccupations. We can see why the notion of the hermeneutic circle, above all other types of method, has tended to carry the mood of romantic Christianity into the critical arenas of the twentieth century. We might say of Gadamer and Ricoeur, modifying what Angus Fletcher has said of Coleridge, that hermeneutic "method is the expression, and the experience, of grace as it appears in this life."[7] More importantly for my present purposes, the link between the desire for mental wholeness and the commitment to methodical investigation provides us with the fundamental premise of Schleiermacher's hermeneutic schemes.

The Fourfold Formula: Symmetry and Infinity

Schleiermacher's hermeneutic manuscripts are a complex series of texts. They include the sketchy aphorisms of 1805 and 1809–10; extended drafts on "grammatical interpretation" (1809–10) and on "technical interpretation" (1826–27); a series of elaborated theses referred to as the "Compendium" of 1819 [*die kompendienartige Darstellung*], annotated by Schleiermacher in 1828; and two addresses of 1829 to the Prussian Academy of Sciences, annotated in 1832–33 (HM 21–27). Together, they represent a curious body of writing, ranging from fragments and bare outlines of rules and formulae to extended passages of unusual eloquence displaying all the symptoms of the romantic sublime. It is clear that hermeneutics is, for Schleiermacher, a passionate endeavor. He calls into question every human word, spoken or written, and, having made himself the protagonist of an infinite task,

---

[7]Angus Fletcher, "'Positive Negation': Threshold, Sequence, and Personification in Coleridge," in *New Perspectives on Coleridge and Wordsworth,* ed. Geoffrey Hartman, English Institute Essays (New York: Columbia University Press, 1972), 147.

generates a method designed to approximate the total understanding it is impossible to gain.

From his earliest notes on hermeneutics, Schleiermacher's terms for the "objective" and "subjective" reconstruction of a text are "grammatical" and "technical" interpretation, respectively.[8] This second pair of terms comprises the founding binarism from which all elaborations derive: "Grammatical interpretation: To understand the discourse and how it has been composed in terms of its language. Technical interpretation: To understand the discourse as a presentation of thought. Composed by a human being and so understood in terms of a human being." Schleiermacher insists simultaneously on the mutual necessity of both modes:

> Grammatical interpretation: Not possible without technical interpretation. Technical interpretation: not possible without grammatical interpretation.

> Grammatical interpretation. Viewed in isolation, the ideal is to understand in complete abstraction from technical interpretation [to the point where "the person and his activity disappear and seem to be merely an organ of the language"]. Likewise, in technical interpretation, the ideal would be to understand in complete abstraction from grammatical interpretation [until "the language and its determining power disappear and seem to be merely an organ of the person, in the service of his individuality"]. (BO 69, 161)[9]

The two terms refer to textual aspects. They are complemented by a pair of interpretive methods. "Comparison" [*Vergleichung*], the "historical" approach, is supplemented around 1819 by "divination" [*Divination*], or "immediate intuition" [*Anschauung*], resulting in the fourfold combination of two textual aspects (grammatical and technical) and two treatments of them (comparative and divinatory). Grammatical and technical interpretation are both preoccupied with a problem of unity. The first focuses on the unity of conceptual meaning [*Bedeutung*] that can be inferred from the multiple senses [*Sinnen*] of a word, the second on the internal connectedness of larger units of style. In 1819 Schleiermacher is able to state, "The rules for the art of interpretation must be developed from a positive formula, and this is: 'the historical

---

[8]Around 1828 the much-debated term "psychological" interpretation is sometimes substituted for and sometimes designates a subdivision of technical understanding.

[9]See also Aphorism #48 (HM 49): "If every spoken statement is viewed with language at the center, all personal nuance disappears, except in the case of the true artist of language who individualizes the language anew."

and divinatory, objective and subjective reconstruction of a given statement'" (HM 171, 111). Since each interpretive approach can be paired with each textual aspect, the resulting diagram forms a chiasmic image of romantic totality, the chiasmus that, as Christensen says, "figures rather than resolves [the] will to interpretation."[10]

Despite the ease with which such formulations lend themselves to symmetrical statement—and the manuscripts, as one would expect, show a strong tendency to parallelism—they are asymmetrical in application. In this asymmetry Schleiermacher's ambition to be an artist, a genius, of interpretation becomes visible. Neither the grammatical nor the technical approach, proceeding according to its own internal logic, can judge what proportion of the task of understanding belongs to it. The decision about the relative emphasis to be placed on grammatical or technical interpretation depends on the interpreter, the locus of this methodological dialogue.

The required exercise of readerly intuition in adjudicating the claims of language and author makes hermeneutics itself the object of hermeneutic art. But Schleiermacher's curious silence about the nature of art and authority in the interpreter—striking after the polemics against art in *On Religion* and *Soliloquies*—exhibits his characteristic reticence in the presence of the question of power. The task of combining grammatical and technical interpretation is "artful" because it produces a finite representation of an infinite amount of information. Schleiermacher's earliest notes, perhaps as early as 1805, already link the impossibility of complete knowledge, the compensatory substitution of hermeneutic method, and the artful character of the reader's discretionary freedom, as does the draft of 1809–10. "Because of this double-character of understanding, interpretation is an art"; the "art lies in knowing when one side should give way to the other." Since, in any hermeneutic instance, "complete knowledge is impossible, it is necessary to move back and forth between the grammatical and psychological sides." Schleiermacher adds, with a willfulness that arises from no other logic than the need for interpretive self-determination, "No rules can stipulate how to do this" (HM 59, 100).[11]

---

[10]Jerome Christensen, *Coleridge's Blessed Machine of Language* (Ithaca: Cornell University Press, 1981), 27.

[11]The art of hermeneutics corresponds to the art of composition, for authorial creativity calls forth the inventiveness of the reader or listener. The writer is present only as the problem of the work's origin. Schleiermacher does not permit literary genius to condescend to the interpreter but insists on a similar originality: "every individual constructs language; . . . every understanding of a given text contributes to understanding the language. Consequently, the same principle operates in both" (HM 42; see also 97).

The autonomy of the reader and the eternal romantic aspiration toward completeness form a pair of complementary desires.[12] Together, they generate the theory of an art of hermeneutics which creates understanding as something "finite and definite," a positive response in the realm of representation to an infinitely receding horizon. Hermeneutics offers a solution to the laments about the unending labor of scholarship recorded in Schleiermacher's letters of the 1790s, a way of bringing labor and inspiration together: "the task is infinite, because in a statement we want to trace a past and a future which stretch into infinity. Consequently inspiration is as much a part of this art as of any other. Inasmuch as a text does not evoke such inspiration, it is insignificant" (HM 111). The experience of reading becomes a sequence of herculean efforts in this laborious but artful methodology. In every area the task is "infinite," an adjective that pervades the hermeneutic manuscripts. The possible senses of a single word are infinite in number; the historical data about an author's linguistic context and generic influences are infinite; and the particulars of authorial biography are infinite. "Infinite" becomes a synonym for "unknowable," a provocation to work, not to transcendence.

The compensatory nature of hermeneutics is not only due to the fact that we can never constitute perfect knowledge, however. Just as often, Schleiermacher attributes the necessity of method not to the infinitude of facts to be known, but to chronic misunderstanding. The epigraph to the hermeneutic writings could be taken from the *Confidential Letters on Lucinde:* "the talent for misunderstanding is infinite." Schleiermacher calls for a "more rigorous practice of the art of interpretation . . . based on the assumption that misunderstanding occurs as a matter of course, and so understanding must be willed and sought at every point." Only out of the "negative formulation" of Schleiermacher's fourfold schema of *misunderstanding* can the "positive formula" emerge. If there is such a thing as immediately comprehensible ("artless") language, it is not worthy of interest: "The distinction between artful and artless interpretation is not based on the difference between what is familiar to us and what is unfamiliar, or between what is spoken and what is written. Rather it is based on the fact that we want to understand with precision some things and not others" (HM 110, 108).[13]

---

[12]McGann discusses the necessary failure of romantic systems in *The Romantic Ideology*, 47.

[13]Relationships of fulfilled understanding are not normative for Schleiermacher's hermeneutics. Understanding comes closer to prevailing in the *Dialektik*, in which thought itself is necessarily a social process moving toward consensus. Even in that

The artfulness of hermeneutics derives, therefore, from the desire and interest of the interpreter. Schleiermacher's insistence on a general hermeneutics makes legitimate "such authors as newspaper reporters or those who write newspaper advertisements." In the first of the 1829 Academy addresses, he defends the hermeneutic dignity of "works which have no outstanding intellectual content, for example . . . stories narrated in a style similar to that normally used in ordinary conversation to tell about minor occurrences, a long way from artistic historical writing, or . . . letters composed in a highly intimate and casual style [or] . . . epigrams." In the fascination with the style of "ordinary conversation" or its surrogates, "highly intimate and casual" letters, we can detect the source of Schleiermacher's preoccupation with the mind of the author—the ghost that floats through twentieth-century hermeneutic philosophy as the specter of psychologism. Although Schleiermacher frequently refers the hermeneutic problem back from text to mind, he is in fact convinced that full understanding evades us in the psychological or interpersonal domain as well. Even "personal impressions" of immediate speech "must be interpreted," a process that is "never certain." Although he argues that interpretation has "the same aim as we do in ordinary listening," he stresses the role of frustration in causing that aim to be pursued: "I often make use of hermeneutics in personal conversation when, discontented with the ordinary level of understanding, I wish to explore how my friend has moved from one thought to another or try to trace out the views, judgments, and expectations which led him to speak about a given subject in just this way and no other" (HM 36, 181–83).[14]

---

work, however, dialogue arises from the participants' knowledge of the merely relative validity of their individual perspectives (see Manfred Frank, ed., *Hermeneutik und Kritik, mit einem Anhang sprachphilosophischer Texte Schleiermachers* [Frankfurt am Main: Suhrkamp, 1977], 97. Even the "potentiating linguistic spirit" of Christian churches, constituted by the discourse of their members, is founded in their need for differentiation from all other institutions (Aphorism #51, HM 50). Trutz Rendtorff's analysis of Schleiermacher's conception of the church is useful in extending my analysis of the desire for community at work in Schleiermacher's hermeneutics. Rendtorff discusses religion as "a particular mode of communication" and traces the implications of this characterization for the systematic structure of religion in Schleiermacher's works. Both Hegel and Schleiermacher, he writes, "recognize the Christian present . . . by the mediate way of a logical system" adapted to historical communities. *Theology: The Systematic Function of the Church Concept in Modern Theology,* trans. Reginald H. Fuller (Philadelphia: Westminster Press, 1971), 118.

[14]Elsewhere in the same extended passage he concludes, "The practice of hermeneutics occurring in immediate communication in one's native language" is "essential for our cultured life" (HM 182).

In focusing on the issue of "psychologism," the purported confusion between persons and texts, commentators on hermeneutics have missed the true cause of this blurring, which is the strength of the reader's self-regard. By responding to writing as if it were speech, and speech as if it were writing, Schleiermacher's representative reader satisfies both the need for intimacy and the need to apprehend an analytical totality.[15] The fourfold formula marks an intentional swerve away from the trajectories of transcendental idealism and from the transumptive will of Hegel. Its back-and-forth, both-and, shuttling, inclusive motions represent a decision to avoid the style of philosophical presumption. But we feel the strain. The construction and revision of the formula and the prospect of the labor that will be expended in meeting its demands suggest that hermeneutic method is doubly motivated, by the pleasures of theoretical mastery as well as by the longing for wholeness.

Grammatical Interpretation

Grammatical interpretation ("To understand the discourse . . . in terms of its language") is the earliest component of Schleiermacher's hermeneutics to take shape, the earliest in several senses. Its sphere, comprised of word meanings, inherits the techniques and problems addressed by Schleiermacher's predecessors, who focused on the linguistic complexities of the Bible and of classical texts. Grammatical interpretation thus predates Schleiermacher's hermeneutic innovations, though of course it is modified by them. Grammatical interpretation is predominant in his earliest manuscripts, the aphorisms. It is presented first in all subsequent hermeneutic manuscripts. "Language is the only presupposition in hermeneutics. . . . Grammatical interpretation comes first because in the final analysis both what is presupposed and what is to be discovered is language" (HM 55).

Nonetheless, the initiatory status of grammatical interpretation does not signify a priority of value. Grammatical tactics divide language

[15]Wolfgang Iser, who is closely involved with hermeneutic concerns, though not identified with philosophical hermeneutics, discusses the relation of text and reader in terms of its "asymmetry" but comes to a different conclusion: while "the asymmetry between text and reader stimulates a constitutive activity on the part of the reader," the text's "blanks" and "negations" create a structure which in turn "controls the process of interaction." *The Act of Reading: A Theory of Aesthetic Response* (Baltimore: Johns Hopkins University Press, 1978), 166–70.

into tradition and the individual talent; they precede consideration of the author because of their negative logic. The task of grammatical interpretation is to "construe . . . meaning from the total pre-given value of language and the heritage common to the author and his reader" in order for the individual creativity of the work then to be sharply distinguished from its conventional elements. It locates authorial art by defining it as what the conventional use of language is not. In practice, what this entails is a "precise determination of any point in a given text" in the light of "the use of language common to the author and the original public" (HM 70, 117).

To personify this mode of reading in terms of gender, it is masculine but antiheroic in character by virtue of its penchant for hard work and discipline. The "point" at which grammatical interpretation aims is the individual word. The exposition of grammatical procedures describes the exhausting prospect of arriving at the meaning of a word inductively, on the basis of a potentially infinite number of examples. This task is occasionally described in exalted terms as the resolution of multiplicity into unity, but this is not its prevailing mood. The slow accumulation of the senses [*Sinnen*] that constitute a "word-sphere" of unified meaning [*Bedeutung*] must start in the assumption that every word is problematic (including what Schleiermacher calls "formal" or "structural" elements, such as particles and inflections). Every use of a word "involves an infinite, indeterminate multiplicity" of contextual possibilities, and the word may be used in a given work, genre, or era innumerable times (HM 51, 79, 119, 42, 76, 121).

Consequently, when Schleiermacher turns to examples of how grammatical interpretation proceeds, it is difficult to feel that "science" is "constantly renewing itself from the center of its intuition." Except for a few moments when the "organic connections" of "coordinating and subordinating" grammar begin to sound like a fable of interpersonal relations, the "determination of the word . . . by a process of elimination" does not seem radiant with philosophical intuition (HM 128–29). One is reminded of Schleiermacher's complaints during the 1790s about the "unspeakable trouble," the "torment," it cost him "to grasp . . . a [philosophical] book."

The variability of meaning, which requires so much effort to understand, pervades the whole field of figurative language. Schleiermacher takes pains to clarify this and so should we, for it is through this admission of indeterminacy that the laboriousness of grammatical interpretation shades into its divinatory alter ego. The "distinction between the literal and the figurative. . . . disappears," Schleiermacher writes, because the method for analyzing them is the same. Every word is read in context, and almost every context is to some extent figurative: "There . . . arises a pretension that scientific expressions should be 'exact,' but this pretension can never be fulfilled. There are always terms that are commonly called 'figurative,' and even when that does not seem to be so, it is only because the terms are no longer grasped genetically." It is the task of philosophy, "the center of all science," to understand words as a "living terminology" constantly in transition between figurative instability and "the hegemony of the concept," or unified meaning. What might be called the density of differentiation, the multiplicity of *Sinnen* characteristic of words in a mature language is a philosophical opportunity: "duplicity of expression . . . is the basis for higher meaningfulness" (HM 119, 73–74, 87).[16]

Mirroring the "higher meaningfulness" of language, the collection of data about linguistic history "belongs to a higher understanding" than that experienced by the author. This comprehension is "higher" because it is self-conscious, and self-conscious because it is a willed solution to misunderstanding. "The statement that we must consciously grasp an author's linguistic sphere . . . implies that we understand the author better than he understood himself." *Because* "difficulties arise . . . we must become aware of many things of which the author himself was unaware" (HM 131–32, 85, 118–19). The phrase "to understand the author better than he understood himself," persistently associated by later writers with Schleiermacher's purported desire for empathic contact with the author's mind, in this rationalized area of hermeneutic theory is based on the reader's remoteness from linguistic habits automatic to the writer he studies. Temporal distance and the ethic of hard work needed to overcome it give hermeneutic understanding its priority of value over the author's unreflecting linguistic competence.

The defense of hard work nevertheless breaks down tellingly at a key juncture in Schleiermacher's reasoning, where the divinatory impulse, although unnamed, begins to make itself felt. In the 1809–10 draft on grammatical interpretation he starts to present the notion of the hermeneutic circle as a solution to the problem of distinguishing a word's unity of meaning from its particular variants. Because "this essential unity is never found as such [without the adulteration of the particular], it can never be presupposed"; rather, "unity is to be

16See also Aphorism #6 (HM 52).

sought." This logic leads to the theory of the hermeneutic circle: "Consequently, the task of grammatical interpretation is divided into two parts: (1) the task of determining the essential meaning from a given usage and (2) the task of ascertaining an unknown usage from the meaning." Elsewhere, Schleiermacher predicts the success of the hermeneutic circle as an interpretive strategy more dramatically, as in the second address to the Prussian Academy: "As soon as we turn to a new part we encounter new uncertainties and begin again, as it were, in the dim morning light. It is like starting all over, except that as we push ahead the new material illumines everything we have already treated, until suddenly at the end every part is clear and the whole work is visible in sharp and definite contours" (HM 76–78, 198).

In the passage of 1809–10, however, we see what can happen when one interrogates the hermeneutic circle too closely (HM 76–78). A series of questions exposes the limits of this solution and rapidly propels Schleiermacher into a regression that leads to thoughts of children, savages, and the primacy of feeling. "How does one get hold of the meaning?" he asks. "That is, how does one first arrive at a given usage and then go farther? How does one learn to understand in the first place?" The need to "go farther," to go back to "the first place"—the rhetoric of the readerly drive that motivates hermeneutic theory—impels Schleiermacher to reflect on the process of language acquisition. He describes this as an exact though unconscious replica of grammatical interpretation:

> For a child every instance of relating a name to an object must seem indefinite. It does not become definite until after many comparisons. . . . Only by means of associating and comparing particular meanings does one begin to grasp the inner unity. The inner unity is that which is representable in every particular instance of the intuition [that is, every time the word is used]. But since the completeness of the particular is never reached, the task is unending.

The quest for a point of origin prior to hermeneutic labor, conflated with the desire to "get hold of . . . meaning" in an absolutely satisfying way, leads to a paradoxical vision of a childhood without hermeneutic innocence. The nostalgia we anticipate in Schleiermacher's text at the moment of temporal regress does not emerge. The surrogate for the "inner unity" of the text is the inner feeling of the interpreter. As it is throughout the whole range of Schleiermacher's theological and philosophical works, "feeling" is a supremely ethical sensation, almost a self-explanatory one. In his inability to believe in a possible "completeness of the particular," Schleiermacher shifts again into the interrogative and answers his own questions in a passage of brilliant density: "Is there any substitute for this completeness? And even if one had such a substitute, would there be any guarantee that one had grasped the inner unity accurately? The guarantee could not be another rule having to do with method. It could only be feeling [*Gefühl*]. Thus this feeling [of unity] must be the substitute for completeness." Feeling arrives to compensate for the inadequacies of method, just as emotional prose responds throughout this passage to the endlessness of the hermeneutic circle. But at the point where divination, the intuitive apprehension of authorial creativity, is about to become crucial, feeling itself is referred to grammatical confirmation, albeit of a continually shifting kind: "The foundation for the certainty of this feeling must be that every given usage may be easily coordinated to the presumed unity and that this coordination is appropriate to the character of language. But this is confirmed only by analogy with several other unities, and it therefore becomes certain only along with others." The intuitive sense of "ease" and "appropriateness," stricken with anxiety about divinatory mysticism, must be backed up by historical or comparative method.

The passage closes by making explicit the dissatisfactions that produced it and by accepting them once more. This resolution is brought about by the image of the primitive, a figure that predictably appears with the child in romantic theories of language. In the very earliest stages of linguistic development, primitive societies have a certain knowledge of their entire language which even the children of nineteenth-century Europe cannot attain. "Grasping the character of a language by means of the reflection of the totality of thinking in that language is possible," Schleiermacher suggests, "only in the case of primitive peoples living close to nature." Schleiermacher's sense of the fallen condition of the modern interpreter again reveals the extent to which hermeneutics is a compensatory strategy. "One who has lost his philological innocence [*Unschuld*] must for the most common cases rely on philological science. The task can be completed only by approximation" (HM 76–78).

Throughout this passage Schleiermacher has asked questions to which the strategies of the hermeneutic circle have been an admittedly imperfect answer, second best in the light of the wish for an immediate or early certainty about meaning. The hermeneutic circle characterizes, rather than resolves, problems of understanding. Its compensatory status points us toward an explanation of why Schleiermacher needed to introduce divination into his hermeneutic system. Only with the assistance of immediate intuition is the hermeneutic circle transformed into a source of comfort, however temporary, rather than unease.

Technical Interpretation

Schleiermacher always conceived of hermeneutics as a dialectical process organized by a binary set of terms, grammatical and technical interpretation. The grammatical approach is the more stable of the two. Over the twenty-five years spanned by his hermeneutic manuscripts, its tasks and methods do not markedly change, though the energy expended on their description diminishes. Fully described later than grammatical interpretation, technical interpretation appears to balance its opposite term neatly. Once the tactics of comparison and divination are elucidated to complete the fourfold process of understanding, one would expect a certain stabilizing of all four terms.

The association of technical interpretation with divination undermines this symmetry, however, despite Schleiermacher's efforts to keep the four terms in balance. As grammatical interpretation ("understanding by reference to the language") had as its aim the determination of the unity of the word-sphere, technical interpretation ("understanding by reference to the one who speaks") pursues an analogous synthesis: it "is chiefly concerned with the over-all coherence [of the text] and with its relation to the universal laws for combining thoughts." Because of its capacity for the perception of textual unity, technical interpretation executes the inaugural plunge into the hermeneutic circle, "an overview" or "preliminary [reading]" of the whole in which grammatical observations may then be situated. "At the very beginning [of technical interpretation] . . . one must immediately grasp the over-all coherence. The only way to do this is by quickly reading over the whole text" (HM 69, 166–67, 83, 57). Technical interpretation is associated with beginnings of at least three kinds. Its grasp of textual unity qualifies it to begin the hermeneutic endeavor, despite the competing claims of grammatical interpretation; it is oriented to what is new in language, that is, to individual style as linguistic innovation; and it seeks to understand the origin of that style in the author's mind, although Schleiermacher provides no vocabulary or methodology for psychological analysis.

The psychological element of discourse inheres in textual transitions, connections, and discontinuities and requires no reference to the author's mind. If "unity may be reduced to style, in the higher sense of the term," then to understand the author need not entail the kind of telepathic empathy that the later Schleiermacher is frequently assumed to desire. In the 1819 "Compendium" the reader's inability to read minds gives rise to his or her compensatory mastery of style. And in the realm of readers all things are equal: "with respect to the objective [grammatical] aspects [of the work], the author had no data other than we have." In the 1820s Schleiermacher increasingly discredits the writer's special authority: "It is normally supposed that the most direct way to find the inner unity of the work is to examine the author's own statements at the beginning or at the end. This is wrong. In many writings what the author declares to be his subject matter is quite subordinate to the actual theme." Putting oneself "inside" the author, then, is the same thing as reading "between the lines" of the text, a process in which the reader's mind fills in the gaps in order to produce a coherent interpretation (HM 69, 112, 168, 182).[17]

Technical interpretation, true to its character as "a development of the beginning," views content as "what moved the author" and form as "his nature moved by that content." Its goal is to "grasp how the work is a necessary undertaking of the author," and "a sense for this necessity emerges only if the genesis of the text is never lost from view." The problem of "genesis," especially when it is bound to individual unity that is known to be "indescribable," leads to divination (HM 166, 172, 148).

Two kinds of motivation are at work in writing, according to Schleiermacher: primary and secondary thoughts, occasionally also called "purpose" and "idea." The purpose, or primary thought, refers to the author's conscious choice of subject matter prior to composition and to the declared logic of his or her argument. It is the ideas, the secondary thoughts, that present a hermeneutic challenge. The idea is

[17]When Schleiermacher links hermeneutics to dialectics (the "art of thinking") the tension between the "communality" of speech as shared thought and the need for interpretation, once the "internal speech" of thought is externalized, becomes evident in a subdued way. "Communality" means only that hermeneutics is necessary: "Since the art of speaking and the art of understanding stand in relation to each other, speaking being only the outer side of thinking, hermeneutics is a part of the art of thinking. . . . Speaking is the medium for the communality of thought, and for this reason rhetoric and hermeneutics belong together and both are related to dialectics. . . . Thinking matures by means of internal speech, and . . . speaking is only developed thought. But whenever the thinker finds it necessary to fix what he has thought, there arises the art of speaking. . . . every act of understanding is the reverse side of an act of speaking, and one must grasp the thinking that underlies a given statement" (HM 97).

the theme that actually emerges in the text as written. Secondary thoughts are unplanned spin-offs or deviations from the intended direction of argument or exposition: "a free train of thought. . . . aroused in him [the writer] in the course of his work." Individual creativity inheres largely in these "secondary representations" (HM 154–56).

Despite his numerous references to the mental origin of the work and to the mental surprises that created it, Schleiermacher never actually wants to get into the author's mind. What he wants is the sensation of recovering the experience of textual genesis. He values the artistic work because it calls forth the art of hermeneutics. Because "composition" provides him with evidence of "the way the connections between the thoughts have been constructed," empathic contact with the author emerges out of the minutiae of composition, which tend, therefore, to take on the status of symptoms or behavioral data (HM 147). Schleiermacher will take whatever biographical information he can get, but technical interpretation presupposes his remoteness from the person. The psychology that matters is that of the interpreter, and what most matters about the reader is desire, not knowledge. Since this desire is attributed to any "artful" reader, psychology is even here the wrong word. Regardless of our psychic individuality, not because of it, we are drawn to literary origins.

Divination

Schleiermacher's conflation of author and style allows empathy to be oriented to writing, albeit writing endowed with all the attributes of mind. "The hermeneutics of the spirit, insofar as it is not encompassed by the hermeneutics of the sense, lies beyond the scope of hermeneutics altogether" (HM 212). Since form provides adequate evidence for the divinatory recognition of the spirit that made it, a kind of psychologism is at work. The "method" (ill-named as such) of divination is the primary vehicle of Schleiermacher's desire for contact with another subjectivity. Whether the subject is a text or an author, the gift it ultimately provides is the reader's enhanced self-esteem. For divination is a pleasurable indulgence in antiscientific thinking, carefully contained within the flexible rationalism of the hermeneutic formula.

After emerging as the necessity for "immediate intuition" around 1809–10, divination is integrated into hermeneutic procedure at the very end of the 1819 Compendium, the "Kompendienartige Darstellung." By the time of the Addresses to the Prussian Academy it has become Schleiermacher's central theme and, in his mind, one of his chief contributions to hermeneutic theory. This tendency is consistent with the rest of his theological and philosophical corpus, which is filled with efforts to define in abstract language the redemptive process of intersubjective understanding. In *The Christian Faith* this concern takes the form of a phenomenology of religious consciousness; in the *Dialektik* it surfaces in the imperative of consensual concept formation; in the hermeneutic manuscripts it appears as divination.

As technical interpretation must alternate with its complement, grammatical interpretation, so divination must refer back to comparison. Making explicit what has been implicit all along, Schleiermacher characterizes the two methods in terms of gender:

> By leading the interpreter to transform himself, so to speak, into the author, the divinatory method seeks to gain an immediate comprehension of the author as an individual [*das Individuelle unmittelbar aufzufassen sucht*]. The comparative method proceeds by subsuming the author under a general type. It then tries to find his distinctive traits by comparing him with the others of the same general type. Divinatory knowledge is the feminine strength in knowing people; comparative knowledge, the masculine.

> Each method refers back to the other. The divinatory is based on the assumption that each person is not only a unique individual in his own right, but that he has a receptivity to the uniqueness of every other person.

> This assumption in turn seems to presuppose that each person contains a minimum of everyone else, and so divination is aroused by comparison with oneself.

As the conscious link between divination and "the feminine strength in knowing people" so powerfully shows, the divinatory method ushers into hermeneutics the scenario of *Confidential Letters on Lucinde, On Religion,* and *Soliloquies.* In the description of how the reader comes to know the author, we encounter a theoretical allegory: the community of understanding forms through discourse between androgynes in whom masculine individuality and feminine receptivity to it [*Empfäng-*

---

[18]See Sara Friedrichsmeyer's discussion of how the association of woman with the nonrational made her the object of desire for male philosophers, in *The Androgyne in Early German Romanticism* (Bern: Peter Lang, 1983), 51.

lichkeit] peacefully coexist.[18] "Comparison does not provide a distinctive unity. The general and the particular must interpenetrate, and only divination allows this to happen," Schleiermacher writes (HM 150–51).[19]

The symmetry of these complementary temperaments may be illusory, however, for divination tends to unsettle the balance between them. Since under the rubric of technical interpretation, divination undertakes to understand the same textual attribute as comparison—individuality—and since it accomplishes this effortlessly and instantaneously, it threatens to replace research with intuition. Why shouldn't this alternate perceptual mode render methodical comparisons obsolete? Divination is consistent with Schleiermacher's critique of alienated logic. He turns to it because "it is impossible to characterize the 'perfect understanding of style' in terms derived from the metaphorics of decoding," as Manfred Frank, one of the most acute readers of Schleiermacher in our century, remarks. "What is made commensurable by the 'comparison' cannot be the 'new,' . . . the as-yet incomparable of a phrase just heard, unless a conjectural hypothesis ('divination') had already made the . . . individual combinatory manner of the author . . . commensurable . . . by a leap of the imagination or an originary 'guess.'"[20]

The power of divination to outperform comparison suggests that within Schleiermacher's systematic hermeneutics resides the temptation to abandon systems altogether. He wants divination to play a double role, as the opposite of comparison in the fourfold strategy of hermeneutics ("We must employ both methods in both aspects" [HM 192]) and also as the energy that initiates, subsumes, or exceeds other kinds of understanding. The divinatory tendency of Schleiermacher's imagination strains the symmetrical apparatus designed to limit it. He strives to permit divination only as an opening move and a last resort, framing the methodical work of comparison. He says repeatedly that the hermeneutic results of comparison and divination are identical, except in their temporality: intuition apprehends instantaneously the whole that comparative study forms slowly, inductively.

Despite their identical conclusions, only divination that has been validated by comparison is worthwhile. Divination "becomes certain

---

[19]Frank observes, further, "an individual praxis can become social praxis only when it successfully effects a rupture in the repertoire of the grammatical." Frank, *Hermeneutik und Kritik*, 34.

[20]Ibid., 49.

only when it is corroborated by comparisons. Without this confirmation, it always tends to be fanatical" (HM 151). The reference to the
"fanatical" marks divination as the extremism against which symmetry
must be constituted. In the end Schleiermacher prefers systematic procedure over spontaneous receptivity. The balanced relationship of textual attributes (grammar and technique) and their corresponding readerly approaches (comparison and divination) win out over positioning
the reader in a "feminine" stance with regard to the work.

The 1829 addresses ["Akademiereden"] exhibit an easy and unin-
hibited tone more characteristic of *On Religion* or of Schleiermacher's
letters than of the rest of the hermeneutic manuscripts. It is impossible
not to feel that these qualities are bound up with Schleiermacher's
apparent agenda: the judging of his contemporaries and predecessors
in the field of hermeneutics, including the philologists Friedrich Ast
(1778–1841) and Friedrich August Wolf (1759–1824), and the setting
forth of the advantages of his own system. He seems to feel that
divination is his own particular creation, despite its connection to Ast's
notion of "spiritual" interpretation and to Wolf's ideal of perfect communication with the author.[21] The tendency of divination to destabil-
ize the fourfold logic of interpretation is surely related to its association
with Schleiermacher's own philosophical inventiveness.

The error in calling divination a "method" quickly becomes apparent. The addresses focus on the sensations of beginning and ending,
providing no work to fill the gap between the two. Divination is the
attraction to unknown origins and the pleasure in contemplating them.
Anything laborious required in the passage from mystery to illumination is relegated to the comparative method or to the field of grammatical interpretation. As pure desire and its projected fulfillment,
divination elides the domain of method.

Divination enters these texts as a series of rhetorical indulgences in
the poetry of quest romance oriented to lost beginnings (HM 193–95).
In the first address, moving back to the individual discovery of language in childhood, Schleiermacher reflects, "Even as I am dealing
here with the completion of the [hermeneutic] operation, I am driven
back almost involuntarily to the very beginning." As he has once
before, he associates the beginning of both writing and interpretation
with the linguistic experience of the child. He has not forgotten that he

---

[21]Richard E. Palmer, *Hermeneutics* (Evanston: Northwestern University Press, 1969),
75–83, and Hans Frei, *The Eclipse of Biblical Narrative* (New Haven: Yale University
Press, 1974), 300–302.

has described language learning as a form of grammatical interpretation and tries now to reconcile that suggestion with the "temptation" of a more intuitive theory. The involuntary nature of this 'drive,' like the reference to the potentially "fanatical" character of divination, hints again at the effort to keep receptivity under control. "This very beginning" of hermeneutics, he continues,

> is the same as when children begin to understand language. . . . Children do not yet have language, but are seeking it. Nor do they know the activity of thinking, because there is no thinking without words. With what aspect, then, do they begin? They do not yet have any points of comparison. . . . Are we not tempted to say that each child produces both thinking and language originally, and that either each child out of himself by virtue of an inner necessity engenders them in a way that coincides with the way it had happened in others or gradually as he becomes capable of a comparative procedure he approximates others. But in fact this inner movement toward producing thoughts on one's own, although initially stimulated by others, is the same as that which we have called "the divinatory."

As Schleiermacher tries to read his dialectic of hermeneutic methods back into early stages of development, he feels "tempted" to explain language acquisition as pure divination, the result of "inner necessity." At the same time, he is still drawn to a less mystical theory of mimetic comparison, which attributes inner necessity to the child's comparison of himself or herself with others. Divination, an "inner movement toward producing thoughts on one's own," prevails, though its beginnings may be in external stimuli. He concludes, "This divinatory operation . . . is original and the soul . . . shows itself to be wholly and inherently a prescient being [*ein ahnendes Wesen*]."

At this point Schleiermacher stops trying to establish the similarity between adult interpreters and children who are learning to speak and loses himself in admiration of the magnificence of these first beginnings:

> With what an enormous, almost infinite, power of expression does the child begin! It cannot be likened to later developments, nor to anything else. . . . These first activities of thinking and knowing are so astonishing that it seems to me that when we smile at the false applications which children make of the elements of language they have acquired—and to be sure often with all too great consistency—we do so only in order to find consolation or even to take revenge for this excess of energy which we are no longer able to expend. (HM 193–94)

The child's "power of expression" is manifested in the ability to "use," "reproduce," or "grasp" the "images" that form the basis for word-spheres or word meanings. Schleiermacher does not explain or really comprehend the process by which this occurs. What matters more is his sensitivity to his own emotions when confronted by such energy. The response he imagines—the smile of consolation and revenge—is an ironic experience of unassuageable desire in several moods: loss, envy, and vicarious gratification.

Trying to recover from this condition, Schleiermacher claims kinship with the child once again, not on the basis of the adult's quantum of energy but on that of our ongoing capacity for beginning again: "Viewed in this light, whenever we do not understand, we find ourselves in the same situation as the children, although not to the same degree. . . . On such occasions, we can always begin with the same divinatory boldness." The boldness of the adult has the compensatory logic that imbues all of Schleiermacher's hermeneutics. Like Wordsworth, he modulates from the sublimity of childhood to the sociability of mature, if "sluggish," knowledge: "we ought not simply contrast our present situation to those immense beginnings in childhood, for the process of understanding and interpreting is a whole which develops constantly and gradually, and in its later stages we must aid each other more and more." This aid takes the form of offering "to others points of comparison . . . which themselves begin in this same divinatory way." Translated into temporal terms, speed—a trope of imaginative energy—is exchanged for richness: "the soul . . . the more it possesses, becomes more sluggish, in inverse proportion to its receptivity" (HM 194–95).

Society is important because it provides a field for differentiating the self. As Schleiermacher wrote in the passage with which I opened the subject of divination, "each person contains a minimum of everyone else, and so divination is aroused by comparison of oneself" (HM 150–51). Here Schleiermacher's reader has become too ethical to be narcissistic but, as the hermeneutic manuscripts repeatedly show, is not averse to taking pleasure in distinctiveness. Whereas the true narcissist seeks gratification in his or her reflected image, as in the *Soliloquies,* this figure becomes absorbed in the contemplation of others who are partly the same, partly different. The enrichment of collective cultural life is ethically consistent with the individual reader's momentary sense of achieved objectivity. Or, put another way, objectivity sanctions Schleiermacher's version of the will to power, the will to understand.

Since power and truth are joined in the linking of conceptual mastery with philosophical objectivity, the potential of hermeneutic pleasure to foster private egotism at the expense of the community of scientific discourse is blocked.

The temperate pleasures of self-love are immanent in the sensations of conclusive understanding. The condition sought by the reader is the "divinatory certainty" that results from reconstructing the genesis of the written work. Out of the "dim morning light" in which reading begins comes conclusive illumination: "suddenly at the end every part is clear and the whole work is visible in sharp and definite contours." When divination and comparison have both been taken as far as they can go, "the internal process [of creation] has been made so trans-parent . . . that, since what has been intuited is a thought and since there is no thought without words, the entire relationship between the production of the thoughts and its formation in language is now fully and immediately evident" (HM 185, 198, 193). Such thematic and rhetorical shifts persistently bring together metaphors of unmediated vision and the achievement of understanding. Stylistic heightening and hermeneutic success coincide so regularly in Schleiermacher's two ad-dresses that one wonders if the necessity for the divinatory method does not have more to do with the kind of writing it permits than with the hermeneutic work it accomplishes.

Schleiermacher describes the authority the reader may legitimately claim through a kind of pleasure principle, or principle of "enrich-ment." In the process, he confronts the charge of psychologism and defines both authors and texts as means to the end of readerly represen-tation. "Historical reconstruction[,] which we undertake in order to comprehend better a work of some author[,] will achieve true excel-lence," he asserts, "not merely because it clarifies the work in question but also because it enriches our own lives and the lives of others." Recognizing the heroic tonality in this statement, he goes on: "Such enrichment is sublime, and it should be added to our consideration of works so that we do not produce trivialities which demean ourselves and our scientific labor" (HM 207).

I cannot resist here introducing Emerson, a voice out of my own past, in order to point out what is at stake in Schleiermacher's her-meneutic ethics. "Culture," Emerson proclaims, "is the suggestion . . . that a man has a range of affinities through which he can modulate the violence of any master-tones that have a droning preponderance in his scale, and succor him against himself. Culture redresses his balance, revives the delicious sense of sympathy, and warns him of the dangers of solitude and repulsion."[22] In this passage a "range of affinities" with others different from oneself rescues one from the violence and monotony of temperament. The moral contrast between preponderant "master-tones" and the "succor" of "delicious . . . sympathy" indicates that cultivated discourse is an ethical imperative. Society "redresses" and balances the extremes of self-reliance. Emerson is never committed to the tempering virtues of culture for more than a paragraph at a time, but at such moments he articulates one of the key ethical features of romantic theories of understanding by grounding objectivity in interpersonal exchanges.

What Emerson allows us to see more clearly is the extent to which Schleiermacher's hermeneutic tactics are governed by ethical criteria. To translate Emerson's terms back into Schleiermacher's, the "violence" of the individual corresponds, in a morally chastened form, to the ability to subsume or incorporate the author into an understanding so complete that it generates a feeling of confidence and pleasure. Schleiermacher's reader must test and share his or her certainty in the realm of science, in order to ensure its contribution to collective "enrichment." But this interpreter has already situated the saving difference of unlikeness in the dialectics of understanding itself. The reader is obligated to test divinatory conclusions against grammatical interpretation, which functions as the internalized conscience of the research community. The act of reading itself is an exercise in redressing imbalance, as the interpreter oscillates between the author's individual and cultural attributes and between his or her own artful and scientific tendencies.

Schleiermacher regards his own theorizing about divination as in itself creative. In a series of intricate readings of Wolf and Ast in the second address to the Prussian Academy, he brings forward the need for artistic intuition in understanding in order to amplify the heretofore impoverished role of divination. The reflexivity of this strategy, of hermeneutic theory conducted through applied hermeneutics, is extremely dense. Schleiermacher exercises his own creativity by developing the idea of readerly inspiration in a commentary on Wolf's notion of interpretive art. This associational chain accounts for much of the rhetorical urgency of the addresses.

In the second address Schleiermacher suddenly becomes defensive

---

[22] *The Conduct of Life*, in *The Complete Works of Ralph Waldo Emerson*, Centenary Edition (Boston: Houghton Mifflin, 1903–4), VI, 136–37.

about divination. It "seems so underdeveloped and thin in comparison with [grammatical interpretation]," he concedes, "that it would seem completely improper to give it a place equal to the other in a new hermeneutics." And again: "how trivial this method looks" (HM 206–7). These passages partly constitute a rhetorical ploy leading to the claim of the "sublime" benefit of divinatory fulfillment. But they also reveal Schleiermacher's awareness of the mildly deviant quality of a strategy like divination in the context of philological tradition (although, viewed in the larger context of German criticism after Herder, it is of course a development to be expected).[23]

Schleiermacher's response to Wolf in both addresses shows how willfully and with what apparent disingenuousness he sought out the element of artistry in established works on hermeneutics and made it his own. He zeroes in on Wolf's "very surprising" stipulation that the interpreter needs the ability to "perform the actual operations which the ancients did . . . in a free and individual fashion." Schleiermacher presents himself as confounded by Wolf's suggestion. "For my own part," he confesses stodgily, "I would have been content to understand . . . fluency . . . as the mature fruit of long-term studies" merely. Like a pedant indignant at the sudden demand for artistry, he asks, "How then can Wolf demand such art from us as the admission fee . . . to the shrine of the science of antiquity? And by what honest means are we supposed to attain it?" Schleiermacher chooses not to acknowledge the most "magical" quality of divination, its effortlessness, and treats it as the means to "fluency," not as fluency itself: "Assuming there is no magical way [Zaubermittel], I see no other than that of . . . adopting a procedure that is, fortunately, not merely imitative, but also divinatory—methods that would ultimately lead to fluency as the fruit of study" (HM 186–87).

The turning point in this oddly oblique presentation comes when Schleiermacher takes Wolf more figuratively. "Fluency," he now observes, effectively directs us to "something other" than philology, in-

---

[23]Frei, The Eclipse of Biblical Narrative, 285–86, 282–306 passim. Frei's extended discussion of the way meaning moves, gradually and not without contradiction, from text to reader, and especially of the role of Herder in emphasizing the meaning-creating spirit of the reader, indirectly supports my arguments for the primary importance of the reader in Schleiermacher's hermeneutics. At the same time, Frei is more convinced by Kimmerle's view of the psychologistic later Schleiermacher than I am (290). See also Hermann Patsch, "Friedrich August Wolf und Friedrich Ast: Die Hermeneutik als Appendix der Philologie," in Ulrich Nassen, ed., Klassiker der Hermeneutik (Paderborn: Schöningh, 1982), 76–107.

terpretive access to "the internal intellectual activity of an author."
"Herewith," Schleiermacher announces, "a new understanding of this
side of interpretation is opened to us." By the end of the second address, Schleiermacher has once again taken full responsibility for the
idea of divination. "If it is a mistake, though I do not think it is, to
assign both of these tasks [comparison and divination] to the interpreter, then it is my fault alone, for my guides do not accept this view"
(HM 188, 208). This sentence is laden with negativity—the double
negative of "not being mistaken," the characterization of originality as
a "fault" which his mentors "do not accept." His pleasure in divination
seems to have disappeared beneath his own modesty. In the realm of
interpretive ethics, however, the disavowal of pride may be as certain
an indicator of aspiration as an open celebration of it.

In view of divination's unsettled character, or Schleiermacher's character shifts in its vicinity, it is difficult to evaluate the status within it of
the desire for a community of understanding. The first definition we
looked at from the hermeneutic manuscripts strongly voiced this impulse. "Divinatory knowledge is the feminine strength in knowing
people. . . . a receptivity to the uniqueness of every other person"
(HM 151). If we follow the implications of the phrase "feminine
strength" [*weibliche Stärke*], we are led deeply into the relationship
of the image of community to the unreconciled logical and intuitive
modes of hermeneutic understanding. Schleiermacher's inconsistency
arises from the question of the direction of understanding. Does it
operate in one direction only, in the reader's dialectical but not dialogical response to texts, utterances, and their authors? Or is it bidirectional,
the intersubjective construction of a "life world," to use Habermas's
romantic term, in which readers and authors/texts act on each other?

The extent of the reader's communal spirit varies with the degree of
Schleiermacher's subliminal femininity at any given moment. Receptivity, the vision of understanding as communion, is bound up with
the phenomenon of speech. Speech, in turn, "the medium for the
commonality of thought," is associated with woman. In Schleiermacher's defense of "feminine knowledge" as a talent required in social
as well as textual affairs, he links speech, as the discourse of an individual's "whole being," to the dynamics of conversation arising from
"shared life": "The immediate presence of the speaker, the living expression that proclaims that his whole being is involved, the way the
thoughts in a conversation develop from our shared life, such factors
stimulate us far more than some solitary observation of an isolated text
to understand a series of thoughts as a moment of life which is break-

ing forth, as one moment set in the context of many others" (HM 97, 183). But such claims are rare, "moment[s] of life" that stand like islands of grace in the mediated universe of approximate understanding. Their position is analogous to that of women, who stand out as the self-conscious linguists of desire in male intellectual society.

Schleiermacher, Philosophical Hermeneutics, and the Question of Gender

Since the mid-1960s, hermeneutic philosophy has displayed a persistent ambivalence toward its romantic past and particularly toward Schleiermacher. Since Heinz Kimmerle published Schleiermacher's hermeneutic manuscripts in 1959, the crux of the debate has been his relative emphasis on authorial psychology as opposed to language.[24] The contest between the psychological and the linguistic is a version of

[24]The question of how "psychological" Schleiermacher's hermeneutic theory became has been the focus of debates over its value since Kimmerle's edition, which contained a powerfully influential interpretation of Schleiermacher's theoretical development. According to what might be called the currently orthodox view of Schleiermacher's hermeneutics, which has persuaded Gadamer, Ricoeur, and scholars like Palmer and Weinsheimer, Schleiermacher's work can be divided into a brilliant early phase, in which he focused on language, and a conventionally romantic second stage, in which he lapsed increasingly into the hermeneutics of empathy. This reading of Schleiermacher's texts serves the need of recent hermeneutic philosophers both to acknowledge their precursor and to accentuate their difference from him, a difference of which "linguisticality" is the sign. It is to the credit of Manfred Frank that he has argued strongly from a broadly informed theoretical position against Kimmerle. (The most accessible statement is Frank's article, "The Text and Its Style: Schleiermacher's Theory of Hermeneutic Language," trans. Richard Hannah and Michael Hays, *Boundary II* 11, 2 (1983): 11–28. See also *Das Individuelle Allgemeine: Textstrukturierung und -interpretation nach Schleiermacher* (Frankfurt am Main: Suhrkamp, 1977).

Late in life Schleiermacher did distinguish two aspects of technical interpretation, designated "psychological" and "technical," respectively. Insofar as the former "focuses . . . upon how thoughts emerged from the totality of the author's life" and the latter "upon how a set of thoughts arose from a particular thought or intuition" in the process of composition, it is clear that the desire for empathic intuition operates strongly in Schleiermacher's system (HM 223). My argument in the present study is that the register of desire operates throughout Schleiermacher's career, not simply in its later stages, and throughout twentieth-century hermeneutic discourse as well.

For the relevant bibliography, see Hans-Georg Gadamer, "The Problem of Language in Schleiermacher's Hermeneutics," *Journal for Theology and the Church* 7 (1968), 68–85; Heinz Kimmerle, "Hermeneutical Theory or Ontological Hermeneutics," in *History and Hermeneutik,* ed. Wolfhart Pannenberg et al. (New York: Harper & Row, 1967), 107–21; Paul Ricoeur, "Schleiermacher's Hermeneutics," *Monist* 60,2 (1977): 181–97.

the larger problem facing hermeneutic theorists, the tension between allegiance to a philosophical rigor that must eschew personification and desire for an ethic of communion that redeems the objectified relationships of technological society. This conflict accounts for the unresolved simultaneity in Schleiermacher's hermeneutics of comparison and divination, which arrive at the same goal by different interpretive paths. Recent hermeneutic writings display a similar tension between philosophy's need to purify itself of subjectivity and its dreams of a life world experienced as a "Thou."[25]

This predicament has discursive consequences in the work of Hans-Georg Gadamer and, to a lesser extent, that of Paul Ricoeur and Jürgen Habermas. In all three it takes the form of a constant emphasis on the metaphoric status of terms like "voice, "conversation," "question and answer," or even "incarnation."[26] Gadamer insists on the nonliteral meaning of his key words, sometimes laboriously: "It would be wrong to think that . . . what is experienced in tradition is to be taken as the meaning of another person, who is a 'Thou.'" The thing thus designated, rather, is "a meaningful content detached from all bonds of the meaning individual." Nonetheless, in the next phrase Gadamer personifies content once again as "a genuine partner in communication, with which we have fellowship as does the 'I' with a 'Thou.'"[27]

Gadamer calls attention to his metaphoric patterning, for example, by setting up a comparison of "the hermeneutic phenomenon" to "the model of the conversation between two persons" in order to reveal what "these apparently so different situations have in common."[28] These gestures dissociate Gadamer from what he perceives as the more literal use of dialogue and empathy in romantic hermeneutics. Nevertheless, the pervasiveness of such figures of speech in post-Heideggerian hermeneutic writings suggests that they are needed not for logical reasons— their logic is constantly being corrected—but for affective and ethical ones. Metaphors of community, receptivity, and conversation constitute an ethical code that seems to require this strongly figurative dimension, in addition to more methodical articulation.[29] Such language be-

---

[25]Hans-Georg Gadamer, *Truth and Method,* trans. and ed. G. Barden and J. Cumming (New York: Continuum, 1975), 321–22, 404.

[26]Ibid., 252, 321, 341, 333, 385.

[27]Ibid., 321.

[28]Ibid., 340–42.

[29]In the region of the ethical the difference between argumentative and figurative language is never clear, as when Gadamer writes, "Understanding is a modification of the virtue of moral knowledge. It appears in the fact of concern, not about myself, but

trays the uneasiness of hermeneutic philosophers in the presence of romanticism in general, Schleiermacher in particular, and, more universally, in the presence of metaphor itself.[30] What is striking, where inherited metaphors are so active, is the entire absence of the ambiguous figure of woman. For the image of the speech community to be acceptable to modern philosophers, its earlier figurative link with the feminine had to be extinguished.

Joel Weinsheimer makes the best possible case for the superiority of Gadamer's hermeneutics over Schleiermacher's and for a clear and genuine difference between the languages of contemporary and romantic hermeneutics. Weinsheimer's commentary, however, like Gadamer's *Truth and Method* itself, treats Schleiermacher polemically as embodying errors that Gadamer has corrected. This dichotomized mode of argument makes both philosophers appear excessively consistent, given the fact that the basis of their affinity is precisely the instability caused by the lurking ghost of divination.

When, over time, the "alienation of voice" leaves us only with "the meaninglessness of writing," Weinsheimer explains, the mediating strategies of hermeneutics ensure that "the past does not live still but rather again, and the more fully for being interrupted." Gadamer emerges as sophisticated and tough-minded in his insistence that the "given of hermeneutics is 'a consciousness of loss and alienation'" and in his Hegelian affirmation of "difference [as] the condition of, rather

---

about the other person. Thus it is a mode of moral judgment" (*Truth and Method*, 288). Insofar as understanding involves dealing with utterances, texts, and gestures, Gadamer's insistence here on concern for "the other person" invokes the full romantic drama of hermeneutic dialogue.

[30]Domna Stanton links the motif of the mother in feminist theory with the privileging of metaphor as the means to "a transportation of meaning beyond the known." This relationship among woman, metaphor, and transcendence likewise prevails in the hermeneutic tradition and is one basis for its hidden affiliation with feminist theory. "Difference on Trial: A Critique of the Maternal Metaphor in Cixous, Irigaray, and Kristeva," in Nancy K. Miller, ed., *The Poetics of Gender* (New York: Columbia University Press, 1986), 157–82.

For a criticism of current hermeneutic philosophy from a different angle than my own, see Walter Benn Michaels, "Against Theory 2: Hermeneutics and Deconstruction," *Critical Inquiry* 14 (1988): 50, 58. Benn Michaels's argument is logical but surprisingly ahistorical. He demonstrates that, "for hermeneutics, a text means what its author intends but also necessarily means more," which enables him "to attack the hermeneutic account of the role played by linguistic convention in constituting textual identity." Benn Michaels's defense of authorial intention could be substantially reinforced and complicated by investigating the anxiety that the problem of authorial psychology has generated over the whole history of hermeneutics.

than the obstacle to, assimilation and appropriation." Schleiermacher materializes at this point in Weinsheimer's argument, as in Gadamer's, as "the initial wrong turn . . . toward methodologism in the human sciences."[31]

> The task of interpretation has been uprooted [by Schleiermacher] from the context of intelligent consensus within which the authentic life of understanding gets constantly negotiated. Now it has to overcome a complete alienation. The imposition of an artificial apparatus that is supposed to open up whatever is alien and make it one's own takes the place of the communicative ability in which people live together and mediate themselves along with the tradition in which they stand.[32]

Both Weinsheimer and Gadamer view divination as Schleiermacher's naive attempt to overcome the unintelligibility of an estranged tradition "and thus return directly to the past as it originally was."[33] They see quite clearly that, in his hermeneutic formula, divination compensates for method or system. What they fail to recognize is that, through the persistence of a romantic code of metaphor, divination is a corollary of the Gadamerian critique of method as well. Instead of occurring after misunderstanding, as in Schleiermacher's hermeneutics, divination (by other names) takes place before it.

Gadamer, who loves the human voice even more than Schleiermacher, uses it to symbolize immediate understanding spontaneously experienced in the present. "Misunderstanding does not always come first," he writes. "There is always a world already interpreted," a realm of "artless language," transparent speech, and "infinite dialogue."[34] By characterizing tradition as dialogue, Gadamer gratifies the same interest in immediacy expressed in the psychological tendencies of Wilhelm Dilthey and the divinatory impulses of Schleiermacher.[35] The stance of receptivity derived from Schleiermacher's rhetoric of divination is car-

---

[31]Joel C. Weinsheimer, *Gadamer's Hermeneutics: A Reading of Truth and Method* (New Haven: Yale University Press, 1985), 129–31, 214.

[32]Hans-Georg Gadamer, *Reason in the Age of Science,* trans. Frederick G. Lawrence (Cambridge: MIT Press, 1982), 130.

[33]Weinsheimer, *Gadamer's Hermeneutics,* 131.

[34]Hans-Georg Gadamer, "Text and Interpretation," 1981 lecture, University of Michigan.

[35]Wilhelm Dilthey's article, "The Development of Hermeneutics," ed. and trans. H. P. Rickman, *Selected Writings* (New York: Cambridge University Press, 1976), 246–63, is largely responsible for the persistent view that Schleiermacher yearns constantly for empathic communion with authors. This text by no means reflects either Dilthey's whole view of Schleiermacher or the whole range of Schleiermacher's hermeneutic thinking.

ried into the modern hermeneutic arena under the rubric of voice, which now becomes a locus of comprehensibility.

Against Weinsheimer, then, I would argue that Gadamer's failure to remember the complex mixture of impulses which produced Schleiermacher's hermeneutic formula dooms him to repeat the gestures he wishes to avoid. He associates Schleiermacher with an excess of method ("artificial apparatus"), the technological thinking that represents modern "alienation." By splitting Schleiermacher's hermeneutics into hyperrational method and mere empathy, Gadamer reinforces both his own distaste for method and his claims for more sophisticated feeling states. He espouses, however, romantic hopes for "the authentic life" of "intelligent consensus" and "a moral attitude" opposed to "objectivation" and favoring an ethos of "participation," "concern," and "affection." He wants hermeneutics to be a philosophy of quasi-Christian intersubjectivity in which understanding is "not a form of domination but of service" [*nicht Herrschafts- sondern Dienstformen*].[36] In the context of such views the engagement with nonpersonal tradition begins to look like a way to avoid the discourse of psychology toward which they tend. By caricaturing Schleiermacher in this precise way, Gadamer can present his own hermeneutic theory as modernist while returning to romantic moods, minus the divinatory or empathic feminine.

The hermeneutics of Ricoeur similarly reveal the continued energy of a romantic conception of understanding. This is a continuity denied by his assertion that, in complicating the ostensibly psychologistic nineteenth-century view of understanding, he is moving "Beyond Romanticist Hermeneutics." The relative autonomy of the text, its separation from living speech, is a fortunate fall or "productive distanciation," according to Ricoeur. The fall from speech to writing means that "the primordial, the original" language is lost. Immediate communication, that "wonder" of "being-together" (which, I have argued, Schleiermacher denies even to speech), is no longer possible. In the aftermath of this event the "deepest wish of hermeneutics is to conquer a remoteness" between the text and the interpreter, a temporal gap (between past and present), and a linguistic difference (between speech and writing).[37] How does the interpreter overcome these distances?

[36]Gadamer, *Reason in the Age of Science*, 130; "Text and Interpretation"; *Truth and Method*, 278.

[37]Paul Ricoeur, *Interpretation Theory: Discourse and the Surplus of Meaning* (Fort Worth: Texas Christian University Press, 1976), 2, 43, 15; "The Language of Faith," in *The Philosophy of Paul Ricoeur,* ed. Charles E. Reagan and David Stewart (Boston: Beacon, 1978), 228–29; "Existence and Hermeneutics," in *The Philosophy of Paul Ricoeur,* 101.

Ricoeur, believing that he is at this point correcting Schleiermacher, rejects as illegitimate the ambition to know the mind of the author. "Authorial meaning" (as Schleiermacher himself had believed) "becomes properly a dimension of the text to the extent that the author is not available for questioning." The absence of the speaker results in a surplus of meaning. The second part of the hermeneutic dialectic now occurs in the "struggle between otherness and ownness" by which the reader appropriates the work: "Reading is the remedy by which the text is rescued into proximity."[38]

Reading is also the way the reader is rescued, however, in a specifically ethical sense. Ricoeur's reader encounters in multiple meanings "the surging up of the possible," "the grace of the imagination." He or she is freed from the "egoistic and narcissistic ego" that seeks possession, for Ricoeur prohibits fantasies of power. He contrasts the "self," which proceeds from the understanding of the text, to the "ego," which claims to precede it. "The text," he writes, "gives a self to the ego."[39] Ricoeur is nowhere more like Schleiermacher than in this desire to create a more virtuous reader.

Habermas gives the ethical speech community a role in his social theory which is more delimited and more self-conscious in its idealizations than its place in the hermeneutics of either Gadamer or Ricoeur. "The goal of coming to an understanding," he states, "is to bring about an agreement that terminates in the intersubjective mutuality of reciprocal understanding, shared knowledge, mutual trust, and accord with one another." His "theory of illocutionary action" takes as its theme the "establishment of interpersonal relations." Speakers "are always already orientated to those validity-claims, on the intersubjective recognition of which possible consensus depends." They act counter to institutional systems in a realm of what one might call domestic informality, where the "everyday certainty . . . characteristic of background knowledge in the life-world" prevails.[40]

The historical background of the ideal speech community is investigated by Habermas in *Knowledge and Human Interests*. His sympathetic

---

See also his essays, "The Hermeneutical Function of Distanciation" and "Appropriation," in *Hermeneutics and the Human Sciences*, ed. and trans. John B. Thompson (Cambridge: MIT Press, 1981).

[38]Ricoeur, *Interpretation Theory*, 30, 35, 43.

[39]Ibid., 94–95.

[40]Jürgen Habermas, *Community and the Evolution of Society*, trans. Thomas McCarthy (Boston: Beacon, 1979), 3, 33; "A Reply to My Critics," in *Habermas: Critical Debates*, ed. John B. Thompson and David Held (Cambridge: MIT Press, 1982), 227.

analysis of the necessarily circular logic of Dilthey's divinatory hermeneutics indicates the extent to which his theory of the ideal speech community is derived from romantic philosophies. For Habermas, Dilthey's acceptance of a divinatory element in hermeneutics points to the inherently paradoxical nature of the hermeneutic enterprise. Hermeneutics, as the art of understanding the ordinary language of individuals, is by virtue of its object an impure theory. "Only statements of a pure language can be completely understood"; conversely, with "linguistic expressions . . . linked to a concrete life context," "complete understanding is impeded." Divination is the symptom, within the hermeneutic tradition, of our inability wholly to grasp the "ineffably individual" context that "ordinary language" makes "communicable." The hermeneutic circle is defensible, according to Habermas, because understanding requires treating ordinary language as "the articulation of a life context, which represents an individual meaning that cannot be wholly grasped in general categories."[41]

In the works of Habermas divination is not the power of immediate intuition, but rather the symptom of imperfect understanding. Nevertheless, because this resistance to pure logic characterizes the quasi-domestic therapy of the informal speech community, the romantic links among understanding, speech, and community persist. They persist, however, without any recognition of the conventionally feminine character of this conversation. Like the hermeneutic school with which he takes issue, Habermas avoids noticing that the ideal speech community is based on complex metaphoric equations arising from the inherited blending of gender roles with ethical attitudes. In the hermeneutic tradition after Schleiermacher, in which at least certain aspects of Habermas's writings must be included, the conscious connection of the value of speech communities with the feminine and the divinatory has been repressed or evaded, the feminine more completely so than the divinatory. This history of forgetting produces, in part, the current failure of hermeneutic thought to admit into its discourse an analysis of its own desires.[42]

Such evasion may represent a kind of progress, a move away from

[41]Jürgen Habermas, *Knowledge and Human Interests,* trans. Jeremy J. Shapiro (Boston: Beacon, 1972), 169–70, 164, 163, 172.

[42]The most detailed discussion of the relationship of the critical theory of Habermas to feminist theory has been undertaken by Nancy Fraser, who sharply criticizes his failures to reflect on the question of gender while seeking to elaborate his thought in a feminist direction. "What's Critical about Critical Theory? The Case of Habermas and Gender," *New German Critique* 35 (1985): 97–131.

earlier mythologies according to which intuition and analysis are marked according to gender. A less sanguine argument seems more plausible, however. Hermeneutic philosophy—and the critical theory of Habermas to the extent that it draws on hermeneutic values—has not corrected its unconsciously gendered associations but has forgotten they were ever there. Over the course of the nineteenth and twentieth centuries, as philosophy became more phobic about the remnants of sensibility that stubbornly persisted in its discourses, the gender-specific meaning of these ideas was suppressed. This fending off of the memory of romanticism occurred not only in order to exclude the feminine, but also to exclude the suspect modes of thought for which the feminine was the metaphoric vehicle: the romantic (including 'romantic love'), the psychological, and the figurative. Hermeneutics is left with a desire for ethical consensus—and an aversion to the history of that desire.

It is perhaps incongruous, at this point, to introduce the language of feminist theory, for it has been pointedly ignored in the discourse of philosophical hermeneutics, and the reverse is also largely true. Kristeva's acerbic characterization of Heideggerian "care" as "a metaphor for . . . . the mother or the nurse. . . . promising something beyond the eternal frustration that it simultaneously proclaims" is the most direct statement of a feminist distaste for the unconscious feminine associations that pervade hermeneutic as well as Heideggerian philosophy.[43]

But if there is feminist resistance to philosophical evocations of the maternal, there are also feminist parallels and analogues. The image of the speech community, of the "dialogue of love," is central to both feminist and hermeneutic theory. To the feminist imagination, this configuration has taken the form of "the female world of love and ritual" or, more philosophically, the "speaking-among-women" within which "speaking (as) woman" can occur.[44] For hermeneutic theorists, dialogue descends from the androgynous conversation in which masculine reason is supplemented by feminine intuition. This common ground of feminism and hermeneutics reflects not agreement, but

---

[43]Julia Kristeva, *Revolution in Poetic Language,* trans. Margaret Waller, intro. Leon S. Roudiez (New York: Columbia University Press, 1984), 129.

[44]Carroll Smith-Rosenberg, "The Female World of Love and Ritual: Relations Between Women in Nineteenth-Century America," in *A Heritage of Her Own,* ed. Nancy F. Cott and Elizabeth H. Pleck (New York: Simon & Schuster, 1979), 311–42; Luce Irigaray, *This Sex Which Is Not One,* trans. Catherine Porter (Ithaca: Cornell University Press, 1985), 134–36.

rather a shared idiom of desire. The speech community in which understanding takes place, for Gadamer, Ricoeur, and others, offers a moral alternative to the world of exploitative relationships reflected in theories of aggression, pathology, and mere signs.[45] Similarly, in much feminist writing the community of women's speech (the place of the mother) serves as moral ground for a revised history of authority.[46]

A key difference between feminist and hermeneutic positions emerges in the writing of Elisabeth Schüssler Fiorenza, who works in the area of biblical interpretation, the traditional domain of hermeneutics. Linking the ideal of community with the necessity for aggression, she rejects the hermeneutic evasion of conflict: "feminist biblical hermeneutics stands in conflict with the dialogical-hermeneutical model developed by Bultmann, Gadamer, and the New Hermeneutic [a theology oriented to the work of Bultmann]. . . . Its goal is not 'identification with' or 'consent to' the androcentric text . . . [but] critical solidarity with women in biblical history." Feminist interpretation "begins with a *hermeneutics of suspicion*"—Gadamer's term for theories that reject the ethos of participation—and culminates in "a *hermeneutics of creative actualization*" of self and community in the church of women (author's emphasis). Communities, for Schüssler Fiorenza, are intrinsically oppositional.[47] The connection between legitimate aggression and the speech community within which aggression is suspended, if not prohibited, marks a distinctive shift away from hermeneutic dialogue. It also swerves away from romantic literary representations of dialogue, such as those by Schlegel and Schleiermacher, as well as from romantic

[45]Gadamer, drawing on Ricoeur's usage, contrasts the Nietzschean tradition of the hermeneutics of suspicion to the hermeneutic ethos of "participation." "The Hermeneutics of Suspicion," in *Hermeneutics: Questions and Prospects,* ed. Gary Shapiro and Alan Sica (Amherst: University of Massachusetts Press, 1984), 54, 64–65. For his critique of language as a sign system, see *Truth and Method,* 377–78.

[46]The impression of common ground is strengthened by the conjunction of the hermeneutic critique of scientific rationality and the feminist analysis of science. Beyond the more obvious parallels between the hermeneutic and feminist critiques of the myth of scientific objectivity and its supporting ideology of the rational subject, it is worth acknowledging the relationship between a book like Gadamer's *Reason in the Age of Science* and one like Sandra Harding's *The Science Question in Feminism* (Ithaca: Cornell University Press, 1986) or the discussion of science in Luce Irigaray's *Ethique de la différence sexuelle* (Paris: Les Editions de Minuit, 1984), 117–21, as works that explore the conditions under which a new theory of science can be formulated. See also Stanton on the relationship between the maternal metaphor and the metaphor of voice, in "Difference on Trial," 166–68.

[47]Elisabeth Schüssler Fiorenza, *Bread Not Stone: The Challenge of Feminist Biblical Interpretation* (Boston: Beacon, 1984), 140, 15, xiv.

perceptions of Platonic dialogue, both of which tolerate considerable conflict.

Once we shift our attention to nontheological feminist theory, we find a similar link between feminist aggression against existing philosophies and a feminist ethos of concord within the circle of women's language. One of the most informed articulations of this stance comes in Irigaray's version of "I–Thou" conversation. In her attack on categorically objectified relationships Irigaray imagines an "I" and a "Thou" taken beyond, if nonetheless alluding to, phenomenological intersubjectivity. In "feminine syntax," she writes, "there would no longer be either subject or object." Instead, speaking as a woman and among women "would involve nearness, proximity, but in such an extreme form that it would preclude . . . any establishment of ownership, thus any form of appropriation" (would preclude, in Ricoeur's terms, any "ego"). This syntax would be generated by the desire for community expressed in "appeals to move, to be moved, together." The "tightly woven systematicity" of rational male discourse, "the countable," is surrounded by the looser web, field, or fluid of feminine language. The circle of speech resists the social and verbal forms of masculine rationalism which, as Adrienne Rich has observed, fails "to identify and assimilate its own surreal or nonlinear elements."[48]

Given the resemblance between the feminist version of the speech community and the one constructed by hermeneutic philosophy, the radical communicative and metaphoric value ascribed by Irigaray to the female *body* has a distinct value as a way of insisting on feminine difference. The structure of Irigaray's *Ethique de la différence sexuelle* reveals the interdependence of feminist desire and the feminist critique of desire. Her argument exposes the way the nostalgic longing for the feminine within masculine culture blocks the emergence of a feminine language community. In order to empower the *feminist* longing for a "space-time" in which such a language can develop, Irigaray grounds her ethics in a renovated sense of touch, in the "pre-discursive" caress, the gesture of desire that knows itself as such. I find it difficult to participate in Irigaray's move from critique to myth-making. The possibility of renovating romanticism from within the feminine—which, with her evocations of the divinatory, the infinite, and the maternal, is precisely what she is up to—seems undermined in advance by her exposure of philosophy's desires. And yet the ethical and political

[48]Adrienne Rich, *Of Woman Born: Motherhood as Experience and Institution* (New York: Norton, 1976), 62.

clarity that goes along with Irigaray's regenerated romantic metaphors tempts us to concede their ongoing efficacy.[49]

In a spirit of synthesis that seeks to link what Irigaray puts asunder, Jean Bethke Elshtain attempts to mediate between feminism and the disciplines of psychology and social philosophy. The figurative equation between speech and community creates, for Elshtain, the point common to both feminist theory and critical theory. She proposes a blend of three elements: "psychoanalytic discourse" informed by feminism, Habermas's ideal speech situation, and feminist discussions of "female moral reasoning and maternal thinking." The closeness of Habermas's ethics to those of the feminist project emerges, she argues, in his notion of the "life world" made possible by "ideal speech," a world where "domination is absent; and reciprocity pertains between and among participants." Her task in this article is somewhat similar to my own, that is, to unveil a kind of cultural forgetfulness. She reviews how feminist theorists have unknowingly "recapitulated . . . earlier arguments on language that erode the search for emancipatory feminist speech" and attempts to supply, from existing models, a more sophisticated view.[50]

In proposing Habermas as one of her exemplary theorists, however, Elshtain repeats the history of error she seeks to correct. For Habermas describes a feminized environment from which the specifically feminine has been excluded so completely that it now requires a feminist supplement. If Elshtain is clear about the way feminism has adopted theoretical approaches to language which confuse or betray its orientation, she is less clear about the way the theoretical material to which she turns as a substitute has expelled the feminine. The hermeneutic tradition stands as a reminder to feminists that the ideal of feminine conversation descends to us, in part, through the ambivalent patriarchies of romantic literature and philosophy.

[49]Irigaray, *Ethique de la différence sexuelle*, 108–9, 143, 173–99.

[50]Jean Bethke Elshtain, "Feminist Discourse and Its Discontents: Language, Power, and Meaning," in *Feminist Theory: A Critique of Ideology,* ed. Nannerl O. Keohane et al. (Chicago: University of Chicago Press, 1982), 133, 144, 131.

PART II

COLERIDGE

CHAPTER 4

The Littery Literary Man
and Lady-Like Wholeness

Coleridge and Schleiermacher

One is tempted to locate Schleiermacher, Coleridge, and Fuller, three writers who operate within the force field of German idealism, at increasing cultural distances from German romantic philosophy, with Schleiermacher closest to the center, Coleridge further off, and Fuller most remote of all. But such an approach would impute a normative status to the conventions of philosophical writing over against the more "literary" prose of "philosopher-critics"; it would ascribe particular authority to Germany as the source of the idealist tradition and treat England and America as progressive deviations from it.[1] And finally, since this critical narrative implies a causal structure as well, it would preclude compelling insights into the redundancy of romantic anxieties about critical aggression and the overdetermined paths by which these anxieties were generated and through which we now encounter them.

In her discussion of the risks of comparative studies for feminist critics, Alice Jardine observes that comparison is "a nineteenth-century concept" structured by "a certain analogical logic." "In order to posit an autonomous [theoretical] object," she comments, the comparative

---

[1]Rosemary Ashton, *The German Idea: Four English Writers and the Reception of German Thought, 1800–1860* (Cambridge: Cambridge University Press, 1980).

scholar proceeds "by means of measurement with a common unit": "one compares *A* to *B* according to a model. This model can be an 'idea,' 'principle,' 'politic,' or 'structure' over which the comparativist has complete control.[2]

Ambivalence toward aggressive forms of analytical thought, expressed in the gendered language of ethical sensation, is the unifying "idea," "politic," and "structure" of the present study. My defense against the charge of comparativism, I suppose, is to argue that it is worth doing precisely because the texts I examine, the theoretical texts of philosophy and criticism, became the medium for comparative studies in the late eighteenth and nineteenth centuries. In local circumstances—in Berlin, in Nether Stowey and Keswick, and in Boston—philosophical language derived its meaning from its status as a method of abstraction. "Metaphysics" was appropriated from elsewhere in the culture ("elsewhere" than literature and its associated vocations) or from another culture altogether (Germany). Despite the capacity of the idea of "Reason" to operate within various contexts having in common a specific need for ethical or ideological classification, Reason was always perceived as external to its local use. The alien character of Reason was figured outside Germany as "German," "metaphysical," or "blasphemous." In Germany reason became ambiguously conflated with system-formation itself. The comparativism of my approach, therefore, imitates the transmission of romantic analytical idioms and documents their history as local configurations that are nevertheless self-consciously analogical.

In addition to the convenience of idealism as a commodity for export, other historical factors help account for the strength of certain shared themes in the works of Schleiermacher and Coleridge. Both men were sons of clergymen, born within four years of each other (1768 and 1772, respectively). Both left home for school, Schleiermacher at fifteen, Coleridge at ten on the death of his father. Separation from the family intensified the tendency of both to seek substitutes for family members and led to the mood of pathos in their portrayals of domesticity. Both were drawn into vicarious relationships with women, evident in Schleiermacher's friendship with other men's wives and in Coleridge's attraction to their sisters. Schleiermacher was nurtured in the family circle of the Dohnas, then in the circle of Henriette

---

[2]Alice Jardine, *Gynesis: Configurations of Woman and Modernity* (Ithaca: Cornell University Press, 1985), 14. Jardine quotes from Michel Foucault, *The Order of Things* (New York: Random House, 1970), 55.

Herz in Berlin, then as a spiritual third party to his wife's first marriage. Coleridge was drawn to the Evans family, a widowed mother and her three daughters; to Robert Southey, who was inseparable from involvement with the Fricker sisters (one of whom Coleridge married); and to William and Dorothy Wordsworth and their later intimates Mary Hutchinson (eventually William's wife) and Sara Hutchinson. Both Schleiermacher and Coleridge rationalized their dependence on feminine sympathy as conducive to philosophical labor and its necessary antidote.

During the 1790s the odd surrogate families of Schleiermacher and Coleridge brought them into close but problematic associations with poets, if we can extend this flexible rubric to Friedrich Schlegel. Schleiermacher's friendship with Schlegel and Coleridge's with Wordsworth reveal a similar pattern of sentimental but power-haunted relationships between men, mediated by women within the same circle. Reconstituting the family in this unorthodox way gives rise to discourse of the kind we have already discovered in Schleiermacher, pervaded by metaphors of speech, especially dialogue; metaphors of family, friendship, or church as dialogically constituted; metaphors of the feminine as the conversational realm of pity and sympathy; and metaphors of system or method as the masculine alternative or supplement to domestic wholeness.

At the same time, the disturbing figure of the poet–friend–brother comes to embody the whole problem of vocational choice, so bound up with the symbolic relationships between labor and masculinity and therefore also with the question of ethical stance. Wordsworth, as the poet of feminine pathos in poems like "The Female Vagrant," "The Thorn," and "The Ruined Cottage," and Schlegel, as the celebrant of the erotics of feminine intuition in *Lucinde,* offered identification with the womanly as an expression of homosocial sympathy between men. But there was something in Wordsworth's and Schlegel's respective commitments to the aesthetic which put Coleridge in particular, but Schleiermacher too, in a position of deviance, rebellion, or correction toward it. Theories of understanding provide the idiom used by Coleridge and Schleiermacher in constructing an independent basis for personal and moral authority.

The question of genre evolved in Germany and England in ways that are sufficiently unlike each other to warrant a somewhat different approach to Coleridge's texts. For Schlegel, the preeminent German theorist of genre, the powers of criticism were expressed by destabilizing generic definitions to the point where habitual classifications broke down. Schleiermacher was certainly affected by Schlegel's generic inventiveness, but affected as though by a model for human behavior, not for writing. His attraction to the genres of dialogue, correspondence, and the "address" shows the extent to which literary dramas of intersubjectivity appealed to him. But he swerved away from the formal self-consciousness of the Berlin and Jena romantics because he believed that aesthetic criticism, including genre theory, blocks a productive theory of subjectivity; this opinion did not preclude his meticulous attention to genre in the hermeneutic operations of grammatical interpretation and comparison.

One need only look at the demographics of fiction in England and Prussia in the 1790s to understand why generic questions became so much more overtly ideological in Coleridge's context. "The novel," for Coleridge, stood for a large, middle-class population of readers; an established economy of writers and reviewers; and at times for the widely regretted female addiction to narrative sensation. "The novel," for Schleiermacher, stood for *Lucinde,* intended and almost universally received as an attack on bourgeois domesticity. Schleiermacher rejected fiction because it was produced by aesthetes; Coleridge because it was not.

Whereas ethical ambivalence toward critical aggression becomes apparent in Schleiermacher's hermeneutic writings in the asymmetries of understanding, for Coleridge it takes the form of a reflexive preoccupation with genre itself, which stands preeminently for the choice (or fate) of the identity of poet or philosopher-critic. Critical prose stands in a synecdochal relation to critical thinking. Coleridge's investment in the production and reception of reflective essayistic prose is such that only the value of this mode as a figure for critical intellect can account for his defenses of it. If periodical prose and its book-length adaptations (*The Friend*) stand for their critical content, it becomes less surprising that such nonfictional forms should bear an immense burden of social discipline.

The fact that critical prose—its production, media, and audiences— is inseparable from Coleridge's anxieties about his ethical stance has partly to do with the highly developed role of the press in English ideological conflict. One way of thinking about Coleridge's generic mission in *The Friend* is as an attempt to formulate a kind of nonfictional prose that is not the textual equivalent of party politics.[3] The

---

[3]Some excellent books illuminating the political culture of eighteenth-century England have appeared in the 1980s. They include Marilyn Butler, *Romantics, Rebels, and Reactionaries: English Literature and Its Background, 1760–1830* (Oxford: Oxford Univer-

ethical and the nonpartisan were closely identified throughout the eighteenth century, and Coleridge's claims for philosophical criticism bank on the perceived value of disinterestedness. Politics and textuality were more remote from each other in Germany, even after Napoleon's invasion of Prussia in 1806 brought political crisis to the citizenry. Although Schleiermacher cannot be said exactly to have missed the French Revolution, he did not stake either his professional activities or his personal values (except for his conspicuous judiciousness) on supporting or opposing it. In a letter to his father written in February 1793 he comments on "the miserable death of the King of France," but the real subject of the letter is Schleiermacher's position *outside* political contagion. He sympathizes with the revolution without lapsing into the "fatal vertigo" of wishing to imitate it; he has "impartially loved" it because his support is conditional on the behavior, not the programs, of the French. Opposed on principle to capital punishment, he abhors both the execution and those who condemn it for the wrong reasons; he drifts through the party labels of political arguments suspected by all and understood (as usual) by none: "and poor I, who very seldom have an opinion on any particular subject, much less belong . . . to any party, I am regarded by the democrats as a defender of despotism and a supporter of routine, by the hotheads as a politician who turns his coat according to the wind . . . by the royalists as a Jacobin, and by rational people as a senseless fellow with too long a tongue" (BR I 107–8; BW I 280–81).

Schleiermacher's face-to-face encounter with French troops in 1806 produced a sense of revulsion, but not the fascinated, hysterical, long-distance revulsion of Coleridge toward "Jacobins." Schleiermacher emerged as a nationalist during the period of the occupation, his commitment oscillating between a restored Prussia and a unified Germany. His views first coincided with the policies of the Prussian government under Friedrich Wilhelm II during the occupation and the overlapping period of attempted reforms and then became increasingly antipathetic as the Prussian regime came under the conservative influence of Austria.[4] Despite these involvements, however, he never feels his integral personality to be threatened by the overproduction of pamphlets and

---

sity Press, 1981); Olivia Smith, *The Politics of Language, 1791–1819* (New York: Oxford University Press, 1984); Jon Klancher, *The Making of English Reading Audiences (1790–1832)* (Madison: University of Wisconsin Press, 1987); and Ronald Paulson, *Representations of Revolution: 1789–1820* (New Haven: Yale University Press, 1983).

[4]Jerry F. Dawson, *Friedrich Schleiermacher: The Evolution of a Nationalist* (Austin: University of Texas Press, 1966), chaps. 4–8.

newspapers; politics never functions in his writings on interpretation as an expressive drama of urgent personal belief; and hermeneutic understanding is not constituted as the antidote to ideology. Politics enters into Coleridge's writing, by contrast, as a crisis for the writing subject. By 1800, Coleridge had linked the French to all the literary and social qualities he opposed. The consequent overtness of politics in Coleridge's handling of critical ethics leads us in a different direction than in the case of Schleiermacher.

The question of politics has a renewed importance in the context of recent interest in relationships among history, criticism, and ethics. If Coleridge and Schleiermacher sought a kind of power in proving their sophistication about morality, we seek to be moral by showing our sophistication about power. The choice of the term "ethics" or "ideology" marks the style of critics interested in the question of power (and who is not?).[5] The advantage of the word "ethics," with its old-fashioned ring, is that it reminds us that we inherit interpretive reflexes from centuries in which ethics and morality were considered genuinely explanatory of intention, behavior, and writing. The advantage of "ideology" is that it reveals the material, systematic, and interested character of ethics.[6]

The value of J. Hillis Miller's oddly skewed polemics on the ethics of reading lies in the clarity with which he sets forth the purported competition between ideology and ethics. Ethics, for Miller, is precisely the nonideological; it is constituted by the purity and difference of the uniquely literary. His either/or construction, despite its insights into the ethical claims of deconstructive approaches, has to resort to idiosyncratic definitions of the ethical in order to avoid recognizing the common qualities of ethical and ideological reading. Miller blocks this recognition only by expunging the habitual reference of the word

[5]Barbara Herrnstein Smith's term, "value," arouses some of the same issues but in a way that reveals considerable dislike of either ethical or ideological identifications. It is closely linked to a "heterogeneous" style, contingent on an experiential flux that anxiously avoids being defined in terms of specific histories of power. See "Contingencies of Value," *Critical Inquiry* 10 (1983): 11. The word "history," in recent critical usage, has become a loose synonym for an orientation to the history of the cultural constructions of power.

[6]For a discussion on the relationship between the "self-evident political pertinence" of feminist criticism and its ethical significance, see Tobin Siebers, *The Ethics of Criticism* (Ithaca: Cornell University Press, 1988), 186–219, esp. 195–96, where he discusses the relationship between a "victimary mythology" and the tendency to associate theory with violence, and 206–7, where he connects "the poetics of suffering" in romanticism, Freud, and feminist theory.

"ethics," a word that, insofar as it names the negotiations between conviction and behavior, can be pressed to acknowledge a structural resemblance to theories of "ideology," with *their* history of debate over the relation of system to subject. Miller swerves away, therefore, from the resonant connotations of "ethics," which blur any categorical difference between ethical and ideological sensitivity. He even resists the term "ideology" in order to avoid the "vague and speculative" thinking that would look for points of contact between ethical and ideological critique.[7] As Siebers observes, the "environment" of the ethics of criticism "is no longer exclusively textual, nor is it wholly political."[8] Rather, literary ethics is presently constituted by the experience of subjective response to the moral content of ideological positions.

The ongoing debate about the meaning of these highly charged terms is reflected in recent discussions of both Schleiermacher and Coleridge. In Coleridge criticism we find a reaction quite different from the response of hermeneutic philosophers to Schleiermacher. Recent interpretations of Schleiermacher's writings attempt to suppress the divinatory and feminine aspects of romanticism while reviving the tropes of I-Thou dialogue and the speech community; readings of Coleridge's texts long ago passed through this phase. As Murray Krieger argued in *The New Apologists for Poetry* (1956), the tendency to engage in "an uncompromising prejudice against romanticism coupled with an invocation of romantic and Coleridgean concepts" typified the work of Hulme, Eliot, Ransom, and others.[9] The subsequent redignifying of romanticism extends back to Krieger's book itself.

Since Krieger made those comments, the theme of love has come to pervade writing on Coleridge in a curious way, although this stage of Coleridge criticism appears now to have yielded to other preoccupations. More precisely, Harold Bloom's view that Coleridge "always needed more love than he could get" emerged for a time as his defining quality.[10] Numerous critics dwelt on the question of whether Coleridge himself was or is lovable and why. Particularly in the opposition between the responses of Walter Jackson Bate and Norman Fruman, the problem of sympathy for Coleridge quickly became involved with

---

[7]J. Hillis Miller, *The Ethics of Reading* (New York: Columbia University Press, 1986), 4–5.

[8]Siebers, *The Ethics of Criticism,* 1.

[9]Murray Krieger, *The New Apologists for Poetry* (Minneapolis: University of Minnesota Press, 1956), 35.

[10]Harold Bloom, *The Anxiety of Influence* (New York: Oxford University Press, 1973), 248.

the evaluation of Coleridge's own capacity for sympathetic response and then with the vexed issue of plagiarism. Coleridge presents the critic with the apparent necessity of reconciling his appetite for love with shifty compositional ethics. Readers either assuage or deplore the complaint of insufficient care that Coleridge inflicts on us when he has just done something blameworthy.

Bate's portrait of Coleridge depends on the denial of aggressive impulses performed in the modern critic's script of free indirect discourse:

> He needed . . . to reassure himself, that he was a benevolent man. And he *was* benevolent. The constant protest that this was so . . . was not because he was trying to hide any deep aggressions. It was because he had quickly learned—or felt—that . . . he was outside the pale of an older, more respectable company. . . . His deepest need was to prove that in this waif-like irregularity there was nothing harmful or vicious: as little . . . as the friendly albatross when, also from outside the pale . . . it appears on the ship of human voyagers: able, with its wide spread of wing, to travel so far; awkward when not in flight; unaccustomed to the habits of men, but eager for their company; and altogether well-meaning. . . . And was he not, in his own way, always seeking to return home—return to the hearth, the domestic and simple virtues, the humanly direct and unpretentious?[11]

Bate taps the reader's sympathy for Coleridge's "waif-like" pathos by ascribing to Coleridge a remarkably "ethical unconscious."[12] After using a loosely Freudian idiom to deny our suspicion of repressed aggression, Bate undermines this denial by suggesting that Coleridge's violence is self-directed—quite a different proposition, but an equally moral one. Coleridge's life, he proposes, is constructed as "an act of 'blessing,' and in the older meaning of that term: a surrender, a giving, which assumes sacrifice."[13] Hence, Bate argues, Coleridge needs to deprecate himself in order to be vicariously gratified through the accomplishments of others—and in order to be blessed, in turn, by his critics.

Fruman, at the other extreme, is compelled by his indignation at such deluded pity to write a long book showing why Coleridge is not lovable. (The short answer to this question is, because his false statements about plagiarism are intentional lies and he is morally account-

---

[11]Walter Jackson Bate, *Coleridge* (New York: Collier Books, 1968), 49.
[12]I take this phrase out of its context in Siebers's *The Ethics of Criticism*, 159.
[13]Bate, *Coleridge,* 50.

able for them.) The tension between love and judgment in Fruman's book is nowhere more open than in the Introduction, which justifies a ruthless, even violent, methodology in the name of sympathetic understanding:

> it may appear at times that Coleridge has been thrust into the dock to be harried by a remorseless prosecutor intent upon diminishing a literary giant. But my purpose has been to understand, sympathetically understand, this infinitely complex man. The seemingly pitiless scrutiny of his letters and notebooks, the rude intrusion into his most private thoughts and feelings, all has but one end in view, to make some sense out of the riven life of this baffling genius.

One could not hope for a better example of the romantic association between analysis and violence: close reading borders on intellectual rape, and moral evaluation resembles inquisitorial harassment. Fruman's guilt about his own aggressiveness is nearly Coleridgean in its desire for atonement. The passage closes: "let me say that I began this lengthy study with profound respect and a sense of deep personal affection for Coleridge. So have I ended."[14]

Reactions of sympathy and blame in binary opposition have provoked interpretations of Coleridge which refuse to indulge in either. Beverly Fields, for example, in a persuasive reading of Coleridge's family romance, finds in the paradoxical logic of psychoanalysis a way of avoiding both empathy and disapproval.[15] The value of psychoanalytic interpretation, for Fields, is precisely that it links the lovable personality to suppressed violence and confounds the critic who wants to have one without the other.

Jerome Christensen, too, deals with the way in which "writing and morality are primordially connected." Christensen reveals the alertness of deconstructive criticism to ethical questions and its capacity for hesitantly defending the moral dilemmas of the parasite, the counterfeiter, and the plagiarist. Christensen's starting point, like my own, is the opposition between "the moral blanket" of Fruman's accusations and the "moral remission" of Bate's sympathy. Christensen regards Coleridge's self-disparagement as the symptom of a wish to dominate: "submission to authority is a strategy of conquest, ambivalence a kind

---

[14]Norman Fruman, *Coleridge: The Damaged Archangel* (New York: George Braziller, 1971), xix.

[15]Beverly Fields, *Reality's Dark Dream: Dejection in Coleridge* (Kent, Ohio: Kent State University Press, 1967), 4–5.

of power." But the manipulations of self-pity, while they express a desire for authority, do not abuse it: "The anxiety of the marginalist is owed to the fact that his resourcefulness is always derived, his freedom licensed, as it were, by his host—the authority on which he obsessively relies and which he compulsively disrupts." Sensitive to the analogy between romantic metaphors of textuality and of the family, Christensen restates his point in terms of domesticity. The "politic aggressiveness of the marginalist" can also, he suggests, be said to derive from the anxiety of living in a "borrowed home," a trope that gains its specifically philosophical prestige from Heidegger.[16] Christensen does not want his view of Coleridge to be dictated by the pathos of a parasitic or homeless state external to the securely placed reader; rather, he wants our ethical equality to Coleridge to arise out of a sense of our own marginality. To live in a "borrowed home" is to hover between the condition of the vagrant and the condition of full domesticity she solicits; we oscillate, in other words, between victimage and nurture. In Christensen's canny adaptation of eighteenth-century moral sensibilities we can glimpse a subdued version of Coleridge's sentimental ethics.

"The Improvisatore"

In Coleridge's texts domestic nurture closely neighbors nightmare visions of female "LIFE-IN-DEATH" (PW 194). Both the sisterly and the gothic aspects of the feminine provoke claims of masculine difference as logical event: desynonymizing, distinction, dissevering, dissection. The gendering of rational states and strategies makes philosophy an aspect of the self and the self a site of cultural conflict. One of Coleridge's most revealing portrayals of the interpretive predicament, "The Improvisatore" of 1827, illustrates the difficulty of sorting out eros from interpretation in his writings.

"The Improvisatore" is remarkable less for the poem with which it concludes (composed *"ex improviso"),* though this is intriguing enough, than for the prose dialogue with which it begins. The dialogue resembles the conversations and epistolary fictions composed by the early German romantics, in which the discourse of the Berlin salons was transformed into hermeneutic drama. As in Schlegel's *Lucinde* or

---

[16]Christensen, *Coleridge's Blessed Machine of Language* (Ithaca: Cornell University Press, 1981), 38, 177, 109.

Schleiermacher's *Confidential Letters,* the conversation concerns the relationship of language to love. Dialogue issues from the understanding that results from erotic loss. "The Friend," as the avuncular extemporizer is called, becomes able to communicate the meaning of the word "Love" through the failure of his own romantic quest. The half-fatherly, half-brotherly friendship of "a man turned of fifty" for the two young women who question him signifies that the role of confidant, advisor, and explicator is incompatible with an immediate experience of love (PW 463).

In the poem "improvised" to answer the last question posed to the Friend in the prose dialogue—"Surely, he, who has described [love] so well, must have possessed it?"—Coleridge connects the failure of love analogically and causally to the failure of poetry (PW 466). As in the Dejection ode, interpretive strength and vicarious feeling are what remain once direct possession of the beloved is lost. The possibility of creating understanding out of failure works best in relation to women or to God. For Coleridge best sustains the fiction of lost powers when imagining a female auditor or when expressing his dependence on divine mercy. The link between the feminine and the sacred, forms of rescue and comfort, suggests a peculiarly Coleridgean mode of what Schleiermacher called divination.

The "Friend" is called on first to define love and then to "interpret" the feeling that his definition arouses in Katherine and Elizabeth. The subject of love is broached through poetry—a clear instance of the relation of theme to genre—when Katherine tries to remember the words of "the ballad that Mr. —— sang so sweetly." Just as the sensation of understanding will be felt, later in the dialogue, before it can be articulated, so here, at the beginning, the Friend can recall the sense but not the words of the ballad: "I do not recollect the words distinctly. The moral of them, however, I take to be this. . . ." Although he gets his "nick-name" from his powers of invention, "by perpetrating charades and extempore verses at Christmas times," the Improvisatore's most evident talent is the ability to paraphrase feminine intuition through quotation. Elizabeth queries, "What are the lines you repeated from Beaumont and Fletcher, which my mother admired so much?" (This glance in the direction of the mother reinforces the avuncular character of the young ladies' "Friend.") The passage from *The Elder Brother* ("We'll live together, like two neighbour vines") elicits the main point of the conversation: "But is there any such true love?" (PW 463–64).

In this mediating role the Improvisatore differs significantly from de

Stael's Corinne, whose performances are erotically irresistible though grounded in a secret genealogical torment that keeps her from full romantic gratification.[17] Before the Friend can be induced to offer an opinion on the nature of love, there is some telling byplay on the subject of his qualifications. He suggests that a man of his age might be expected to give both "a less confident answer" than his girlish auditors and, in the light of his Christmas charades, a less "serious" one. "Serious!" he exclaims. "Doubtless. A grave personage of my years giving a Love-lecture to two young ladies, cannot well be otherwise." He plays ironically with the image of his remoteness from their incipient amours: "It will be asked," he continues (quoting again), "whether I am not the 'elderly gentleman' who sate 'despairing beside a clear stream', with a willow for his wig-block." Having proved that he is in love with neither of the girls, he finally launches into a lecture on love by way of another allusion, this time to a "well-known ballad" of Burns (PW 463–64).

The Friend's superior memory for literature is symptomatic of his power to speak intuitively; nevertheless, he is pretentiously embarrassed at having to shift from banter to "discourse," a shift for which the lyric text provides the hinge: "Well, well, I will be serious. Hem! Now then commences the discourse; Mr. Moore's song being the text." Then he launches into the abstract analysis demanded by the two girls, a parody of Coleridgean desynonymizing: "Love, as distinguished from Friendship, on the one hand, and from the passion that too often usurps its name, on the other—" At this point he is irreverently interrupted by Eliza's brother but resumes in the full swing of definitional momentum. He distinguishes love from both friendship and lust by attributing to it the powers of self-expression ("communicativeness" and *"utterancy* of heart and soul") and receptive understanding ("a peculiar sensibility and tenderness of nature") (PW 464). Love, then, is communicated understanding. It grasps the meaning of "outward and visible signs," the "detail[s] of sympathy" radiating from the beloved. As the Friend is doing at this very moment in the dialogue, love translates nonverbal communications into spoken utterance of a surprisingly abstract but ostensibly feminine sort.

The object of definition shifts from the word "love" to the sensations of love brought to consciousness by the process of definition itself:

[17]Germaine de Stael, *Corinne, or Italy,* trans. and ed. Avriel H. Goldberger (New Brunswick: Rutgers University Press, 1987).

Eliza: There is something *here (pointing to her heart)* that *seems* to understand you, but wants the *word* that would make it understand itself.

Katherine: I, too, seem to *feel* what you mean. Interpret the feeling for us.

The emotion supplied by women and the linguistic supplement offered by the male join in an allegory of the kind of one-to-one correspondence between "signs" and "sacrament within" which Coleridge is all the while trying to describe. Understanding is staged as the process by which intuition is half-verbalized in a circle of female friends. A man theorizes in their midst, but on a theme and with listeners that soften the analytical edge of his distinctions. Fortunately, Coleridge is capable of appreciating the potential absurdity of the situation. In response to the Friend's lecture on love, Eliza exclaims, "What an elevating idea!" to which Katherine, the voice of irony and doom, remarks, "If it be not only an *idea*" (PW 464–65).

In reply to the request for further interpretation the Friend launches into a characterization of the loving subject which embodies allegorical union: "a confirmed faith in the nobleness of humanity . . . brought home and pressed . . . to the very bosom of hourly experience." The happy pair, faith and experience, represents the attempt on the part of the self to be a kind of home, an unstable attempt, since faith produces "seeking" and the experience of fulfillment does, too. Love inheres in "that *willing* sense of the insufficingness of the *self* for itself, which predisposes a generous nature to see, in the total being of another, the supplement and completion of its own;—that quiet perpetual *seeking* which the presence of the beloved object modulates, not suspends, where the heart momently finds, and, finding, again seeks on." The beloved must be the object of other-directed desire *("seeking"* completion) and, "possessing the same or the correspondent excellence," must also be a mirror image of the lover's virtues, available to be appropriated or interiorized (PW 465).

Defining the "last and inmost" of "the concentric circles of attachment" in terms of mutual appropriation requires the Friend to distinguish love from mere self-love. His attack on vanity provokes a satiric catalog of vices culminating alliteratively in "a sort of solemn saturnine, or, if you will, *ursine* vanity, that keeps itself alive by sucking the paws of its own self-importance." Individuals thus afflicted are tormented "by *never forgetting themselves*" (PW 465–66). This sudden shift of mood within "The Improvisatore" typifies the interdependence of the tones of love and assault in Coleridge's prose generally. "The

Friend," called on to philosophize about love but not to possess it, practices a verbal style in which the celebratory definition of the "last and inmost circle" of love requires a righteous moral judgment against all pretenders. Even in a little work like this, preoccupied with the sympathetic exchange of intuitive and critical forms of understanding, distinctions are noticeably aggressive.

The poem that follows, itself a dialogue among uncertain impulses and moods, tells the story of the Friend's own romantic loss and thus explains how he came to be a theorist of love. With all the self-pity of which Coleridge is capable, it narrates the death of Fancy, the inability to obtain "fair fulfillment of . . . poesy," and the failure of Hope.[18] The story, which answers and evades Eliza's question ("Surely, he, who has described [love] so well, must have possessed it?"), can be told only in poetry, though the Friend responds briefly in prose: "If he were worthy to have possessed [love], and had believingly anticipated and not found it, how bitter the disappointment!" Stage directions follow: "(*Then, after a pause of a few minutes*), ANSWER, *ex improviso*" (PW 466). The first four stanzas of the poem conform to the narrative of loss established as early as 1796, in "Lines on an Autumnal Evening" (see below). Having suffered the collapse of the hope of love, which is almost preferable to the real thing, the speaker is also abandoned by Fancy, the poetic equivalent of hope. Although a faint promise of "Contentment" glimmers unconvincingly at the end of the poem, the rewards of understanding are restricted to the prose frame (PW 466–48).

Coleridge's need to connect the longing for lost love to the capacity for understanding is never, as far as I can tell, reconciled with his narrative of the desynonymizing mind that takes pleasure in aggressive statements of difference, unless perhaps this can be said to occur in the elaborate religious formulas he constructs in the last decade and a half of his career. The moment he reconciles difference, he is back in the feminine mode that cannot negotiate or really converse with "method"

[18]Coleridge's pathos, not for the first time, is derived from Wordsworth's "Lucy poems," which spoke so strongly to Coleridge's sense of himself as a lost child:

> Doubts toss'd him to and fro:
> Hope keeping Love, Love Hope alive,
> Like babes bewildered in a snow,
> That cling and huddle from the cold
> In hollow tree or ruin'd fold.

> (PW 467, lines 30–34)

but can only lovingly heal its divisions. In "The Improvisatore" an even more complex situation prevails. Feminine understanding is mediated by the male translator, who makes his auditors conscious of their intuitions. But the interpreter is drawn under the sway of the inchoate feeling of the girls who question him, for his definitions of love cannot organize the account of his own unhappiness.

A notebook entry of 1815 suggests the extent to which Coleridge thought of a "literary Man" as being not only the temperamental antithesis of "a well-attuned and sensitive female mind," but also marginal even to the standard binary characterizations of the sexes. The position is an ethical one. If the writer ruins "all non-pertinent Objects" in his room for the sake of his productions and if the lady, who lacks "the callus of an extreme Stimulation," banishes the artist's mess in order to have "the whole . . . Space *in keeping,*" only the person who contains attributes of both—or neither—refrains from destruction. Coleridge contrasts the *"Artistical . . .* Sense of the Beautiful" to "the pleasure in Beauty, modified by the sense of Propriety, and Rank in Life."

> See an artist's Room, see a *littery* literary Man's Room!—all in disorder— much dirt, more Confusion—but here and there some exquisitely finished Form or Combinations of Form—in the production, no less than in the contemplation of which the Painter . . . annihilates for ⟨himself⟩ all non-pertinent Objects, which *co-exist* with his compositions only to the Eye of his Visitors—. Now a well-attuned and sensitive female mind must have the whole of the given Space *in keeping*—it requires the callus of an extreme Stimulation to be able to endure . . . the scattered Books, fluttering Pamphlets, & dusty Paper-wilderness of a Wordsworth.—I know but two individuals, who combine both, viz—Lady-like *Wholeness* with creative delight in *particular* forms—& these are Mr. Robert Southey, Poet Laureat &c &c &c, and Mr. Sam. Tayl. Coleridge, whose whole Being has been unfortunately little more than a far-stretched Series of Et Ceteras. (N III 4250 29.175)

The literary man—inevitably, Wordsworth—"annihilates" all "non-pertinent Objects"; the "disorder" of his "Paper-wilderness" suggests that he has drained the orderliness from life in order to invest it in "some exquisitely finished Form." The "fairest part of the most beautiful Body"—a phrase from Chapter 12 of *Biographia Literaria*—is created here only by the sacrifice of life to art (BL I 234). The feminine mind, by contrast, turns the room into a work of art, though its "wholeness" is merely "Lady-like," or decorous, not "exquisitely finished."

Coleridge and Southey are a strangely doomed pair of androgynes at the end of this entry. As usual, for Coleridge, Southey stands for the most extreme kind of compulsiveness, the drive to straighten up both works and lives. The three "&c"s attached to his name undercut Coleridge's praise, as it is always undercut. And Coleridge, despite the fact that he includes himself in the category of persons who are both lady-like and creative, suggests at the end that he is beyond the pale of either, "a far-stretched Series of Et Ceteras." His stance in this passage indicates a strong sense of being neither male nor female, but rather, as in "The Improvisatore," the bachelor dwelling among women who makes theoretical improvisation his home away from home.

Family, Authority, and
Generic Choice: 1789–98

Coleridge creates the analogy between ethics and genre specifically to cope with his own resentment. Criticism of Coleridge, preoccupied with his turn from poetry to prose, has sustained this tendency. As part of the code of literary definition, genre implies evaluation, judgment, consumption. Aggression, therefore, is always likely to operate in generic transactions. Like any phenomenon associated with aggression, genre became something that Coleridge obsessively negotiated and justified. All English writers in Coleridge's lifetime were well aware that style functioned as an ideological allegory, an image of social tensions among literary consumers. But Coleridge's unusually strong sense of writing as the medium of ideological and cultural contagion led to unprecedented efforts of generic containment. To pursue Coleridge's actions in the domain of critical prose, we need to begin with an overview of his early writings, which are quite differently configured from the works I take up subsequently, *Biographia Literaria* and *The Friend*.

My oblique point of entry into the generic topography of Coleridge's poetry and prose in the 1790s is the topos of the family, a cluster of scenes and arguments that includes references to family relationships and settings, as well as to related social and political issues. This last rubric covers, for example, Coleridge's negative response to William Godwin's theoretical abolition of the family and the positive familial basis of the Pantisocratic experiment.[19] Merely enumerating the range of meanings attached to the family in Coleridge's early works breaks down certain categorical presuppositions. Family and "philosophy"— the latter comprised of political ideals, religious speculations, and ethical reflection—are impossible to separate. Retirement takes its meaning antithetically from war; the prophetic mount looks down at the domestic "cot" in its pastoral dell; brothers imply a commitment to universal fraternity; and women supply the sympathetic milieu in which such fraternal idealism can operate in an unalienated fashion. It is important to acknowledge that, though understanding is an aspect of the familial, I am ranging well beyond the particular dynamics of the ethics of understanding here to show its relationship to other ethical desires.

The figures and themes I have identified as familial are barely visible in Coleridge's published prose during the 1790s, including his sermons and lectures. In the same period, however, his poetry accommodates both domestic desire and public debate. By 1802, the year of the verse letter to Sara Hutchinson which became the Dejection ode, a reversal is underway. Coleridge's poetry is almost wholly given over to hope and loss arising from the yearning for familial nurture. As in "The Improvisatore," analysis is characterized as a symptom, and political comment disappears. But in the prose of *Biographia Literaria* (1817) and *The Friend* (1809–10, 1818) the feminine and its related familial virtues emerge as the necessary context for reason.

Early Poems: The Prospect and "Lone-Whispering Pity"

Coleridge's poems on the French Revolution are structured by contrasts between landscapes corresponding to the familial and the analytical.[20] The voice of political prophecy speaks through a hypermasculine, hyper-Miltonic sublime that transforms history into allegory. In the opening lines of "The Destiny of Nations," for example, a grandiose subject justifies both the ambition of the poet and his choice of an allegorical style:

[19]Anthony John Harding, *Coleridge and the Idea of Love* (Cambridge: Cambridge University Press, 1974), 21–23.

[20]"The Destruction of the Bastille" (1789); "Religious Musings" (1795); the visions of Joan of Arc eventually assembled as "The Destiny of Nations" (1794–96; 1817); "Ode to the Departing Year" (1796); and "France: An Ode" (1798).

> Auspicious Reverence! Hush all meaner song,
> Ere we the deep preluding strain have poured
> To the Great Father, only Rightful King,
> Eternal Father! King Omnipotent!

Allegory, in turn, corresponds to the abstractions that occur to the individual who looks out over the widest prospect.[21]

> For what is Freedom, but the unfettered use
> Of all the powers which God for use had given?
> But chiefly this, him First, him Last to view
> Through meaner powers and secondary things
> Effulgent, as through clouds that veil his blaze.
> For all that meets the bodily sense I deem
> Symbolical, one mighty alphabet
> For infant minds.
>
>   (PW 131–32, lines 1–20)

The theme of godly freedom leads directly to "the unfettered use / Of all the powers" of the poet, powers both rhetorical (the heavenly sky-scape of blazes, clouds, and beams) and intellectual (mastery of the "mighty alphabet" of "sense").

In less grandiose portions of these poems the naturalized equivalent of "Symbolical" vision is the view from the mountain, the "burst of prospect" from which "the whole World / Seem'd *imag'd* in its vast circumference" ("Fears in Solitude," PW 263, line 215; "Reflections on Having Left a Place of Retirement," PW 107, lines 39–40). In "Life," an important sonnet of 1789, the discovery of a therapeutic view lifts the poet beyond his private grief—significantly associated with the feminine—to reveal an implicitly collective landscape that "seems like Society."[22] "Musing in torpid woe a Sister's pain," he is stirred by a "glorious prospect" of "Wood, Meadow, verdant Hill, and dreary Steep." The sight, instantly allegorized, becomes a vision of the speaker's future and of the present arrangement of Coleridge's poetry:

---

[21]See my "Aggressive Allegory," *Raritan: A Quarterly Review* 3 (1984): 100–115.

[22]Karl Kroeber, "Coleridge's 'Fears': Problems in Patriotic Poetry," *Clio* 7 (1978): 361–63. I have benefited as well from Stuart Peterfreund's "Coleridge and the Politics of Critical Vision," SEL 21 (1981):585–604. Virtually all of John Barrell, *The Idea of Landscape and the Sense of Place, 1730–1840: An Approach to the Poetry of John Clare* (Cambridge: Cambridge University Press, 1972), is pertinent, especially chap. 1. See also Robert Sternbach, "Coleridge, Joan of Arc, and the Idea of Progress," *ELH* 46 (1979):248–61.

> May this (I cried) my course through Life portray!
> New scenes of Wisdom may each step display,
> And Knowledge open as my days advance!
> > (PW 11–12, lines 9–11)

The leap from self and sister to "Life" and "Knowledge" exhibits in the most transparent way a simple contrast between autobiography and analysis which corresponds in turn to the familiar symbolic topography of feminine valley and masculine "steep."

Throughout the poetry of these years such prospective moments correspond to an emphasis on brotherhood distinct from the desire for a domestic circle of wives, sisters, and children. The stresses of fraternity are suggested by parallels between the public language of "Religious Musings" and the disturbing poem to Coleridge's elder brother, "To George" (1797). "Musings" equates sublimity with fraternity:

> Tis the sublime of man,
> Our noontide Majesty, to know ourselves
> Parts and proportions of one wondrous whole!
> This fraternises man.

Humanity's "common sire" is its "common centre," the cause of "sacred sympathy" among members of "the vast family of Love" (PW 113–14, lines 126–29, 148). This is precisely the condition Coleridge describes as existing among his brothers in "To George": "fraternal love / Hath drawn you to one centre." He has had to create for himself a family based entirely on relationships with women, however: "I've rais'd a lowly shed, and know the names / Of Husband and of Father" but, quite pointedly, not that of "Brother" (PW 174, lines 13–14, 34–35). In his prophetic poems Coleridge speaks as the seer whose vision of the whole locates him in the nation's "common centre." The poetry of visionary politics provides a language for the ego strength that vanishes when he writes of literal brotherhood.

"Kubla Khan," built up out of the accumulating anxieties of threatening fathers ("Ancestral voices prophesying war"), demonic mothers (the "woman wailing for her demon-lover"), and mediating sisters (the "damsel with a dulcimer"), is Coleridge's climactic poem in the prophetic vein. The poet whose paradisal revelation strikes "holy dread" into others is a figure adapted from the sacred politics of the more cumbersome poems on the French Revolution and the Revolutionary Wars. "Kubla Khan" alters the hierarchies that structured those texts.

Its concluding invocation of the singing damsel transposes the mostly vertical axis of Xanadu into the horizontal pattern of dance. The poem resists the division into domestic valley and public-spirited mountain. In a wholly demonic place there are no safe familial sanctuaries or self-congratulatory overviews. The poet prays for a manifold influx of verbal energies—decree, wail, and song—which will make him the center of a weaving, irradiated circle (PW 297–98). It is the single instance of such reflexive empowerment in Coleridge's work.

Throughout Coleridge's poetic career the images of sister, mother, and wife (or of all three merged into a single figure) are the focus of powerful desire, often in the form of mourning or nostalgia. During the 1790s this desire is evident in Coleridge's sonnets on the death of his sister and the birth of his son; in "To George"; in the Conversation Poems; and in the images of home in "Rime of the Ancient Mariner." The poems most pertinent to my developing arguments about Coleridge's later prose, however, are those in which feminine domesticity must negotiate with public prophecy. Carl Woodring captures the major dichotomies baldly in a chiasmic chapter title: "Ideas and Feelings: Pity versus Power."[23] The domestic occurs as a moment in the prophetic, by which it is displaced or absorbed; or, conversely, the prophetic occurs in domestic life and is disciplined by it.[24]

---

[23]Carl Woodring, *Politics in the Poetry of Coleridge* (Madison: University of Wisconsin Press, 1961), 45. Woodring's survey of Coleridge's poems of the early 1790s, though not oriented to questions of gender, includes some striking observations on Coleridge's grotesque portrayal of Catherine the Great, who emerges as the feminine antithesis of Pity. Pity, for Woodring, is more strongly associated with the bonds among radical young men than with the feminine (49, 45–48).

[24]Thomas McFarland, the critic who most strongly emphasizes Coleridge's and Wordsworth's commitment to the family (as a version of "the significant group"), also defends the tradition of romantic conservatism more fervently than any other American critic. In order to resist the threat posed by the "Jacobin mania of our own era," he makes romantic conservatives the occasion for an essay in defense of the current validity of "Wordsworthian" politics—including, it seems, the following program: Cold War sentiments ("The communist societies have been no less murderous and repressive than were the Nazis—a fact that the noble indignation of Solzhenitsyn has been drumming into the reluctant conscience of our time"); a defense of the death penalty ("in our own day, it could as cogently be argued that any man's birth diminishes me"); and an attack on abortion ("the same humanitarian feeling that wishes to protect and conserve criminal life is unconcerned by the exposure and dissipation of foetal life"). The deep homosocial loyalty and antifeminist anxiety of McFarland's conservatism should be obvious, derived as it is from an anti-Jacobin brotherhood consisting of Burke, Coleridge, Wordsworth, Arnold, Schopenhauer, Leavis, Ortega y Gasset, and others. *Romanticism and the Forms of Ruin: Wordsworth, Coleridge, and the Modalities of Fragmentation* (Princeton: Princeton University Press, 1981), 214, 196, 207, 211, 172–215 passim.

Given the dualistic logic of "Religious Musings," "Fears in Solitude," and "Reflections on Having Left a Place of Retirement," which provided us with examples of the masculine political prospect, it is not surprising that they also illustrate the way prophecy is plagued by domesticity. Or, to use more anachronistic metaphors, the way the cottage becomes a launching pad for sublimity, a kind of tonal trampoline necessary to radical aspirations. In "Reflections" the speaker narrates a progressive ascent from his "low Dell" to the "stony Mount" from which all of England seems to be visible. He then rises to the more abstract plane of theory on which "the bloodless fight / Of Science, Freedom, and the Truth in Christ" unfolds. The poet's idyllic condition precipitates an anxious reaction; his guilt feelings reveal the tug of home:

> I was constrain'd to quit you. Was it right,
> While my unnumber'd brethren toil'd and bled,
> That I should dream away the entrusted hours
> On rose-leaf beds, pampering the coward heart
> With feelings all too delicate for use?

The brotherhood of masculine laborers charges the poet with effeminacy, with having joined "The sluggard Pity's vision-weaving tribe!/ . . . Nursing in some delicious solitude / Their slothful loves and dainty sympathies!" The allure of pity, however, is not in "nursing" one's tastes but in being nurtured. Even as the poet imagines an active future, he looks forward to the homesickness that will pervade it: "Yet oft . . . My spirit shall revisit thee, dear Cot!" (PW 105–8, lines 44–48, 63–65).

"Fears in Solitude" reverses the order of emotions in "Reflections" but repeats its ambivalent structure. This time the poet begins by resenting the demands of general sympathy. But as he broods on the impending invasion, he is stricken by a sense of shared national guilt, as though the whole country has lapsed into an escapist pastoral. In order that England may be spared the "evil days" when "all-avenging Providence" will exact retribution, the poet calls for purgatorial battle. He ends by returning from military masculinity to domestic sentiments, but with the crucial substitution of "dear Britain," "my Mother Isle!," for his actual family. While wending his way homeward through the rural setting of the final verse paragraph, he reads the wide prospect as an image of "society— / Conversing with the mind." Conversation, so often dependent on feminine receptivity, here includes society at large, or at least, in Coleridge's much-mediated way, the thought of society. But the source of sociable desire, "thoughts that yearn for human kind," is none other than "my own lowly cottage, where my babe / And my babe's mother dwell in peace" (PW 256–63, lines 44–124, 215–32).[25]

The universal brotherhood formed by philosophical speculation is not always pestered by a sense of transgression, as in "The Eolian Harp," nor is the domestic imagination always as repressive as it is in that poem.[26] "Lines on an Autumnal Evening" (1793) domesticates the story of poetic election.[27] The poet-protagonist begins by withdrawing his muse, Fancy, from nature and directing it to the unnatural mind, "Disappointment's wintry desert." In retrospect Fancy merges with the desired "Maid" who once met him with a kiss. The poem unfolds in the manner of a quest romance as the protagonist seeks to repeat this encounter with the beloved, whose crucial attribute is the voice that "seems in each low wind . . . to float / Lone-whispering Pity in each soothing note!" (PW 51–54, lines 9, 35–36). "Pity" is the word that divides receptivity from power for Coleridge. It frequently designates maternal and sisterly care, the family Coleridge wished he had, but later refers also to Wordsworth as the poet of the recurring pathos of homelessness.

In "Lines on an Autumnal Evening" pity elicits divination, not quest. The speaker cultivates extrasensory intuition in his own neighborhood. He feels the maid's presence in his local wanderings but prefers luxuriating in sensuous fantasies to gaining possession. Such desire—or, since it remembers the initial kiss, nostalgia—is the essential poetic condition. The poet prays for "the wizard's rod" or "the power of Proteus" in order to transform himself into the landscape where he knows his muse lurks:

[25]See also the poem in *The Watchman*, "To Mercy" (W 166–67), in which England as the pregnant mother is befouled by the Oedipal Pitt; and Karl Kroeber, "Coleridge's 'Fears': Problems in Patriotic Poetry," 354.

[26]In "The Eolian Harp" the speaker's whiff of the "intellectual breeze" takes place during an escape from the conjugal cottage to the "slope / of yonder hill," the locale of generalizing vision. On his return, one glance from the "heart-honour'd Maid" who represents his anxieties about theoretical adventure is enough to make him renounce "vain Philosophy's aye-babbling spring." This reaction ensues even though the most philosophically speculative portion of the poem (the "one Life" passage) was added only in 1828, more than thirty years after its original publication in 1796 (PW 100–102, 101n).

[27]"Lines on an Autumnal Evening" is a revision of "An Effusion at Evening" (1792) (PW 49–50).

A flower-entangled Arbour I would seem
To shield my Love from Noontide's sultry beam:
Or bloom a Myrtle, from whose od'rous boughs
My Love might weave gay garlands for her brows.
When Twilight stole across the fading vale,
To fan my Love I'd be the Evening Gale;
Mourn in the soft folds of her swelling vest,
And flutter my faint pinions on her breast!
(lines 57–66)[28]

The female breast is the physiological emblem of Coleridgean pity, the locus of maternal eroticism.[29] The desire for indirect access to the beloved is reinforced by the curious verb "Mourn." This tendency seems to accept and even to enjoy the speaker's intimate but unconsummated relation to the suddenly large woman who tucks the infantile breeze into her "vest."

The autumnal evening has been forgotten in the pursuit of mental associations, as it will be again in "Dejection: An Ode"; the storm that intrudes on "Dejection" appears figuratively in this earlier poem as well, but to little effect. The speaker establishes the temporal distance between his present self and his remembered fantasies by comparing himself to a "Savage" who has fallen asleep under a clear sky but who awakens to "The skiey deluge, and white lightning's glare." The poem ends by lingering in the earlier time or place, near the "native brook" that catches up the feminine qualities of the maid. The conceit that likens the stream to Quiet's dimpled cheek ("Where soften'd Sorrow smiles within her tears") and compares memory to a chaste vestal shows that the protagonist of "Autumnal Evening" still yearns for a pitying mother (lines 71–74, 79–90). As early as 1793, then, *before* his major poetry, Coleridge associates poetic power with loss. This makes

[28]This scene anticipates Keats's "Ode to Psyche," except that Keats's mind becomes the bower Psyche will inhabit, whereas Coleridge, transformed into the enclosing landscape, wants to be *enfolded* by Love.

[29]But see Fields's suggestion that "the recurrent image of the child on the mother's lap" (a scenario in which the breast is, of course, prominent) is an "elaboration" of an earlier scene and that "the lap Coleridge longed for was his father's, a reassuring place of comfort where he could deny, by means of affection, his feelings of anger and hostility." Her observation concerning the link between the comfort provided by his gentle father and the religious vocation with which his father was strongly associated complicates my argument in Chapter 6 about the association, in Coleridge's later prose works, between religion and the feminine. *Reality's Dark Dream*, 42.

it difficult to read "Dejection," also addressed to an inaccessible muse, as a reliable explanation of the failure of Coleridge's poetic career after 1800. In fact, the fable of the poet who seeks the elusive care of a quasi-maternal figure or broods on her absence organizes most of Coleridge's great poems and a number of unread ones.

Knowledge, Love, and Power in the Early Prose: 1795–96

> I commenced an harangue . . . varying my notes through the whole gamut of eloquence from the ratiocinative to the declamatory, and in the latter from the pathetic to the indignant. I argued, I described, I promised, I prophecied; and beginning with the captivity of nations I ended with the near approach of the millenium[*sic*], finishing the whole with some of my own verses describing that glorious state[.] (BL I 181)

The difference between the *Lectures on Politics and Religion* of 1795 and Coleridge's contributions to *The Watchman* of 1796 is not due to the lapse of a year between them.[30] The former emphasizes the relation of knowledge to love, and the latter, the relation of knowledge to power. Anxiety about the violence of repressive governments, suffering mobs, and debate itself calls up, in the *Lectures,* themes familiar from the domestic strain of Coleridge's poetry. He prefers benevolence to mental strength; consequently, as in the poems of the same period, his prophecies are tempered by a guilty awareness of the transgressions inherent in political life. *The Watchman,* however, in which he writes not as an author but as "Editor" and "Contributor," calls forth a voice of remarkable decisiveness, pragmatism, and even aggressiveness. The motto of the sheet reads, "That All may know the TRUTH; / And that the TRUTH may make us FREE!" (W 197, 3). His self-characterization as a truth-teller replaces the prophetic Watchman with the zealous but tough newspaperman.[31]

---

[30]The *Lectures* includes Coleridge's six lectures on "Revealed Religion, Its Corruptions and Political Views," "Consciones ad Populum, or Addresses to the People," his "Lecture on the Slave Trade," and several lectures on English politics and the conduct of the war with France. For the context of these works, see the Editors' Introduction, as well as E. P. Thompson's criticisms of their account in "'Bliss was it in that dawn': The Matter of Coleridge's Revolutionary Youth and How It Became Obscured," *London Times Literary Supplement* no. 3623 (1971): 931–32.

[31]Michael G. Cooke, though overly schematic, offers fine insights on the phenomenology of moods which underlies generic affinities, in *Acts of Inclusion: Studies Bearing on an Elementary Theory of Romanticism* (New Haven: Yale University Press, 1979), 3–11.

The lecturer of 1795 attributes his anxiety to the violence of the political situation in which he finds himself. Wandering "in the maze of POLITICAL ENQUIRY," the best-intentioned citizen "must tread over Corses, and at every step detect some dark Conspirator against human happiness" ("On the Present War"). The vehemence of debate persuades him that to engage in political discussion is to risk physical danger.[32] "They, who in these days of jealousy and Party rage dare publicly explain the Principles of Freedom," he declares in the "Advertisement" for "A Moral and Political Lecture," "must expect . . . to be entitled like the Apostles of Jesus, 'stirrers up of the People, and men accused of Sedition.'" England's crumbling social decorum, furthermore, is a sign that the country is teetering on the brink of uncontrollable civil violence, for which France is the ever-present image. By dwelling on the savagery of his times, Coleridge dramatizes his role as "Metaphysical Reasoner" and religious apologist. In these early attempts to identify philosophy with faith, he argues that philosophy is necessarily benevolent, part of the "beautiful fabric of love" rent by "the system of Spies and Informers" (LPR 53, 17–18, 95, 59–60).

The links between philosophical consistency and the ethic of nonviolence appear utterly transparent to the lecturer. In order "to place Liberty on her seat with bloodless hands," he shows "the necessity of forming some fixed and determinate principles of action to which the familiarized mind may at all times advert" ("A Moral and Political Lecture"). What principles fix is a barrier against potential aggression by self or others. Even righteousness is dangerous. In language redolent of his negative characterizations of his brother George and of Southey, he warns, "Indignation is the handsome brother of Anger and Hatred—Benevolence alone beseems the Philosopher" (LPR 17–18). From the beginning, philosophy signifies for him a kind of man and a manner of life, and that is why he automatically equates method with morality. The intellectual discipline of self-conscious reasoning is the moral practice that guides him through the maze of political conflict.

It is not only as a barrier against his own irrationality or that of "unstable Patriots of Passion or Accident" that Coleridge values philosophy. He asserts "the necessity of *bottoming* on fixed Principles" as a policy of active reformation. His view of applied philosophy emerges

---

[32]The material danger of violence facing Coleridge and his radical friends is attested to by E. P. Thompson, "Disenchantment or Default? A Lay Sermon," in *Power and Consciousness,* ed. Conor Cruise O'Brien and William Dean Vanech (New York: New York University Press, 1969), 155–68; and by Smith, *The Politics of Language,* 57–67.

most interestingly in his description of the two classes of persons who call themselves "professed Friends of Liberty." The first group is well-intentioned but timid, oscillating with "the winds of Rumor" from republicanism to aristocracy. A benevolent temper is useless to members of this class: "Their sensibility unbraced by the co-operation of fixed principles, they offer no sacrifices to the divinity of active Virtue." If the lack of philosophy among the virtuous produces ineffectiveness, the same deficiency in "the second Class" threatens to usher in political apocalypse. "Unillumined by Philosophy and stimulated to a lust of Revenge by aggravated wrongs," persons in this group engage in sacrifices of a more appalling kind, which "would make the Altar of Freedom stream with blood, while the grass grew in the desolated Halls of Justice." This lurid prose, of which I have cited only a portion, makes explicit philosophy's function as the antidote to violence. Only logical rigor can save the populace from "frightful Names" (LPR 5, 8–9).

Into this polarized milieu Coleridge wants to introduce a "small but glorious band" of "thinking and disinterested Patriots," the first draft of the clerisy. This "unresisting yet deeply principled Minority," whose principles are "fixed" but not oppositional, "gradually absorbing kindred minds shall . . . become the whole." Family resemblance is the basis for Coleridge's communal model of wholeness, unlike Schleiermacher's system of collective difference. "Kindred" affection is the analogue of a Christian utopia, where Jesus is "son," "Friend," and "neighbor" and where Godwin's proposed extermination of the family is controverted: "general Benevolence is begotten and rendered permanent by social and domestic affections. Let us beware of that proud Philosophy, which affects to inculcate Philanthropy, while it denounces every home-born feeling. . . . The paternal and filial duties discipline the Heart and prepare it for the love of all Mankind" (LPR 12, 218, 163, 46).[33]

The equivalence of knowledge and love is nowhere clearer than in

---

[33]See the "Editors' Introduction" for the case in favor of the centrality of Godwinism as "the real opponent in Coleridge's mind during the inception and preparation of the lectures" (LPR lxvii); and see Thompson, "'Bliss was it in that dawn'" for an opposed viewpoint: "By neglecting the alternatives to Godwinism, the editors . . . leave us with a Coleridge who is a total individualist, in a unique posture, swatting hostile ideologies like wasps on every side" (931). On the whole, I find Thompson's position more persuasive, although on the particular issue of the family, and all that it stands for, Coleridge's antithetical reaction to Godwin may dominate.

the argument that the "purifying alchemy" of the human sciences may "transmute the fierceness of an ignorant man into virtuous energy."[34] The rhetoric surrounding this visionary cell of philosophical patriots firmly establishes the connection between the philosopher and the prophet. The passage ends with the allegorical prospect that corresponds, in so many of Coleridge's poems, to political commitment. As the "visionary cell" advances, "These soul ennobling views bestow the virtues which they anticipate. He whose mind is habitually imprest with them soars above the present state of humanity, and may be justly said to dwell in the presence of the most high. Regarding every event even as he that ordained it, evil vanishes from before him, and he views with naked eye the eternal form of universal beauty" (LPR 8–13).

In *The Watchman* Coleridge similarly commits himself to methods of analysis and argument. "KNOWLEDGE IS POWER," his "Prospectus" declares, and ensuing numbers show to what extent this includes his own power.[35] Philosophy produces self-assertion, not, as in the 1795 lectures, benevolence. "I ought to be considered in two characters," he explains to a correspondent, "as the Editor of the Miscellany, and as a frequent Contributor." Both "characters" are negatively defined by

[34]The philosophical minority must approach radicals with "the healing qualities of knowledge." I am reminded here of a television advertisement for the health maintenance organization marketed by the medical school of the University of Michigan. From an elevated perspective, the viewer looks down at a sequence of images that proceed from cave drawings to Renaissance manuscripts to scenes of early industrial technology and finally to a high-tech computer-generated picture of the human body accompanied by the only words yet to appear on the screen: "Knowledge heals." The link between the superior analytical perspective and the ethical claim to healing is vividly apparent.

[35]David Simpson remarks on Coleridge's need to inject difference and dialectical contraries into the process of speculation, in *Irony and Authority in Romantic Poetry* (New York: Macmillan, 1979), 120–21. David V. Erdman, in "Coleridge as Editorial Writer" (in *Power and Consciousness*, ed. O'Brien and Vanech, 198), comments on Coleridge's sense of his own influence at a later date: "In a newspaper poem in September [1802], with an image deceptive with the modesty of the poet-journalist who feels his power as imponderable but real, who can variously estimate it as decisive in a vast balance or as nil, Coleridge presents himself as the gentian daring to grow within a few steps of the glacier. . . . 'venturing near, and . . . leaning over the brink of the grave,' now usually the brink of renewed war. Only a little less innocent-seeming is the grain of sand (or the shout) that precipitates an avalanche. This image-cluster . . . is functional in most of the essays of 1802 leading to a climax in a 'speculative' prophecy in January, 1803, called 'Our Future Prospects.' In the whole series we see Coleridge fascinated by the not quite believable idea that his nearly weightless words may tip the teetering balance of world power."

their forceful criticism of *The Watchman*'s main texts: reprinted accounts of parliamentary debates, domestic politics, and foreign affairs.
Without apology, he admits to "the intemperance of a young man's
zeal." "Does the Spirit of Meekness forbid us to tell the Truth?" he
demands. The personality of critical "truth-teller" and antiauthoritarian commentator yields Coleridge real pleasure in his own antagonism (LPR 197, 194–98).

The subject of method, which pervades *The Watchman*, takes the
form of instruction on effective argument. "Method" does not possess
the meanings it will acquire two decades later in the "Essays on the
Principles of Method." Here it signifies not the avoidance of conflict,
but the assault of judgment on error. The mode of abstraction Coleridge recommends is distinctly reductive. Vaguely evoking the mood
of experimental science and the hegemonic language theory of the
mid-eighteenth century, he vigorously promotes the value of transparent prose.[36] His call for more logical parliamentary debates conflates the virtues of syllogistic reasoning, the all-encompassing prospect
of the philosophical "eye," and the prestige of the sacred: "the statement and the deductions from it should be holy ground. . . . Thus
each part reflecting its appropriate rays, the eye would be enabled to
catch it readily, to look on it attentively, and to trace its boundaries
with precision" (W 56).[37]

When Coleridge was confronted directly with the charge that abstract
thinking is a form of violence, however, he moved toward the equation
of method and divine love which receives full articulation in the "Essays
on Method." In the "Letter to a Noble Lord" (1796), Edmund Burke
had restated the critique of theoretical government first set forth in

[36]Hans Aarsleff, *The Study of Language in England, 1780–1860* (Minneapolis: University of Minnesota Press, 1982), 227–30; Smith, *The Politics of Language*, chap. 1, "The
Problem."

[37]Coleridge's role as editor entails the pleasurable violence of "abridging and meth-
odizing the arguments," excerpting the crucial portions of debates as reported in the
newspapers, and adding pointed comments and footnotes (W300). The pleasure of
imposing clarity on others evidently is not incompatible with composing one's own
prose according to a more complex logic. Coleridge's response to an essay of Thomas
Beddoes printed in an earlier number of *The Watchman* enjoys just such revisionary
authority. Coleridge focuses on "the *arrangement*" of the work, with its "intermixture of
miscellaneous matter" and chronological, rather than logical, organization. He makes
sense out of the nation's "jumbled discourse" with an editor's self-confident activism.
The editorial voice of *The Watchman* is so forceful, in fact, as to indulge frequently in the
righteous indignation that appeared so threatening in the context of the lectures. If this
speaker can be called prophetic, it is in the vein of Isaiah, "terrible in his eloquent
irony," with whom Coleridge strongly identifies ("Essay on Fasts," W55).

Reflections on the Revolution in France (1790). In the earlier work, contrasting the French Enlightenment to British pragmatism, Burke had categorically opposed the application of philosophical methods to politics: "The pretended rights of these theorists [French *philosophes*] are all extremes; and in proportion as they are metaphysically true, they are morally and politically false." In composing his sweeping rebuttal of Burke's charges in the "Letter," Coleridge was faced with the already-conventional equation between scientific or philosophical analysis and violence. The "hard . . . heart of a thorough-bred Metaphysician," Burke had written, approaches "the wild malignity of a wicked spirit" and, indeed, resembles "the principle of Evil himself, incorporeal, pure, unmixed, dephlegmated, defecated, evil!" (a paradoxical catalog, if evil is both "pure" and "defecated"). Mere geometricians and chemists, bearing "the dry bones of their diagrams," are, by comparison, just "indifferent" to the "feelings and habitudes" of "the moral world" (W 34n).[38]

Coleridge responds with equal fervor by defining abstract or theoretical disciplines as heroic expressions of universal love and by equating vision with rationality. He charges that the "vile . . . system" described by Burke wrongs

> the Metaphysician who employs the strength and subtlety of reason to investigate, by what causes being acted on, the human mind acts most worthily; the Geometrician, who tames into living and embodied uses the proud possibilities of Truth, and who has leavened the whole mass of his thoughts and feelings with the love of proportion; and the Chemist, whose faculties are swallowed up in the great task of discovering those perfect laws by which the Supreme Wisdom governs the Universe! (W 34)

Without directly addressing the question of the morality of analytical logic, Coleridge draws on the high-minded motives of those who employ it and the divinity of the natural world they explore in order to defend theoreticians from the charge of cruelty. Only in the acknowledgment that the mathematician "tames into living and embodied uses the proud possibilities of Truth" does he indirectly concede that mastery is one of the pleasures of science. He swerves away from this suggestion by letting the chemist be "swallowed up" by universal laws. The real attraction of theory, for Coleridge, is the theme of

---

[38]Edmund Burke, *Reflections on the Revolution in France*, ed. J. G. A. Pocock (Indianapolis: Hackett Publishing Co., 1987), 54.

rigor, for it is not "Truth" that is thus made "proud," but the meta-physician, the geometrician, the chemist, and the editor.

Burke enters Coleridge's text as the figure in whom the problematic character of prose is most fully embodied and brings with him all the difficulties entailed in the transition from the lectures and journalism of the 1790s to Coleridge's reflections on them in *Biographia Literaria*. Despite the changes that occur in his claims for critical prose between 1796 and 1817, when Burke emerges again as the model for the *"scientific* statesman, and . . . *seer,"* Coleridge continues to locate the writing of philosophical criticism within the triangle marked out by knowledge, love, and power (BL I 191).[39] The reorientation of Coleridge's prose writing which takes place between 1796 and his return from Malta in 1806 has generally been thought to pertain to the question of political "apostasy," the turn from Unitarian radicalism to Anglican apologetics, and to Coleridge's lost confidence in poetry. I prefer to approach these changes through the shifting meanings of the feminine in the social topographies of criticism.

[39]Coleridge had begun his review essay by praising Burke, whose powers he increasingly admired as his own politics became more conservative. Addressing other critics of Burke in 1796, he writes, "Nor can I think his merit diminished, because he has secured the aids of sympathy to his cause by the warmth of his own emotions, and delighted the imagination of his readers by a multitude and rapid succession of remote analogies. It seems characteristic of true eloquence, to reason *in* metaphors; of declamation, to argue *by* metaphors" (W 30–31).

CHAPTER 5

"Woe Is Me That I Am Become a Man of Strife"

Abstruse Research and Vicarious Gratification

Biographia Literaria, in addition to everything else it intends and desires, is a discourse on the ethics of criticism, and specifically on criticism as written. Because the genres of criticism convey speculation on understanding, interpretation, and judgment, Coleridge equates them with these uneasily compatible enterprises. To state the dynamics of *Biographia Literaria* in these terms, of course, excludes nothing. Genre, for Coleridge, is a figurative expression of an author's entire cultural predicament. Throughout *Biographia Literaria* (written in 1815, published in 1817) he assumes that modes of writing are traceable to the material and psychological conditions of the author and, therefore, to the characteristics "of particular countries and a particular age" (BL II 14). To choose prose or poetry, or a subgenre of either, is to make a social gesture. This is why Coleridge's "life in letters" is at once heterogeneric and obsessed with generic purification. The essayistic prose of *Biographia Literaria* and *The Friend* becomes synonymous with criticism, and criticism becomes a term that can range from political journalism to book reviews, from "practical criticism" to encounters with Wordsworth's prefaces, and from autobiography to philosophy. The *Biographia* takes the form of a series of distinctions drawn between degrees and kinds of aggression. Since criticism bears the burden of

Coleridge's anxieties about intellectual violence, an investigation of ethical tensions necessarily leads us to his rhetoric of generic choice.[1]

Faced with the politics of genre in the *Biographia,* therefore, we come up against the much-debated question of Coleridge's double "apostasy": his renunciation of radical sympathies and his turn away from poetry as a primary vehicle for ambition.[2] If we examine these changes from a feminist perspective, we can make better sense of Coleridge's

---

[1]Gérard Genette sets forth the argument against traditional generic criticism in "Genres, types, modes," *Poétique* 32 (Nov. 1977): 408. Faced with the importance of genre for a writer like Coleridge, one needs also to adapt the observations of Claudio Guillen, who argues for the significance of genre as an authorial gesture in *Literature as System: Essays toward the Theory of Literary History* (Princeton: Princeton University Press, 1971), "The Uses of Literary Genre," 122. I concur with many of the discussions of romantic writings which point to the way such texts unsettle and exacerbate the whole question of genre. The argument that a particular kind of writing (the dialogue? the fragment?) represents, above all others, "a privileged battlefield for the question of genre as such," a way of questing for "a kind of 'beyond' of literature itself," seems less and less persuasive. There appear to be so many candidates for the ultimately antigeneric genre that I have had to abandon my own favorite choice, romantic nonfictional prose. See Philippe Lacoue-Labarthe and Jean-Luc Nancy, "Genre," *Glyph Textual Studies* 7 (Baltimore: Johns Hopkins University Press, 1980): 3, 11. Increasingly, I agree with at least one of Jacques Derrida's versions of his "law of genre": "Every text participates in one or several genres, there is no genreless text; there is always a genre and genres, yet such participation never amounts to belonging." The ways in which texts make generic statements about themselves, in what Derrida calls the "genre-clause," comprise an idiom of resistance as well as identification and become unusually reflexive and critical of genre theory itself at many moments of literary change. "La Loi du genre/The Law of Genre," trans. Avital Ronell, *Glyph* 7 (1980): 212.

[2]Recent treatments of Coleridge's "apostasy" take into account, as explanatory factors, the depth of alienation suffered by English Jacobins in the late 1790s and early years of the new century (E. P. Thompson, "Disenchantment or Default? A Lay Sermon," in *Power and Consciousness,* ed. Conor Cruise O'Brien and William Dean Vanech [New York: New York University Press, 1969], 150–52); also Coleridge's psychological dependency on an atmosphere of sympathy or at least on the habitual quest for one (Karl Kroeber, "Coleridge's 'Fears': Problems in Patriotic Poetry," *Clio* 7 [1978]: 370–71); and, finally, the existence of an "uncanny" strategy of proleptic apostasy in advance of a permanent change of mind about either politics or poetry (Jerome Christensen, "The Rhetoric of Apostasy," *Critical Inquiry* 12 (1986): 769–87). Christensen argues that Coleridge's political apostasy, as it generated defensive retrospection in the form of metaphysical apologies, was an essentially critical innovation, one that implicates all modern critics in apostasies of their own. Christensen chooses not to address the question of biographical causality, or addresses it through the "always already" process of referring "apostasy" backward from the late to the early Coleridge, then from the early Coleridge to the late Burke. Although this strategy simply replicates the same set of questions with reference to Burke, it stays closer to the obsessive persistence of Coleridge's anxieties than more teleological narratives.

redefinition of the uses of poetry and criticism. For in Coleridge's texts the feminine signifies an acute sense of difference between the psychological and the political realms and, at the same time, their intimate contiguity.

The scheme implicit in Coleridge's writings of the 1790s and sketched in the preceding chapter can be reduced to the following narrative: poetry is constituted by mutually generated scenes of mountaintop prophecy uttered in a spirit of radical patriotism and vignettes of a pitying muse in domestic retirement expressing the conversational ethic of nature. Coleridge's prose, in *The Watchman* or the *Lectures on Politics and Religion,* while concerned about its own participation in conflict, nevertheless delivers fierce political pronouncements. This configuration lasts until Coleridge's departure for Germany with the Wordsworths in the autumn of 1798. The interval spent in Germany seems not to have affected this set of practices decisively, although it strengthened Coleridge's habit of simultaneously evading and idealizing the family. On his return in 1799, he faced an atmosphere of political repression and anticipated domestic unhappiness. This combination of circumstances blocked his oscillation between activism and retirement. Both elements of the vision that had structured the works of the previous decade had been altered. Coleridge was left with the problem of how to speak with authority in the absence of an anti-authoritarian cause and how to celebrate sympathy without a spiritual home.

Most of this chapter is given over to strategies of critical self-authorization in *Biographia Literaria.* In this opening section, therefore, I pause to consider Coleridge's revised account, *in his poetry,* of critical thinking. Coleridge met Sara Hutchinson a few months after his return from Germany; she soon represented poetry as "the voice of mourning," all the poetry Coleridge would write henceforth and much that he had written already (BL I 221). Wordsworth and Hutchinson together embody Coleridge's poetic condition: William as the poet of both philosophical reflection and of vagrancy; Sara as the responsive mercy that assuages homelessness while being itself unavailable. Poetry and love are conflated by Coleridge as forms of permanent longing ("The still rising Desire still baffling the bitter Experience, the bitter Experience still following the gratified Desire" [N I 1454]) and are made mutually explanatory. The verse letter to Sara ("A Letter to ———") marks the point at which the long-established yearning for pity's feminine voice—the unconsummated, virtual love typical of poems like "Lines on an Autumnal Evening" [1796] and "The Nightengale" [1798]—finds an autobiographical correlative.

From the perspective of poetry, Coleridge defines critical speculation as the consequence of the "abstruse research" that has transformed poetry into its own epitaph. Sara's place as an absent object corresponds to the epitaphic quality of the feminine in Coleridge's later writing. "Fear of Parting," he writes in a notebook entry of 1803, "gives a yearning so like Absence as at moments to turn your presence into absence" (N I 1334). Coleridge's prose, though it admits the "voice of mourning" only in a highly idealized fashion, can incorporate it more fully than the poetry of loss can introject critical content. We need only turn to the "Prospectus" of *The Friend* (1809) to see how "Dejection" becomes an ethical condition characteristic of a whole generation. The forthcoming periodical will include among its "chief Subjects"

> Sources of Consolation to the afflicted in Misfortune, or Disease, or Dejection of Mind, from the Exertion and right Application of the Reason, the Imagination, and the moral Sense. . . . In the words "Dejection of Mind" I refer particularly to Doubt or Disbelief of the moral Government of the World, and the grounds and arguments for the religious Hopes of Human Nature. (F II 18–19)

The verse letter to Sara Hutchinson, "A Letter to ———", contains Coleridge's diagnosis of the affective perturbations resulting from suppressed emotion. The poem is structured by an overdetermined sense of guilt produced by the speaker's knowledge that, in complaining of the "Indifference or Strife" of his own home, he has produced unhappiness and illness in the Wordsworths'; the letters preceding this one have been carriers of misery. Infectious logic also governs the way domestic unhappiness affects thought. Philosophy ("abstruse research"), a repressive strategy or anodyne prescribed by the speaker for himself, is contagious: "that, which suits a part, infects the whole." Like opium, it is addictive ("almost grown the temper of my Soul"), so that it replaces desire for the feminine with a theoretical habit (lines 164, 266–70).[3] "A Letter," then, focuses on the dubious ethics of em-

---

[3] All citations from "A Letter to ———" are taken from Stephen Maxfield Parrish, ed., *Coleridge's Dejection: The Earliest Manuscripts and the Earliest Printings* (Ithaca: Cornell University Press, 1988). I refer to the Cornell Manuscript, 21–34. Line numbers are cited parenthetically in the text.

pathy and the need to make already mediated gratification even more indirect.

The figure of the new moon with "the Old Moon in her Lap" parallels the speaker's one direct experience of nurture remembered later in the poem:

> the happy night
> When Mary, Thou, & I together were. . . .
> Dear Mary!—on her Lap my head she lay'd. . . .
> And on my Cheek I felt thy Eye-lash play—
>
> (lines 99–107)

The inhabitants of the night sky form an idealized family of self-sufficient but loving spirits, a gathering of persons linked by allusion ("dear William's Sky-Canoe!") to the Wordsworth/Hutchinson circle (line 23).[4] More elaborate stellar mediations end up reinforcing the spectatorial alienation that is the principal symptom of homelessness. The stars change from a perceived reality to the figurative basis of a private ritual in which mutual blessings are exchanged.

Coleridge recalls "sky-gazing in 'ecstatic fit'" from "the barr'd window" of his schoolroom, the childhood equivalent of abstruse research, perhaps, and the origin of his subsequent "Vision" of the stars. At such moments he would muse to himself on men's universal delight "to see a Maiden's quiet Eyes / Uprais'd, and linking on sweet Dreams by dim Connections / To Moon, or Evening Star, or glorious western Skies—." In the crucial phrase, "linking on sweet Dreams by dim Connections," the maiden appears to be associating her thoughts of love with moon and stars, as Coleridge is attaching his thoughts of her to the same celestial panorama. A few lines later this fantasy of eye contact, mediated by the moon and stars, seems to be lived out in the sphere of feeling:

---

[4]Lines 35–41 are reminiscent of the gloss to "The Rime of the Ancient Mariner," composed for *Sibylline Leaves* of 1817: "In his loneliness and fixedness he yearneth towards the journeying Moon, and the stars that still sojourn, yet still move onward; and every where the blue sky belongs to them, and is their appointed rest, and their native country and their own natural homes, which they enter unannounced, as lords that are certainly expected and yet there is a silent joy at their arrival" (PW 197). The reference to "lords" is striking here, as the moon is clearly feminine in the verse that is being glossed, as well as in Coleridge's other poetic descriptions of the night sky.

I feel my Spirit moved—
And wheresoe'er thou be,
O Sister! O Beloved!
Thy dear mild Eyes, that see
Even now the Heaven, *I* see,
There is a Prayer in them! It is for *me!*
And I, dear Sara! *I* am blessing *thee!*

(lines 92–98)

The exchange of glances by way of the moon mirror is too symmetrical, the relationship between the lovers too evenly balanced, to be
tolerable for long. Coleridge's memory of his lover in the attitude of
"the conjugal and mother Dove," which follows, is also too good to be
true. In the rest of the poem the speaker places himself in a priestly or
even monkish relation to the family in which Sara is "nested with the
Darlings of [her] Love" (lines 325–27, 217). This relation will evolve
into that of the Improvisatore whose "Vigils" on behalf of young
women take the form of quotation and commentary.

The "Letter to ———" is an explanation, an apology, and, in the
end, a justification of "the fretting Hour, / Then when I wrote thee
that complaining Scroll / Which even to bodily Sickness bruis'd thy
Soul!" In relation to Sara and her circle, Coleridge has the capacity only
to inflict pain. Through the negative influence of the vicarious lover,
the poem is obliquely preoccupied with effort and efficacy. To "for-
sake / All power, all hope of giving comfort" causes the speaker to
promise that in the next life he will have better work habits. In heaven,
he vows, his heart will adorn itself with a bridegroom's Wordsworthian "Coronal" and "wear away / In no inglorious Toils the manly Day" (lines 114–18, 175–76, 135–40). Happy marriage and hard
work go together. And in this glancing reference to the problem of
"manly" productivity and vocation lurks also the question of criticism.

The verse letter contains a compressed interpretation of Coleridge's
studies—the "work" of philosophical criticism, celebrated in the prose
writings—as both pathological symptom and emotional defense. "Abstruse research," theoretical criticism, understands its relation to the
family unusually well in this poem. The letter of complaint that made
Sara sick carried Coleridge's disease into the domestic sanctuary that
should have been its antidote. But contagion is the logic of vicarious
gratification. The "wither'd branch upon a blossoming tree" is in
jeopardy of either infecting the organism on which it depends or of
being wholly dissevered from it. The "philosophical critic" invented

by Coleridge in the decade following the verse letter, not surprisingly, is a strong opponent of social and political epidemics.

The Twenty Years War: Wordsworth's "Preface"

In Coleridge's several attempts throughout *Biographia Literaria* to define the difference between poetry and prose, the generic line is most sharply drawn in his account of the public reception of Wordsworth's 1800 "Preface" to *Lyrical Ballads*. Coleridge demonstrates that his own critical text, like Wordsworth's preface, deploys theory in the service of aggressive intentions. His commentary on the "Preface" tries to drive Wordsworth from the field of criticism, where he is shown to be not only wrong, but incompetent. Having ceded genius to Wordsworth, Coleridge cannot tolerate incursions into the domain that is now the basis for his self-regard.

He sets out to prove that theories of poetry stated in prose, not poetic experiments themselves, incite angry responses. The "Preface" is "the true origin of the unexampled opposition which Mr. Wordsworth's writings have been since doomed to encounter." Poetic lapses that "would have been either forgotten or forgiven" otherwise "provoked direct hostility when announced as intentional, as the result of choice after full deliberation" (BL I 70–71).

Coleridge assigns the responsibility for the "twenty years war" triggered by the "Preface" to the fatal interaction of the poet's revisionary fervor and his readers' consequent disquietude. The energy of Wordsworth's "disgust or contempt" in the "Preface" and the errors of his position were due, writes Coleridge, to "his predilection for a style the most remote possible from [that] . . . which he wished to explode." Francis Jeffrey's position was not so far from that of Coleridge himself when he referred to Wordsworth's essay as a "flagrant [act] of hostility" (BL I 74, II 90, I 71n).[5]

Coleridge's exposition of the psychology of reception focuses on the

[5]Paul de Man displays his characteristic aversion to explanations that invoke aggression when he describes the romantics' segregation of poetry and prose in terms of a superstitious anxiety about "power" and "authority" without introducing the notion of conflict: "Common sense tells us that poetry and philosophy are modes of discourse that should be kept distinct: to couple such power of seduction with such authority is to tempt fate itself. Hence the urge to protect, as the most pressing of moral imperatives, this borderline between both modes of discourse." "Wordsworth and the Victorians," in *The Rhetoric of Romanticism* (New York: Columbia University Press, 1984), 85.

way "fear . . . predisposes the [reader's] mind to anger." Wordsworth's prose gave evidence of the intentional quality of his poetic
style, and this intentionality was felt by readers as an attack on them:
"they felt *very positive,* but were not *quite certain,* that he might not be in
the right, and they themselves in the wrong; an unquiet state of mind,
which seeks alleviation by quarreling with the occasion of it" (BL I 71–
72). The reader accused of "error" can be made to feel at "fault,"
Coleridge implies in his note to this passage. As the reader's fear is
proportionate to the power of the poet's will, the reader's anger is
proportionate to his or her fear. Only a writer familiar with the therapeutic possibilities of argument could comment with such assurance on
the way quarreling may alleviate an obscure sense of guilt. But it is
more significant that Coleridge takes into account the habitual association of prose with conscious intentions. As the voice of the ego, prose
seeks out conflict.

The critique of Wordsworth's poetics conforms to a similar logic of
defensive aggression, though it is only later in *Biographia Literaria* that
this likeness becomes wholly apparent. After introducing the conflict
between Wordsworth and his critics, Coleridge characterizes himself
as a reader in search of understanding, the aftereffect of emotion. Understanding precedes philosophical criticism as the mind's first response to the sensations of reading. "I no sooner felt, than I sought to
understand" (BL I 82). Understanding is associated with receptivity, as
it is for Schleiermacher, but with a more pronounced nuance of ap-
probation. When Coleridge narrates the development of his "understanding" of Wordsworth's poetry, therefore, he does not enter into
the ritualistic demands for method which make the critic strong; these
come later, making understanding a kind of hinge on which the reader
swings from acquiescence to argument.

From its origin in feeling, understanding proceeds through intuition
toward critical conclusions. "Repeated meditations," his account of
reading continues, "led me first to suspect, (and a more intimate analysis . . . matured my conjecture into full conviction) that fancy and
imagination were . . . distinct." This brief but careful statement of the
place of understanding in Coleridge's interpretive response comes at
the end of the story of his discovery of Wordsworth. And that story,
we recall, began with the end of his remarks on the "twenty years
war." It began, in fact, right after a citation from Aristophanes: "the
contest . . . still continue[s] as undecided as that between Bacchus and
the frogs" (BL I 82, 75–76). The turn from others' wrangling to personal reading, from conflict to wonder, dramatizes the difference between criticism and understanding.

Two meanings, or meaning clusters, are associated with the term "understanding" as Coleridge uses it. The first, and most familiar, defines (the) Understanding as a lesser modality than (the) Reason. It is the faculty or capability that is demeaned in order to glorify Reason; the latter is exclusively oriented to principles, whereas the Understanding "has no appropriate object but the material world in relation to our worldly interests" (LS 68–70).[6] Such definitions transform Understanding and Reason into central characters in a series of antagonistic value judgments. The second type or aspect of understanding, and the one that most concerns me here, is never really defined at all by Coleridge. Understanding enters as the object (or direction) of desire, and with an unmistakably feminine identity. It is manifested either in the context of personal relationships or in argumentative situations in which such relationships are invoked.

The background of such passages in the published works lies in the poems and notebooks of late 1801 and 1802. Unquestionably in connection with Coleridge's friendship with Wordsworth and his involvement with Sara Hutchinson, the mingled themes of understanding, pity, and hope become more pronounced. Understanding that never relinquishes hope is a form of forgiveness, an ethical response akin to the pity that Coleridge always craves: "The unspeakable Comfort to a good man's mind—nay, even to a criminal to be *understood*—to have some one that understands one. . . . The Hope of this—always more or less disappointed, gives the *passion* to Friendship" (N I 1082; see also N I 1022 and PW 416). If male friends perpetually disappoint the desire for understanding grounded on the principle of hope, women are more generous, if equally unavailable. The endlessly longed-for state of being understood repeatedly takes the form of erotic fantasies: "I have no dear Heart that loves my Verses—I never hear them in snatches from a beloved Voice, fitted to some sweet occasion, of natural Prospect, in Winds at Night" (N I 1463). More explicitly: "Sara! Sara! . . . Misery conjures up . . . Forms, & binds them into Tales & Events . . . the Tale grows pleasanter—& at length you come to me / you are by my bed side, in some lonely Inn, where I lie deserted— there you have found me—there you are weeping over me!" (N I 1601). The conjunction, in the first passage, of woman, voice, and poetic receptivity shows how deeply connected Coleridge's sense of

---

[6]The chief exception to this generalization, as James McKusick has recently demonstrated, is Coleridge's *Logic,* unpublished in his lifetime. This treatise, McKusick argues, is "a critique of pure understanding," an understanding that is "identical with the faculty of discourse." *Coleridge's Philosophy of Language* (New Haven: Yale University Press, 1986), 123, 120.

literary understanding is to the feminine capacity for conversational response. As in the texts of Schleiermacher, to be understood is to enter into dialogue, in this case a dialogue blessed by the participation of nature's voices as well as women's. The second notebook entry appears to have less to do with understanding. But insofar as this scene demonstrates that the most desired aspect of woman is her tears of pity as she bends over her prone lover, and insofar as pity is (for Coleridge) the purest form of sympathy, the link to understanding is crucial.

The association between the feminine and the state of *being comforted* accounts for the conservatism of what I have been calling the familial tendency in Coleridge's writings. The analogical chain that joins sympathy, friendship, and family love depends heavily on the inclusion of their institutional embodiments, the neighborhood, the nation, and the church. The clergyman, for instance, a living representative of Coleridge's fluid substitutions, "lives in sympathy with the world." He is "a neighbour and a family-man," the guest of "the rich land-holder" and the "visitor of the farm-house and the cottage"; he may be "connected with the families of his parish or its vicinity by marriage," and since "the revenues of the church are in some sort the reversionary property of every family," he manifests the "essentially moving and circulative" economy of the nation (BL I 227–28).

The minister absorbs the feminine gifts of sympathy from his marriage (a married clergy being the distinguishing feature of the Church of England over against Catholicism) and transforms them into the discursive and material networks that bind together an idealized England. Marriage is the means by which one is "connected" to parish, neighborhood, and country, all of which partake of the conversational activity represented by women. To a great extent, this fantasied suffusion of womanliness throughout national life is a reaction to the perceived violence of radical rhetoric. For Coleridge, the family circle and its widening gyre are the antidote for political conflict. The "feminization" of religion in Coleridge's works is a problem I postpone to the end of the next chapter, but the connection between sympathy and unity is central to the critique of Wordsworth in the *Biographia,* to which we now return.

In Coleridge's account of his first readings of Wordsworth the theme of sympathy borders closely on those of "union" and poetic unity. Coleridge's own alternation between submission and argument is interwoven with his description of the simultaneously disruptive and unifying powers of the poet. The Wordsworth who emerges from this compounded ambivalence displays both sublimely masculine imaginative strength and a pathetic sensibility that affiliates him with the feminine. The first shock of Coleridge's discovery came through his encounter with a strangely disjunctive, even aggressive, poetic style. Wordsworth's "Descriptive Sketches" (1793) struck Coleridge with its "harshness and acerbity," with language "peculiar and strong . . . at times knotty and contorted." The poem was so convinced of its own power to demand "a greater closeness of attention, than poetry . . . has a right to claim" that it provided metaphors for its own strength, or that of its author: "overpowering light," "storm," "floods," and "the fire-clad eagle's wheeling form." The alpine setting of the poem evoked the "glory-smitten summits of the poetic mountain" occupied by Shakespeare and Milton in language that echoes Coleridge's celebration of Shakespeare's "perfect dominion, often *domination,* over the whole world of language," over all other writers save Milton, and, implicitly, over the mind and soul of the reader (BL I 77–78, II 25–28).

Coleridge's analysis of "Descriptive Sketches" is followed by and contrasted to an account of "the sudden effect produced on my mind" by Wordsworth's recitation of a manuscript draft of "Guilt and Sorrow" (1791–94). Wordsworth's style was purified of earlier faults: "There was here no mark of strained thought, or forced diction, no crowd or turbulence of imagery," but rather "manly reflection and human associations." (The strenuousness of "Descriptive Sketches," Coleridge implies, was feminine or demonic, whereas the style of "Guilt and Sorrow," despite its feminine subject, was "manly.") In explaining the unusual impression made by this style "on my feelings immediately, and subsequently on my judgement," Coleridge launches into the "ANCIENT of days" passage, a set piece openly quoted from *The Friend:*

It was the union of deep feeling with profound thought; the fine balance of truth in observing with the imaginative faculty in modifying the objects observed; and above all the original gift of spreading the tone, the *atmosphere,* and with it the depth and height of the ideal world around forms, incidents, and situations, of which, for the common view, custom had bedimmed all the lustre, had dried up the sparkle and the dew drops. "To find no contradiction in the union of old and new; to contemplate the ANCIENT of days and all his works with feelings as fresh, as if all had then sprang forth at the first creative fiat; characterizes the mind that feels the riddle of the world, and may help to unravel it. (BL I 77–80, 80n, 81n)

Coleridge now praises not discontinuity, the first proof of power, but the mental motions that fill the gaps between pairs of opposites, "modifying," "spreading . . . around," carrying on into, and combining. The kind of "union" dramatized here stops just short of wholeness or totality. The "union" of thought and feeling is tantamount to "balance"; "the union of old and new" is a state of noncontradiction; the child's wonder combines with adult knowledge without displacing it. As in the definition of the poet in Chapter 14, Coleridge's language confirms the paradoxes of romantic irony.[7]

The unity brought about by the imagination is not an expression of sympathy. That it should not be is perhaps unexpected. After all, the mental and textual dramas of reconciliation contained in Coleridge's definitions of poetry, poets, and reading would seem to fit neatly into the chain of analogical substitutions which ranges from feminine conversation to the dialogue of social classes. What could better be used to defend the ethic of sympathy than the idea of unity? But it is another, secondary theme that carries the burden of sympathy in Coleridge's discussion of Wordsworth.

Coleridge finds Wordsworth's sympathy, an intuition associated with the heart and with heartfelt response, in his tales of mothers and children—"Guilt and Sorrow," "The Thorn," "The Mad Mother." Although Coleridge does not mention in Chapter 4 the subject matter of the poem that so impressed him, the fifth of the six "Beauties of Wordsworth's Poetry" enumerated in Chapter 22 is "meditative pathos," explicitly linked to maternal themes. This "pathos," or "sympathy," like the imagination itself, represents "a union of deep and subtle thought with sensibility," which emerges in poems like "The Affliction of Margaret ———" ("The Ruined Cottage"). Coleridge quotes Margaret's tale, commenting on the psychological realism of the speaker's associations but surely also appreciative of the infant's therapeutic suckling at its mother's breast (BL I 79, II 150–51).

It is not surprising that Coleridge looks to Wordsworth for a friend's passionate understanding and even pity. Wordsworth's ambivalence toward the maternal paradoxically supplies the scripts for Coleridge's envy and longing. Dramatizing his own imaginative death in the

---

[7]In the poet a more deeply reconciling "spirit of unity" that *fuses* its materials "by that synthetic and magical power . . . [the] imagination" brings about the "balance . . . of opposite or discordant qualities." The poet's influence on readers similarly hovers between unity and distinction: "the whole soul" is brought into activity, but only through "the subordination of its faculties to each other, according to their relative worth and dignity" (BL II 16).

poem, "To William Wordsworth," Coleridge shows how Wordsworth's power to speak "Into my heart" led to "a heart forlorn." Wordsworth's poetry, then, works in a way analogous to erotic love itself: the "pangs of Love, awakening as a babe / Turbulent, with an outcry in the heart" are now among the flowers "Strewed on my corse, and borne upon my bier." The pathos of receptivity infantilizes the reader in a pleasurable if ultimately disturbing way: "In silence listening, like a devout child, / My soul lay passive" (PW 403–8, lines 2, 61, 65–66, 74, 95–96).

In Chapter 4 of the *Biographia,* as soon as Coleridge has finished quoting himself from *The Friend,* understanding as an aggressive mode of inquiry nudges aside understanding as a sympathetic mood. "I no sooner felt [Wordsworth's excellence]," he announces, "than I sought to understand." "Repeated meditations" led him "to suspect," and a "more intimate analysis" brought the "full conviction" that "fancy and imagination were two distinct . . . faculties." At once, the ceremony of "desynonymizing" announces the entry of the "philosophical critic," and Coleridge's task changes abruptly from understanding Wordsworth to establishing principles on his behalf (BL I 82, 85). The first principle is the method of differential naming itself, which marks the self-assertion of the formerly "passive" reader. Coleridge fastens on his own procedures in "establishing the actual existences of two faculties generally different," through which he intends to "furnish a torch of guidance to the philosophical critic; and ultimately to the poet himself. In energetic minds, truth soon changes by domestication into power; and from directing in the discrimination and appraisal of the product, becomes influencive in the production" (BL I 85). The value of desynonymizing definitions becomes clear. "Domesticated" into "power" by method, truth puts the poet under the influence of the critic.

Why does the philosophical critic always call himself into being through desynonymizing gestures? In a footnote, Coleridge ascribes differentiation to evolution, not destruction. With the "instinct of growth, a certain collective, unconscious good sense" is always "working progressively" in language, like the division of one-celled organisms (BL I 82, 83n). This benign metaphor, however, cannot conceal an implicit aggression. Coleridge has to push two words apart with the lever of "principle" to create a space for the philosophical critic to enter.

He first uses the word "desynonymizing" in a notebook entry of January 1803. The well-known pairs of words subjected to obsessive differentiation begin to crystallize around 1800: "genius" and "talent" appear in the *Morning Post* essay on Pitt in that year; "fancy" and "imagination" in a letter of 1802; "imitation" and "copy" in a notebook entry of 1804. As James McKusick notes, Coleridge's history of linguistic change suggests that "innovation gradually shifts from the poet to the philosopher as culture becomes more advanced."[8] It is on the basis of this process of linguistic differentiation that, in the midst of his chapter on fancy and imagination, Coleridge claims to have made criticism creative.

"To admire on principle," he concludes, "is the only way to imitate without loss of originality." He agonizes over the implications of "originality," a word that reverberates through the last two paragraphs of Chapter 4. The reader is invited to "[chastise] my self-complacency" in having once taken "some little credit to myself" for establishing "the diverse meaning" of "fancy" and "imagination." Intoning the Wordsworthian phrase "There was a time," Coleridge relinquishes the "conceit" that hoped for public favor. Like most romantic pasts, however, this one rises up a few lines later, when Coleridge returns to what is really at stake in this chapter, the differences between Wordsworth and himself. If Wordsworth focused on the poetic manifestations of fancy and imagination, he, Coleridge, will "investigate [their] seminal principle": "My friend has drawn a masterly sketch of the branches with their *poetic* fruitage. I wish to add the trunk, and even the roots as far as they lift themselves above ground, and are visible to the naked eye of our common consciousness" (BL I 85, 88). The superior masculinity of philosophical criticism ("the seminal principle") reverses the botanical order of things to add the trunk and roots of the tree last. This does produce an organic whole, but backward. Desynonymizing, dividing a trunk into two branches, bears fruit. Prose, coming after poetry, claims to be its source. If one needed evidence that philosophical criticism is unnatural, this little allegory would provide it.

In a letter of July 1802 to Southey, Coleridge comments on Wordsworth's "Preface" in a way that demonstrates the close connection in his mind between enforcing difference and mediating the conflicts that arise from it. "I rather suspect that some where or other there is a radical Difference in our theoretical opinions respecting Poetry," he remarks disingenuously. His response will be to "[act] the arbitrator between the old School and the New School," although his negotiations promise to take the prescriptive form of introducing "some plain,

[8]McKusick, *Coleridge's Philosophy of Language,* 96–99.

& perspicuous, tho' not superficial, Canons of Criticism respecting Poetry." The movement from difference to arbitration is reflected in Chapter 14 of the *Biographia,* the beginning of the long struggle with Wordsworth which constitutes the second volume. Having announced that he thinks it "expedient to declare once for all, in what points I coincide with his opinions, and in what points I altogether differ," Coleridge characteristically turns first to an explanation of his own differential procedure. His effort both to attack and to defend Wordsworth is justified through a methodological allegory in which difference necessarily leads to unity. "The office of philosophical *disquisition* consists in just *distinction,*" he begins forcefully, then at once reassures us about his motives: "it is the privilege of the philosopher to preserve himself constantly aware, that distinction is not division" (BL II 10–11, 10n)

In *Biographia Literaria,* however, the energy of differentiation is so great and the commitment to any form of unity is finally so qualified that Coleridge's reassurances have to be taken as expressions of desire rather than as statements of procedure. The purpose of Volume II is to evict Wordsworth from the domain of prose, where he is ineffectual and Coleridge dominant. The worst offense, and the one that triggers the greatest outpouring of argument, is Wordsworth's dictum, *"There neither is or can be any essential difference between the language of prose and metrical composition."* Nearly all of Coleridge's criticisms pertain to the consequences of this central error. Describing the "defects" of Wordsworth's poetry, for example, he attributes them to the poet's attempts to apply his linguistic ideal: "his only disease is the being out of his element; like the swan, that having amused himself, for a while, with crushing the weeds on the river's bank, soon returns to his own majestic movements on its reflecting and sustaining surface" (BL II 60, 120–21). Behind this powerful simile lies the intent to keep separate the creatures of water and land, poetry and prose. The riverbank is reserved for Coleridge, who habitually associates himself with awkward birds; the swan, after "crushing the weeds," is returned to his proper "element."

By intruding a moral purpose on his poetry, Wordsworth has not only damaged his proper style but has usurped the task of prose. He has tried to unite truth with pleasure, a union Coleridge severs in the name of philosophy. The "*immediate* object" of moral truth "belongs to the moral philosopher," he insists, "and would be pursued . . . with far greater probability of success, in sermons or moral essays, than in an elevated poem." And in case this is not emphatic enough, he argues that failing to maintain the distinction between truth and pleasure will "destroy" those "not only between a *poem* and *prose,* but even between philosophy and works of fiction" (BL II 130).

He glances in the direction of a hypothetical synthesis ("the blessed time shall come, when truth itself shall be pleasure"), only to remind Wordsworth that it is "the poet's office" to depict humanity as it "actually exists," leaving it to the philosopher "first to *make* it what it ought to be." The unity of truth and pleasure and, by Coleridge's own analogy, of prose and poetry, is postponed to the millennium, leaving him free to eject his friend simultaneously from prose and from philosophy. "I reflect with delight," he remarks in Chapter 18, "how little a mere theory . . . interferes with the processes of genuine imagination in a man of true poetic genius" (BL II 130, 59–60). His delight, it is safe to say, comes not only from his experience of the authority of Wordsworth's proper voice, but from his ability to show that Wordsworth can be mastered when he ventures into the critical arena.

"A Chapter of Requests and Premonitions"

Chapter 12 of the *Biographia* comprises Coleridge's explanation of how he would have us read him. The title, "of requests and premonitions concerning the perusal or omission of the chapter that follows," contains a veiled threat of disaster to any reader who makes the wrong choice about Chapter 13. Indeed, the function of Coleridge's philosophical language in Chapter 12 is to construct a typology of the reading public on the basis of its aggressiveness or receptivity toward him.[9]

The chapter begins with the theme of understanding, this time in the service of Coleridge's differential rigor. Here understanding becomes part of a moral dichotomy that contrasts friendly to hostile readers, and the "adage or maxim" on understanding is phrased as a challenge: *"until you understand a writer's ignorance, presume yourself ignorant of his understanding."* The types of readerly attitudes available to us preclude sympathy among equals. The options include superior understanding (such as he attains in reading "a treatise of a religious fanatic"), "rever-

---

[9]My discussion of Coleridge's construction of his audience owes a good deal to Jon Klancher's "Coleridge: The Institutions of a Misreading Public," in *The Making of English Reading Audiences (1790–1832)* (Madison: University of Wisconsin Press, 1987), 150–79.

ential" ignorance (such as he feels toward Plato), or, antithetical to both, the "contemptuous verdict[s]" of *"fashionable"* readers who "dismiss" idealism as "Jargon" (BL I 232–33). If one is not capable of one of the two philosophically informed stances, interpretive mastery ("understanding the author better than he understands himself") or filiopiety, one is relegated to the prevailing brutality of typical British readers and critics.

Coleridge's principal request of the reader is to practice a nonviolent hermeneutics. This kind of understanding is associated not with philosophical criticism at all, but with the nonverbal intuition of women. The reader must assuage his (Coleridge's) "anxiety of authorship" by either "pass[ing] over the following chapter altogether" or by "read[ing] the whole connectedly." To explain why it is best to read "connectedly," Coleridge (in the passage I have used as an epigraph) draws on metaphors of gender familiar to us from his poems:

> The fairest part of the most beautiful body will appear deformed and monstrous, if dissevered from its place in the organic Whole. Nay, on delicate subjects, where a seemingly trifling difference of more or less may constitute a difference in *kind*, even a *faithful* display of the main and supporting ideas, if yet they are separated from the forms by which they are at once clothed and modified, may perchance present a skeleton indeed; but a skeleton to alarm and deter. (BL I 233–34)

The "anxiety" Coleridge confesses has more to do with being misunderstood than with not being read, and it generates the metaphor of that "delicate subject," the female body. The woman whose parts are "dissevered" from one another stands clearly for the fate of Coleridge's text at the hands of the reader who subjects Chapter 13 to the wrong kind of reading. "Christabel" is the source of the woman made "deformed and monstrous," whose "fairest part" is almost certainly Geraldine's horrifying breast, which makes for the "difference in kind" between her and Christabel. In this context the fable asks that the reader take responsibility for turning innocence into evil, Christabel into Geraldine. In an anticipatory way Coleridge attributes his own deformation of Chapter 13 to the reader, who, whether she or he skips the chapter or misunderstands it, must share his guilt.

Nevertheless, the reader who strives merely for connectedness will be wrong, too. Appreciation of the whole depends on the proper understanding of difference. Coleridge represents mistreatment by readers who fail to grasp this principle as the severing of his skeletal ideas from the "forms" of language and argument, their clothing or (more drastically) their flesh. The preternatural overtones of the chapter title, "requests and *premonitions*," are echoed in the image of a skeleton that rises up here to "alarm and deter" the would-be reader. To violate an "organic whole" is to risk the avenging specter of the death one has caused. Again, the image of the refined and beautiful woman—the "delicate subject" par excellence—is transformed into that of "LIFE-IN-DEATH," the demonic female of the Mystery Poems. Victimization, Coleridge threatens, turns lovers into avengers.

The closing sentences of the paragraph shift to the contrast between an ideal "unprejudiced" reader and the reader clothed in "prior systems." As Coleridge moves away from his experience as the object of critical scrutiny and toward an assault on the public, metaphors of the feminine diminish, although not metaphors of the body. "I shall not desire the reader to strip his mind of all prejudices," Coleridge writes regretfully, "or to keep all prior systems out of view during his examination of the present." He, at least, will not disjoin flesh from skeleton. He has not yet "discovered the art of destroying the memory . . . without injury to its future operations," he observes ironically, registering again, in his hypersensitive way, the extent to which objectivity is associated with violence (BL I 234).

If he manages not to demand the death of memory in the individual reader, Coleridge certainly does not feel bound to treat his audience collectively as an organic whole or according to the ethic of connection. Fearing the reader who would do violence to his book, Coleridge tries to exclude him in advance by means of philosophical definitions. With an ominous bow, he states that the "extent of my daring" is to formulate a test "by which it may be rationally conjectured beforehand, whether or no a reader would lose his time, and perhaps his temper, in the perusal of this . . . treatise." The diagnostic test is to be self-administered by the reader, who must thus internalize Coleridge's distinctions. The test consists of asking oneself whether one is a materialist who "receives as fundamental facts . . . the general notions of matter, spirit, soul, body" and so on. If the answer is yes, then "for him the chapter was not written" (BL I 234–35).

This antidemocratic use of philosophical criteria shows precisely how attributing violence to the reading public may justify conservative uses of theory and method. All of Coleridge's distinctions imply hierarchies, and this one is no exception. With much fanfare, he proclaims the "courage" it takes "to tell the truth" about differences of ability in an age in which the whole "PUBLIC" is presumed to constitute the literary audience: "I say then, that it is neither possible or necessary for all men, or for many, to be PHILOSOPHERS." Philosophical consciousness "lies beneath or . . . *behind*" (but really, as we quickly find, above and beyond) "the spontaneous consciousness natural to all." He designates "the domain of PURE philosophy" as "properly . . . *transcendental,*" a word that in turn provokes a long footnote on the making of distinctions (BL I 235–39).

The effort to exclude threatening readers from philosophical texts by means of philosophy itself is palpably defensive. Yet as therapy it works. As soon as he assumes a philosophical posture, Coleridge ceases to feel like the reader's feminized victim and moves toward a heroic prospect that yields a vision of a powerful feminine enigma. He does so by numbering himself among the masculine "few" who, by "measuring and sounding the rivers of the vale," infer that "the sources must be far higher and far inward." The "sources" pursued by such questers recede into the riddle of Nature herself, in the character of the Sphinx:

> How and whence . . . the ascertaining vision, the intuitive knowledge, may finally supervene, can be learnt only by the fact. I might oppose to the question the words with which Plotinus supposes NATURE to answer a similar difficulty. "Should any one interrogate her, how she works, if graciously she vouchsafe to listen and speak, she will reply, it behoves thee not to disquiet me with interrogatories, but to understand in silence, even as I am silent, and work without words." (BL I 239–41)

Coleridge celebrates Nature's way of resisting those who "interrogate her," her silent preference for intuitive nonverbal understanding. As in "The Improvisatore," the dialogue of philosophy with the feminine produces feelings that may be associated with words but are not conveyed by them. As though to emphasize the link between understanding and love, Coleridge adds a footnote on Plotinus in which he glosses "understand" as the sociable mode of intuition best expressed in "our own idiomatic phrase, *'to go along with me.'*" Mother Nature and intuition meet in a sanctuary that criticism has created but cannot enter. In the words of Plotinus, cited by Coleridge, "we ought not to pursue [Nature] with a view of detecting its secret source, but to watch in quiet till it suddenly shines upon us." Receptivity defines what Coleridge now terms "the philosophic imagination" or "the sacred power of self-intuition," which is more closely related to the sympathetic mode of understanding than to the secondary imagination of

Chapter 13 or the poetic genius of Chapter 14. Meanwhile, the obscurity of such intuition reinforces the sociological message: "philosophy cannot be intelligible to all" (BL I 240–43). The materialist must look on with the alienated desire of the voyeur.

As though to confirm the special rigor of philosophy, Coleridge begins to draw on the German texts out of which he constructs the rest of the chapter. They have a particular value in this context as the embodiments of metaphysical system-making. The usefulness of the plagiarized arguments is surely no greater than the advantage of borrowing the identity of German philosophers, with their collective aura of profundity.[10] Coleridge exploits Schelling (and, to a lesser extent, Leibnitz, Jacobi, and Kant) "to make some preliminary remarks on the introduction of POSTULATES in philosophy" and then to set up the idealistic framework within which "the deduction of the imagination" will unfold. These extended appropriations make a visible impact on the appearance of Coleridge's book. The "two cases" pertaining to the objective and the subjective are organized under two numbered statements, one "Either," the other "Or." These are followed by the ten theses, with occasional "scholia," which set forth the necessity for grounding the knowledge of existence in "the absolute self, the great eternal I AM" (BL I 247, 275, 255, 257, 264). Although the content of these items is largely derived from Schelling, the form is not. It is a stylistic allegory of a British image of German philosophy and, thus, incarnated, descends like a deus ex machina into Coleridge's text in response to his manifold "premonitions."

The *sensation* of "system" is as important as its content. Having promised qualified readers entry into the rarefied heights of transcendental idealism and having terrorized unqualified ones with the threat of finding themselves in "a land of darkness, a perfect *Anti-Goshen,*" Coleridge lives up to both predictions by introducing postulates and theses. The chief characteristic of the journey toward philosophical utopia is the sequential logic that strives to achieve "a methodical ascent to the imagination"; logic, in other words, that replicates Miltonic nature "by gradual scale sublim'd" to spirit, as we read in one of Coleridge's epigraphs to Chapter 13 (BL I 243, 295).[11] His reliance on plagiarized texts in this portion of the *Biographia* is both the effect and

[10]Rosemary Ashton, *The German Idea: Four English Writers and the Reception of German Thought, 1800–1860* (Cambridge: Cambridge University Press, 1980), 36–37.

[11]Jerome Christensen, *Coleridge's Blessed Machine of Language* (Ithaca: Cornell University Press, 1981), 169.

the cause of anxiety about his readers: the effect, because the exclusion of unqualified readers is validated by the inaccessible hyperphilosophical persona of the plagiarized sections; the cause, because reliance on German authorities makes Coleridge worry more about how readers will react to his "abstruse" prose.

When another Coleridge does return, in the guise of "Your affectionate,&c.," the letter-writer of Chapter 13, it is to fret about his readers once more. In the phony letter from a friend there is an element of boredom or impatience with the philosophical demonstration he has assembled from German books. Coleridge may desire to have the *Biographia* read as a connected whole, but the kind of syllogistic connectedness that takes over these chapters does not, finally, hold his interest. Philosophical prose compels him most when it is motivated by a specific anxiety or antagonism. Such energies lead Coleridge into plagiarism, and they lead him out of it. He reanimates his prose by creating a crisis involving his relation to his audience.

A literary life, however dedicated to communication of various kinds, is not the place for a treatise on "the Logos or communicative intellect in Man and Deity," Coleridge-as-correspondent insists. On the basis of the rule of truth in advertising, according to which generic conventions may determine purchasing decisions, to violate the patterns of a literary life is to impose on the reader. The strongest argument against continuing in this vein is that the reader will be "almost entitled to accuse you of a sort of imposition on him" and respond with the anger Coleridge has been anticipating since the beginning of Chapter 12. The ontological instability of "the PUBLIC" allows it to enter into Coleridge's complex fear of his own capacities for inflicting and inciting aggression. His concern about the reception of his works is linked to his belief in the aggressiveness of their philosophical or critical content. He characterizes the encounter between such texts and their potential readers through metaphors of transgression and conflict, scenarios of violation and "blame" (BL I 303–4). In Chapter 12 he assumes that his readers will experience philosophical discourse as an "imposition," which, indeed, he partly intends it to be.

The brusque but passionate conclusion to Chapter 13, in which Coleridge delivers "the main result" of the chapter that might have been, is staged as a rapprochement with the reader whose time and patience have just been saved. It is no accident, of course, that this gesture coincides with the advent of the imagination. For the imagination enters to promise that philosophy is well-intentioned; that "at all events it struggles to idealize and to unify"—and what is being united here, if not the philosophical critic and his readers? The undoing energy of the secondary imagination, which "dissolves, diffuses, dissipates," is not identical to the critical processes of differentiating, defining, and desynonymizing. Desynonymizing fixes words in relations of momentary stability; the secondary imagination releases "fixed and dead" objects into a state of fluidity. By renaming the differential method of criticism so as to transform it into the first stage of imaginative operations, Coleridge once again brings poetics into line with ethical imperatives. Universal frames—"all human Perception" and "the eternal act of creation"—reach out to reassure us. The effort of the "conscious will" to live up to this cosmic tolerance reflects a similarly comforting intent. Our suspicions might well be once more aroused, however, by the final negative differentiation that segregates the imagination ("on the contrary") from Fancy (BL I 304–5).

"The *viva sectio* is its own delight"

To Coleridge, the common danger of the media of literary and political debate—quarterlies, magazines, and newspapers—lies in their combined assault on the proper distinction between the public sphere and the family, that is, the whole private or internal domain of home and subjectivity. "Political and religious zealots" bring about the "transfer of the feelings of private life into the discussions of public questions," he argues, while book reviewers perpetrate "an unjustifiable intrusion on private life." It is not surprising, then, that when he takes up (or takes on) these media in *Biographia Literaria* his sensitivity becomes more explicit. Journalistic aggression confirms the trend by which "readers in general take part against the author, in favor of the critic" (BL I, 197, 219, 30). Coleridge might appear to have placed himself in the critical camp after having dispensed critical advice to Wordsworth. But his representations of the threat posed by reviewers derive their fantastic energy from the fact that his own private life had been the subject of critical remark. As the victim of journalistic criticism, the philosophical critic defends himself by borrowing the virtues of authors.

Not accidentally, Coleridge's first sustained attack on the quarterlies comes in the chapter on the "irritability of men of Genius." An essay on the etiology of aggression introduces the question of the proper conduct of criticism. Coleridge asserts that "men of the greatest genius" are not prone to anger or "fanaticism." They possess a "calm and tranquil temper," content to dwell "in an intermundium" where the shocks of reality are mediated by the imagination.[12] But Coleridge is more interested in shifting the blame for "irritability" to the critic than in exonerating poets. Critics in the grip of vengeful passions are failed aspirants to literary greatness, frustrated by the conscious gap between desire and performance which betrays itself "in suspicious and jealous irritability." Coleridge's self-incriminating arguments implicate him little by little in the violent temper he deplores. He admits that "indolence" and "mental cowardice" have caused his failures, then has to dissociate himself from the "testiness or jealousy" typical of would-be geniuses. His grotesque autobiographical parable clears him of harboring the desire for fame and depicts fame itself as victimization, while implying that he has become famous in spite of himself: "I have laid too many eggs in the hot sands of this wilderness the world, with ostrich carelessness and ostrich oblivion. The greater part indeed have been trod under foot, and are forgotten; but yet no small number have crept forth into life, some to furnish feathers for the caps of others, and still more to plume the shafts in the quivers of my enemies, of them that unprovoked have lain in wait against my soul" (BL I 30–33, 38, 44–46). The ostrich is oblivious of its offspring until they ornament its enemies. Coleridge's carelessness of intent is crucial to his claim of geniality; his claim of continued interest in his productions is fundamental to his defense of the true author's right to "self-defence." The paradoxes of his confession result from the desire to have aggression and to hate it, too.

Indignation on his own behalf finds a habitual outlet in Coleridge's portrait of the critic as *fanatic*. The word "fanatic" functions as the threshold connecting literary criticism to politics. If the individual reviewer is "liable to superstition and fanaticism," a whole class of such individuals constitutes a political and social threat. Devoid of the heart's self-centering flame, they "seek in the crowd . . . for a warmth in common, which they do not possess singly," until they become a mob: "Cold and phlegmatic in their own nature, like damp hay, they heat and inflame by co-acervation; or like bees they become restless and irritable through the increased temperature of collected multi-

---

[12]Steven Knapp undertakes a lengthy and persuasive reading of how the imagination, as it emerges in the contest between critics and geniuses in Chapter 2 of the *Biographia,* is introduced to save the mind from "fanatical violence," and how, in order to accomplish this, the imagination must imitate fancy's rapid substitutions. *Personification and the Sublime: Milton to Coleridge* (Cambridge: Harvard University Press, 1985), 25, 28–32.

tudes. Hence the German word for fanaticism . . . is derived from the swarming of bees." In a less colorful account of the same evolution from mental inadequacy to savage demagoguery, Coleridge traces the change of "scriblers from idleness and ignorance" into "libellers from envy and malevolence," and thence to "that most powerful . . . adulation, the appeal to the bad and malignant passions of mankind" (BL I 30, 41). Individual fault enlarges to social crisis fast enough to induce panic. But it is only such terror that permits Coleridge to emerge as the hero of private morality and to inhabit, momentarily, the sanctuary of domestic life.[13]

Coleridge's account reveals some indecision as to whether critical abuse results from the internal pressures of a particular psychological type or from self-delighting malice. Despite his attempts to give a social and psychological explanation of the practices that turn ordinary men into savage reviewers, he falls back, in verses written for the occasion, on attributing such impulses to pure sadism, the critic's "own personal malignity," or, worse, a "*habit* of malignity in the form of mere wantonness":

> No private grudge they need, no personal spite:
> The *viva sectio* is its own delight!
> All enmity, all envy, they disclaim,
> Disinterested thieves of our good name:
> Cool, sober murderers of their neighbour's fame!
>
> (BL II 109)

[13]Coleridge inflates the threat to authorial peace still more in the fables of language machines to which Christensen has attended so carefully. Less malevolent than the vindictive mob but also emptier of meaning, "language, mechanized . . . into a barrel-organ," takes over "the manufacturing of poems." In Chapter 21 Coleridge savagely proposes a "critical machine" in the shape of a windmill as a better alternative to the *Edinburgh Review* as it was then conducted. Whichever metaphor prevails—mob or machine, collective viciousness or inhuman economy—irritable criticism is likened to modern systems that appear to operate in the "absence of all foundation." The circumstance of anonymity strengthens the sense of unreality and turns "synodical individuals" (Marvell's phrase) into "*counterfeits*" (BL II 111, I 31, 42). Grounded in neither personality nor value, the critic's mind must fill itself instead with a "quick change of objects"; thus disconnected from moral interiority, reviewers "kindle . . . into violent and undisciplined abuse . . . literary detraction, and moral slander." Conforming to the Coleridgean logic of vicariousness, hollow men prey on those who possess true selves. See Christensen, *Coleridge's Blessed Machine of Language*, 184–85, 206–7; Klancher, pointing to later, non-Coleridgean examples, discusses what he calls the "master sign" of "mechanism" in ways that shed light retroactively on the *Biographia* (*The Making of English Reading Audiences*, 69–73). See also Knapp on the mechanical substitutions of the fancy in *Personification and the Sublime*, 35–36.

The association between critical "malignity" and experimental science (the *"viva sectio"*) makes explicit a set of associations that structures Coleridge's view of the ethics of thinking. His shifting personifications of science invest it with qualities of both metaphysics and natural science, and both methodologies carry the danger of cruelty. Chapter 9 provides the most direct exploration in the *Biographia* of the connection between the science of philosophy and critical aggression. At the beginning of the chapter its contents are announced: "Is philosophy possible as a science, and what are its conditions?—Giordano Bruno—Literary aristocracy, or the existence of a tacit compact among the learned as a privileged order—The author's obligations to the Mystics;—to Immanuel Kant—" and so on through Fichte, Schelling, and "English writers to Saumarez." The proximity of the question of science to the elitist practices of "the learned" prepares us for an allegorical history of metaphysics in which "science" becomes not a system, but an instinct, a drive, "an affectionate seeking after the truth" and truth's "correlative," Being (BL I 140–42).

The parable of the "secret and tacit compact among the learned" is taken wholly from Schelling's *Darlegung des wahren Verhältnisses der Naturphilosophie zu der verbesserten Fichte'schen Lehre* (1806). It must have been irresistible to Coleridge, for it makes intellectual history a story of boundaries and transgression, conspiracy and persecution. The extent to which Schelling's allegory spoke to Coleridge's own indignation about philosophy's place in English life is evident in his rhetorical interpolations. Although the charges against the learned ring strangely in a book in which we can discern the emerging notion of the clerisy, the conflict between false science and true and the transgressive nature even of the latter wholly correspond to Coleridge's own anxieties. The combined tendency of his modifications of Schelling's language is to strengthen the connection between philosophy and religion. Coleridge emphasizes the legitimacy of the "truly inspired," chastises Pharasitical intellectuals with citations of scripture, and exacerbates Schelling's moral contrast between the "haughty priests of learning" and the "living waters" of revelation (BL I 147–49, 147–49n).

The need to find a Christian basis for philosophy expresses not simply Coleridge's belated orthodoxy, but also his sense of the internalized conscience of philosophy itself, a conscience whose task it is to keep in check the negativity of critique. Metaphysics contains piety as a moral reflex. In Schelling's parable, for example, "free thought" is not only a victim of persecution but, almost by nature, a "transgressor" subject to immediate repression: "The few men of genius among the learned class, who actually did overstep this boundary, anxiously avoided the appearance of having so done." Persecutions carried out by antispiritual scholars arise, then, not simply from malevolence, but from fear of "the true depth of science and the penetration to the inmost centre" (BL I 148). For Coleridge, the danger lies not in the chaotic energy of immediate revelation, but in the implicit sacrilege of bringing analysis to bear on the spirit.

Coleridge admires the "Sage of Koenigsberg" for his contributions to "the only . . . pure science" (metaphysics) and looks to him for help in "pacifying the unsettled, warring, and embroiled domain of philosophy." But clearly, "pure science" is no guarantee against conflict and may be its source. One purpose of Coleridge's celebration of popular mystics, which surrounds the long excerpt from Schelling on the conspiracy of the learned, is to develop a philosophical identity based on nonviolence or, to be more precise, reluctant violence. Coleridge portrays the "uneducated man of genius" as caught in a double bind: fundamentally peace-loving, yet possessed by the internal spiritual imperative to bear witness, he draws down on himself the fury of the skeptics. Without the expertise possessed by "those, to whom reasoning and fluent expression have been as a trade learnt in boyhood," such persons are drawn into the civil wars of philosophy: "Woe is me that I am become a man of strife, and a man of contention,—I love peace: the souls of men are dear unto me: yet because I seek for Light every one of them doth curse me!" Coleridge's "gratitude" for the nurture of such writers qualifies his praise of Kant, for the unorthodox sincerity of simple mystics helped "prevent my mind from being imprisoned within the outline of any single dogmatic system." Such systems, including the grand march of German philosophies on which Coleridge relies before and after this statement, are affiliated with the vivisectionist impulse. The testimony of the mystics confirms Coleridge's loyalties to the intuitive domain and his "presentment, that all the products of the mere *reflective* faculty partook of DEATH" (BL I 297–98, 150, 152).[14]

[14]One of Coleridge's alternatives to the political and philosophical languages that surround him is the science of political prophecy, and its avatar is Edmund Burke: "He referred habitually to *principles*. He was a *scientific* statesman; and therefore a *seer*. For every *principle* contains in itself the germs of a prophecy; and . . . the prophetic power is the essential privilege of science" (BL I 192; see also 203). The notion of political prophecy is unfolded at greater length in *The Statesman's Manual,* written after but published before *Biographia Literaria.* According to the hermeneutic logic of that volume, prophecy is science or history operating "prospectively," in the realm of effects

Reviewing is the crux, for Coleridge, of all discussions of critical ethics. The use in reviews of "intimate knowledge" of the author is the moral equivalent of sacrilege, rape, and the destruction of art: "[the reviewer] steals the unquiet, the deforming passions of the World into the Museum; into the very place which, next to the chapel and oratory, should be our sanctuary, and secure place of refuge; offers abominations on the altar of the muses; and makes its sacred paling the very circle in which he conjures up the lying and prophane spirit." If principles are the soul's "mother-tongue," the individual personality is its "sanctuary." To charge Coleridge with domestic irregularity becomes paradigmatic of the violence of all anonymous reviews, in which the namelessness that shields the reviewer encourages his assault on the author. The wounds that rankled most, the ones that Coleridge protests in a pained and indignant note to Chapter 3, had been inflicted in 1799. George Canning had appended a note to his poem, "New Morality" (published in *The Beauties of the Anti-Jacobin*), in which he referred to Coleridge's nonattendance of chapel at Cambridge and charged that he had subsequently deserted his family: "He has since married, had children, and has now quitted the country, become a citizen of the world, left his little ones fatherless, and his wife destitute" (BL II 109–10; LS 24, BL I 67–68).[15] Canning had made the most of his chance to treat blasphemy and domestic irresponsibility as the natural consequences of radical sympathies. For Coleridge, who cultivated a notion of the family as the sanctified antithesis of politics and the analogue of grace, such accusations became the epitome of the destructive effect of popular print media.

In the *Biographia* the subject of reviewing unfolds chiefly in Chapter

---

rather than causes: "[The Bible's mystery] contemplated under the relations of time presents itself to the understanding retrospectively, as an infinite ascent of Causes, and prospectively as an interminable progression of Effects—" (LS 49–50). The primary benefit of defining the Bible as the foundation of science and the origin of principle lies in the power of such a gesture to heal the split between analysis and at-homeness, a theme made most explicit in *The Statesman's Manual*: "At the annunciation of *principles,* of *ideas,* the soul of man awakes, and starts up, as an exile in a far distant land at the unexpected sounds of his native language, when after long years of absence and almost of oblivion, he is suddenly addressed in his own mother-tongue. He weeps for joy, and embraces the speaker as his brother" (LS 24). From the "oblivion" of philosophical "exile," the language of home and religion returns the soul to relationships of consanguinity.

[15]The charge would be alluded to again by the *Edinburgh's* "Christopher North" in the wave of adverse criticism that greeted the *Biographia*. See J. R. de J. Jackson, *Method and Imagination in Coleridge's Criticism* (London: Routledge and Kegan Paul, 1969), 8–14, 323–50.

3, in which Coleridge examines the "merciless and long-contin-
ued . . . cannonading" he and Southey have received from the literary
press. In Chapter 21, "Remarks on the present mode of conducting
critical journals," he is similarly provoked by Jeffrey's review of *The
Excursion* (1814) to defend Wordsworth from the "more intimate
knowledge" that transforms "censure" into "personal injury" and "sar-
casms" into "personal insults." Like the rest of the Wordsworth circle,
Coleridge regarded Jeffrey's review as particularly savage, insofar as
Jeffrey had frequently expressed his sympathy for Wordsworth's poetry and had visited with Southey and Coleridge during a trip to Keswick in 1810 (BL I 50–51, II 109).[16]

Nevertheless, at the same time he includes himself in the group of
writers whose private life has been violated, Coleridge is determined to
separate himself, in the public mind, from the "Lake School." "Be it,
that . . . my literary friends are never under the water-fall of criticism,
but I must be wet through with the spray . . . ?" he inquires. He
distinguishes his own position by asserting principles of "fair and philosophical" investigation (BL I 55, II 107). Principles are both the sign
of Coleridge's own personality and the means of enforcing impersonality in others. They let him speak aggressively as the philosophical
critic while restraining the invasive reviewer. The function of principles in family life, however, poses an ethical problem less easily resolved. Reasoned criteria may defend domestic culture against the pry-
ing curiosity of the reviews and their subscribers. But how can the
family nurture philosophy without at the same time being wounded by
it? Significantly, Coleridge handles these questions in the hypothetical
idiom of advice, and his solution takes on the quality of fantasy.

In Chapter 11 ("An affectionate exhortation to those . . . disposed
to become authors") Coleridge makes a sustained attempt to shield the
would-be author from the life of a professional writer. He proposes
changes in the mode of literary production, exhorting the young men
who form his imagined audience, "NEVER PURSUE LITERATURE AS A
TRADE." He advises them to select "a profession, i.e. some regular
employment . . . which can be carried on so far mechanically that an
average quantum only of . . . exertion [is] requisite to its faithful discharge." It quickly becomes apparent that Coleridge is motivated by
economic logic only insofar as he regards economic pressure as the
antithesis to love. A "mere literary man," whose intellectual life is

---

[16]John Clive, *Scotch Reviewers: The Edinburgh Review, 1802–1815* (Cambridge: Harvard University Press, 1957), 151–65.

controlled by the marketplace, is neither loved nor capable of love (BL I 223–24, 228). Advice about the choice of career changes rapidly into guidance in family matters.

The account of the daily routine of an amateur author, presented as an alternative to professional writing, at first seems like a domestic idyll. "From the manufactory or counting-house, from the law-court, or from having visited your last patient, you return at evening . . . to your family," Coleridge imagines himself telling "a dear young friend," "prepared for its social enjoyments, with the very counte-nances of your wife and children brightened, and their voice of wel-come made doubly welcome, by the knowledge that, as far as *they* are concerned, you have satisfied the demands of the day by the labor of the day" (BL I 224–25).

Within the imagined bliss of the family circle, however, occurs an-other, deeper withdrawal from the women one lives with to the soli-tude of the study and the masculine companionship of books, "so many venerable friends with whom you can converse." With a spirit "free from personal anxieties," the young man may be liberated from the present to find the ancient authors "still living." Coleridge appar-ently feels he has moved his dilettante too peremptorily into the study, however, and remembers that the women are being neglected: "But why should I say *retire?* The habits of active life and daily intercourse with the stir of the world will tend to give you such self-command, that the presence of your family will be no interruption. Nay, the social silence, or undisturbing voices of a wife or sister will be like a restorative atmosphere, or soft music which moulds a dream without becoming its object" (BL I 225). As always for Coleridge, the idealized "wife or sister" embodies sympathy and intuition that do not need to be articulated (hence the "social silence" that he finds so "restorative"). Nevertheless, a marked evasion of women is apparent here, first in the sense of women as a source of "demands" to be "satisfied" and then in their function as something to retire from.

Coleridge's need to limit feminine authority takes the form of en-couraging men's absence from home as well as retirement within it. The idealized sensation of the "restorative atmosphere" of domesticity, with resident women as the *genii loci,* depends on the careful manage-ment of a separate masculine sphere. One of the advantages of a career in the church, he suggests, is that one need not spend too much time in the female-dominated home. One has "a superior chance of happiness in domestic life, were it only that it is as natural for the man to be out of the circle of his household during the day, as it is meritorious for the woman to remain for the most part within it" (BL I 228–29). Women occupy an ambiguous position between the economy of public life and the domestic realm of male imaginative culture. They are the fireside muses whose sympathy the imagination requires, but they also signify the contamination of the marketplace. They bring into the family—as into the text—unsettling demands for economic productivity and conventional notions of masculine success. Silence and "undisturbing voices" communicate feminine support, but when conversation becomes an "object" requiring response, one suspects that woman has suddenly betrayed herself to society. Coleridge retreats from feminine intuition as the conduit for popular culture, even as he constructs it as a nuance to be desired.

CHAPTER 6

The Daughter of Logic

The Ghost Dance of History

In an essay of 1941, published in a volume with the Coleridgean title *The Intent of the Critic,* John Crowe Ransom employed a political analogy that indicates just how persistent is the association of nonfictional prose with certain abuses of authority: "A poem is, so to speak, a democratic state, whereas a prose discourse—mathematical, scientific, ethical, or practical and vernacular—is a totalitarian state."[1] Ransom's dictum reflects the ideological polarities of the 1940s as much as Coleridge's defense of philosophical prose depends on those of the late eighteenth century. The position expressed here is not precisely parallel to Coleridge's opinions in *The Friend* about the differences between poetry and prose. It does, however, share several fundamental assumptions with Coleridge's essays: first, that one may describe genre in ethical terms; second, that every ethical stance has a political equivalent; and third, that nonfictional prose—be it "mathematical, scientific, ethical, or practical and vernacular"—is at least partly defined by its power to operate in the name of rigor, subordination, and control.

Coleridge never employs so invidious a comparison as Ransom's democratic and totalitarian states when contrasting poetry and prose.

[1] John Crowe Ransom, "Criticism as Pure Speculation," in Hazard Adams, ed., *Critical Theory since Plato* (New York: Harcourt Brace Jovanovich, 1971), 886.

Nonetheless, centralized planning or conceptual control sustained over time—what he elsewhere calls "Method"—constitutes for him the "Wonderfulness of Prose." Prose, the epitome of bookishness itself, marks its possessors as the objects of "admiration":

> prose must have struck men with greater *admiration* than poetry. In the latter it was the language of passion and emotion; it is what they themselves spoke and heard in moments of exultation, indignation, etc. But to have an evolving roll, or a succession of leaves, talk continuously the language of deliberate reason in a form of continued preconception, of a *Z* already possessed when *A* was being uttered,—this must have appeared *god*-like. I feel myself in that state when in perusal of a sober, yet elevated and harmonious, succession of sentences and periods I abstract my mind from the particular passage, and sympathize with the wonder of the common people who say of an eloquent man, "He talks like a book."[2]

The Friend, like the *Biographia,* presents itself as a revision of the modus operandi of contemporary periodical prose, above all, of the language of "these viperous Journals, which deal out Profaneness, Hate, Fury, and Sedition throughout the Land." *The Friend* offers an antidote to the combative discourse of journalism; the 1809 title page displays that sure mark of polemical intent, a denial of factional interest: "A Literary, Moral, and Political Weekly Paper, excluding personal and party politics, and the events of the day" (F I 98, II 1). Although periodical literature represents a set of practices to be reformed, however, it is only a part of what *The Friend* rejects. In the *Biographia* the constitutive antithesis of nonfiction prose is poetry; in *The Friend* it is the novel. The generic code by which Coleridge links journalism to the novel, Jacobin politics, anonymous reviewing, and gossiping women is what really governs the thematic structure of *The Friend.*

The *Biographia,* in which the feminine is resented as the voice of economic demand but desired as understanding, is a far more tolerant text. In *The Friend* the feminine is aggressively cast out by Coleridge's reform of public discourse and by his construction of method. The womanly qualities he would like to repress, however, keep returning in *The Friend* and in ways that erase the essayist's difference from either the demonic energy of contagious femininity or the silent recep-

---

[2] *The Literary Remains of Samuel Taylor Coleridge,* ed. H. N. Coleridge (New York: AMS Press, 1967), 2:226–27.

tivity of the feminine victim. The hysterical and effeminate Rousseau becomes a strangely sympathetic figure. Maria Eleanora Schöning, whose rape Coleridge pointedly narrates as nonfiction, takes on the divinatory aura of Sara Hutchinson. At the point when he actually confronts his role as narrator of violence, Coleridge first half-identifies with the rapist and then recoils with horror at how close he has come to the gothic violations of taste perpetrated by Matthew Lewis in *The Monk*. Finally, in the "Essays on the Principles of Method," the binary contrast between the methodical man (Hamlet) and the antimethodical woman (Mistress Quickley [Coleridge's spelling]) breaks down as method comes to be defined in terms of desire instead of in terms of control. The virtues and solaces associated throughout Coleridge's career with the feminine are, by the end of the "Essays on Method," transposed into religious constructions in which method becomes the route to hope and pity.

In *The Friend,* then, to return to the exclusions that eventually cause Rousseau to materialize, Coleridge acknowledges periodical writing as his generic locale and seeks to stake out new ground within or adjacent to it on which to gather "a lesser Public." "The present Work," he declares, will counter the prevailing trends of "periodical Literature" by putting "information" before "amusement," before, that is, "the gratification either of the curiosity or of the passions." The friendly essayist immediately treats the "Fable of the Maddening Rain"—in which public mania is literally as arbitrary as the weather—as proof of the "*entertainingness* of moral writings" and of their healthful effects.[3] The immediate issue in this opening essay is the vexed relationship of pleasure to "the love of knowledge," an emotion "always preceded by thought, and linked with improvement" (F I 14–15, 10).

Coleridge admits that it has been "a heavy disadvantage" to begin *The Friend* with the prospect of a "slow and laborious ascent" before him in the form of difficult philosophical explanation. If he begins in "despondency," though, he ends in enthusiasm, using the famous metaphor of the reader with a "Chamois-hunter for his guide." He called this glamorous evocation of masculine effort in ascending the mountain of methodical argument "the finest passage in the *Friend.*" Sublime alpine settings advantageously combine the exaltation of the view from the peak with the sense of virtuous work expended—"the

---

[3]See also the quotation from one of his own poems on "medicinable powers" (F I 23) and the "Prospectus" to the 1809 edition (F II 18–19).

blood of toil from our own feet"—in having attained it (F I 19, 55–56).[4]

The peculiarly high value placed on self-reliance throughout *The Friend,* evident in the attempt to motivate readers to grapple with *The Friend* itself, has a superficially Emersonian flair. As in Emerson's essays, the call to individual commitment dares the reader to mental independence and to the Spartan rigors of intellectual "austerity." Coleridge defines his texts as "works which cannot act at all" without calling "the reasoning faculties into full co-exertion with them." Twenty years later, Emerson would arouse his readers with the possibility of instantaneous upward changes of state, but Coleridge draws on the imagery of ascent in order to convince his audience of the desirable slowness of their progress through "the longest apprenticeship." "Histories" are full of "accounts of noble structures raised by the wisdom of the few, and gradually undermined by the ignorance and profligacy of the many." Work, "the intensity and permanence of . . . action," constitutes history; the refusal to continue that labor in the act of reading destroys it (F I 22, 61–62). History as the vertical structure produced by work is set over against the flattened surface of culture created and then acted on by gothic hallucination or hysterical association.

Of all writers, Coleridge, the one most castigated for procrastination and a lack of self-disciplined effort, becomes a scourge of the general "aversion" to "continuous reasoning."[5] He insists paradoxically on

---

[4]The simile of the chamois hunter leads directly into an instance of what might be called the imperial sublime, in which Coleridge asks his reader to examine "the journals of our humane and zealous missionaries in Hindostan" for proof of the "exhaustion" experienced by the "natives" when trying to comprehend "the simplest chain of reasoning." The same individuals, however, are able "to swing by hooks passed through the back, or to walk on shoes with nails of iron pointed upward on the soles," proving that "all this . . . demands so very inferior an exertion of the will than to *think*" (F I 55–56).

[5]This tirade continues, enlarging its object from modern readers to works of "true modern taste": "videlicet, either in skipping, unconnected, short-winded asthmatic sentences, as easy to be understood as impossible to be remembered, in which the merest common-place acquires a momentary poignancy, a petty titillating sting, from affected point and wilful antithesis; or else in strutting and rounded periods, in which the emptiest truisms are blown up into illustrious bubbles by help of film and inflation. 'Aye!' (quoth the delighted reader) 'this is sense, this is genius! this I understand and admire! I have thought the very same a hundred times myself!'" (F I 26). See also Matthew Corrigan on Coleridge's attack on lazy readers, *Coleridge, Language, and Criticism* (Athens: University of Georgia Press, 1982), 9–13. Frances Ferguson demonstrates that Burke's theory of the sublime is, among other things, an anxious reaction to the beautiful—the domestic, the social, and the feminine. "The Sublime of Edmund Burke,

"co-exertion" in the fraternity of wisdom and also on a doubly determined isolation, enforced both by the solitude of thought and by the
rejection of readers who prefer accessible texts. He can write as both
leader and victim, therefore, and in both roles can present himself as a
hero of labor. Coleridge argues, in a way consistent with his emphasis
on intention and motive throughout *The Friend,* that the reading subject makes the difference between legitimate and deplorable pleasures:
he classes "information" pursued without moral aspirations "among
the gratifications of mere curiosity, whether it be sought for in a light
Novel or a grave History." The moral qualities of the reader are so
consistently matched with his or her selection of genre that genres
become metonymies of their audiences, and vice versa. Novels, taking
on the guilt of their consumers, come to stand for "mere curiosity,"
whereas nonfictional prose, inevitably historical, is conflated with the
"delightful effort" made by its more disciplined devotees (F I 62, 15,
17).[6]

In *The Friend* each of Coleridge's negative categories—the novel,
France, English Jacobins, and the illogical discourse of women—
repeats the destructive dynamics of the whole of culture. France, of
course, provides Coleridge with the most fully articulated picture of a
country suffering from the maddening rain of revolution. But all the
elements of this anxiety-inducing series of negative terms are damned
together as forms of instantaneous gratification. They are bound by
Coleridge's condemnatory logic, which proposes delay, especially the
delay imposed by labor, as a form of control. The serial structure of his
polemic on behalf of work, however, mimes the feminine powers of
negativity itself. He is right, at least in terms of his own procedures, in
claiming that "aversion to all intellectual effort is the mother evil of all
which I had proposed to war against, the Queen Bee in the hive of our
errors and misfortunes, both private and national." The ahistorical
pleasures of fiction are motivated by the same hungry curiosity that
stimulates journalism in "this age of literary and political *Gossiping.*"
Consumers of novels and newspapers, in the *"sans-culotterie* of their
Ignorance," are seduced equally by the *"Anglo-gallican* taste" and the
cry of "THE SOVEREIGNTY OF THE PEOPLE—HURRA!" The connections
among all enemies of reflective labor—connections based on the analo-

---

or the Bathos of Experience," *Glyph Textual Studies* 8 (Baltimore: Johns Hopkins
University Press, 1981): 75.
   6Corrigan, *Coleridge, Language, and Criticism,* 112–16.

gy to the multiple symptoms of a single malady—emerge repeatedly in Coleridge's near-hysterical catalogs: "*Tell-truths* in the service of falsehood we find every where . . . from the elderly young women that discuss the love-affairs of their friends and acquaintance at the village tea-tables, to the anonymous calumniators of literary merit in reviews, and the more daring malignants, who dole out discontent, innovation, and panic, in political journals" (F I 9, 22, 210, 20, 212, 49–50).

The "infectious feeling of insecurity" arising from all mental activity not grounded in the moral substance of effort pervades "the field of imagination." Coleridge's "soul-sickening sense of unsteadiness" grows with the perceived spread of "epidemic distemper" within a culture he thinks is contagiously ill. The picture that results is at once sublime and disgusting:

> And could we bring within the field of imagination, the devastation effected in the moral world, by the violent removal of old customs, familiar sympathies, willing reverences, and habits of subordination almost naturalized into instinct . . . and above all, if we could give form and body to all the effects produced on the principles and dispositions of nations by the infectious feelings of insecurity, and the soul-sickening sense of unsteadiness in the whole edifice of civil society; the horrors of battle, though the miseries of a whole war were brought together before our eyes in one disastrous field, would present but a tame tragedy in comparison. (F I 120, 210)

Coleridge's discussion of "the Origin and Progress of the Sect of Sophists" in the second section of *The Friend* offers another version of the attack on French vices. Here he also links cognitive instability to antipatriarchal sentiments. Once the Sophists had resolved "to separate ethics from the faith in the Invisible," they were thrown open to "accidents of an ever-shifting perspective." *The Friend's* history of "prostituted genius" offered on the open market instead of earned through slow transmission from one generation to the next is a thinly veiled account of eighteenth-century subversions: "they offered to the vanity of youth and the ambition of wealth a substitute for that authority, which by the institutions of Solon had been attached to high birth and property, or rather to the moral discipline, the habits, attainments, and directing motives, on which the great legislator had calculated . . . as the regular and ordinary results of comparative opulence and renowned ancestry" (F I 436, 441, 438–39). Against the loss of differentiation that makes history a gothic nightmare, Coleridge constructs the principles of antifictional, anti-French, and antifeminine prose.[7]

In representing political anxiety through the atmospheric effects of the gothic, including the drama of hysteria both male and female, Coleridge draws on idioms derived ultimately from the political culture of seventeenth-century England and continuing to operate at least through representations of the European revolutions of 1848. A certain class of British and later American spectators reflecting on Continental upheavals from 1789 on visualizes history as a prospect or "field." Within the huge but claustrophobic scope of this scene, especially when viewed by a threatened observer, the proliferating mimesis brought about by revolution makes language, manners, and domesticity into the interchangeable parts of culture. The "abrupt, broken, and unpredictable sequences of events" that define revolution become joined to the sense of excessive relatedness by which every aspect of public and private life is drawn into a panic-inducing chain of symptoms.[8]

The complexity of France as the demonic and seductive antithesis of England reinforces the associative structure of contagion in *The Friend*. One of the most frequent infiltrators is what Jon Klancher has called "the radical in the text." This "shadowy, antithetical figure" inhabits

[7]I agree with Jerome Christensen's sense that the debilitating effects of novels, Jacobinism, and anonymous reviewers conform to "an erotic dynamics which reflects the entropic curve of the male in a sexual act," "the unchecked, associative trajectory of desire towards death." I am dubious, however, about his suggestion that Coleridge's supplemental gestures are designed to sustain the textual equivalent of "erotic play" which keeps the circulation of the body politic in constant motion. To turn Coleridge's obsessive binary logic and the negative and exclusionary gestures that flow from it into forms of textual "autoeroticism" drains from Coleridge's writing the ethical difficulty associated with the aggressiveness of prose and of criticism itself. "Politerotics: Coleridge's Rhetoric of War in *The Friend*," *Clio* 8 (1979): 354, 348, 357. See also Christensen's *Coleridge's Blessed Machine of Language* (Ithaca: Cornell University Press, 1981), 205–7, on French style, novels, and mechanistic association.

[8]This conjunction of the seditious, the feminine, the satanic or anti-Oedipal, and the ghostly has its English basis in the politics of the preceding century and their subsequent aestheticization. One might think of Dryden's "Annus Mirabilis" (1666) in this connection, for example. Dryden characterizes the Fire of London as the return of the political repressed, the intangible but destructive presence of the "ghosts of traitors," its "shining sheet" of flame likened to the dance of "Dire night-hags" (lines 889, 986, 990–91). *John Dryden,* ed. Keith Walker, The Oxford Authors (New York: Oxford University Press, 1987), 60–63. See Ronald Paulson, *Representations of Revolution (1789–1820)* (Yale University Press, 1983), 39–40, 43; see also 45, 50–51, and discussions of the Miltonic allegory of Satan, Sin, and Death.

or haunts the writing of hegemonic authors and partly generates it.[9] Coleridge focuses on the obvious figures—Rousseau, Paine, and their ideological result, Napoleon—figures so obvious, in fact, as to be anything but "shadowy." Paine, though a more conventional and definite figure than Coleridge's Rousseau, also induces the dematerializing effects of revolution. "Paine's Rights of Man," Coleridge charges, contains "the essence of JACOBINISM, as far as Jacobinism is any thing but a term of abuse, or has any meaning of its own distinct from democracy and sedition" (F I 178–79).

"Jacobinism" functions in Coleridge's text precisely as the signifier of words devoid of "essence," as the mark of "democracy and sedition" and *therefore* of metonymic substitution. This has the effect of flattening history into an ethically malleable surface that can acquire positive or negative meanings. Coleridge concentrates on Paine's discussion, in Part II of *Rights of Man* (1792), of taxation as the product of monarchical and aristocratic corruption and as the cause of poverty. Rejecting Paine's logic of addition and subtraction, Coleridge introduces the metaphor of economic circulation. The enthusiasm inspired in him by this transferential figure culminates in a prose ode in praise of the "NATIONAL DEBT" and the British "*system* of credit" as "the cement" which has bound together "all the interests of the state" (F I 178–79, 229, 233). "Circulation" is the counterpart, among the virtuous, of "contagion" among the vicious. Circulation cements, contagion dissolves, but both account with equal efficiency for the propagation of a moral condition throughout a social system. The structural similarity of circulation and infection, both of which explain cultural uniformity and neither of which is original with or unique to Coleridge, suggests that the gothic surface of hysterical history is connected to persistent desires for as well as fears of relatedness.

If Paine is the Jacobin apologist in *The Friend,* Rousseau is its most remarkable case history. Paired with Martin Luther in Coleridge's comparative study of the "similarity in their *radical* natures," Rousseau emerges as the victim of an age that could not discipline or contain

---

[9]Jon Klancher, *The Making of English Reading Audiences (1790–1832)* (Madison: University of Wisconsin Press, 1987), 28. The radical is by no means the most alien figure in Coleridge's text. England and France are brought together under the rubric of European civilization and are set over against "the brutal Russian," the "imbruted African," "the African Negro or the South American Savage" (F I 195, 518, 102n, 512–13). The parable of the African and the missionary sets forth in the most explicit way the imperialist tendencies of "method."

his hysterical tendencies.[10] In the first "Landing-Place," intended for the reader's rest and pleasure, Coleridge produces gothic vignettes in honor of historical reflection. According to his own links among fiction, curiosity, passive enjoyment, and wandering mental associations, the "Essays Interposed for Amusement" provide the proper context for a fantastic version of history. Coleridge pairs first Erasmus and Voltaire, then Luther and Rousseau, "in this our new dance of death, or rather of the shadows which we have brought forth—two by two— from the historic ark." The point of this shadow dance, he suggests, is to test the relative influence of temperament and culture. Given two individuals of similar personalities, what difference do historical circumstances make? The "heroic LUTHER," subjected to this mode of analysis, emerges as eerily similar to "the crazy ROUSSEAU, the Dreamer of lovesick Tales, and the Spinner of speculative Cobwebs; shy of light as the Mole, but as quick-eared too for every whisper of the public opinion; the Teacher of stoic *Pride* in his principles, yet the victim of morbid *Vanity* in his feelings and conduct!" (F I 127, 132).

Eighteenth-century culture, Coleridge argues, was not substantive enough to resist being drawn into Rousseau's etherealizing net, whereas Luther's less flexible milieu kept his fantasy life under better control. In introducing the first of the "Landing-Place" essays, Coleridge tries to articulate the uncanny effect by which history generates moods of recognition and recurrence. He decries the "restlessness to understand" that causes some to personify godly providence as a "Harmonist." He goes on nonetheless to evoke restlessness of a different kind in an attempt to explain what it feels like to encounter "the analogies of nature, revolving upon herself," and their mimetic antithesis, "the masquerade figures of cunning and vanity." Likening the "sense of *recognition*" to the auditory effect of the music of a great composer, he describes how "the present strain . . . seems not only to recal, but almost to *renew,* some past movement." Having "modified the Present by the Past," the composer proleptically constructs the future as well ("weds the Past *in* the Present to some prepared and

---

[10]Edward Duffy's remark that, in Blake, "prophetic wrath" is "directed against some hyphenated chimera always named Voltaire-Rousseau" seems applicable to this section of *The Friend* as well. In his discussion of the comparison of Luther and Rousseau, Duffy views Coleridge's text, as I do, as evincing an "ambivalent attitude toward 'crazy Rousseau'—a not unadmiring demonization," and an effort to contain a "peculiarly eruptive" energy. *Rousseau in England: The Context for Shelley's Critique of the Enlightenment* (Berkeley: University of California Press, 1979), 57, 62–68.

corresponsive Future"). In the process of reception the same thing takes place for the listener; "retrospection blends with anticipation, and Hope and Memory (a female Janus) become one power with a double aspect" (F I 129–30).

Coleridge's musical analogue is stabilized by the interior experience of composer and auditor. But when he turns to history, the "charm" of "pleasurable sensation" is replaced by "intellectual complacency," and temporality becomes double-faced in a more disturbing way. The "female Janus" comes to preside over the inability to distinguish "analogies of nature" from "masquerade figures." Coleridge offers the comparison of Rousseau and Luther as exercise for the judgment and fancy. In bracketing (or "abstracting") "questions of evil and good" by focusing on such historical contrasts and "the *mode* of producing them," he creates the phantasmagoric resemblances, the surface intensities, that he attributes to the mental life of Luther and Rousseau (F I 129–31). For both figures display, in their thoughts and behavior, the uncanny resemblance of piety and sedition once moral content has been evacuated, leaving only the surface, which is structured solely by style.

The basis of Rousseau's likeness to Luther is the "almost superstitious hatred of superstition" felt by both. Indeed, the lengthier discussion of Luther dwells on the issue of his superstition and above all on the phantasmic devil that provoked the ink blot on the wall of Warteburg ("the result and relict of [an] author-like hand-grenado"). The episode, according to Coleridge, was the product of a half-dreaming, half-waking condition associated with the nightmarish confusion of mental and bodily sensation. The fact that Luther is possessed by holy, not worldly, images during his struggle to translate the Bible protects the virtue of his superstitious agon. But Luther's mental fictions, "angry fancies . . . recollections of past persecutions . . . uneasy fears and inward defiances and floating Images of the evil Being," coalesce as or "condense themselves into" perceived diabolical realities. Coleridge links gothic scenarios to uncontrolled mental associations, but both have material historical effects, to whit, the Reformation and the Revolution (F I 133, 137, 142).[11]

The connection between apparitions and surface phenomena or threshold effects becomes explicit in Essay III of the first Landing-

---

[11]Coleridge derives his account of Luther from Jonas Ludwig von Hess, *Durchflüge durch Deutschland, die Niederlande und Frankreich* (7 vols., Hamburg, 1793–1800) (F I 136). This is also his source for the equally hysterical narrative of "The Life of Maria Eleanora Schöning" in the second Landing-Place of *The Friend* (F I 342).

Place. Here Coleridge sets forth his "Ghost-Theory" in terms of the metaphor of window glass, a surface that contains the images of both objects seen through it and objects reflected in it. The fascinating way in which the landscape, the fire, and Coleridge's books ("lettered, as it were, on their backs with stars") are able to fuse by virtue of their two-dimensional ontology finds its more disconcerting analogues in the way apparitions are projected onto reality itself (F 144–45). And, ultimately, onto history as a "field" or plane in which the depth that allows us to distinguish between objects and reflections vanishes.

Rousseau, whose unchecked sensibility transformed a culture more permeable than Luther's into a subtler kind of ghost story, exhibits the more significant likeness to Coleridge himself, a resemblance based on "the strange influences of his bodily temperament on his understanding; his constitutional melancholy pampered into a morbid excess by solitude; his wild dreams of suspicion; his hypochondriacal fancies of hosts of conspirators all leagued against him." Rousseau inhabits a historical arena of contrived indeterminacy or instability. Imagine Luther in eighteenth-century Geneva, Coleridge demands, "and Luther will no longer dream of Fiends or of Antichrist—but will he have no dreams in their place? His melancholy will have changed its drapery; but will it find no new costume wherewith to cloath itself?" (F I 134, 143). Coleridge emphasizes the restless activity generated by French theorists, who "usurping the name of reason [the Human Understanding] openly joined the banners of Anti-christ, at once the pander and the prostitute of sensuality, and whether in the cabinet, laboratory, the dissection room, or the brothel, alike busy in the schemes of vice and irreligion. . . . Prurient, bustling, and revolutionary this French wisdom has never more than graced the surfaces of knowledge."[12] The surface becomes the trope of instability.

Rousseau is more than a signifier for the idea of France, however. He displays what I have called (following Eve Sedgwick) the gothic but what might also be called (drawing on Neil Hertz's discussion of the politics of male hysteria)[13] the hysterical aspects of Coleridge's own writing. By hysterical writing, in this context, I mean writing that is obsessed with the body as the threshold of the imaginary. Such writing tends to conflate personal symptoms with cultural discourses and thus to be overwhelmed by a phantasmagoria of historical analogies. Not

[12]From *The Statesman's Manual*. Cited in Duffy, *Rousseau in England*, 66.

[13]Neil Hertz, "Male Hysteria under Political Pressure," in *The End of the Line: Essays on Psychoanalysis and the Sublime* (New York: Columbia University Press, 1985).

surprisingly, Rousseau is the most feminine, as well as the most "prurient," of radicals: "His sensibility, which found objects for itself, and
shadows of human suffering in the harmless Brute, and even the
Flowers which he trod upon—might it not naturally . . . have wept,
and trembled, and dissolved, over scenes of earthly passion, and the
struggles of love with duty?" Rousseau's "pity, that so easily passed
into rage," marks him as a sexually ambiguous figure. Once Rousseau
"had slipped the cable of . . . faith," he was subject to a dangerous
volatility in his bodily and sexual identity symptomatic of his philosophical ailment (F I 143, 133).[14] He dramatizes the slippage between
revolutionary politics and the feminine, both of which signify precisely
the logic of slippage, contagion, or metonymy. Every term in Coleridge's series of analogical effects, therefore, represents the analogical
effect itself. The resulting mood is at once claustrophobic and agora-
phobic, for Coleridge frightens himself with scenes at once limitless
and (because their contents all have the same meaning) redundant.

The affinity between Coleridge and his portrait of Rousseau unsettles the notion that English romantics are blessed with a greater degree
of sanitive balance than French ones. In doing so, it also lends credence
to recent investigations of the notion of male hysteria. Hertz approaches the subject by way of a political cartoon of 1792, a parody of
Burke's *Reflections on the Revolution in France* in which the serene female
figure of British Liberty is contrasted to the demonic Medusa of French
Liberty, "a hideous and fierce but not exactly sexless woman" with "a
decapitated male at her feet." He goes on to trace the figure of the
terrifyingly sexual female as it embodies the anxieties felt by Hugo,
Tocqueville, and other observers of the events of 1848. Male hysteria
arises, Hertz suggests, through the "linking of what is politically dangerous to feelings of sexual horror and fascination." Images of what is
"sexually equivocal or positively effeminate" connote the "dissolution
of hierarchical difference" and the resulting "incitement to . . . semiotic restlessness."[15] Such reflections shed considerable light on Coleridge's characterization of Rousseau and especially on "semiotic restlessness" in Coleridge's texts. For Coleridge's own political hysteria is

[14]For Coleridge's objections to Rousseau's theory of human equality and to the
derivation of government from reason in *Du contrat social,* see F I 159, 191–202.

[15]Hertz, *The End of the Line,* 162, 168, 185, 176. Catherine Gallagher's response
includes the suggestion that the reactions Hertz analyzes can be viewed as "a much
more historical and a much less hysterical phenomenon" (196), a caution that applies to
the present instance as well, although the descriptive impact of the term "hysteria" is
indispensable.

aroused, almost willfully, by his belief that the surface constituted by
Jacobinism, journalism, female gossip, and domestic unease preys on
the depths of constitutionality and the subject. The metaphor of disease
creates a hyperbolic, uncontainable threat that legitimates dread as the
basis for public policy. The surface becomes sublime, if perversely so.

The role played in this hysterical dynamic by Coleridge's private
experiences of dread raises all the difficulties one might expect to face
in working out the relationship between subjectivity and ideology.[16] If
we look again at Coleridge's characterization of Rousseau, we can see
how close his case history comes to autobiography. Coleridge diag-
noses Rousseau's disease as an infectious relation of body, consciousness, and politics. Specifically, Rousseau inhabits the space between
sleep and waking, the scene of greatest anxiety for Coleridge, where he
is hyperconscious of the body and of the nightmares that the body both
produces and feels inscribed on it. The "strange influences of . . .
bodily temperament on . . . understanding"—the relationship between "hypochondriacal fancies" and paranoia ("hosts of conspirators
all leagued against him")—become models for and refractions of collective disturbances.

The intervals of waiting to fall asleep or of awakening contain the
elements of Coleridge's hysteria: a preternatural awareness of particular parts of the body and of the skin as the organ of touch, which at
such times displaces the eye (N I 1414); an equally acute consciousness
of the mind's associative wanderings, usually guided by somatic stimuli (N I 1597, 1601, 1827); and finally, the sense of impending or just-
experienced nightmares in which the image of the demonic female
persistently dominates.[17] In addition to the haunting female dream
figure, Coleridge associates the bodily terror of falling asleep (marked
by the sudden "Sense of diminished Contact") with being born (the
loss of the "Contact" of "the womb") *and* with the suffering of women
in childbirth (N I 1414).[18] This conjunction of symptoms displays the
characteristic hysterical use of bodily afflictions as both the cause and

[16]In what follows, I am referring only to female figures of horror, ignoring, for the
moment, the place of the desirable pitying and nurturing female in Coleridge's writings. Clearly, the two are interdependent: nights of fear lead to days of dependence on
the presence or thought of Sara Hutchinson and her imaginary sisters.

[17]See Beverly Fields, *Reality's Dark Dream: Dejection in Coleridge* (Kent, Ohio: Kent
State University Press, 1967), 34–56.

[18]See also the melodramatic comparison of gastric pains to childbirth (N II 2092) and
the reference to muscular fatigue (in the thighs) so great as to produce "hysterical
weeping" (N I 1487).

the characters of the mind's "pictographic script."[19] The signifying function of the body creates the "theatricality" of hysteria, its ability to multiply symptomatic expressions, to become "a malady of representation."[20]

In a notebook entry on the psychology of dreams, Coleridge hypothesizes that "the Origin of moral Evil" is somehow related to "the *streamy* Nature of Association." "Thinking" [which, he says, "= Reason"] "curbs & rudders" this substrate of experience, in which the "diseased Currents of association" contaminate the whole mind with "Vice." "Do not the bad Passions in Dreams throw light . . . upon this Hypothesis?" he asks (N I 1770). Nightmare, then, is not only the condition in which life-in-death appears in terrifying forms; it is the state in which the purest actions can change into evidence of the mind's capacity for evil. The worst horror of dream derives from the sleeper's inability to maintain the distinctions between real and unreal; Coleridge finds this so unnerving that he identifies it as *in itself* immoral.

We find the waking equivalent of the "streamy" associations of sleep in Coleridge's meditation on the mysterious incompatibility of "deep feelings" with distinct notions. The union of such feelings with "obscure ideas" is restricted to conceptions "necessary to the moral perfection of the human being." In other words, the combination of mystery and emotion is legitimate only in the religious sphere, and logical rigor must be systematically applied to every other area of thought. For to "connect with the objects of our senses the obscure notions and consequent vivid feelings . . . due only to immaterial and permanent things" is "profanation." The "bedimming influences of custom, and the transforming witchcraft of early associations," constantly threaten to invade the domain of the understanding and must be controlled. The "preventive, the remedy, the counteraction" of streamy association, Coleridge insists in triplicate, is "the habituation of the intellect to clear, distinct, and adequate conceptions" in all things secular (F I 106).

If such education is missing, an entire nation experiences a hysterical condition, or the pains of sleep. When "deceit and superstition" encounter therapeutic truth, they become more dramatic, "the extravagances of ignorance and credulity roused from their lethargy, and angry at the medicinal disturbance—awakening not yet broad awake . . . blending the monsters of uneasy dreams with . . . real objects."

---

[19]Mary Jacobus, *Reading Woman* (New York: Columbia University Press, 1986), 209.
[20]J. Laplanche and J.-B. Pontalis, *The Language of Psychoanalysis*, trans. Donald Nicholson-Smith (New York: Norton, 1973), 194–95.

The "fury and violence of imposture attacked or undermined in *her* strong holds" results in a kind of mass haunting apparent only to the truth-teller himself (emphasis added). The step from the streamy psychopathologies of everyday life to "the satanic Government of Horror under the Jacobins" is a short one. The "Delirium" of dream that is "the height . . . of mere association" erupts into public life in "the contagious nature of enthusiasm, and . . . the acute or chronic diseases of deliberative assemblies" (F I 67, 193–94; N I 1770).

The case of Coleridge/Rousseau confirms the definition of male hysteria as "hysteria about women."[21] If Coleridge is afflicted by dread of the feminine, however, he is also tormented by his identification with it, assuming femininity as the sign of his suffering. With Coleridge, then, we encounter a form of male hysteria which does not simply react to woman as an intermittently demonized power or knowledge.[22] For him the feminine signifies the vacuity that occurs when meaning is felt to wander through mental and bodily associations, precisely the syndrome in which the political and the subjective meet in (and as) an unstable surface. Coleridge is able to portray Rousseau as the origin or cause of the French Revolution (and thus of Coleridge's own hysteria) and also as a victim or fellow sufferer of hysteria, his double. The complexities of this move make it possible for Coleridge to exploit hysteria as a political reaction to Jacobinism and, at the same time, to identify with its pathologies.[23]

The terror of the gothic results from the multiplication of surfaces sustained by references to apparent depths but doomed to correspondence and proliferation.[24] *The Friend* exhibits this conventional structure in the specter of feminine gossip and novel-reading. Insofar as *The*

[21]Jacobus, *Reading Woman*, 200–202; Hertz, *The End of the Line*, 126. Like Hertz, in his reading of Freud's account of Dora, Jacobus discovers a mimetic hysteria (a "confusion of tongues") in male analytical discourses challenged by the language of female hysterics.

[22]Alice Jardine suggests that a similar phenomenon, called by her "male paranoia," is a response to "a woman who *knows* anything." *Gynesis: Configurations of Woman and Modernity* (Ithaca: Cornell University Press, 1985), 97.

[23]I have benefitted, in writing this section, from Jane Gallop's treatment of feminist discussions of the Dora case, in *The Daughter's Seduction* (Ithaca: Cornell University Press, 1982), 132–50; and from Dianne Hunter, "Hysteria, Psychoanalysis, and Feminism: The Case of Anna O.," in *The (M)other Tongue: Essays in Feminist Psychoanalytic Interpretation,* ed. Shirley Nelson Garner et al. (Ithaca: Cornell University Press, 1985), 89–115.

[24]Eve Sedgwick, *The Coherence of Gothic Conventions* (London: Methuen, 1986), 12–13, 165–70.

Friend associates dread with contamination, it is consistent with its hysterical logic to fear the most facile modes of literary communication. At this point we might well recall Burke's image of Rousseau as a youthful interloper who enters "the sacred family circle, seduce[s] the wife or daughter, and undermine[s] the authority, indeed take[s] the place of the father-husband." In Ronald Paulson's summary:

> Burke develops the model in . . . *A Letter to A Member of the National Assembly* (1791), where he argues that Rousseau has become for the revolutionaries a figure "next in sanctity to that of a father," and following his example, they encourage tutors "who betray the most awful family trusts and vitiate their female pupils" and they "teach the people that the debauchers of virgins, almost in the arms of their parents, may be safe inmates in their house. . . ."[25]

In *The Friend* the novel, poetry, and periodicals—all, here, associated strongly with curiosity's appetite in the female reader—act like Burke's Rousseau to seduce both sons and daughters under the very eyes of the patriarch of the breakfast table. Coleridge fears that the admirer of contemporary literature who fails to examine with sufficient care "the books which are to lie on his breakfast-table" may suffer "the punishment of [his] indiscretion in the conduct of [his] sons and daughters" (F I 41–42). The seditious eroticism of the young Rousseau, undermining the domestic intimacies of an upper-class family, has been dispersed throughout the literary marketplace.

The portrait of Rousseau in *The Friend* is clearly just one episode in Coleridge's response to *"Anglo-gallican"* thinking. A more explicit demonstration of the connections among French intellectual habits, prose style, "habitual novel reading," and the gossip of women comes in the "Letter to R. L.," in which he defends the style of *The Friend* against charges of "obscurity."[26] Coleridge argues that the "abstruseness" complained of by readers is not only necessary but desirable. Ideological conflict is played out in stylistic terms as he contrasts his preference for "the stately march and difficult evolutions" of seventeenth-century authors to "the epigrammatic unconnected periods of the fashionable *Anglo-gallican* taste": "I can never so far sacrifice my judgement to the desire of being immediately popular, as to cast my sentences in the French moulds . . . for those to comprehend who

---

[25]Paulson, *Representations of Revolution*, 62–64.

[26]Coleridge never printed the letter critical of *The Friend*, which Southey had written at his request (see F II 498–99).

labour under the . . . pitiable asthma of a short-witted intellect" (F I 20). In referring to "Anglo-gallican" taste, Coleridge is exploiting a stereotypical view of the curt, pert, or pointed style, as it was called in the seventeenth century. By the late eighteenth century this style had become a critical stereotype only: no one wrote that way anymore. Long associated with French writers, its English practitioners—best known for the dislike they engendered—were Collier and L'Estrange. The prejudice against this too-facile, too-clever prose absorbed Coleridge's distaste for the neoclassical couplet. By 1799 it had become connected to his feelings about the French Revolution, which gave an old rhetorical criticism political life.[27]

Coleridge joins the French style to the French Revolution on the basis of their common contempt for an intellectual work ethic. Philosophical virtue must be earned by the most masculine "effort" and "exertion," the antithesis of "the habit of receiving pleasure" through "habitual novel reading." The logic of his associations is not hard to follow. Sentences are made long (and thus difficult) by chains of internal "connections," "the *hooks-and-eyes* of the memory"; the devices of apposition, subordination, parallelism, and qualification needed to express a complex idea are further required to retain that idea in the mind. The complication of syntax itself does not make sentences memorable, but rather the labor and time expended in establishing their meaning. Excessively short sentences "in the French moulds," novelistic plots that act on the mind like an addictive drug, and the false stimulations of journalism all produce the ghostliness of the political condition he deplores.[28] Lest anyone doubt that Coleridge is issuing a call to a more heroic and masculine prose held together by "the cement of thought as well as of style," he likens the debility of the novel-reader to the state produced by feminine gossip:

> those who confine their reading to such books dwarf their own faculties, and finally reduce their understandings to a deplorable imbecility. . . . Like idle morning visitors, the brisk and breathless periods hur-

[27]George Williamson, *The Senecan Amble: Prose Form from Bacon to Collier* (Chicago: University of Chicago Press, 1951; reissued 1966), chap. 11, "Pert Style in Neo-Classic Times."

[28]Coleridge writes, in notebook entries of 1803, that "the Philosopher of London & Paris" asks himself, "How can I by verbal association so alter, or dislocate, these sentences, by dialectic art, as to make them appear a contradiction in Terms." The consequence, he fears, will be a prose style consisting of nothing but "Proverbs and Apologues," "Maxims, Aphorisms, & Sentences," like that popular "among the French, the beginners of this Style" (N I 1758, 1759).

ry in and hurry off in quick and profitless succession; each indeed for the
moments of its stay prevents the pain of vacancy, while it indulges the
love of sloth; but all together they leave the mistress of the house (the
soul I mean) flat and exhausted, incapable of attending to her own concerns, and unfitted for the conversation of more rational guests. (F I 20–
21)

Coleridge's conceit enjoins the feminine soul to behave in a more
manly or "rational" fashion.

Unlike the *Biographia*, *The Friend* largely excludes or represses the
familial sphere as an object of desire and as an analogue of intuitive
understanding. Instead, such longing enters *The Friend* in the association of the proleptic force of method with the redemptive possibility of
hope. The more violent casting out of the feminine in *The Friend* can be
accounted for only in terms of the ethics of antifeminine writing. For
whether one looks at Coleridge's personal circumstances in 1809–10,
when the original periodical was composed in the company of the
Wordsworths and with Sara Hutchinson as amanuensis; or in 1812, in
the aftermath of the quarrel with Wordsworth; or in 1818, after Coleridge had come to regard the Gillmans of Highgate as yet another
surrogate family, there is no biographical evidence that his personal
need for domestic consolation should not be expressed as insistently in
The Friend as in the *Biographia,* written in the same period, or in his
poems.[29]

The dedication of the 1818 edition to "Mr. and Mrs. Gillman," in
gratitude for his "hope" for Coleridge and her ability to blend "the
affectionate regards of a sister or daughter with almost a mother's
watchful and unwearied solicitudes," provides further evidence that
the domestic arena is as much on Coleridge's mind as ever (F I 4).
Expression of these desires is blocked in most of *The Friend,* however.
The exclusionary dynamics of prose take over as Coleridge seeks to
call into being an audience of male readers constituted by an agreed-on
rejection of the feminine, the popular, and the radical.[30] Indeed, such

[29]As I noted in Chapter 4, the 1809 "Prospectus" of *The Friend* leads one to expect
echoes of the Dejection ode, offering as it does "Consolation to the afflicted in Misfor-
tune, or Disease, or Dejection of Mind, from the Exertion and right Application of the
Reason, the Imagination and the moral Sense" (F II 18–19).

[30]Coleridge's personal circumstances do illuminate the emphasis on male relationships in *The Friend* to some extent. After his return from Malta, and particularly after
his intimacy with the Wordsworths had ended, he fantasized more and more about
becoming the philosophical confidant of young men. His sons and nephews were
nearing maturity (Hartley went to Cambridge in 1815), which made this persona more

an audience seems already to have been formed by the common suffering of its members from the viral effects of "Anglo-gallican" culture. The taint of femininity in all things French intensifies this homosocial desire for a positive critical identity, even as the feminine haunts the masculine domain through representations of hysterical masculinity, such as Rousseau.[31]

These exclusive gestures once again raise questions pertaining to critical violence.[32] What sort of aggression is compatible with—or constitutive of—critical integrity? Coleridge confronts an ethical dilemma arising from the need to reconcile forceful moral judgment

---

plausible. Some vicarious familial pleasure became available in addressing his sons' generation. This kind of relation is made apparent by the author of the "Mathetes" letter reprinted in *The Friend* and by Wordsworth, whose "Answer to Mathetes" was written at Coleridge's request. The theme of this exchange is the fate of "noble and imaginative spirits . . . who in the amiable intoxication of youthful benevolence" are most at risk of error. This portion of *The Friend* repeats in a nonfictional context the major plot of the eighteenth-century novel, "the history of a pure and noble mind" as it encounters the dangers of "seduction" and "infatuation" (F I 379, 378, 384). By becoming a "Friend" to younger men, Coleridge could enter into the world of homosocial bonds without confronting the anxieties produced either by the figure of the elder brother or by that of the mother. And he is free to write the story of his own younger self. In the process of responding (compulsively) to William Hazlitt's charge of apostasy, Coleridge adopts a curiously nostalgic tone toward his earlier politics, a kind of autoavuncular sympathy, an extension of friendly pity toward himself. See F I 223–27.

[31] Eve Sedgwick, *Between Men: English Literature and Male Homosocial Desire* (New York: Columbia University Press, 1985), 1–20. Coleridge's discussion of "the origin and progress of the sect of sophists" in the second section of *The Friend* is another version of the attack on the French vices of instability, irreligion, and egalitarian sentiment. Once the Sophists had resolved "to separate ethics from the faith in the Invisible," they were thrown open to "accidents of an ever-shifting perspective" made worse by the "itinerancy" that followed from "selling wisdom and eloquence" (F I 437–39). Like the French encyclopedists, Coleridge's Sophists directly threaten the foundations of patriarchal influence. See also F I 46–47.

[32] Klancher's definition of the aims of the "romantic ideology" is valid as a statement of Coleridge's practice in *The Friend*: "to rule in and rule out the possible readings of social and cultural discourses contested throughout the social realm." Coleridge seems to me to believe less in "the clerisy" as a literal social institution than Klancher's reading permits. Coleridge no doubt is moved by the desire for a community of "co-exertion," but the theory of prose unfolded in *The Friend*, dictated as it is by the need "to rule in and rule out," leaves little area to be collectively occupied. *The Friend*, then, is less a call for a new class of readers than an expression of Coleridge's need to find sources of "hope" in the realm of public discourse. There is no question that the effect of Coleridge's prose works was to reinforce the gender specificity of critical prose and its link with aggression. But his "romantic ideology" was more of an expression of social anxiety and desire than it was a successful intervention in the literary marketplace. *The Making of English Reading Audiences*, 136, 151.

with a peaceable manner. To use more psychological language, he wants to be both strong and likable. He evades this double bind by sanctioning "the free infliction of censure in the spirit of love" (F I 124). His strategy is grounded in differences between context and conscience, the Understanding and the Reason. These contrasts in turn lead him to argue that all human beings are equal enough to be held accountable not only for their actions but for the consequences of their actions, while being unequal enough to require their submission to traditional authorities.

The opening section of *The Friend*, devoted to the economies of "the Communication of Truth," holds individuals responsible for the origin, transmission, and reception of their opinions. Coleridge distinguishes sharply between mere verbal accuracy and moral truth, in which "we involve likewise the intention of the speaker, that his words should correspond to his thoughts in the sense in which he expects them to be understood by others." Defining "veracity" as the duty "to convey truth" protects those with honorable intentions. If it is "the wish and design of the mind to convey the truth only," then "any positive error" is almost certainly "the fault or defect of the Recipient, not of the Communicator." If authors do not prudently consider "the matter, the manner, and the time of their communications"—particularly their auditors' "habits of reasoning" and "predominant *passions*"—then they do not merit the exemptions granted by Coleridge to the moral individual. Persons who appeal to irresponsible auditors are members of the "Anglo-gallican" cultural conspiracy: "whether the faulty cause exist in our choice of unfit words or our choice of unfit auditors, the result is the same and so is the guilt" (F I 42–45, 48–49, 81).[33]

The public policy of truth-telling exposes the ideological direction of Coleridge's theory of the will. And the argument about the universal accountability of individuals on the basis of will derives from the mother lode of Coleridgean "desynonymizing," the difference between Reason and the Understanding. As we pursue his handling of this binary construction, we can see clearly how *the* Understanding, when involved dualistically with *the* Reason, signifies the ethical opposite of the sympathetic or receptive understanding so often repre-

[33]When Coleridge applies this line of reasoning to the question of libel laws, he concurs with the government's opinion that both price and mode of publication are reliable signs of authorial intention. To appeal to the wrong audience is proof of demagoguery. See Olivia Smith, *The Politics of Language, 1791–1819* (New York: Oxford University Press, 1984), 64.

sented in his texts as feminine. In the realm of Reason, will, and conscience, everyone is equal: "as the Reasoning consists wholly in a man's power of seeing, whether any two ideas, which happen to be in his mind, are, or are not in contradiction with each other, it follows of necessity, not only that all men have reason, but that every man has it in the same degree. . . ." Since conscience requires only knowledge of one's own intention, all men are equal in conscience, as well as in Reason. But equality of reason and conscience permits the huge sphere of the Understanding—the sphere of publication, reading, and political discourse—to be governed by inequality: "when we . . . speak, not exclusively of the *agent as meaning* well or ill, but of the action in its consequences, then of course experience is required, judgment in making use of it, and all those other qualities of the mind which are so differently dispensed to different persons, both by nature and education." The essay concludes, not surprisingly, by congratulating itself on having exposed the "gross sophism" of Rousseau's political theory: "And though *the reason itself* is the same in all men, yet the means of exercising it, and the materials (i.e. the facts and ideas) on which it is exercised, being possessed in very different degrees by different persons, the *practical Result* is, of course, equally different—and the whole ground work of Rousseau's Philosophy ends in a mere Nothingism." Coleridge accuses Rousseau of refusing to leave the idealizations of Reason for the necessary pragmatism of social life. There is no possible route from Reason to "positive and conventional laws" governing human society except by way of the Understanding. Government exists only "where individual landed property exists"; property is always unevenly divided; and only the Understanding is adapted to negotiating the distinctions of wealth, class, power, suffrage, and learning which organize the quotidian world of inequality (F I 159, 199–200).

When Coleridge is preparing to hold his antagonists responsible for the effects of their writings, he includes the "consequences" of action in the sphere of will, rather than in the realm of understanding and reception. When he wants to enlarge the area of inequality, however, he ascribes the consequences of moral action to the differentiated realm of the understanding. Either way, the distinction between reason and understanding serves Coleridge's aggressive impulses by enlarging the category that is associated with culpable behavior.

Through logical tactics such as these, Coleridge purports to establish his moral superiority to "elderly young women" given to gossip, "anonymous calumniators of literary merit," and "daring malignants, who dole out discontent, innovation and panic, in political journals."

He contrasts his own "asperity of censure," based on methodical arguments and derived from Law, Principle, and Reason, to the less acceptable aggression of "the illiterate perpetrator of 'the Age of Reason.'"
Paine "must have had *his* very conscience stupefied by the habitual
intoxication of presumptuous arrogance." In fact, an entire essay,
which concludes with these passages, is given over to the definition of
"ARROGANCE, or Presumption." "The probable charge of ARROGANCE,"
writes Coleridge "it was my hope to guard against" (F I 49–50, 32, 27).

The criteria that place Coleridge in a superior ethical position to
Paine are predominantly intellectual, even academic, pertaining mostly
to what he calls "logical courtesy." One symptom of arrogance, he
charges perversely, is "plagiarism," or that moral equivalent of plagiarism brought about by the author having "neglected to possess himself . . . of the information requisite for [a] particular subject." This
definition evades the possibility that "abstruse research" itself can become a form of plagiarism, as, of course, it was in Coleridge's case.
Furthermore, it accentuates the arbitrariness of his logic throughout
The Friend—or rather, it points up the logic of his arbitrariness. For the
term "arrogance" makes "the law of fair retaliation" legitimate (F I 29–
31). The "arrogant" absence in others of the moral category of method
justifies Coleridge's own methodical aggression.

The portrait of the hero of method in the "Answer to Mathetes"
(preparatory to the "Essays on Method") confirms the link between
analytical logic and mental strife. Imagine the following combat, Coleridge proposes. "Range against each other as advocates, oppose as
combatants, two several intellects," one an "adversary" of "impetuous
zeal," the other a "more advanced mind" that "not only sees that his
opponent is deceived; but . . . *how* he is deceived." The spectatorial
violence of method permits, in the end, an "irresistible" gentleness:

> versed in the secret laws of thought, he can . . . pierce infallibly all the
> windings, which false taste through ages has pursued—from the very
> time when first, through inexperience, heedlessness, or affectation, she
> took her departure from the side of Truth, her original parent.—Can a
> disputant thus accoutered be withstood?—to whom, further, every
> movement in the thoughts of his antagonist is revealed . . . who, there-
> fore, sympathises with weakness gently, and wins his way by for-
> bearance; and hath, when needful, an irresistible power of onset,—
> arising from gratitude to the truth which he vindicates . . . as his own
> especial rescue and redemption.

Here history is a far cry from the "dance of death" induced by sympathetic identification with Rousseau. The "history of society" is a form of knowledge based on an apprehension of depth, just as familiarity with "the secret laws of thought" creates an expertise based on access to the interior subject. Armed with these modes of cognition, the "riper mind" moves hierarchically ("through all the gradations") and is able to "pierce" the effects of his adversary's "windings." He imposes height and depth on surfaces.

Method, the conspiracy of "the secret laws of thought," aspires to be both a mode of power and a mode of love. As both a constructive and a negative tactic, it modulates easily from one degree of intellectual aggression to another. By virtue of its associations with rhetorical pathos and logical rigor, method possesses the capacity, at one and the same time, to serve strategies of exclusion and of hope.[34] Since method attacks in the name of planning, foresight, and anticipation—and, in its most sacred aspect, in the name of hope and faith—it ultimately lays claim to the rights of prophecy (F I 402).

The Sorceress of Pleasure and the Priest of Diana: Fiction in *The Friend*

Nonfictional prose, as the term itself shows, is constituted over against fiction, as soon as fiction acquires a sufficiently clear historical identity.[35] Once prominent in the literary economy, in Coleridge's view, the feminine loses its silent or tacit quality and enters into the babel of degenerate gossip that assaults the masculine imagination. It is not surprising, then, that fiction would seem to violate the sanctuary of the home by broadcasting its secrets. The feminine refuge crumbles as its interior life is taken up into the realm of textual commodities.

---

[34]On Coleridge's place in the history of relationships between logical and rhetorical conceptions of method, see the fine article by Paul K. Alkon, "Critical and Logical Concepts of Method from Addison to Coleridge," *Eighteenth Century Studies* 5 (1971): 97–121.

[35]For the economic conditions that formed part of this process, see Jane Spencer, *The Rise of the Woman Novelist* (London: Basil Blackwell, 1986), 11–14. Nancy Armstrong's *Desire and Domestic Fiction: A Political History of the Novel* (New York: Oxford University Press, 1987) sets forth a similar but more ambitious argument about "The Rise of Female Authority in the Novel" and the socioeconomic function of fiction. Her adaptations of Foucault's theory of epistemic change designate a later period than the one Spencer focuses on as the point when feminine discourse emerges in the novel. The strategies that Armstrong locates in the 1790s and others that she places as occurring between 1818 and 1848 (pp. 161–72) seem to me to be already conventional by the time of the French Revolution.

In an "age of personality," Coleridge fears, the relation between public and private realms is inverted.[36] The very inwardness of private character loses its "solid WELL-BEING" in the fluidity of self-revelation. A class of *"public* characters" has appeared, comprising "wretched mis-users of language" who focus exclusively on persons rather than ideas. Such texts infiltrate the private home, which is the proper domain of reading; they "introduce the spirit of vulgar scandal and personal inquietude into the Closet and the Library, environing with evil passions the very Sanctuaries, to which we should flee for refuge from them!" The assault of such "scandal-bearers" on "the home-bred strength" of reason reverses the vice of the female gossip, who retails family secrets among her acquaintance. But for Coleridge, "the most garrulous female Chronicler, of the goings-on of yesterday in the families of her neighbours and townsfolk" performs the same dangerous sorcery as the men of letters who can write only about each other (F I 358–59, 39).

Some such link between women and fiction, but extending also to gossip, curiosity, and newsmongering, is necessary to account for the status of fiction in *The Friend*. Despite the fact that Coleridge is not particularly upset by the proliferation of women writers and is disturbed by the taste of woman readers mostly to the extent that men have come to share it, he senses that the cultural trends he dislikes are related to the changing discourse of the feminine. Crucial to the generic character of moral nonfiction is the ability to speak as the defender of the home and of the purity of women—even, occasionally, to speak *as* a suffering woman—and yet, insistently, to be unlike them: "Pleasure, most often delusive, may be born of delusion. Pleasure, herself a sorceress, may pitch her tents on enchanted ground. But Happiness (or . . . solid WELL-BEING) can be built on Virtue alone, and must of necessity have Truth for its foundation" (F I 39).

The problem with novels has to do with the kind of pleasure they

---

[36]An even more vehement tirade on the same subject occurs elsewhere in *The Friend:* "in this AGE OF PERSONALITY, this age of literary and political *Gossiping* . . . the meanest insects are worshipped with a sort of Egyptian superstition, if only the brainless head be atoned for by the sting of *personal* malignity in the tail . . . the most vapid satires have become the objects of a keen public interest purely from the number of contemporary characters *named* in the patch-work Notes. . . . In an age, when even Sermons are published with a double Appendix stuffed with *names*—in a generation so transformed from the characteristic reserve of Britons, that from the ephemeral sheet of a London Newspaper to the everlasting Scotch Professorial Quarto, almost every publication exhibits or flatters the epidemic distemper" (F I 210).

offer and the way such pleasure operates in the mental life of the reader. That is why Coleridge is so concerned with the effect of novel-reading on the memory. The basis of communication and indeed of morality lies in the ability "to contemplate the past in the present, and so to produce . . . continuity in . . . self-consciousness." When men "have ceased to look back on their former selves with joy and tenderness," they are reduced to "fragments," "self-mutilated, self-paralysed" (F I 40–41). The unifying power of memory is at the heart of every one of Coleridge's valued terms in *The Friend*: political continuity, sacred history, the prophetic scope of methodical thought, the density of a connected prose style, and finally the belief that one's own past displays not apostasy, but consistency.

Despite his emphasis on the "tenderness" of temporal continuity, Coleridge argues, in his refutation of Rousseau's *Du contrat social,* that we cannot and indeed should not remember *feelings* of political disillusionment. To elucidate the difference between the memory of thought and the memory of feeling, he introduces a literary parallel: "Those of my readers who at any time of their life have been in the habit of reading Novels may easily convince themselves of this Truth by comparing their recollections of those stories, which most excited their curiosity and even painfully affected their feelings, with their recollections of the calm and meditative pathos of Shakespeare and Milton." "Curiosity," the psychological antithesis of memory, is the motive most persistently associated with the novel by Coleridge. The "mere excitement of curiosity and sensibility" makes possible "the habit of receiving pleasure without any exertion of thought," which "may be justly ranked among the worst effects of habitual novel reading." And since the "exertion of thought" is the foundation of an integrated personality, the escape into novelistic sensation is finally dehumanizing— like, Coleridge goes on to say, the frenetic visiting that debilitates "the mistress of the house" (F I 179, 20–21).

In Coleridge's first published responses to gothic romances the novel by a male author (potentially his double, like Rousseau) upsets him far more deeply than similar books by women. In his comments on books by Ann Radcliffe and Mary Robinson, the relationship between novel-reading and curiosity is fully worked out. The romance is a "contest of curiosity on one side, and invention on the other," described in highly erotic language: "curiosity is kept upon the stretch from page to page, and from volume to volume, and the secret, which the reader thinks himself every instant on the point of penetrating, flies like a phantom before him, and eludes his eagerness till the very last moment of protracted expectation."[37] Coleridge tends to regard the gothic romances written by women as an unfortunate detour in the progress of taste which will (he hopes) be followed by a return to the style of Smollett, Fielding, and Sterne. When "satiety [banishes] what good sense should have prevented. . . . real life and manners will soon assert their claims." If the works of Ann Radcliffe and Mary Robinson can be treated as relatively harmless, however, the same cannot be said for Coleridge's view of *The Monk* (1796). The "libidinous minuteness" of Lewis's writing and the crucial indicators after his name, "M. G. Lewis, Esq. M.P.," makes him a serious cultural threat. The combination of "impiety," "voluptuous images," and the prestige of public office elicit calls for parental censorship, even in 1796, when Coleridge was still a radical: "the Monk is a romance, which if a parent saw in the hands of a son or daughter, he might reasonably turn pale."[38]

The episodes of suffering portrayed by Lewis "with no hurrying pencil" display an authorial "brutality" toward the reader compared to that shown by "him who should drag us by way of sport through a military hospital, or force us to sit at the dissecting table of a natural philosopher." The gothic novel, in its voyeuristic sexual curiosity, is allied with medical and scientific forms of analytical violence (the *"viva sectio"*). Needless to say, Coleridge is even more infuriated by Ambrosio's surprise at the fact that Antonia (his victim) has remained ignorant of sexual matters despite her diligent Bible study—because her "prudent mother" has given her an expurgated version of the sacred writings. Ambrosio's belief that books lead to erotic knowledge is the antithesis of principled reading: "a mind may be so deeply depraved by the habit of reading lewd and voluptuous tales, as to use even the Bible in conjuring up the spirit of uncleanness. The most innocent expressions might become the first link in the chain of association, when a man's soul has been so poisoned . . . he might extract pollution from the word of purity, and, in a literal sense, turn the Grace of God into wantonness."[39]

[37]*Coleridge's Miscellaneous Criticism,* ed. Thomas M. Raysor (Cambridge: Harvard University Press, 1936), 356–57.

[38]Ibid., 370, 378, 382, 374–75. See also Coleridge's letter on the novels of Scott, in *Collected Letters of Samuel Taylor Coleridge,* ed. E. L. Griggs (Oxford: Oxford University Press, 1971), V 34; also his reference to *Tom Jones* (F I 49) and defense of the "sunshiny, breezy spirit" of Fielding against the "close, hot, day-dreamy continuity of Richardson," in the *Marginalia,* CC V II 693.

[39]*Coleridge's Miscellaneous Criticism,* 375. On the authorship of Coleridge's writings on gothic novels, see Charles I. Patterson, "The Authenticity of Coleridge's Reviews of

To explain why he has paid "particular attention to this work," Coleridge cites its "unusual success," its occasional "real merit," and the fact that "the author is a man of rank and fortune." "Yes!" he exclaims, "the author of the Monk signs himself a LEGISLATOR!—We stare and tremble" as though Lewis himself were a gothic specter.[40] As the narrator of scenes of seduction and rape, Lewis partakes of the guilt of his protagonist. This is a position Coleridge will find himself approaching in the nonfictional story of Maria Eleanora Schöning. In that context he will insist that the truth of his story prevents him from being implicated in the narrative of Maria's rape. Lewis, by contrast, choosing to invent such a tale and to tell it with apparently voyeuristic leisureliness, dissects the bodies of women and forces the reader to watch. Because the relationship of a male writer to his female characters replicates the structure of Coleridge's own identification with the feminine, he never refers to female authors as the cause of his trouble. The female apparitions of his nightmares constantly haunt him, but in the realm of language he recognizes them mostly in texts by men.

The crisis of promiscuity to which Lewis contributes is denounced in the motto of the seventh essay of *The Friend,* on the communication of truth: "how are we to guard against the herd of promiscuous Readers?" For if authors write in the vernacular, "we divulge the secrets of Minerva to the ridicule of blockheads, and expose our Diana to the Actaeons of a sensual age." The solution is distinctly Coleridgean: "It will be enough, if we abstain from appealing to the bad passions and low appetites, and confine ourselves to a strictly consequent method of reasoning" (F I 51–52). In the context of *The Friend* the references to Minerva and Diana are scarcely accidental, for the female virgin has two roles. She represents the wisdom of the soul guarded by learned men from the "promiscuous" public. But she also represents the pure object on behalf of which wisdom is necessary. In this capacity she inhabits the domestic sanctuary guarded by reason and "strictly" fenced about by method.

Two paragraphs after Coleridge contrasts the "sorceress," Pleasure, to the "solid WELL-BEING" of Truth, he makes it clear that what Truth protects from Pleasure is the purity of the family. The exercise of Truth, in this case, requires paternal censorship brought to bear on the

Gothic Romantics," *Journal of English and German Philology* 50 (1951): 517–21, and David V. Erdman, "The Extent of Coleridge's Contributions to the *Critical Review,*" *Bulletin of the New York Public Library* 63 (1959): 433–42, 445n.

[40]*Coleridge's Miscellaneous Criticism,* 376.

"lax morality" of the age, an epidemic that "extends from the nursery and the school to the cabinet and the senate":

> the patrons and admirers of such publications may receive the punish-
> ment of their indiscretion in the conduct of their sons and daughters. . . .
> The suspicion of methodism must be expected by every man of rank and
> fortune, who carries his examination respecting the books which are to
> lie on his breakfast-table, farther than to their freedom from gross verbal
> indecencies, and broad avowals of atheism in *the title-page*. For the exis-
> tence of an intelligent first cause may be ridiculed in the notes of one
> poem, or placed doubtfully as one of two or three possible hypotheses, in
> the very opening of another poem, and both be considered as works of
> safe promiscuous reading "virginibus puerisque:" [for girls and boys] and
> this too by many a father of a family, who would hold himself highly
> culpable in permitting his child to form habits of familiar acquaintance
> with a person of loose habits, and think it even criminal to receive into his
> house a private tutor without a previous inquiry concerning his opinions
> and principles.

This passage sets forth in concrete terms the intrusion of "the spirit of vulgar scandal and personal inquietude" into "the Closet and the Library," "the very Sanctuaries" of "refuge," where both girls and boys are feminized. The patriarch, who is dominant in the public realm by virtue of his "rank and fortune," translates public into familial power by becoming a closer reader. Careful study of the text marks the responsible exercise of parental discipline; the footnotes and hypothetical suggestions of poems and novels may be as morally revealing as the social text of reputation and conduct. The basis for ethical criticism is a "strictly consequent method of reasoning." Coleridge's view of censorship in the home is thus consistent with his approach to the question of government censorship of the press. He prefers to have the freedom of the press constrained not by prior legal restraint, but by libel laws that hold each author personally responsible for the effects of publication (F I 41–42; see also 72–75, 77–82). He is irresistibly drawn to the figure of the moral individual, forced to establish lines of ethical demarcation, as the potential hero or villain of reason.

If the father fails to practice critical method in the family setting, he will betray the sanctuary it is his duty to guard and become subject to the sorcery of pleasure. The man "alienated" from his own proper powers will resemble Hercules, who "in the evil day of his sensual bewitchment, lifts the spindles and distaffs of Omphale with the arm of a giant," dressed in female garb. The father has to avoid becoming effeminate in order to protect the feminine. After this threatening glimpse of the degraded Hercules, Coleridge invokes the goddess whose temple is profaned. To violate "our own moral being," he writes, "implies the same sort of prudence, as a priest of Diana would have manifested, who should have proposed to dig up the celebrated charcoal foundations of the mighty Temple of Ephesus, in order to furnish fuel for the burnt-offerings on its altars." More than the deprived goddess herself, he emphasizes ritual "foundations" and the structural integrity of the temple, systems that protect priests from "sensual bewitchment" (F I 36, 38–39).

The figure of the paternal censor can be taken as emblematic of the way much of the argumentative and figurative language of *The Friend* tries to insist that nonfictional prose is to fiction as masculine is to feminine and as method is to understanding. The critic's identity depends on establishing all three sets of antithetical differences, but such dichotomies, as we have repeatedly discovered, are subject to constant slippage; it is against the epidemic of association that they are erected in the first place. In generic terms this epidemic lurks in the way philosophical prose relies on the techniques of fiction. Novelistic episodes—above all, "The Story of Maria Eleanora Schöning"—become the vehicles for woman to reenter the text as both the giver and the recipient of pity. Coleridge then has to confront, in his guilty feelings about narrating the tale of her suffering, his own violence toward the feminine throughout *The Friend*.

Coleridge's halfhearted acquiescence to his readers' desire for "rational entertainment" is followed in the 1809 edition by a "miscellany" of two sonnets by Wordsworth, two prose "Specimens of Rabbinical Wisdom," and his translation, the "Hymn Before Sun-Rise, in the Vale of Chamouny." But *The Friend* is at war with the impulse to be popular. Coleridge really can write only for those capable of discovering the "intrinsic beauty" of truth itself, with "the illustrations . . . appropriate to it." The three "Landing-Places" of the 1818 edition are devoted to such "illustrations." The style of the landing-places is intended to combine the elevation of prose with the restfulness of fiction. The superior perspective of a "magnificent stair-case" remembered by Coleridge from his childhood provides the title of the "Landing-Places," and the metaphor of the "prospect" is explicit: "from the last and highest [landing-place] the eye commanded the whole spiral ascent with the marbled pavement of the great hall from which it seemed to spring up as if it merely used the ground on which it rested." The principles of a mode between fiction and nonfiction, which we might

call the "biography of mind," are set forth in one of the essays of the
second Landing-Place. Coleridge exerts himself to distinguish the
"spirit of genuine Biography" from the biographical "mania" of the
present "age of personality." The wrong kind of biography exhibits
the same uncontrolled associations that infect the novel. Comprising
"huge volumes of . . . minutiae," these "garrulous" biographies gratify only "the cravings of worthless curiosity" and "the habit of gossiping in general" (F II 151, 153–58; I 148–49, 356–57).

True biography, by contrast, is devoted to the analysis of "greatness
in the *mind,*" a clear assault on effeminate genres. Incidents that act
only on the sensual curiosity of the reader must be excluded, along
with "unprovoked abuse and senseless eulogy" that pander to a culture
obsessed with personal fame. Against the "ensnaring meretricious *pop-
ularness* in Literature" biography marches into battle, "all robustness
and manly vigor of intellect, all masculine fortitude of virtue" (F I 24).
The fullest demonstration of the principles of biography comes in
Coleridge's "Sketches of the Life of Sir Alexander Ball" in the third
Landing-Place. Coleridge had served as Ball's secretary in Malta when
Ball was the island's High Commissioner. As Ball's life exemplifies the
power of principle over accident, so Coleridge's "Sketches" illustrate
the attention to the moral architecture of experience proper to biographical writing.[41]

"The Story of Maria Eleanora Schöning," the first essay in the second Landing-Place and the one immediately preceding the essay on
biography, seems at first to serve the same ends as the "Life of Ball."
Coleridge places it "joining on to the section of Politics" as "proof of
the severe miseries which misgovernment may occasion in a country
nominally free" (F I 341). The account traces the survival of the heroine's moral purity through a hair-raising series of sufferings, assaults,
and injustices. Maria Schöning, whose mother died in childbirth,

[41]Numerous examples of such moral biographies appear in *The Friend,* some of
which I have already touched on. The comparison of the *"radical* natures" of Erasmus
and Voltaire, Luther and Rousseau in the first Landing-Place (F I 129–34) is prepared for
by a similar treatment of Charlemagne and Napoleon in the section on the communication of truth (F I 83–90), although some of these experiments have more in common
with the story of Maria Eleanora Schöning. Coleridge's essay on biography includes an
extract from the *Life of . . . North,* which serves both as a good example of the genre
and as a model of style: "his language gives us the very nerve, pulse, and sinew of a
hearty healthy conversational [and resoundingly masculine] *English"* that properly conveys "the kindly good-tempered spirit of the passage" (F I 359).

nurses her father in destitute circumstances until his death. At age seventeen, deprived of all their property by revenue officers and eventually locked out of her own house, she is raped on her father's grave. Eventually, she is rescued by a friend, Harlin. Harlin's ailing husband dies; the two women struggle against the most extreme poverty. Harlin desperately contemplates killing her infant so that the court, on her arrest, might place her older child in an orphanage. Maria offers herself and Harlin up to the authorities as already guilty of infanticide, in order to save the children—and Harlin's eternal soul. Even after the innocence of both has been revealed to the court, the execution of Harlin proceeds and Maria dies before she can be put to death (F I 342–55).

Maria's story initially anticipates a political conclusion, as the appearance of revenue officers and judges as villains suggests. Coleridge remarks several times in his introduction that the events he is about to describe could not have occurred "under a wise police and humane government" (in England), but are due to the "oppressive, and even mortal, taxation" of certain German states. But violence is not perpetrated solely by governmental systems. Revenue officers and judges enforcing irrational laws do account for the fact that Maria has no home and is left wandering helplessly to her father's grave. The man who rapes her there, however, is a mystery of human depravity, an unidentified "monster."

The entry of the rapist into the narrative causes a crisis of generic identity. The initial emphasis on heartless bureaucrats and unfair tax laws has been displaced by Coleridge's characterization of Maria herself. Her perfect innocence transforms the story, which began as a parable of injustice and inequity, into a confrontation between virtue and vice in the tradition of the novel of seduction. The account of injustice and the tale of violation are nevertheless connected, for Maria's purity makes her unable to speak in explanation and self-defense to the magistrates, who repeatedly misinterpret her. Silence, virtue, and victimage go together as Maria becomes inarticulate in the presence of authority: "not a word could she say for herself. Her tears and inarticulate sounds—for these, her judges had no eyes or ears" (F I 342, 347, 345).

Her silence at this crucial juncture is all the more striking given the fact that she has just been characterized in terms of her voice, a voice that conveys not purity alone, but the whole configuration of Coleridge's desire for the feminine:

The *peace, which passeth all understanding,* disclosed itself in all her looks and movements. It lay on her countenance, like a steady unshadowed moonlight: and her voice, which was naturally at once sweet and subtle, came from her, like the fine flute-tones of a masterly performer, which still floating at some uncertain distance, seem to be created by the player, rather than to proceed from the instrument. If you had listened to it in one of those brief sabbaths of the soul, when the activity and discursiveness of the thoughts are suspended, and the mind quietly *eddies* round, instead of flowing onward—(as at late evening in the spring I have seen a bat wheel in silent circles round and round a fruit-tree in full blossom, in the midst of which, as within a close tent of the purest white, an unseen nightingale was piping its sweetest notes)—in such a mood you might have half-fancied, half-felt, that her voice had a separate being of its own—that it was a living something, whose mode of existence was for the ear only: so deep was her resignation, so entirely had it become the unconscious habit of her nature, and in all she did or said, so perfectly were both her movements and her utterance without effort and without the appearance of effort! (F I 343)

Deirdre Coleman has traced the connection of this passage to Sara Hutchinson's work on *The Friend* with Coleridge and to Coleridge's notebook entries about her, including "Phantom," a manuscript poem of 1805. As Coleman notes, "Coleridge projects onto Sara his own momentary sensation of being totally fixed and absorbed in the object of his love."[42] Or perhaps "totally . . . absorbed" is too strongly put. The vicarious distance at which one hears flutes or birds or at which the bat hovers from the unseen nightingale marks precisely the relationship of Coleridge to the feminine sanctuaries he imagines. Maria's "unconscious habit" of "resignation" results in a posture that eschews both "effort" and "the appearance of effort": the defining attributes of masculine interpretation. The essential life of Sara/Maria speaks "for the ear only," the organ of sympathetic receptivity. The relationship between Sara/Maria's voice and Coleridge's ear dramatizes the feminine mode of understanding "which passeth all understanding"— understanding supplemental but unavailable to either logic or discourse.

The excessiveness of the passage, in which Coleridge's feelings for Sara Hutchinson enter into the tale of Maria Schöning, caused Southey

---

[42]For a full discussion of the basis for the identification of Maria Schöning and Sara Hutchinson, see Deirdre Coleman, "A Horrid (German) Tale in *The Friend* (No. 13)," *Wordsworth Circle* 12 (1981): 265–69; I quote from 266.

to note that it is "too beautiful for its place" in *The Friend*.[43] The lyricism is "too beautiful," too feminine, in the context of the moral, political, and biographical parables of the landing-places. But for Coleridge beauty is inseparable from victimage and ensuing depredation. In the novelistic "myth of female innocence and male guilt," one kind of excess predicts the other.[44] The extremes of mood corresponding to this plot—horror at and sympathy for the feminine—parallel Coleridge's own moral anxieties in *The Friend*. He casts out the feminine as sorceress but encounters her again as the nightingale whose rape he has guiltily written.

Before he narrates the rape of Maria Schöning, Coleridge confesses that he "can scarce summon the courage to tell, what I scarce know, whether I ought to tell." He invokes the contrast between his factual account and novels in order to justify proceeding with the tale: "Were I composing a tale of fiction, the reader might justly suspect the purity of my own heart" and would legitimately "resent" this episode "as an outrage wantonly offered to his imagination." Like "Monk" Lewis, the author of novels of seduction and rape is responsible for the impure heart of his male protagonist and is likewise guilty of "an outrage wantonly offered" to the (feminine) virtue of the reader. By writing nonfiction, Coleridge (until now) has been keeping his own heart pure and his readers' innocence intact. Then, remarkably, he begins to sympathize with the rapist:

> As I think of the circumstance, it seems more like a distempered dream: but alas! what is guilt so detestable other than a dream of madness, that worst madness, the madness of the heart? I cannot but believe, that the dark and restless passions must first have drawn the mind in upon themselves, and as with the confusion of imperfect sleep, have in some strange manner taken away the sense of reality, in order to render it possible for a human being to perpetrate what it is too certain that human beings have perpetrated. (F I 346)

Faced with the mystery of depravity, Coleridge draws on his notebook entries on the relationship of dreaming, guilt, and the body to identify with the "brutal" individual who raped Maria on holy ground. The mind's "dark . . . passions" produce a dream-like state in which "the

---

[43]Cited by Coleman from Southey's *Memorials of Coleorton*, in "A Horrid (German) Tale," 265, 268n.

[44]Spencer, *The Rise of the Woman Novelist*, 112.

sense of reality" is lost in "confusion." The illusion of unreality then allows disinhibited appetites to turn their dream into violent reality. If fiction is related, by virtue of its streamy associations, to nightmare, the rapist acts out a novelistic delusion. And like other aspects of the novel, it proves contagious. It frightens the theorist of nonfiction into sensations of guilt—sensations for which there is ample *textual* reason in the aggression toward feminine qualities which *The Friend* repeatedly displays.

The narrator, after a brief remark on the moral hazards of German churchyards, dwells on the gothic aftereffects of Maria's ravishment: the torments of shame ("Guiltless, she felt the pangs of guilt"); her preternatural sense of her father's rejection ("she imagined that she heard her father's voice bidding her leave his sight. . . . His last blessings now sounded in her ears like curses"); and the predictable atmospheric details ("in the deep and dead silence the only sounds audible were the slow blunt ticking of the church clock, and now and then the sinking down of bones in the nigh charnel house") (F I 347). The rest of the story contains the complicated account of the way Harlin and Maria manage, through an excess of innocence, to die. Coleridge makes no further effort to resist fictional style.

The public discourse of the eighteenth and nineteenth centuries could not compose the biography of a woman in the sense that Coleridge composed a philosophical biography of Alexander Ball. The tale of Maria Schöning attempts to narrate as history the political and social circumstances of a crime, but the nature of the crime causes both history and biography to be sexualized, transposed into the language of the novel.[45] As a preface to the essay on biography, the story of Maria Schöning calls that methodical genre into question in advance, for it entirely unsettles Coleridge's relationship to the exemplary mind or situation. Maria's feminine subjectivity evokes his ambivalent pathos at redundant spectacles of victimage: her actual sufferings, the narrator's pain in contemplating them, and his aggression in telling the story. He is unable to say what she stands for, finally, because he cannot sustain, in the face of such powerful demands on his pity, the defenses against the feminine that prevail in so much of *The Friend*. Nor will the reader of the "The Story of Maria Eleanora Schöning" be surprised when, in one of the most sustained of those defenses—the "Essays on the Principles of Method"—the gendered opposition of method and metonymy also comes undone.

---

[45]Armstrong, *Desire and Domestic Fiction*, 183–84.

Method and Mistress Quickley:
"Essays on the Principles of Method"

In one of the extraordinary dreams recorded in the notebooks of 1803 and 1804, Coleridge describes a female apparition that haunts the realm of pure intellect.[46] She represents logic but also sabotages its development by seducing the philosopher:

> My Dream—History of Scotus, deranged as a youth / imagining himself in the Land of Logic, lying on the Road & in the Road to the Kingdom of Truth, falls into a criminal Intercourse with a Girl, who is in Love with him, whom he considers as the Daughter of the King of the Land/— impersonation & absolute *Incarnation* of the most Abstract—. Detected he defends himself on this ground. O it was a wild dream, yet a deal of true psychological Feeling at the bottom of it. (N I 1824)

The "Land of Logic" in which this ambiguous female dwells is itself a dream world. Coleridge becomes Scotus in a state of deranged imagination, entering into a pilgrim's progress of philosophy. It would not be surprising to find logic disrupted by "criminal Intercourse with a Girl." The Coleridgean twist in this dream comes with the girl's relationship to "the King of the Land"—or, at least, her apparent relationship, for we know only that the protagonist "considers" her "as" such. But he seems to have convincing grounds for his belief. She is not only the "impersonation" but the "absolute *Incarnation*" of the "most Abstract"—logic? Truth? At any rate, though the intercourse may be "criminal," she appears to be the legitimate daughter of sovereign logic, by virtue of her ideality. Scotus "defends himself on . . . [the] ground" that he was seduced by the image of the object of his philosophical quest.

As Kathleen Coburn points out, this dream shares elements with another dream narrative of the same period. The earlier dream is also set in a land of logic, a melange of images from Christ's Hospital and Cambridge. Coleridge is harassed by an assortment of male figures: "a fat sturdy Boy who dabs a flannel in my face," "Friends" who "join in

---

[46]As Coleridge's notebooks have become more accessible, these dreams have become a focal point for interpretations of his life and works. Even in nonfeminist criticism the images of women in the dream narratives have been understood to possess unusual intensity and importance. See, in particular, Norman Fruman's *Coleridge: The Damaged Archangel* (New York: George Braziller, 1971), 385, 391–92, for his discussion of this dream, and Field's *Reality's Dark Dream*, 57–63.

the Hustle against me," and "a little weak contemptible wretch" who, in "a former Dream," had assaulted Coleridge's scrotum. Through this crowd of male associates and tormenters "rushes a university Harlot"; this figure "in white with her open Bosom certainly was the Cambridge Girl," Coleridge comments. She is half protective, since she takes him away from the group of "Friends" who are leagued against him, but she is also predatory. She "insists on my going with her," he escapes, and "she overtakes me again / I am not to go to another while she is 'biting'—these were her words /—this will not satisfy her" (N I 1726). This woman, with her aggressive sexuality, is quite different from the incarnation of the abstract Coleridge encounters in the later dream. Emerging from the chaotic "Hustle" created by Coleridge's fellow students, she represents the antithesis of logic. And yet, like the princess of the Kingdom of Truth, the harlot is a distillation of the speculative domain. As the "Scotus" dream makes clear, the horror of the Land of Logic inheres in the fact that it can be invaded by the body's appetites. But the mind also can divert itself from its narrow road by creating or discovering a feminine simulacrum of truth, possibly even truth itself, in a relationship of love or passion quite distinct from the protagonist's relationship to his expected intellectual goal. In the realm of truth (or, it is safe to say, of method) the philosopher who seeks pure reason somehow finds himself in love with it.

The "Essays on the Principles of Method" and the other essays in the last section of *The Friend* ("On the Grounds of Morals and Religion") resemble the world of Duns Scotus's dream.[47] Rationality and desire are both incompatible and indistinguishable. Method is introduced in its conventional guise as the rational authority of masculine discourse, in relation to which woman stands as the negative other. But also, and increasingly, method is an application of religious hope—the hope of persons for one another and of the individual for salvation. And since hope is related to sympathy, nurture, and divinatory understanding, method has a womanly nuance. Method is not merely a logical or a rhetorical mode, but a mode of transcendental desire. It exceeds (though it does not deny) rationalism through an "intuition" or "faith" oriented to "Being" and "Revelation" (F I 460, 514, 516). The methodical mind thus moves continuously between apparently opposite per-

---

[47]For background on the "Essays on Method," see Alice D. Snyder's edition of *Coleridge's Treatise on Method, as Published in The Encyclopaedia Metropolitana* (London: Constable & Co., 1934). She includes commentary on the difference between the *Treatise* and the "Essays," as well as the "Prospectus" of the Encyclopaedia Metropolitana and relevant manuscript fragments. See also James R. de J. Jackson, *Method and Imagination in Coleridge's Criticism* (London: Routledge & Kegan Paul, 1969).

spectives: the point of view of the scientist or prophet who sees law revealed in hierarchical patterns and the point of view of the believer whose sense of cosmic proportion comes from yearning toward his place in an intellectually defensible system.[48]

The "Essays on the Principles of Method," then, exemplifies the problem that we face in approaching all of Coleridge's later philosophical-theological works. For as he merges the legitimate reductions of science with the Christian soul's private need for strength, the gendered metaphors of difference apparent in so many earlier texts become more difficult to isolate. The meaning of this growing ambiguity is unclear. To the extent that the philosophical system becomes the way to mercy, has the realm of logic absorbed the feminine into itself? Has the masculine reason suffered a crisis of conscience and become feminized? Or does the Christian method Coleridge recommends in *The Friend* manifest the brotherhood of the clerisy, with its antifeminine tendencies?

In the eight "Essays on the Principles of Method" Coleridge relies even more than he usually does on the stereotypical difference between masculine logic and feminine association. Although this binary configuration rapidly becomes irresolute, in the chapters devoted to method it is the dominant metaphor. He begins with a polemical question: "What is that which first strikes us, and strikes us at once, in a man of education?" Coleridge "does not discover method abstractly, he discovers it in the man," in the personal matrix of motive and intention.[49] The "difference" that "so instantly distinguishes the man of superior mind that . . . 'we cannot stand under the same arch-way during a shower of rain, *without finding him out,*'" inheres in the purposiveness of his talk, "the unpremeditated and evidently habitual *arrangement* of his words, grounded on the habit of foreseeing, in each integral part, or . . . sentence, the whole that he then intends to communicate. However irregular and desultory his talk, there is *method* in the fragments" (F I 448–49).[50] Coleridge at once juxtaposes the discourse of

[48]As Elinor S. Shaffer concludes, "Coleridge's analysis yields the insight that culture is not rational; that it cannot be maintained by reason; yet that the culture of his own society has always been accompanied by a claim to rationality, and that the irrational culture must itself die if it cannot maintain its touch with that claim." "Metaphysics of Culture: Kant and Coleridge's *Aids to Reflection,*" *Journal of the History of Ideas* 31 (1970): 218.

[49]Christensen, *Coleridge's Blessed Machine of Language,* 233–34.

[50]Coleridge's essays on method evince what Paul K. Alkon has referred to as the "ambivalence towards displayed method" apparent in English critical thought on method in the eighteenth century. Despite the fact that Coleridge set himself against the unconnected or aphoristic essay, calling for a connected style that would rejoin "interest

the "man of education" to "describing or relating" as performed by "an ignorant man." The uneducated speaker's account has not undergone method's metamorphosis but replicates the order of experience: "the objects and events recur in the narration in the same order, and with the same accompaniments, however accidental and impertinent, as they had first occurred to the narrator. The necessity of taking breath, the efforts of recollection, and the abrupt rectification of its failures, produce all his pauses; and with exception of the *'and then,'* the *'and there,'* and the still less significant *'and so,'* they constitute likewise all his connections" (F I 449). The serial "ands" of "unpremeditated" talk are a verbal image of the materials of manual labor, laid out in an operational sequence instead of an interpretive one. Metonymy is the antithesis of method. When the opening contrast between two men, one "educated" and one "ignorant," is immediately recast in the comparison of Mistress Quickley and Hamlet, metonymy is clearly defined in terms of both class and gender.

As in the subsequent discussion of Shakespeare's reflective prince and "easy-yielding" landlady, however, the difference between the learned man and the laborer becomes blurred. In this case it does so through Coleridge's raising up of the worker. The temporality of method is the source of its power to spiritualize the everyday. In the domestic economy of all classes the "first merit" is "that *every thing is in its place.*" Like "clock-work," regular habits "at once divide and announce the silent and otherwise indistinguishable lapse of time":

> But the man of methodical industry and honorable pursuits, does more: he realizes its ideal divisions, and gives a character and individuality to its moments. If the idle are described as killing time, he may be justly said to call it into life and moral being, while he makes it the distinct object not only of the consciousness, but of the conscience. He organizes the hours, and gives them a soul: and that, the very essence of which is to fleet away, and evermore *to have been,* he takes up into his own permanence, and communicates to it the imperishableness of a spiritual nature. . . . it is less truly affirmed, that He lives in time, than that Time lives in him. His days, months, and years, as the stops and punctual marks in the records of duties performed, will survive the wreck of worlds, and remain extant when time itself shall be no more. (F I 449–50)

---

in transitions with concern for sequential order," the nature of the Coleridgean text itself is sufficient evidence of his own "ambivalence" on the subject. "Critical and Logical Concepts of Method from Addison to Coleridge," 103, 120. In this passage the quoted portion is from Samuel Johnson. See F I 448n.

A moment of extraordinary interest, this ode to the spiritual ordering of time finds in male work a common ground that temporarily erases class differences. And compounded with the brief transcendental emotion this affinity inspires, of course, is Coleridge's sense of the link between the salvation of his soul and being able to live up, at last, to the "moral being" of time expressed in work.

As Coleridge turns to his Shakespearean examples, however, the shift from labor to literature corresponds to the reappearance of social distinctions, acting together to prove the pertinence of cultural inequality. His three representatives of the "uncultivated" as opposed to the "well-disciplined" understanding are Pompey the Clown in *Measure for Measure,* the Nurse in *Romeo and Juliet,* and, of course, Mistress Quickley in *Henry IV Part I.* Each of these figures could be used to show how authority figures attempt to fend off comic narrative or, more specifically, how they resist the comic narratives of opportunistic women. For since Pompey's highly circumstantial self-defense before the justice centers on his wife and on the influence of the bawdy Mistress Over-done, all three examples conflate metonymic literalism with women's lasciviousness and gossip. But Coleridge refers only in passing to the Nurse and the Clown, so we will concentrate, as he does, on Mistress Quickley.

The passage Coleridge cites contains "Mrs. Quickley's relation of the circumstances of Sir John Falstaff's debt to her." In the context of the "Essays on Method" it is meant to demonstrate that the discourse of "the uneducated" is produced by "an habitual submission of the understanding to mere events and images . . . independent of any power in the mind to classify or appropriate them." But another reading is possible. Mistress Quickley's tirade tries to hold Falstaff to his proposal. Her indignation takes the form of an outpouring of precise details in order to make it impossible for him not to remember his promise. Every part of the episode, whether logically connected to the discussion of marriage or not, makes it harder for Falstaff to pretend that he does not recall it. Quickley does not slip inadvertently into uncontrolled associations but deliberately summons the whole sensory record of the occasion in order to conjure it up in Falstaff's memory (and, she hopes, his conscience):

FALSTAFF. What is the gross sum that I owe thee?

Mrs. QUICKLY. Marry, if thou wert an honest man, thyself and the money too. Thou didst swear to me upon a parcel-gilt goblet, sitting in my dolphin chamber, at the round table, by a sea-coal fire, on Wednes-

day in Whitsun week, when the prince broke thy head for likening his
father to a singing-man in Windsor—thou didst swear to me then, as I
was washing thy wound, to marry me and make me my lady thy wife.
Canst thou deny it? Did not goodwife Keech, the butcher's wife, come in
then and call me gossip Quickley?—coming into to borrow a mess of
vinegar: telling us she had a good dish of prawns—whereby thou didst
desire to eat some—whereby I told thee they were ill for a green wound,
&c. &c. &c. [Henry IV II i 74–86 (var.)] (F I 450–51)[51]

The question "Canst thou deny it?" reveals the essentially judicial style
of this prosecutorial narration. By insisting that Mistress Quickley's
thoughts are not connected by self-awareness, Coleridge assimilates
her to the female gossips and novel-readers who are damned elsewhere
in *The Friend* as the agents of "Anglo-gallican" culture. Her narrative
comprises images "interlinked" only by "time and place," he charges,
and thus is structured by the associative epidemic that infects literary
periodicals, reform politics, and family morals.

Hamlet then enters as the antithesis of Mistress Quickley; he personifies the "enviable results" of the "science of Method." To set up a
contrast between two narrative passages, Coleridge selects Hamlet's
account of his voyage to England, as told to Horatio. By italicizing key
lines in two long selections from Act V, scene ii, he makes the point
that "all the digressions and enlargements consist of reflections, truths,
and principles of general and permanent interest, either directly expressed or disguised in playful satire." At the same time, he claims,
Hamlet has the material facts under control, "not one introduced
which could have been omitted without injury to the intelligibility of
the whole process" (F I 451–52). Leaving aside such atmospheric rhetoric as the picture of "My sea-gown scarf'd about me, in the dark,"
Coleridge seeks to demonstrate that method does not dispense with
circumstantial narrative, but organizes it.

In this attempt he is not entirely successful. The marked portions of
Hamlet's speeches do leap up to generalization: "There's a divinity that
shapes our ends, / Rough-hew them how we will"; " 'Tis dangerous
when the baser nature comes / Between the pass and fell incensed
points / Of mighty opposites." But Hamlet's exemplary status as the
methodical man is undercut by the pointed question addressed by
Horatio, "How was this sealed?" In light of the omission this query

<hr/>

[51]The same text is used to make a similar point in J. J. Engel's *Schriften* XII (Berlin,
1806). Engel's works were also the source of the "rabbinical" tales in *The Friend* and
other borrowings. See F I 370n, 451n.

exposes, Coleridge concludes, "we should find both *immethodical;* Hamlet from the excess, Mrs. Quickley from the want, of reflection and generalization . . . Method, therefore, must result from the due mean or balance between our passive impressions and the mind's own re-action on the same." This statement suggests that Hamlet and "Mrs. Quickley" are somehow symmetrical in their deviations from method. The dualism of Coleridge's presentation reinforces this: "We wished to bring forward, each for itself, these two elements of Method," he explains, to present "each of the two components [form and matter] as separately as possible." Nonetheless, Hamlet's "exuberance of mind . . . interferes" only with "the *forms* of Method," whereas Mistress Quickley's "sterility of mind . . . is wholly destructive of Method itself." The presence or absence of *"the leading Thought,"* the mental "INITIATIVE," becomes the final criterion of method. Hamlet's excessive reflectiveness is continuous with the perfect mean of "genial method" in "To be? or not to be?"[52] Quickley's alleged mental passivity establishes her as the opposite, the negation, of method: "the uneducated and unreflecting talker overlooks *all* mental relations, both logical and psychological; and consequently precludes all Method, that is not purely accidental. Hence the nearer the things and incidents in time and place, the more distant, disjointed, and impertinent to each other, and to any common purpose will they appear in his narration" (F I 453–55).

By scrutinizing the relationship between method and the theme of sovereignty in Coleridge's examples, Christensen makes sense of why Coleridge sees Hamlet's irony as well as his generalizations as an aspect of method. But Christensen does less well with Mistress Quickley. He subscribes to Coleridge's reading of her speech as an expression of "the anarchic whirl of her seamy establishment" and a symptom of "her immethodical mind and . . . spindrift world."[53] Like Coleridge, Christensen treats Quickley only as representative of the indeterminacy into which even the most methodical mind can slip, without tracing how she disappears from the transcendental equations of the "Essays on Method." In fact, Mistress Quickley's discourse sustains its difference; it is not translated into a moral or philosophical term that can enter into the chiasmic logic of *The Friend*.

Mistress Quickley belongs neither to the spiritualized labor of the

---

[52]As in Coleridge's use of the term "genial criticism," the word "genial" here seems to designate genius joined with conscience and desirous of sympathy.

[53]Christensen, *Coleridge's Blessed Machine of Language,* 248–49; see also 258, 262–63.

"shrewd and able" worker nor to the digressive reflections of Hamlet. A case could be made for reading the associative stories told by comic characters in Shakespeare's plays as proofs in which the density of remembered detail is itself evidence of the legitimacy of the speaker's demand. According to such an interpretation, Quickley's language could be viewed as motivated by foresight, intention, and classification. Coleridge even provides an opening for such a conclusion when he considers the exceptions to the rule that "from the confluence of innumerable impressions . . . the mere passive memory must . . . tend to confusion." In cases like that of Lear's "thunder-bursts," for instance, "the predominance of some mighty Passion takes the place of the guiding Thought, and the result presents the method of Nature, rather than the habit of the Individual" (F I 456). Mistress Quickley's determination to make Falstaff see the light fails to qualify as a sufficiently mighty passion, however. If too methodical to function simply as the indeterminate "eddy" within method, her speech still cannot be drawn into the "amicable exchanges" of the understanding.[54] Details of the body, food, and furniture verify her memory of Falstaff's proposal in the service of self-interested justice. She articulates the somatic domain, the threshold of sensation. In Mistress Quickley's tirade the close conjunction of wounding, wooing, and eating resists the elevations of method more than the speech's syntactic structure does. Like Hamlet in the graveyard, Mistress Quickley might well be asking, "Why may not imagination trace the noble dust of Alexander, till he find it stopping a bung-hole?" "Flying from the sense of reality" into the Land of Logic is hastened by contemplating the scatalogical aspects of the real (F I 455).[55]

There is another side to the dynamics of gender in the "Essays on Method," however, a side that does not enter into the contrast between Hamlet and Mistress Quickley. In the parts of the dedication referring to Mrs. Gillman or in the description of the magical voice of Maria Eleanora Schöning, the intuitive aspect of the feminine enters the "Essays" as divination. As in Schleiermacher's hermeneutic theory, feminine intuition does reason's work without the analytical effort of the masculine intellect. Method takes effort and results in an articulated retrospective narrative of its procedures. "Sense," which comes in obliquely as feminine understanding, arrives at the same conclusions.

[54]Ibid., 258.
[55]See Snyder, ed., *Coleridge's Treatise on Method,* 26–35, for Coleridge's more comprehensive discussion of Shakespeare's genius in that context.

But because it is nonverbal, having renounced explanation as a form of aggression, Sense cannot either know or tell how it got there.

In the "Postscript" appended to one of the essays that lays the groundwork for the "Essays on Method," Coleridge defines modes of creativity. The definitions of Genius, Talent, and Cleverness are familiar enough to any reader of Coleridge as faculties that produce a hierarchy of mental operations. But the characterization of "Sense" presents femininity as a labor-saving strategy for the philosophical male. Intervening between the second and third faculties, Talent and Cleverness, "Sense" is distinguished by its mental style rather than by its results: "By SENSE I understand that just balance of the faculties which is to the judgment what health is to the body. The mind seems to act *en masse,* by a synthetic rather than an analytic process: even as the outward senses, from which the metaphor is taken, perceive immediately, each as it were, by a peculiar tact or intuition, without any consciousness of the mechanism by which the perception is realized" (F I 419).

One can trace here the series of associations which leads Coleridge to the feminine. "Sense" is likened to a bodily state, to a healthy organism acting synthetically, *"en masse."* The comparison to physiological well-being immediately produces the opposition between consciousness and the body and then the link between consciousness and effort. Immediate perception, "without any consciousness of the mechanism by which the perception is realized," is attained without work. "Tact" and "intuition" refer to thinking that mimes the body's spontaneity and ease. And by the time we arrive at such words as "tact," we are very close to personifications of the feminine:

> This is often exemplified in well-bred, unaffected, and innocent women. I know a lady, on whose judgment, from constant experience of its rectitude, I could rely almost as on an oracle. But when she has sometimes proceeded to a detail of the grounds and reasons for her opinion— then, led by similar experience, I have been tempted to interrupt her with—"I will take your advice," or, "I shall act on your opinion: for I am sure, you are in the right. But as to the *fors* and *becauses,* leave them to me to find out." (F I 419–20)

The balance in such women between cultivated habit, on the one hand, and the absence of reflectiveness, on the other, is precarious. They must be "well-bred" but "unaffected and innocent." Culture must have taken hold without making its mark. Intuition is instantaneous and therefore without an awareness of sequence or internal causality. The advantage of manners, apparently, is that the finer aspects of judgment are taught without analysis. The "lady" of unusual "rectitude" arrives at the proper opinion even ahead of Coleridge, who is occupied with "the *fors* and *becauses.*" But her charm (to him) lies in the fact that she cannot account for her position. She is not a comic figure in the manner of Mistress Quickley. Though she draws a smile from Coleridge as he contemplates the disproportion between her will and her understanding, her sympathetic powers protect her from the satire aimed at Shakespeare's comic narrators.

The importance of such women in creating a sense of community and safety becomes evident in Coleridge's closing remarks on the politics of "Sense." This faculty manifests "a desire to remain in sympathy with the *general mind* of the age or country, and a feeling of the necessity and utility of *compromise.*" Transforming sympathy into compromise, and compromise into constitution, he concludes, "If Genius is the initiative, and Talent the administrative, [then] Sense is the *conservative,* branch, in the intellectual republic" (F I 420). Embedded in this statement is the equation between harmony in the family and the political soundness of English life. The influence of English women, working through their private circles, preserves national unity. In the face of religious, party, and class tensions, what "sensible" understanding conserves is the will to community itself. Fixed political opinion yields, through such mediations, to the salutary wish "to remain in sympathy."

The "Sense" of women, which is both extrasensory and commonsensical, has a strong affinity to the religious direction of method. Here and in Coleridge's subsequent prose writings, a totalizing system of philosophical Christianity is increasingly identified with the desire for hope and mercy. As he approaches the "Essays on Method," Coleridge focuses on understanding as a mode of faith. In moments of doubt, when we are forced to make ethical decisions based on "dim and indistinct" apprehensions, understanding must flow from belief, and belief from tradition: "the imperfection of humanity . . . enforces the precept, Believe that thou mayest understand. . . . The Greek verb [*synienai*], which we render by the word, understand, is literally the same as our own idiomatic phrase, to go along with." Method, he states unequivocally, is "inseparable from the idea of God," and therefore scientific "intuition" is synonymous with "stedfast faith" (F I 428, 459; see also F I 325).

Perhaps the best indication that method is an economy of desire comes in its link to processes of transition. If the term means "literally a *way*, or *path* of *Transit*," then what matters most is the continuing aspiration toward systematic vision, not the system itself. The "connective" nature of methodical transition fulfills the need for relationship and, ultimately, for love realized in the realm of ideas. System absorbs the familial. Feelings, which in "Dejection" had to be repressed or evaded through abstruse metaphysics, are now allied with the goals of philosophy. Representing the proper emotional tone is Johann Kepler, whom Coleridge lauds for the spirit that pervades his scientific reasoning and overflows in his "affectionate reverence," "cordiality," and "generous enthusiasm" for his predecessors. Once associated by Coleridge with women, "fervent tones of faith and consolation" characterize the dialogue of God and men and of men with each other. The genealogy of spiritual science displays a lineage constituted by love without resentment or otherness. Faith reveals a system accomplished "when the antithesis between experience and belief . . . [is] taken up into the unity of intuitive reason" (F I 485–86, 519). The "predisposing warmth" of grace brings about the sudden mutual regard of science, philosophy, and religion.

Religion "compels the reason to pass out of itself," as reason has first compelled the subject to pass out of itself. Like the good philosopher, reason strives to determine "the ground of the coincidence between . . . the laws of matter and the ideas of the pure intellect." Once this ground is discovered in religion, the problem of reconciling philosophy and experimental science is solved. God is "at once the *ideal* of the reason and the cause of the material world," and "Religion therefore is the ultimate aim of philosophy"; it supplies "the copula . . . common to all [the Sciences], as integral parts of one system." The horizontal (or chiasmic) movement of the "copula" is what the mind engaged in the transitions of method moves toward. "And this is METHOD," the passage just cited concludes, "the link or *mordant* by which philosophy becomes scientific and the sciences philosophical" (F I 463). The "system," the revealed arrangement of parts and wholes from the perspective of eternity, is the goal of Coleridge's desire.

In most of Coleridge's prose writings the feminine haunts logic as the antidote for the mind's aggressive dissections. As the system of religion takes over this process of ethical compensation, Coleridge treats rationality more kindly. In the process, he shows with unusual clarity the extent to which the ascent toward the abstract is also a journey of moral purification. The "forethoughtful query" of science emerges from "the pure and impersonal reason . . . freed from the limits, the passions, the prejudices, the peculiar habits of the human

understanding, natural or acquired; but above all, pure from the arrogance, which leads man to take the forms and mechanism of his own
mere reflective faculty, as the measure of nature and of Deity." One
can avoid "arrogance" only if the entire realm of the "merely *subjective*"
is left behind. The alternative to such transcendence is violent inquiry
that abuses nature as the German authorities abused Maria Eleanora
Schöning: it "bind[s] down material nature under the inquisition of
reason, and force[s] from her, as by torture, unequivocal answers to
prepared and preconceived questions." The "impersonal reason" produces an absolute but denatured humility. Through "the discipline, by
which the human mind is purified from its idols . . . and raised to the
contemplation of ideas," the realm of experience diminishes in value (F
I 530–31, 490–93). Subjectivity, in this triumph of impersonality, is
not unlike the innocent and tactful woman who helps others to truths
she cannot know.

One might expect, once the systematic nature of thought has been
granted, that Coleridge could regard its abstract character more favorably. But "abstraction" still has almost exclusively negative associations for him.[56] His animus against it does not derive from an aversion
to generalization. Reductions grounded in principle, law, or idea are
admissible; only reductions stemming from the falsely systematic understanding are the mere "outlines and *differencings*" of error. Abstraction represents an alienated relationship between the mind and its objects. The crucial factor in distinguishing abstraction from method is
the subject's grasp of its relative position:

> The ground-work . . . of all true philosophy is the full apprehension of
> the difference between the contemplation of reason, namely, that intui-

---

[56]See Smith, *The Politics of Language,* 22–25, 45–46, 126–44 passim, for the emerging
bias against abstraction, developed (with quite different politics) by Horne Tooke and
Edmund Burke, both of whom influenced Coleridge's position. Coleridge's point of
view on abstraction was not wholly one of opposition. At times he seemed to regard it
as part of all symbolic representation: "The fact is this: the Friend takes the word in its
proper meaning, Abstraho, I draw from. The image, by which I represent to myself an
Oak tree, is no fac simile or adequate *icon* of the Tree, but is *abstracted* from it by my
eye." He goes on, in the margins of *The Friend,* to distinguish between the meanings of
to "draw from" and to "draw" the "attention from" something or to *"leave behind."* A
more accessible distinction in one of Coleridge's marginal notes to *The Friend* links the
process of detaching the mind from a percept to that of constituting the "system-
subject": "from my very childhood I have been accustomed to *abstract* and as it were
unrealize whatever of more than common interest my eyes dwelt on; and then by a sort
of transfusion and transmission of my consciousness to identify myself with the
Object—" (F I 520–21n).

tion of things which arises when we possess ourselves, as one with the whole . . . and that which presents itself when . . . we think of ourselves as separated beings, and place nature in antithesis to the mind, as object to subject, thing to thought, death to life. This is abstract knowledge, or the science of the mere understanding. (F I 515, 520–21)

An intellectual system has become a metaphor for the subject in love with itself. In such "self-affirmation," Coleridge continues, dejection yields to the combined pleasures of autonomy and communion: "It is an eternal and infinite self-rejoicing, self-loving, with a joy unfathomable, with a love all comprehensive." Writ large, this model of the self becomes the structure of the universe. The "economy" of the "irrational creation" reveals how "the powers of the Whole" are "tempered" for particular species. And by a further analogy, humanity "becomes a system in and for itself, a world of its own" (F I 515, 520–21, 517). The vision of the thrice-woven circle that marks the climax of "Kubla Khan" has been accomplished in the kingdom of philosophy. The "Abyssinian maid" of that poem, called on to "revive within me / . . . symphony and song," has been internalized in the "self-rejoicing, self-loving" economy of method, along with the visionary's appreciative audience ("And all should cry, Beware! Beware! / His flashing eyes, his floating hair!" (PW 298).

If, in concluding, we leap over the years between *The Friend* and the works of Coleridge's last decade, we can trace the implications of the relationship between system and desire which has emerged in our reading of the "Essays on Method." The letters on the Scriptures written in the mid–1820s and posthumously published as *Confessions of an Inquiring Spirit* (1840) contain a description of Christian faith as the experience of need and wish fulfillment. But hope and pity, so closely connected with the ethics of understanding which rely elsewhere on figurations of the feminine, increasingly flow from systematic theology instead. *Confessions of an Inquiring Spirit* presents the relationship between readers and the Bible as a hermeneutic dialogue. The communion between "Faith and Scripture" takes the form of "divine reciprocality." On the reader's side, *need* is the crucial attribute: "The needy soul has found supply, the feeble a help, the sorrowful a comfort; yea, be the recipiency the least that can consist with moral life, there is an answering grace ready to enter" (CIS 66, 68). Coleridge grounds his argument against the inspired authorship (and hence against the infallibility) of the Scriptures on the shared experience of need. The doctrine of inspiration turns the biblical poet into an "*auto-*

maton." But if the modern Christian can approach scriptural texts in a spirit of identification, he (the pronoun is unavoidable) will discover "men of like faculties and passions with myself, mourning, rejoicing, suffering, triumphing." These are the confessions, Coleridge begins in the first letter, "of one . . . who—groaning under a deep sense of infirmity and manifold imperfection—feels the want, the necessity, of religious support;—who cannot afford to lose any the smallest buttress." His own sense of dependency and yearning establishes his affinity with biblical authors, "frail and fallible men like ourselves" (CIS 53, 39, 58).

According to the symmetrical logic of the *Confessions,* identification between authors and reader leads to the perfect equivalence of wish and fulfillment. "The truth revealed through Christ" finds "proof of its divine authority in its fitness to our nature and needs." Scripture provides "a correspondent for every movement toward the Better felt in [men's] own hearts," and the test of this correspondence is the experience of answered need: "as long as each man asks on account of his wants, and asks what he wants, no man will discover aught . . . deficient in the . . . many-chambered storehouse" of the Bible (CIS 64, 69).

This is the antithesis of a Freudian theory of desire, in which wish fulfillment must always proceed covertly and emerge through the mechanisms of repression in distorted forms. For Coleridge, religious desire operates in a realm of transparent reciprocity necessarily unlike the experience of dreams. Spiritual "yearnings" within the faithful heart "are not dreams or fleeting singularities, no voices heard in sleep, or spectres which the eye suffers but not perceives." Gratification is evidence of grace: "whatever finds me, bears witness for itself that it has proceeded from a Holy Spirit." And the sense of being found, not surprisingly, is like being in love: "Suppose that the Scriptures themselves from this time had continued to rise in his esteem and affection—the better understood, the more dear; as in the countenance of one, whom through a cloud of prejudices we have at least learned to love and value above all others, new beauties dawn on us from day to day, till at length we wonder how we could at any time have thought it other than most beautiful" (CIS 68, 42, 64).

In a subdued way metaphors of the feminine persist in Coleridge's view of a symmetrical yet affect-laden Christian scheme, as this evocation of a beloved "countenance" suggests. The transformation of the person of Sara Hutchinson into a structure of gratification crystallizes as one of the fundamental elements of Coleridge's later poetry as well as his prose. Family relationships fail in "An Exile" (1805), where intimacy within the catalog of "Friend, Lover, Husband, Sister, Brother!" mocks actual loss (PW 392). Such deprivation then seems to generate the image in "Phantom" (1805) of a radiant female face from which "All accident of kin and birth" has been expunged (PW 393). Indeed, "The Phantom" suggests that Coleridge has consciously accepted Sara Hutchinson's status as a projection of his own needs and desires. "Constancy to an Ideal Object" (1825?) similarly acknowledges as a mental projection the "yearning Thought! that liv'st but in the brain":

> as though some dear embodied Good,
> Some living Love before my eyes there stood
> With answering look a ready ear to lend[.]

If "Hope without an object cannot live," Coleridge wants both to have and to be that object (PW 455–56, 447). Hope is the desire that others will be hopeful, in an extension of faith and belief toward him. "Hope" is also Coleridge's name for the desire that he himself will be able to hope for precisely such hopeful love.

The ambiguity of his conception of hope emerges in "The Pang More Sharp Than All," a poem remarkable for the explicitness of the sexual and familial imagery that supplies his "Allegory." Hope, or Hope's child, once resided with the speaker in a "home of bliss." The flirtatious innocence of this figure, in an extended conceit, is likened to

> the pretty shame
> Of babe, that tempts and shuns the menaced kiss,
> From its twy-cluster'd hiding place of snow!
> Pure as the babe, I ween, and all aglow
> As the dear hopes, that swell the mother's breast—
> Her eyes down gazing o'er her clasped charge,—
> Yet gay as that twice happy father's kiss,
> That well might glance aside, yet never miss,
> Where the sweet mark emboss'd so sweet a targe—
> Twice wretched he who hath been doubly blest!
>
> (lines 11–20)

By the time this stanza ends, hope has been diffused throughout the domestic scene. The child itself represents hope; the mother is "aglow" with her "dear hopes," which shed their radiance over both son and father; and the father, who is blessed with two objects of hope, bestows kisses that cannot miss. The father (in one of Coleridge's longest-recurring fantasies) almost becomes his wife's other child as he gazes at the "twy-clustered hiding place" offered by her breasts. Once the child vanishes, the circle disintegrates. A substitute boy and girl, "twin-births" of a "foster-dame," replace the mother and son. The male twin is "Esteem"; the female, "Kindness," and the poem ends with an expression of grief over the girl's reluctant imitation of Hope: "O pang all pangs above / is Kindness counterfeiting absent Love!" "Still there lives within my secret heart," the poet confesses, "The magic image of the magic Child" (PW 458–59). It is clear enough, I think, that Coleridge gave up on women and on domesticity—which is not to say that he abandons the feminine as an ethic, tone, or stance. It is equally obvious that he never gave up on desire itself or on the desire for desire as a spiritual motion that could lift him toward comfort. The expression, in his later religious writings, of a fundamental need for a divine response fills the void haunted right to the end by the "Phantom" and the "Magic Child."

Nevertheless, if, in fact, there is such a substitution of God for woman as Coleridge's object of Hope—a substitution that, as certain late poems indicate, is never complete or stable—we are still left with the problem of method.[57] For if the figure of love as wife and mother persists in Coleridge's writing of the 1820s and 1830s, however evanescently, the master diagram of the Christian system appears with equal intensity. The figure of the "Noetic Pentad" is evident in numerous versions besides the one that stands at the beginning of *Confessions of an Inquiring Spirit:* in the notebooks of 1818 (N III 4427); in *Aids to Reflection;* in Coleridge's lecture to the Royal Society of Literature, "On the Prometheus of Aeschylus"; in a letter of 1829; and in his marginalia in Southey's edition of *Pilgrim's Progress and Life of John Bunyan* (1830), to mention the fullest examples.[58]

Coleridge was fond of this *topos,* despite at least one editor's distaste for the "uncouth look" of "algebraic symbols" dispersed throughout "the text of an ordinary essay."[59] The diagram maps the synthesis of grammar, logic, and a complex version of the Trinity.[60] The surplus of

[57]See, for example, "Love's Apparition and Evanishment" and "Phantom or Fact: A Dialogue in Verse" (PW 488–89, 484–85).

[58]*Aids to Reflection,* ed. Henry Nelson Coleridge (New York: N. Tibbals, 1872), 130–31; *The Literary Remains of Samuel Taylor Coleridge,* ed. Henry Nelson Coleridge, 2 vols. (London: William Pickering, 1836), II, 343–49; *Collected Letters* VI 816–18; *Marginalia* CC XII, I 806.

[59]"On the Prometheus of Aeschylus," *Literary Remains* II, 342.

[60]For a detailed discussion of the relationship between logic and grammar in Coleridge's *Logic,* written between 1819 and 1828, see James McKusick, *Coleridge's Philosophy of Language* (New Haven: Yale University Press, 1986), chap. 5.

meaning that seems to inhere in formulaic presentation is derived from the sheer concentration of key terms and relationships which the diagram permits. The recurrences of the "Pentad" suggest that it had for its author some of the sublime efficacy of certain prose passages (the "Ancient of Days" piece, for example, taken from the notebooks and used repeatedly).[61] The "Pentad," that is, functions as a rhetorical gesture. For Coleridge, if not for his readers, it delivers the sensation of visionary power—the view from the mountain, if its pyramidical shape can be taken as significant. It yields the sensation of struggling through "the holy jungle of transcendental metaphysics" to the peak of intellectual mastery.[62] Before applying a prose version of this schema to his comparison of Hebrew and Greek 'philosophemes,' he concedes that it "will seem strange and obscure at first reading,—perhaps fantastic. But it will only seem so. Dry and prolix, indeed, it is to me in the writing, full as much as it can be to others in the attempt to understand it. But I know that, once mastered, the idea will be the key to the whole cypher of the Aeschylean mythology."[63]

This diagrammatic apotheosis of method may itself be a kind of "key," although the Casaubon-like pathos of the claim cannot be overlooked. If it is not a key to "the whole cypher"—the reconciliation of philosophy and religion—it may at least provide a key to the dynamics of Coleridge's systems. The tendency to encode desire, to construct a diagrammatic "cypher" for the narrative of yearning and gratification, results in the depersonalized image of the "Noetic Pentad." The divine embrace of the inquiring spirit is transposed into the internal coherence of the system—and vice versa. But the hyperbolic climax of equivalence and relationship represented in the fivefold formula can be understood only as the projected ending of the romance of hope.

---

[61]See F II 73–74, BL I 80, and LS 25.
[62]"On the Prometheus of Aeschylus," *Literary Remains* II, 349.
[63]Ibid., 342.

PART III

FULLER

CHAPTER 7

Performing Interpretation

Within Romanticism

Margaret Fuller (1810–50) intervenes directly in the nineteenth-century characterization of the romantic. Fuller's feminism emerges as a complex rearrangement of the languages available to her, including the traditions of romanticism in its German, French, British, and Boston aspects. The first "romantic" character to take shape in her writing is that of the hero motivated by aspiration and desire. Central to the dynamics of heroism is the problem of aggression, which Fuller very early understood as a problem of gender. Her search for sufficient vent for her antagonisms is informed almost from her childhood with an anxiety that such expressions be socially tolerable. Fuller engages the masculine romantic conflict between receptivity and analytical aggression, therefore, in a way that commits her to occupying simultaneously the positions of the object and the agent of desire, and the roles of lover, analyst, and victim. She inhabits these multiple positions in an style that does not resemble the ambivalent tones we have discerned in the texts of Coleridge and Schleiermacher.

In her writings on women Fuller insists on full rights to the exercise of divination, which she accepts and exalts as a feminine quality. She regards intuition variously as what women are left with when aspiration can find no material form, as an appropriation of masculine ambitions, and as the proof of feminine difference. While demanding all of the powers that male writers had ceded to women—the energies of nurture, understanding, virtue, nonverbal communication—she requires also the prerogatives of the philosophical critic. The defense of woman is also carried out, therefore, in the familiar terms of applied idealism; a prophetic notion of spiritual law provides the basis for both inspiration and attack.

These configurations become fully visible in "A Short Essay on Critics" in the first issue of the *Dial* (1840) and in "The Great Lawsuit: Man versus Men; Woman versus Women" (1843), subsequently expanded into *Woman in the Nineteenth Century* (1844). These writings coincide with the Conversation classes for women conducted by Fuller from 1839 to 1844. The interpreter, a figure enacted in the Conversations after being imagined in her letters, is a representative subject whose knowledge is grounded in pain, purchased by both sympathy and cash, and performed through allegories of universal law. This figure, in its performative context, to some extent reiterates the strategies of Fuller's writing in her studies and translations of Goethe and in her critical and feminist texts of the early 1840s. Since the Conversation classes combine the difficulties of philosophical criticism with the intensities of Transcendentalist friendship and female intimacy, however, the "interpreter" is not identical with the "critic" characterized in Fuller's writings. The ethics of conversation are not precisely the same as the ethics of criticism. But insofar as Fuller thinks through all ethical issues in terms of character, the Conversations, in which she characterizes herself at a transitional moment, have a particular value in the history of how she defines romanticism and the feminine in terms of each other.

What, for Fuller, is the "dialogue of love," then, the scene of discourse that mitigates conflict? For Coleridge, it is that needy state which elicits feminine care, a place where aggression is in abeyance. For Schleiermacher, it is hermeneutic understanding, the most perfectly ethical form of interpretive authority. In Fuller's Conversations the loving dialogue initiated by the central interpreter is the encounter through which strength becomes external, saving the mind from the wounds of its own intensity. It is an allusive and mythologized autobiography—with all the deconstructive ambiguities implied in that generic designation—performed so that others may find their own "law" through identifying with it. This is the same principle of mediation carried out by the critic in "A Short Essay on Critics" and named as the operative term in "The Great Lawsuit." The interdependence, in Fuller's thinking, of character and law, personality and idealism, narrative and allegory, forms the structure that links the Conversations to the texts we will subsequently consider.

Feminist scholarship has made visible the interpretation constructed by Fuller's male acquaintance. This account began with the wishful biography produced in the *Memoirs* compiled two years after her death by Emerson, William Henry Channing, and James Freeman Clarke and with the editorial liberties of her brother, Arthur Fuller, in several collections of her writings. The tradition continued with Octavius Brooks Frothingham (1876), whose chapter on Fuller as "The Critic" of Transcendentalism relies almost entirely on the *Memoirs,* and extended all the way to Perry Miller's foreword to his anthology of Fuller's writings (1963).[1]

The composite portrait derived from these and other writings both suppresses and exaggerates Fuller's sexuality. Her first biographers strove "to make over the moral image of Margaret Fuller," as Bell Chevigny has demonstrated, "especially in the two areas of sacred and profane emotion."[2] Her relationship with Giovanni Angelo Ossoli, the father of her child and probably later her husband, was retrospectively legitimized; her religious orthodoxy insisted on. The tendency to treat Fuller as a strongly sexual presence except in relation to God and her husband produces a schizophrenic result. Fuller appears as a theologically and socially conventional woman who nonetheless overpowered her friends with the "mystical" sympathies, brilliant talk, and physical intensity attributed to passion that had not found normal outlets. Her speech, the metonymic signifier of thought suffused by bodily presence, was characterized as fascinating, hypnotizing, and paralyzing; her texts were judged to suffer from the very rhetoric that succeeded as performance.[3]

I shall return at length to the question of the meanings of speech and writing for Fuller herself. To restore the significance of performance—of gesture, costume, and voice—is crucial for an appreciation of Fuller's reimagining of the romantic, though understandably deempha-

---

[1]Octavius Brooks Frothingham, *Transcendentalism in New England* (Philadelphia: University of Pennsylvania Press, 1959); Perry Miller, ed., *Margaret Fuller: American Romantic* (1963; Ithaca: Cornell University Press, 1970).

[2]Bell Gale Chevigny, "The Long Arm of Censorship: Mythmaking in Margaret Fuller's Time and Our Own," *Signs* 2 (Winter 1976): 452.

[3]Marie O. Urbanski, in seeking to establish Fuller's status as a writer, has documented the tendency to transform Fuller into the legend of her conversation. *Margaret Fuller's* Woman in the Nineteenth Century: *A Literary Study,* Contributions in Women's Studies 13 (Westport: Greenwood Press, 1980), 3–40.

sized by readers seeking to correct the mystifications of the *Memoirs*. Initially, however, it is more important to locate my argument in relation to other feminist perspectives on Fuller.

Feminist criticism tends to understand Fuller's involvement in New England intellectual circles in the light of her subsequent career as a New York journalist and participant in the Italian Revolution of 1848–49. Such accounts contain an implied teleology according to which Fuller's romantic theory of her own identity is separated from the political commitments of 1844 and after. Her sustained encounter with the texts of European and North American romanticism becomes the experience by which she moves somehow beyond or outside of it, into the "moral realism" of social and political engagement. At times this critical narrative reads like an allegory of literary history, in which Fuller's development spans the neoclassicism of her father's eighteenth-century curriculum and the spectrum of romanticism from Goethe to Emerson, to end in the realism of a radical and almost modern engagement with history.[4]

If Fuller's Transcendentalist phase is viewed as something she out-grew, it is also treated as something she grew into, in the late 1830s, as a result of the influence of Emerson. Despite the extraordinary interest of her relationship with Emerson—remarkable in the nuances of attraction, repulsion, self-revelation, and competitive understanding recorded by both parties—he is not as crucial to her development as most accounts of either Emerson or Fuller would have us believe. Although his lectures and essays did have an important impact on the style of her mythopoetic philosophizing, and although the extent of his cathartic aggressiveness in defending the self-reliant hero probably enabled similar language in her own texts, Fuller would have been Fuller without Emerson. And the reverse is also true, despite the fact that Emerson's unsettling friendship with Fuller was far more unique in his experience than hers.

---

[4]See, for example, Chevigny's article, "Growing Out of New England: The Emergence of Margaret Fuller's Radicalism," *Women's Studies* 5 (1977): 87: "Fuller's tendencies, identified in 1841, toward comprehensiveness and social realism would find ultimate expression in Italy. There her recommitment to the body and material reality after the transcendental adventure took the form of revolutionary action." See also Chevigny, *The Woman and the Myth: Margaret Fuller's Life and Writing* (Old Westbury: Feminist Press, 1976), 427 quoted below. Ann Douglas sounds a similar note: "Fuller's life can be viewed as an effort to find what she called her 'sovereign self' by disavowing fiction [associated by Douglas with the romantic novels of de Stael and Sand] for history, the realm of 'feminine' fantasy for the realm of 'masculine' reality." *The Feminization of American Culture* (New York: Avon, 1977), 317.

Her life was characterized by many idealistic, tense, and self-consciously epistolary intimacies. Fuller's early correspondence, which I read closely in this chapter, shows that her aspirations were formed in the mid–1820s by friendships with young men of Emerson's type and eventual acquaintance—disaffected Unitarian intellectuals at Harvard Divinity School—as well as by more ironic but no less literary friendships with women.[5] Emerson appears to offer the structural equivalent, in my chapters on Fuller, of Schlegel's ambiguous importance for Schleiermacher or Wordsworth's for Coleridge. But both Schlegel and Wordsworth are *written into* the texts of Schleiermacher and Coleridge—as provocateurs, as addressees, as objects of interpretation—in ways that I do not see true parallels for in the writings of Fuller, other than in the correspondence with Emerson itself. Emerson's characterization of the romantic figure who serves at once as victim and prophet, critic and interpreter of his society, is rapidly appropriated by Fuller—but not *as* Emerson. Fuller incorporates this figure into her ongoing account of the trials of criticism in a gendered social world; she draws Emerson himself into the patterns of confession and critique which typify her close friendships with other men and women (James Freeman Clarke and Caroline Sturgis, for example). But Emerson does not, I think, decisively organize Fuller's view of the ethics or politics of understanding in her published works.[6]

---

[5]Anne C. Rose gives a very useful account of the social and economic stresses experienced by young Unitarian intellectuals in Boston, in *Transcendentalism as a Social Movement: 1830–1850* (New Haven: Yale University Press, 1981). Her book suggests that Transcendentalism of one form or another had surrounded both Fuller and Emerson from the mid–1820s on and was not something transmitted in a direct line to Fuller from Emerson.

[6]Larry J. Reynolds, in his otherwise timely and useful *European Revolutions and the American Literary Renaissance* (New Haven: Yale University Press, 1988), reiterates the conventional views I take issue with here: first, that in Paris and Rome, Fuller becomes a full-fledged postromantic socialist; second, that Emerson provides Fuller with Transcendentalist notions. To begin with the less important of the two, Reynolds repeats the habitual account of Fuller's relation to Emerson: "Emerson's intellectual brilliance and spiritual integrity stirred Fuller profoundly. Through his public lectures especially, he taught her to value the life of the mind and to challenge the social conventions limiting her personal development. More significant, he also convinced her of the primacy of individualism and the ineffectiveness of cooperative reform efforts, two convictions she would eventually reject in Europe" (57). Despite the fact that both Emerson and Fuller describe the effect of collective activism as personally exhausting, a significant likeness but one not necessarily produced by Emerson's influence, Reynolds's rather unthinking account of Emerson's impact on Fuller is certainly overstated.

As for the more important question of Fuller's radicalism, Reynolds presents Fuller as *both* a radical socialist *and* a romantic prophet without finding any contradiction be-

The whole range of Fuller's cultural and political commitments throughout her life operates within the dynamics of romanticism. If Cora Kaplan is right to argue, as did Fuller herself, that "feminism and Romantic cultural theory emerged as separate but linked responses to the transforming events of the French Revolution," then Fuller's efforts to imagine, experience, and theorize a self-critical feminine subject and her need for the heroic or sublime act make sense as later aspects of the same intertwined constructions. Kaplan uses the history of romanticism to launch her analysis of the struggle within current feminist debate to integrate "social and political determinations with an analysis of the psychic ordering of gender."[7] If we pause at Kaplan's

---

tween the epistemological and ideological construction of those two roles. He simply reads Fuller's ongoing use of transcendental language as a code for socialism: "To Fuller, political change and social change were bound inextricably together, and in the role of prophetess she assumed in her dispatches, she referred to republicanism and socialism together as the 'idea' or the 'thought' or the 'spirit'" (64). I argue in Chapter 8 that Fuller's radicalism is romantic because dramas of romantic subjectivity organize the narrative of historical experience. A Marxist reading of Fuller which does not take into account the problem of subjectivity is not going to be very satisfying.

My final caveat with Reynolds focuses on his claim that "prior to writing her Tribune letters from Italy, Fuller seldom achieved coherence in her writings, a common problem for the Transcendentalists as a group"; *Summer on the Lakes,* he writes, is shaped by mere "whim and fancy" (63). Surely we have gone beyond the point where romantic discourse generally and Fuller's curiously structured and multiple voices in particular can be dismissed as simply incoherent.

[7]"In the heat and light of the revolutionary decade 1790–1800, social, political and aesthetic ideas underwent a kind of forced ripening as the progressive British intelligentsia contemplated the immediate possibility of social change, their thoughts turned urgently to the present capacity of subjects to exercise republican freedoms—to rule themselves as well as each other. . . . Both feminism as set out in its most influential text, Mary Wollstonecraft's *Vindication of the Rights of Woman* (1792), and Romanticism as argued most forcefully in Wordsworth's introduction to *Lyrical Ballads* (1800) stood in intimate dynamic and contradictory relationship to democratic politics. In all three discourses the social and psychic character of the individual was centred and elaborated. The public and private implications of sexual difference as well as of the imagination and its products were both strongly linked to the optimistic, speculative construction of a virtuous citizen subject for a brave new egalitarian world. Theories of reading and writing . . . were explicitly related to contemporary politics. . . ." But the "new categories of independent subjectivity" from the start stimulated the development, Kaplan argues, of an antiromantic socialist tradition: "as the concept of the inner self and the moral psyche . . . was used to denigrate whole classes, races, and genders, late nineteenth-century socialism began to de-emphasize the political importance of the psychic self, and redefined political morality and the adequate citizen subject in primarily social terms. . . . a collective moralism has developed . . . which, instead of criticizing the reactionary interpretation of psychic life, stigmatizes sensibility itself, interpreting excess of feeling as regressive, bourgeois and non-political." Cora Kaplan, *Sea Changes: Culture and Feminism* (London: Verso, 1986), 150–52.

discussion of how politics relates to psychology in the late eighteenth and early nineteenth centuries, however, we are in a position to ask whether Fuller's shift from a literary-philosophical to a social focus represents a decision to critique the romantic sensibility from a point beyond or within it.

In Fuller's case the turn to a new kind of action does not imply a newfound skepticism toward romantic subjectivity. She develops an ironic awareness of the limits of individual autonomy at an early age, and she never substitutes a class or even a social analysis for a theory of the subject, although she comes to see more clearly how class as well as gender constrains personal freedom. She regards the self as the locus of conversation among the many languages of the mind (divination, desire, reason) and of society (family, friendship, economy, nation). But she never, even in Italy, divides collective experience from the interior subject or prefers the former to the latter.

On the contrary, Fuller writes from Italy of national *character*. Revolutionary movements enter her mind as an influx of energy greater than any she can generate within herself; they appear as enactments of her hopes and desires and as the collective expression of the hopes of others; they make manifest in history the spirit of freedom: they are romantic subjects writ large. It is hard to see disclosed in this early letter from Italy the "dramatic and conscious reworking of values, made necessary by Fuller's determination 'to know the common people and to feel truly in Italy,'" which Chevigny claims is present:

> I write not to you about these countries, of the famous people I see, of magnificent shows and places. All these things are only to me an illuminated margin on the text of my inward life. Earlier, they would have been more. Art is not important to me now. I like only what little I find that is transcendentally good, and even with that feel very familiar and calm. I take interest in the state of the people, their manners, the state of the race in them. I see the future dawning. (LMF IV 271)

She does announce a change of "values," perhaps, in substituting scenes of history—"the people, their manners, the state of the race"—for scenes of art and landscape. But "the text of my inward life" still compels her and serves as the locus of her strong feeling for the dawning future. Her response to the Italian Revolution is articulated repeatedly in terms that look back to Herder rather than forward to Marx, and she never is able to regard Italians as anything other than irresistibly picturesque, their faces living images of "the capacity for pure, exalting passion" (NYT May 12 1847).

Writing of a fete in honor of the National Guard, she exhibits a fervor that appears in her personal correspondence as well as in her reports to the *Tribune:*

> All was done in that beautiful poetic manner peculiar to this artist people; but it was the spirit, so great and tender, that melts my heart to think of. It was the spirit of true religion,—such, my Country! as, welling freshly from some great hearts in thy early hours, won for thee all of value that thou canst call thy own, whose groundwork is the assertion, still sublime though thou hast not been true to it, that all men have equal rights, and that these are birthrights, derived from God alone. (NYT Nov 27 1847)

The significance of Fuller's participation in the uprising of 1848–49 appears in the coincidence of the Italian "spirit," which finds its true performance in a "poetic manner," with her own melting heart, itself caught up in the national spirit of America which had its own origins in the "great hearts" of an earlier generation. The spirit of the people moves between its inner and outer sites without ever being divided from the writing subject; indeed, it is the motion of the collective spirit which constitutes the subject as historical: "I find how true was the lure that always drew me towards Europe. It was no false instinct that said I might here find an atmosphere to develop me in ways I need. Had I only come ten years earlier! Now my life must be a failure, so much strength has been wasted on abstractions, which only came because I grew not in the right soil" (LMF IV 315).

Fuller's rejected "abstractions" suggest that Italian nationalism came to supply the psychological function once served by literary and critical inspiration. But the narrative she sees unfolding still tells the story of personal development. Several months later, writing to William Henry Channing, she once again represents her stance toward the revolution as that of a spectator who sees in events the external enactment and general confirmation of a long-held desire: "I have been engrossed, stunned almost, by the public events that have succeeded one another with such rapidity and grandeur. It is a time such as I always dreamed of, and for long secretly hoped to see. I rejoice to be in Europe at this time, and shall return possessed of a great history. Perhaps I shall be called to act. . . . A glorious flame burns higher and higher in the heart of the nations" (LMF V 58–59). In action "the heart of the nations" and her own heart would fuse in the flame of an embodied idea. This is not a renunciation of romantic reflection, with which it is perfectly compatible: "I sit in my obscure corner, and watch the progress of events.

It is the position that pleases me best, and, I believe, the most favorable one. Everything confirms me in my radicalism; and, without any desire to hasten matters, indeed with surprise to see them rush so like a torrent, I seem to see them all tending to realize my own hopes" (LMF V 69).

Fuller's account of her mental state does change after the birth of her son in Italy but in ways consistent with a view of the gendered self as a romantic subject. The encounter of the mother's subjectivity with that of the child fascinates her precisely as a psychological phenomenon. The surviving documents from Fuller's "Roman years" do not bear out, therefore, the view that romanticism had been left behind in Boston. They rather confirm the persistence of constructions that she had worked out as a young woman, constructions that are heterogeneous, plural, and dynamic and thus capable of absorbing changes of locale and opinion. It seems particularly important to be clear about this in view of the fact that feminist critics and theorists are now scrutinizing the historical connections between feminism and romanticism more closely. This examination, in turn, is not a historical accident, but an outgrowth of feminist efforts to work out the theoretical relationship between ideology and subjectivity. The moment in Anglo-American feminism which was served by reading Fuller's radicalism as a rejection of the transcendental subject is past. Fuller's sense of the revisionary critical and social possibilities of that subject—the critique of romanticism from within—provides an opening for the exercise of a differently modulated feminism.

"I have talked myself"

To give a convincing account of Fuller's ability to manipulate, to ends both ironic and sublime, the voices of Augustan wit, sentimental fiction, historical realism, confession, debate, and polemic, we have to begin two decades before the Conversations of 1839–44. In her writings of the years between the completion of her formal schooling (1825–26) and her father's death (1835), we can trace an experimental play of identities from its earliest emergence. Fuller dramatizes the pattern of resistance to the pressure of conventional gender roles, as she feels its increasing constraint, through the juxtaposition of generic idioms. Subjectivity is heterogeneous out of social and psychological necessity. Fuller's represented selfhood encounters its circumstances as the satirist whose ironies derive from the clash between sentimental fantasies and domestic obligations; as the ambitious genius who seeks expressive outlet for her intellectual aspirations; as the conversational-ist and correspondent who demands self-revelation as proof of sympa-thy; as the critic whose aggression is likewise justified by invocations of the central self.

Despite the continuity between Fuller's view of the subject and the psychological focus of English romantic literature, her differences from the romantic generation that came of age during the 1790s—the difference of gender, the difference of the historical moment, the dif-ference of nationality—are so great that her relationship to the ethical dilemmas of Continental and British romanticism is far from obvious. Remote from the arena in which the French Revolution and the emer-gence of an English radical tradition had made romanticism palpably ideological, Americans of a certain class and cultural predisposition encountered romanticism as a profession or vocation.[8] In this tendency Fuller and her generation of New Englanders resemble their British contemporaries, Victorians for whom two generations of romantic writers were remote enough to become usable as types, influences, and exemplars. The history of eighteenth-century romanticism and of its quasi-philosophical yet divinatory critical character had begun to be written: in de Stael's *On Germany* (1813); in *Biographia Literaria* (1817); in Hazlitt's *The Spirit of the Age* (1825); in Carlyle's essays in the *Edin-burgh Review* (1827–32) and *Sartor Resartus* (1830); as well as in the proliferating literature of collected works, biography, and memoir.

The process of transforming romanticism into the object of inter-pretive scrutiny continued in American periodicals—in, for example, the *North American Review* and the Unitarian *Christian Examiner*. Dur-ing the 1830s the pilgrimages of young Harvard faculty to German universities shaped the peculiarly Bostonian mediations that gave Full-er and her circle a sense of romanticism as a scholarly enterprise. They apprehended a mode of cultural inquiry derived from the emerging disciplines of comparative religion, comparative mythology, and com-parative linguistics.[9] Making available the history of romanticism

---

[8]Rose argues persuasively that changes in class relations, economic opportunity, and religious culture in early-nineteenth-century Boston created a generation for which the Transcendentalist critique functioned as a social identity, in *Transcendentalism as a Social Movement*, 17–37, 109–17. See also Henry Nash Smith, "Emerson's Problem of Voca-tion: A Note on the American Scholar," in *American Transcendentalism,* ed. Brian M. Barbour (Notre Dame: University of Notre Dame Press, 1973), 225–37.

[9]Among the members of Fuller's generation and that just preceding it who took advantage of the new German learning—the quintessence of all things "critical" for nineteenth-century America—were George Bancroft, William Emerson, Edward Everett, Frederic Henry Hedge, Henry Wadsworth Longfellow, and George Ticknor.

would be the primary task of the *Dial* (1840–44), self-described as *"A Magazine for Literature, Philosophy and Religion."* The antiauthoritarian and reformist energies of Transcendentalists and other New England intellectuals show the extent to which romantic attitudes were understood to be laden with ideological implications. But despite the exploitation of romantic philosophy in public gestures of cultural revolt, the status of European and British romanticism as the object of private study meant that it was most often transmitted as part of a program of self-definition from which radical discourse or action might or might not flow.

Fuller's education, like that of many British and American writers between 1800 and 1850, recapitulates the eighteenth-century turn from Augustan rationality to heroic reflection. A "Queen Anne's man," her father resolved to educate her as a son and dictated a strenuous neoclassical regime. This he oversaw until his death in 1835 with a scrutiny so intense as to be in itself almost a sufficient model for romantic reflection. That Fuller's self-dramatizing began in resistance to these parental determinations is suggested by the fact that she refused to answer to her baptismal name, Sarah, preferring her middle name, Margaret, instead.[10] By the time Margaret was six, her father would keep her up late for recitations in Latin and English. As she grew older, these performances included oral evaluations of her reading in which "breaks or hesitation" were forbidden and in which the standard of "accuracy and clearness" in speech prohibited vagueness or indecision. "'But,' 'if,' 'unless,' 'I am mistaken,' and 'it may be so,' were words and phrases excluded from the province where he held sway," she wrote around 1840. Indeed, his pedagogical interrogations seem almost designed to train a critic, a critic whose first project is self-analysis. This regime was the vehicle for Timothy Fuller's personal myth of what Margaret Fuller called "heroic common sense" (MMF I 14–18). Fiercely embodied in a kind of vicarious autodidacticism, his fantasy of independence was lived out with greater urgency in his domestic professoriate than in his public endeavors.[11]

---

[10]Michel Foucault's discussion of the proper name of the author in relation to the history of property, textual transgression, and critical practice illuminates Fuller's self-naming in suggestive ways, as Gail Gilliland has pointed out to me. "What Is an Author?" in *Textual Strategies: Perspectives in Post-Structuralist Criticism,* ed. Josué V. Harari (Ithaca: Cornell University Press, 1979), 148–51, 158–60.

[11]As Chevigny astutely observes, there was a tradition of "idiosyncratic behavior and strong opinion" on the paternal side of Fuller's family: "Margaret's grandfather was driven out of town for preaching against the Revolution to his congregation of Minutemen; returning as a farmer, he fought his way back into favor and represented the town at a constitutional convention, where he voted against the document because it recog-

Like all good eighteenth-century reading lists, the one developed by Timothy Fuller functioned according to the conventional juxtaposition of rationality and romance or, in generic terms, of nonfiction and the novel. In the correspondence between father and daughter which begins in 1817, when she is seven, and continues during his annual legislative absences until 1824, she frequently requests permission to read novels and tries to get him to do so as well, appealing to his standards of "reasoning": "I have read papa that Zeluco is a very intelligent sensible book therefore as I assure you I have been a very good girl. I beg you will send me 'carte blanche' to read Zeluco. . . . I have been reading a novel of the name of Hesitation. Do not let the name novel make you think it is either trifling or silly. A great deal of sentiment a great deal of reasoning is contained in it. In other words it is a moral-novel."[12] In her next letter to her father, reading novels becomes entwined with the granting of parental permission and with the "blessing" of the paternal critic. "You will let me read Zeluco? will you not and no conditions," she queries, and she seeks to earn this consent by a demonstration of her capacity for moral criticism. "Have you read Hesitation yet[?]" "I knew you would (though you are no novel reader) to see if they were rightly delineated for I am possessed of the

---

nized slavery. Inheriting this feisty independence, Timothy Fuller worked his way through Harvard, where he was demoted to second place in his class because of participation in a student rebellion. Serving two terms in Congress before becoming Speaker of the Massachusetts house, he opposed the Missouri Compromise in 1820; first in his Jacobin reading and his Jeffersonian principles and later in his loyal and unpolitic support of John Quincy Adams as late as 1832, he showed his political independence. His political stances, his Unitarian faith, and his abrasive personality made him something of a renegade, and he raised his family on the social and political outskirts of Cambridge and Boston, until political discouragement drove him to the country to pursue farming as his father had finally done." (*The Woman and the Myth*, 20).

[12]John Moore, *Zeluco: Various Views of Human Nature, taken From Life and Manners, Foreign and Domestic* (London, 1792). *Zeluco* is a novel about a virtuous young Italian woman and her selfish and abusive husband, duly intermixed with a descriptive tour of the Continent as seen from the points of view of British, German, and Italian characters. Fuller's letter continues: "Miss Argyle the principal heroine has not such superhuman wit beauty and sense as to make her an improbable character. Fitsroy earl of Montague is a sensible well informed man posessing [*sic*] a superior genius and deeply versed in the human character but improbably delicate in his ideas of love. Grosvenor a virtuous well bred youth but inexperienced and possessing ardent [sentence incomplete]. Lady Clervaux a lady whose affections were withered and whose feelings were checked by being taught to believe that fashion is every thing. Sir Thomas has no character. Lord Percival Lorn is a person of very shallow judgement and very malignant feelings two things apparently incompatible" (LMF I 91).

greatest blessing of life a good and kind father. Oh I can never repay you for all the love you have shown me[.] But I will do all I can" (LMF I 91, 94). Her juvenile defense of the value of the novel, directed against his preference for the masculine canon of essays, history, and the classics, replays the central generic competition of the eighteenth century. Out of this keen sense of opposition emerges Fuller's capacity to manipulate literary styles and the conventions of genre.

From a very early moment Fuller engages in the process of constructing her own hybrid form of heroism—and the hybrid quality is as important as the heroic. The stance of aspiring to the "ardors of Search and Action" compounds the topoi of gothic and sentimental fiction, the strenuosity of Roman courage, and the blend of combat and erotic desire peculiar to the quest romance. In its heterogeneous improvisations female heroism becomes a kind of romantic irony; the sublime becomes theater. Stylistic heterogeneity takes on ethical qualities, as it does in so much romantic prose, while it becomes the means of vocalizing autonomous desire in a complex social frame. Fuller's study of "warrior kings" at the age of seven leads two years later to the game in which she assigns royal titles to herself and her siblings ("I as you well know am a queen"). In 1820 she insists that her passionate admiration for the young British woman Ellen Kilshaw is not a novelistic affectation ("I am not romantic, I am not making professions when I say I love Ellen better than my life")—and this in the very letter in which she grapples with her father's dislike of novels (LMF I 159, 89, 94).

Fuller's sensitivity to genre as a field of potential identities makes possible the marvelous expertise in allusion and parody which emerges precociously in her letters to her girlfriends around this time, when she is only ten: "Ah my poor Mary I fear that the die is cast and that you have lost the generous independent noble highminded and spirited Redmond." The same juggling of novelistic, dramatic, and critical personae issues in exuberant ironies. "But what skills it talking?" she writes to Amelia Greenwood a few years later: "I only meant to tell your La'ship my wish was fulfilled. . . . My whole being is Byronized at this moment" (LMF I 101, 164).

Fuller responds to a neoclassical education by transforming it into a drama of quasi-fictive selves. There is never a time when her reading is not fundamentally about constructing her own subjectivity. Her (one hesitates to use the word) juvenile correspondence provides the discursive model for the more sophisticated conversations, personal and epistolary, of her young adult life. After a year at the Prescotts' School in

Groton, Fuller lived with her family in Cambridge from 1825 until their move to the country in 1833. During these years she increasingly comes to terms with sexual difference in a series of negotiations for which the literary voices of her early reading provide the language. Cambridge was a milieu in which masculine and feminine friendships and friendships between men and women could form around serious reading. Fuller's resistance to domestic submissiveness and her commitment to her studies as they become (a) work, however, place her in the highly self-conscious position of gender nonconformity.

Between 1833 and 1835 two episodes coalesced into a kind of parable illustrating the doom of the intellectual female, and Fuller, in her unsurprised way, unquestionably understood them as such. Her studies were interrupted when Timothy Fuller relocated the family in rural Groton in 1833; with his death in 1835 the domestic imperative seemed to have triumphed again. She had to give up a trip to Europe, a sacrifice she regarded at the time and afterward as the confirmation, feared but not unexpected, of everything in herself and her circumstances which demanded a domestication of the heroic. Fuller's mentors, Eliza Farrar and her husband, a Harvard professor, had offered to take her to Europe with them. The opportunity would have given her access to the materials she needed to embark on a true "work," a life of Goethe. In 1842, writing retrospectively, she describes her father's interpretation of such frustrations as commensurate with her "arrogance," though she resists his proleptic chastisement: "My father would often try to check my pride, or, as he deemed it my *arrogance* of youthful hope and pride by a picture of the ills that might come on me,—and all have come of which he spoke, sickness, poverty, the failure of ties and all my cherished plans." She turns against her father in the next phrase ("none of these changes have had the effect he prophesied"), but her reference to her sense of fatality at the time of these events is accurate (LMF III 105).

Before these crises of limitation, Fuller had found her personal community in Cambridge in friendships with William Henry Channing, George T. Davis (a cousin), Frederic Henry Hedge, and particularly in the remarkable correspondence with James Freeman Clarke. When she first arrived in Cambridge after leaving school in 1825, however, her mentors and fellow readers were not male, but female, a community that persisted alongside the later friendships with men and provided one of the key social contexts of the Conversations.

Embodying both intellectual aspiration and the moral self-discipline proper to conventional femininity, her former teacher, Susan Prescott, was deeply associated in Fuller's mind with "Truth and Honor," but also with repression. These meanings are narrated, if not explained, in the autobiographical fiction "Mariana," published in *Summer on the Lakes*. "The remembrance of that evening subdues every proud, passionate impulse," she wrote to Prescott in 1830, referring to the crisis that formed the basis for "Mariana" (LMF I 117, 160). When Fuller returned to Boston, Susan Prescott became her literary confidant.

The theme of "Mariana" is the cost of refusing to compromise in the face of pressure to censure oneself. The protagonist, struggling with the constraints of a girl's boarding school, is not, in any obvious way, either a writer or a critic. She is an artist, however, an actress and dancer of fantastic imagination and energy. Her criticisms are conveyed through the theatrical rebellion of the body, and it is on the body, also, that her rejection by her peers is inscribed. Although Mariana is "very loving, even infatuated in her own affections," she withholds herself from those whose devotion she requires: "there was a vein of haughty caprice in her character; a love of solitude, which made her at times wish to retire entirely, and at these times she would expect to be thoroughly understood, and let alone, yet to be welcomed back when she returned." She dances like "the spinning dervishes of the East," in the grip of the "mystical power" of her own fancy and holding her audience under the spell of her "singular drama," in turn. Her feverish temperament is irritated "by the restraints and narrow routine of the boarding school": "She was always devising means to break in upon it." Again, her rebellion is expressed through the body, particularly through costume, "some sash twisted about her, some drapery, something odd in the arrangement of her hair and dress."[13]

Mariana is given a temporary "vent" in "private theatricals." But she continues to wear rouge even when the performances are over. Theatrical makeup becomes the emblem of her idiosyncrasy, perceived by all to express her claim to superiority, and it is the means of her classmates' revenge. One night she arrives in the dining room to find all of them wearing a spot of rouge on each cheek, a grotesque and universal parody of herself. Afterward, although her bearing is "much subdued," her speech becomes cruelly divisive: "the demon rose within her, and spontaneously, without design, generally without words of positive falsehood, she became a genius of discord amongst them."[14]

---

[13]The story of Mariana appears in Fuller's *Summer on the Lakes, in 1843* (Boston: Little, Brown; New York: Charles S. Francis Co., 1844), 81–83.
[14]Ibid., 83–88.

When she is 'tried' and found guilty of this offense, a psychosomatic episode ensues in which she loses the will to live. She is restored to herself, to the community, and to an ethic of humility and love by a teacher at the school, who narrates the unspecified "griefs" of her "sad life." Having been entrusted with this painful self-revelation by a woman she admires—a communiqué from one victim of resistance to another—Mariana apologizes to her friends and is forgiven. Subsequently, "Mariana could not resent, could not play false." Nor, apparently, could she recapture her power of invention, associated with masculine heroic modes. The "terrible crisis" she had passed through "probably prevented the world from hearing much of her. A wild fire was tamed in that hour of penitence . . . such as has oftentimes wrapped court and camp in a destructive glow."[15]

Although the problem of criticism is nowhere mentioned in the story of Mariana, the dynamics of alienation and belonging which are so crucial to the romantic ambivalence about criticism are played out in an extreme way. Female genius does not formulate itself as argument or intellectual aggression but operates with greater desperation through the codes of behavior and dress. Imagination brings on its own destruction. The community cannot tolerate Mariana's improvisations, which are understood to be negative. She is faced with the choice of penitence or death. To avoid this rigidly constructed fate, Fuller revised her idea of the feminine through experiments with verbal style.

Fuller's first surviving letter after leaving school is to the Marquis de Lafayette, whom she encounters on remarkably knowing terms. "Should we both live," she begins, in her habitual subjunctive, "and it is possible to a female, to whom the avenues of glory are seldom accessible, I will recal my name to your recollection." Her next letter is to Susan Prescott, and it, too, contains a statement of purpose. After describing her daily course of study—Greek, metaphysics, French and Italian literature—she shifts into the playful mock dialogue that so often enables her to make claims of formidable seriousness and grandiosity: "'How,' you will say, 'can I believe that my indolent, fanciful, pleasure-loving pupil, perseveres in such a course?' I feel the power of industry growing every day, and, besides the all-powerful motive of ambition, and a new stimulus lately given through a friend. I have learned to believe that nothing, no! not perfection, is unattainable." "I am determined on distinction," she announces. The rest of the letter is

[15]Ibid., 89–93.

given over to contemplating the project of perfection more real-
istically. The figure she imagines herself becoming is more than a
"succes de societe" but never outside of society. She is concerned with
"grace," "intuitive tact," and "polish"—virtues of performance, tone,
and manner. "Genius" would be insufficient without a circle through
which "the power of pleasurable excitement" can radiate. The ambition to be distinguished is as closely tied to the desire for reputation—
or, as the letter to Lafayette suggests, fame—as to the goal of "perfection" (LMF I 150–52). Fuller wants both to stand out and to belong,
inclinations to which she is persistently loyal.

Regardless of her lighthearted fantasy of escaping from "this blest
age, so philosophic, free, and enlightened," to worship nature "as just
risen from the bath," Fuller's letters to Susan Prescott are exercises in
allusive modeling. "Now tell me," she asks, still balancing "ardent
spirit" and "active employment," fame and belonging, "had you rather
be the brilliant De Stael or the useful Edgeworth?" As this exercise in
comparison suggests, Fuller's reading involved "framing dialogues a-
loud on every argument beneath the sun." "I read very critically," she
asserts, and the link between being critical, being conversational, and
assuming the dilated identities of manifold authors is clear. "Really, I
have not had my mind so exercised for months," she exults. As a result
of her "gladiatorial disposition," she has lost patience with "mere light
conversation"; she studies much, reflects more, and feels "an aching
wish for some person with whom I might talk fully and openly" (LMF
I 153–55)

In the winter of 1829, a decade before the Conversations began,
Fuller responded to an inquiry about her religious opinions, probably
from James F. Clarke. "I have here given you all I know, or think, on
the most important of subjects," the letter ends, "could you but read
understandingly!" The "most important of subjects," religion, calls
forth a degree of resistance worthy of Emily Dickinson. Fuller refuses
dependence even as she mourns in advance over the eventual need to
accept emotional support. Implicit in the rejection of "consolation" is
the wish to escape from the feminine dynamics of "giving or receiving
assistance or sympathy" and to embrace the bleak sublimity of analyzed pain:

> When disappointed, I do not ask or wish consolation,—I wish to know
> and feel my pain, to investigate its nature and its source; I will not have
> my thoughts diverted, or my feelings soothed; 't is therefore that my
> young life is so singularly barren of illusions. . . . the time must come

> when this proud and impatient heart shall . . . turn from the ardors of
> Search and Action, to lean on something above. But—shall I say it?—the
> thought of that calmer era is to me a thought of deepest sadness. (LMF I
> 158–59)

Fuller resists not religion, but the pathos of consolation, as though dependence were a future state that could be dreaded in advance, instead of constantly a present emotional option and pressure. In repudiating the "refuge" or "protection" by which women—"loving or feeble natures"—are normally "soothed," Fuller reveals the extent to which the "ardors of Search and Action" always constitute themselves for her over against conventional comforts. Pride and barrenness are not just the marks of sublimity, but social transgressions that are punished in advance of actual resignation by a mood of "deepest sadness." The Conversations appear to reverse the claims of this letter by electing the "sympathy" of a "visible refuge." I think, however, that the terms are not reversed, but modified. In the Conversations Fuller accepts "consolation" in return for a position of representative centrality, a position from which she performs her quest through pain for meaning.

From her childhood Fuller's heroic figurations are framed by an ironic capacity for social realism which exposes the relativism of all romantic claims. Her fantasies, at such moments, are transposed into parodies of the sentimental. She turns witty manipulations of conventional novelistic language against feminine duties and proprieties. Fuller's parody of the sentimental repeatedly triggers a more wide-ranging irony that draws the whole range of nineteenth-century intellectual fashions into its comical purview. Her distance from the strictures of domesticity is established in one such letter to her close friend Amelia Greenwood by an exaggerated account of the mood produced by reading the English romantics. Pictures of women constrained by familial expectations frame the central paragraph of half-humorous romantic excess. "I have escaped from the parlour where Ive been sitting the livelong eveg [sic] playing auditor to Judge Weston," Fuller begins; "his jokes and anecdotes are pleasant enough but I fairly ache sitting three hours in boarding-school attitude hemming a ruffle and saying never a word. Pa—always thinks my presence gives a finish to the scene;—but I absconded at last to read in solitude over an excellent little supper of dry bread and *lime-water*." Fuller evidently feels that giving "a finish to the scene" and "hemming a ruffle" are domestic obligations of the same kind and degree; her sense of relief at her escape overflows into the savor of her book and spartan repast. The recoil from the double burden of her father's expectations and Judge Weston's anecdotes carries her, in the next paragraph, into a state of Byronic ecstasy. As she describes her sensations while reading Thomas Moore's life of Byron, she feels the west wind of Shelley's ode and the melancholy of Mary Shelley, vicariously saddened when Byron sang one of Moore's songs (see LMF I 165n.) At the same time, the ironic edge of domestic comedy carries over into high romanticism sufficiently to allow Fuller to acknowledge the theatricality of her indulgence.

This portion of the letter opens with Fuller's habitual mock-hyperbole: "How do you live or do you live? I. hope so! Oh days of spring balm and still summery gloss my spirit is inebriate with your delights!" The thought of inebriation conveys the rebellious nature of this fantasy. "You know, Amelia," Fuller confesses, "I've long wished that the customs of society would permit [me] to be intoxicate *only once* as Ive read them to be." As she goes on to describe the experience of "delireum," the natural setting and fantasied participation in the Shelley circle provide a double image of release, a return to an earlier moment of "felicity":

> Well! I was so yesterday; Im sure of it—In the morng I sent into the fields and passed the morng reading Moores Byron and inspiring delight in every breath. *Then* I was *happy*—But after I came home I sat down where the *west* wind could blow on my cheek and read Moore beginning with that song which made Byron's friend's wife so melancholy for three hours or so; and I was in a kind of delireum I read senselessly and dreamed consciously at the same time; I have not been able to read so for ages. My heart was not gay and light as with hope nor proudly throbbing as with—oh words!!—it floated in luxury of realized bliss. No! not *bliss felicity*.—But what skills it talking?—I only meant to tell your La'ship my wish was fulfilled.

Entering into literary history at the point when a woman is on the verge of rewriting romanticism in *Frankenstein,* Fuller is liberated both through and into reading. The power to write the song (Moore), to sing it sadly (Byron), and to hear it with productive melancholy (Mary Shelley) seems to be hers—although composing the narrative of this influx is more difficult: "oh words!!" She refers to this state as a "Byronized" condition: "My whole being is Byronized at this moment." But without a pause she revises "being Byronized" into comprehending Byron: "c'est à dire my whole mind is possessed with one desire—

to comprehend Byron once for all." In that "c'est à dire," reading changes from the construction of subjectivity through identification to the exercise of subjectivity in critical understanding.

Abruptly, Fuller shifts back to the trivialities of social life in Boston. "—I passed yesterday eveg at Mr Higginson's. Miss Storrow was so unkind to herself and me as to have the sick headach.—" The last vignette of the letter contains a glimpse of two friends: "You cant think how droll, dreary, and domestick she and M. looked sewing; writing; —drinking—molasses and water—Adieu" (LMF I 163–65). That romanticism offers an alternative to the gender ideology of the nineteenth-century American middle class is readily apparent. But the fact that this alternative is experienced as an isolated fantasy of the solitary subject and within an ironic social frame is equally clear.

The split between the readerly imagination and the domestic quotidian persists as the basis for an ironic tone that distances Fuller both from domestic boredom and from her own romantic desire. The unifying momentum of her comic sensibility becomes the vehicle for indirect expressions of her internal difference from the descriptions of others, as in this letter to Almira Barlow:

> I have neither fertilized the earth with my tears, edified its inhabitants by my delicacy of constitution, nor wakened its echoes to my harmony,— yet some things have I achieved in my own soft feminine style. . . . I have made several garments fitted for the wear of American youth; I have written six letters, and received a correspondent number; I have read one book,—a pretty piece of poetry entitled "Two Agonies", by M. A. Browne, (pretty caption, is it not?) and J. J. Knapp's trial [in the newspapers]; I have given advice twenty times,—I have taken it once; I have gained two friends and recovered two; I have felt admiration four times,—horror once, and disgust twice. . . . I have had tears for others' woes, and patience for my own,—in short, to climax this journal of many-colored deeds and chances, so well have I played my part, that in the self-same night I was styled by two several persons "a sprightly young lady", and "a Syren!!" . . . "Intelligency" was nothing to it. A "Supercilious", "satirical", "affected", "pedantic" "Syren"!!!! Can the olla-podrida of human nature present a compound of more varied ingredients, or higher gusto? (LMF I 170–72)[16]

Fuller's acute sense of the extent to which her life is determined by

---

[16]Robert N. Hudspeth glosses "olla-podrida" as "A sort of Spanish stew; a miscellaneous mixture" (LMF 172n).

gender permeates the letter. The feminine attitudes of sentimental drama and fiction are parodied throughout: weeping, lament, "delicacy of constitution," poems of agony, and emotional virtuosity that ranges from admiration to horror to disgust. The triviality of the conventional occupations of middle-class women is exposed by the unstoppable boasts about her accomplishments "in my own soft feminine style." Skeptical of social authorities, she has given advice twenty times and taken it once. The price of her recalcitrance, barely touched on, is "patience" with the circumstances that force her to screen her virtues from "glare"—an embrace of humility that is parodied here but stated in wholly serious tones elsewhere.

The most interesting moment in the letter is Fuller's report on how others see her. The theatricality of her own writing—"to climax this journal of many-colored deeds and chances"—is echoed by her pleasurably dramatic sense of social life—"I have played my part." The contrast between the "sprightly" American girl, energetic and clever, and the fascinating but dangerous mythological female—the "Syren" —triggers an ironic catalog of uncomplimentary adjectives. "Intelligency," "Supercilious," "satirical," "affected," "pedantic" register Fuller's delight in the compliments and her amused knowledge of the negative judgments that words like "sprightly" and "Syren" indirectly convey. The crucial thing to be learned from their context in the letter of 1830 is the extent to which literary or allegorical identities express "the goal of my ambition" *and* simultaneously operate in the social sphere as distortions or stereotypes. In her rapid transformations from one style of self to another, in "the olla-podrida of human nature . . . a compound of . . . varied ingredients," Fuller manages with a "higher gusto" at once to stand out and to belong.

This sense of difference operates in other circumstances as the disjunction between her own "talk" and the "self" that is constituted through it. Fuller's sophisticated awareness that talk, costume, gesture, and tone function as signifying practices paradoxically gives rise to apparently naive claims that she is the representative woman, the super-subject who makes her inner life available for others. In performances such as the Conversations the gap between the conventionality of semiotic codes as understood by others and the subject's authentic self-experience is closed through an implied contract that binds all members of the group to an ethic of sincerity.

A more discontinuous relationship between "talk" and "self" emerges in a curious locution at the beginning of a letter of 1832 to Clarke. "I feel quite lost," Fuller writes, "it is so long since I have talked myself." In this context "talked" has the force of a transitive verb. "I have talked myself" means both "I have talked as myself, authentically," and "I have made myself by talking." When she is unable to "talk herself" but nevertheless talks constantly, she begins to feel unreal, "strangely vague and moveable." When internal and external speech fail to correspond, the purpose of conversation, which is to verify the mind's own voice, is defeated. In this more somber mood "vague and movable" sensations give rise not to ironic manipulations of difference but to a renewed quest for a strong intellectual ego: "the time is probably near when I must live alone . . . separate entirely my acting from my thinking world, take care of my ideas without aid . . . answer my own questions, correct my own feelings, and do all that hard work for myself." Fuller defines being "alone" as the separation of the "acting" from the "thinking" world. Her vision of solitude, then, repeats the alienated situation she complains of, the state in which 'talking the self' has proved impossible, leaving subjectivity divorced from conversation. She now oscillates between the fierce recovery of the thinking self that will "take care" of its own "ideas" and a recurring longing for someone "to minister" to her, to answer her "call" with full comprehension. "I am not independent, nor never shall be, while I can get anybody to minister to me. But I shall go where there is never a spirit to come, if I call ever so loudly" (LMF I 178).

In response to the absence of life-giving talk, a readerly and critical identity enters Fuller's discourse. She will accept aid only "from the illustrious dead," from authors; the rest of the letter is devoted to comments on Körner and Novalis. Yet the same choice between solitary wholeness and sociable fragmentation which defines Fuller's personal relationships is now replicated in her approach to literature. In a letter of the previous week to Clarke, Fuller had addressed the problem of constituting the self through reading and of substituting correspondence for talk: "I have not anybody to speak to that does not talk common-place," she begins, "and I wish to talk about such an uncommon person—about Novalis!" The complexities of response are transposed from speech to reading as she goes on to contrast her impressions of Novalis and Goethe. One of Goethe's effects on Fuller is to make her feel "as if I had lost my personal identity" and therefore her voice: "What can I bring? There is no answer in my mind." The "one-sidedness" and "imperfection" of Novalis, by contrast, are a "relief" to Fuller because they inspire her to "write some letters" of criticism (LMF I 177).

Fuller then composes the spiritual biography of a central mind in which lesser, more needy selves find themselves contained. Her protagonist succeeds in ways that are meaningful only as expressing her own will to interpretation. Although this fantasy reads somewhat like Hawthorne's portrait of the feminist heroine Hester Prynne will never be—in other words, as a doom pronounced on the woman who imagines it—it articulates the idea of interpretation as something distinct from criticism, a distinction that seems fundamental to the Conversations:

> I have greatly wished to see among us such a person of genius as the nineteenth century can afford. . . . I had imagined a person endowed by nature with that acute sense of Beauty . . . and that vast capacity of desire, which give soul to love and ambition. I had wished this person might grow up to manhood alone (but not alone in crowds); I would have placed him in a situation so retired, so obscure, that he would quietly, but without bitter sense of isolation, stand apart from all surrounding him. I would have had him go on steadily, feeding his mind with congenial love. . . . I wished he might adore, not fever for, the bright phantoms of his mind's creation, and believe them but the shadows of external things to be met with hereafter. After this steady intellectual growth had brought his powers to manhood . . . I wished this being might be launched into the world of realities, his heart glowing with the ardor of an immortal toward perfection, his eyes searching everywhere to behold it; I wished he might collect into one burning point those withering, palsying convictions, which, in the ordinary routine of things, so gradually pervade the soul; that he might suffer, in brief space, agonies of disappointment commensurate with his unpreparedness and confidence. And I thought . . . such a man would suddenly dilate into a form of Pride, Power, and Glory,—a centre, round which asking, aimless hearts might rally,—a man fitted to act as interpreter to the one tale of many-languaged eyes! (LMF I 166–67)

The "person of genius" in the nineteenth century is unmistakably Margaret Fuller, with her "vast capacity of desire" but also her "retired" and "obscure" position, something Fuller feels even before her family 'retires' to Groton in 1833. Like her, the genius relies on "congenial love" even as he "stand[s] apart from all surrounding him." The capacity for desire is manifest in a "heart glowing with . . . ardor," a word Fuller frequently uses to describe herself. This figure resists "those withering, palsying convictions" that constitute "the ordinary routine of things." He suffers the "agonies of disappointment" that Fuller dreads *avant la lettre* as she moves into the gender dichotomies of adulthood; also like his creator, he has the ability suddenly to assume "a form of Pride, Power, and Glory."

If Fuller's genius resembles herself, he also supplies her defects. He stands apart, but "without bitter sense of isolation"; he can "adore, not fever for," imaginary objects of desire. He can gather ordinary temporality into "one burning point," and above all, he can recover from disappointment to glory. The particular configuration of his triumph is significant. He forms "a centre, round which asking, aimless hearts might rally,—a man fitted to act as interpreter to the one tale of many-languaged eyes!"[17] Well might Fuller comment, in the next phrase, "What words are these!" For her own "asking" heart and her self-gratifying interpretive ambition confront one another here. She is both the "many-languaged" crowd and the hermeneutic master who finds the unifying idea in diverse eyes and tells the one allegorical tale that enables individuals to know themselves and each other. Insofar as this fable combines both the social desire for receptivity and the central figure of genius, it suggests the extent to which she emerges as a romantic critic partly through the Conversations.

The Economy of the Conversations

The emotional range of Fuller's Conversations and the writings that describe or explain them is on display in four accounts of floral gifts, real or imaginary. On April 28, 1844, Fuller wrote to William Henry Channing about "the last meeting of my class," in which affection and presents flow to her from the class members and confirm her status as their "friend":

> We had a most animated meeting. On bidding me goodbye, they all and always show so much goodwill and love, that I feel I must really have become a friend to them. I was then loaded with beautiful gifts, accompanied with those little delicate poetic traits of which I shd delight to tell you. . . . Last, came a beautiful bunch of flowers, passion flower, heliotrope, and soberer flowers. Then I went to take my repose on C's [Caroline Sturgis's] sofa, and we had a most sweet afternoon together. (LMF III 193)

---

[17]Characterizing the representative figure of the age as its "interpreter" is a strategy of some other essays of the period, notably those of Carlyle and Emerson, as in "The Poet," *The Collected Works of Ralph Waldo Emerson*, vol. 3, *Essays Second Series* (Cambridge: Belknap Press of Harvard University Press, 1983), 4.

This exchange, in which Fuller is adequately rewarded, contrasts sharply to a letter to Emerson four years earlier, in which she mentions the present of another bouquet. Reflecting on the gift, abundant in itself, she voices the painful desire for more of what is given in "a very little bit." Her fantasy of compensatory self-indulgence takes revenge on Emerson's own failure of sympathy and comprehension:

> I wish you could see the flowers I have before me *now*. A beautiful bouquet brought me this evening, multifloras, verbenas, fusias, English violets and a lemon branch of the liveliest green. There is but a very little bit of the Heliotrope. It is the flower I love best, but it is rarely given me. . . . When I am a Queen . . . I will have greenhouses innumerable, and I will present every person of distinguished merit with a bouquet every week and every person of delicate sensibility with one every day. If you are there I shall only give you sweet pea or lavender because you are merely a philosopher and a farmer, not a hero, nor a sentimentalist. (LMF II 133)

The gift of heliotrope Fuller receives at the end of the Conversations marks her, according to her own associations, as a queen, a hero, and a sentimentalist. In the context of the Conversations she has been all three: the embodiment, for other women, of certain emotional possibilities—aspiration, confession, imagination, self-exposure. As the emphasis on her clothes and manner in other women's descriptions suggests, she was able to transform herself into a "figure," a metaphor, regarded with fascination as an "interpretation" of some aspect of themselves. At the same time, the appetite for gifts shows the extent of her dependence on their collective gaze.

Fuller's tendency to regard friendship as an economy of exchange bears out Caroline Healey Dall's memory of the way her own gift of flowers had failed to earn Fuller's affection. Instead, the transaction reinforced Dall's exclusion from the intimate possibilities of the Conversations. Caroline Healey, later Dall, almost certainly because of her strong identification with and resistance to Fuller, found her own record of the Conversations compelling enough to publish it, after Fuller's death, as *Margaret and Her Friends:* "I succeeded in getting a beautiful bouquet for Margaret, but was not satisfied as I could find only two or three bits of her favorite flower [the heliotrope]. . . . Margaret took these flowers coldly, to my surprise, for I thought she would smile on them if not on me. It was of this costly treasure, for which I sacrificed many small pleasures, that E. P. P. [Elizabeth Palmer Peabody] said 'it was impertinent for me to offer it.'" Elsewhere in her reminiscences, Dall tells what must be the same anecdote, introducing the idea of an apology that Fuller, the interpreter, misinterprets: "I carried Margaret an exquisite bunch of flowers. I felt that I had annoyed her, and wished her to understand by my flowers that I had not done so intentionally. Flowers were very costly twenty years ago. (I do not know how Margaret received my flowers, but I am confident that she did not see what I meant. Her vivid imagination always refused to read their natural language. For her they spoke an idiom of which I had no notion.)"[18]

Dall is acutely conscious of both the monetary economy of the Conversations, in which she participates, and their emotional economy, which she tries to enter through gift-giving. She is the one who notes how expensive the classes themselves were and understands the cost of her bouquet as emblematic of the emotional "cost" of the Conversations for both herself and Fuller. She resists Fuller on the grounds of her own rival subjectivity: "They thought me self-conceited, when I obeyed an instinct of *self possession,* for I was never yet so enamored of any, as to lose my own centre."[19] Dall's intermittent hostility is what makes her account valuable, apart from the undecidable question of its accuracy as a transcription. Her excluded and resentful position, outside the sentimental closeness of Fuller and her more intimate friends, causes her to describe the Conversations in terms of power relations and material, as well as emotional, dependencies—precisely the kind of definitions other participants resisted.

Like Dall, however, Fuller regards subjectivity as a resource that, when expended, must be replenished or compensated. Outpourings of energy and feeling demand at least recognition in return and desire love most of all. The theme of protecting the imaginative energy of the self runs throughout Transcendentalist writings. For Emerson, the chief argument against political activity was precisely the sense that it would consume the self he had been so long in forming. Behind the American generation of Emerson and Fuller stands the poetry of Wordsworth, preoccupied with the need to justify poetry as labor and to organize a life in which other forms of work do not impinge on it. The tensions among imaginative richness, aesthetic labor, and political expenditure create the dilemmas of subjectivity in its romantic aspects. This tension

[18]Joel Myerson, "Caroline Dall's Reminiscences of Margaret Fuller," *Harvard Library Bull.,* 22 Oct. 1974, 425–26, 419.

[19]Ibid., 417.

extends to numerous scenarios in which interiority is constructed over against collective exteriority: friends, family (at times), society at large or in its needy aspects, nature in its cultural resonances. Fuller's Conversations, in which interiority is communally displayed or invented, present a complex variant of the romantic economy of work and feeling.

The notion of law is the theoretical basis that connects the Conversations to Fuller's "A Short Essay on Critics" and "The Great Lawsuit." As we shall discover in a more amplified way when we turn to those texts, law—eternal ideas realized in personality and history—provides the link between the interpretation of character, on the one hand, and literary and cultural criticism, on the other. Fuller's letters during the late 1830s and early 1840s address her friends with a directness of encounter that asserts itself in the name of the interpretive object—the truth of the ideal inner self. Fuller attributes the same "desire" to both introspection and friendship: the desire to find, in persons, ideas—or the one idea that is the self (LMF II 167–68). The relationship between interpretation and the abstract or allegorical language of the Conversations themselves turns on the definition of personality as idea. The interpreter shows her friends to themselves by "realizing" the principle of their being. In the sphere of human relationships, Fuller believed, the vision of abstract truth discovered in the depth of personality is empowering in its very abstractness or universality.[20] "I loved the realizing of ideas," she explains to Caroline Sturgis in 1840, referring to the period in her life just ended, "and this was easiest in the nearness of mine own persons" (LMF I 167–68). Now, after a significant period

---

[20]It is precisely the heterogeneity of Fuller's idealistic discourse which is missed by Jeffrey Steele in his otherwise timely and illuminating discussion of the process by which Fuller develops a mythology of female archetypes (goddesses, queens, nuns) during this period. In concentrating on this aspect of Fuller's texts and conversation, which is always conveyed by her in a mood of inspiration and sublimity, Steele fails to locate it in relation to the complex range of genres, conventions, and critical strategies which late romanticism was manipulating by 1840. Not least of these relativizing or destabilizing tendencies was the sophisticated romantic view of mythology as a system of figurative substitutions performed by successive cultures, prone to mystification in the interests of power and to the belated sentimentalist's nostalgia for origins. The critical decomposition of the battle spearheaded in America by Boston Unitarians should alert us to caution. It is certainly true, as Steele argues, that Fuller's feminist "mysticism" must be reintroduced into any account of her productions, textual or conversational, but it cannot be understood without grasping also the fact that, like most literary romantics, she *performs* mysticism with a conviction of its meaningfulness but without belief. *The Representation of the Self in the American Renaissance* (Chapel Hill: University of North Carolina Press, 1987), 105–14.

of reorientation or "conversion," "this love of realizing" is directed toward herself.

The psychological change in the fall of 1840 which somewhat alters this demand for the inward possession of the other is usually referred to by students of Fuller as a religious experience or "conversion." The event for which religious language provided sublime metaphors gives rise to expressions of Fuller's desire for a self-entranced solitude and the sense of being "at home" in "the central power, myself." "I know not how again to wander and grope, seeking my place in another Soul," she announces, in an Emersonian vein, to Emerson. "I need to be recognized. After this, I shall be claimed, rather than claim" (LMF II 160).[21]

The equivalence of idealism and subjectivity gives the Conversations their specifically romantic character. Their romantic qualities lie not only in the relationship between truth and self, however, but also in that between interpretation and pain. "We are not merely one another's priests or gods, but ministering angels, exercising . . . the same function as the Great Soul in the whole of seeing the perfect through the imperfect nay, making it come there," Fuller exhorts William Henry Channing. Visionary insight, the "divining sense" of interpretation, is provoked by the other's need. Pain reveals the innermost self, as when Britomart sees Artegall, in the grip of "the evil power," still in a visionary light: "can she doubt therefore him whom she has seen *in the magic glass*" (Fuller's emphasis). In the dynamics of friendship the exchange of pity and self-pity is authentic communication: "I sympathized with you when you said you felt deep compassion for me. I often feel it for myself." In the climax of this letter of July 1841, Fuller identifies herself with the women of the New Testament and bases her claims to insight on the ethic of suffering discipleship. At this point the link between interpretation and the pain of selfhood is understood as profoundly gendered:

The manly mind might love best in the triumphant hour, but the woman could no more stay from the foot of the cross, than from the Transfiguration. And I am fit to be the friend of an immortal mortal because I know both these sympathies. You know I was prepared with you. I drew your lot myself: "Except ye drink his blood ye are none of his." At the foot of

---

[21]Rose, in exploring the relationship between Fuller's friendships with women and her avowed feminism of 1843 and after, suggests that the shift from offering to requiring "confirmation" from others moved Fuller toward publishing feminist statements. Rose's observations are supported by the way the notion of the "soul " or "idea" enables Fuller's radicalism. *Transcendentalism as a Social Movement*, 179–84.

the cross, at the door of the sepulchre I must await the prince my youthful thought elected. (LMF II 214–15)

By locating abstract ideals in the heart of the other person and by making a community of shared pain the condition for access to it, Fuller constructs an ethics of interpretation. The violence she strives to avoid is not simply the hyperrational arrogance of masculine analysis, but fantasies of her own centrality which reduce others to appreciative spectatorship. By turning failure into the revelation of essence, she is able to say that disillusionment has made her more idealistic about her friends, not less. She arrives at the negative quest of Childe Roland: "just to fail as they, seemed best, / And all the doubt was now— should I be fit?"[22] Their failures awaken "a deeper tenderness . . . and a higher hope," she observes to Emerson: "As they fail to justify my expectation, it only rises the higher and they become dearer as the heralds of a great fulfillment" (LMF II 235).[23]

As one approaches the Conversations, one inevitably thinks of the incessant comparisons of Fuller to de Stael's Italian *improvisatrice,* Corinne—identifications that, as Ellen Moers showed some time ago, were felt by virtually every woman writer after 1807 as well as by men less enthusiastic about the spectacle of female empowerment.[24] Cor-

[22]Robert Browning, *The Poems,* ed. John Pettigrew (New Haven: Yale University Press, 1981), I 586, lines 41–42.

[23]The connection between understanding and suffering is closely linked to the end of Fuller's love affair with Samuel G. Ward in the two months preceding the beginning of the Conversations in November 1839. This episode and its consequences strengthen the connection between interpretation and pain which is articulated in more general terms in the letters. In the letter to Ward which begins "You love me no more" (and is signed "Isola"), Fuller refers to the way he has sought to redefine her as his "Mother" instead of as his lover: "You have given me the sacred name of Mother, and I will be so indulgent, as tender, as delicate . . . in my vigilance, as if I had borne you beneath my heart instead of in it. But Oh, it is waiting like the Mother beside the sepulchre for the resurrection, for all I loved in you is at present dead and buried, only a light from the tomb shines now and then in your eyes" (LMF II 91). This passage allows us to locate the origin of Fuller's identification with Christ's mother in Ward's own painfully self-serving epithet; it also displays the critical potential of the mother's capacity to define her figurative son as "dead and buried." The end of Fuller's intimacy with Ward corresponded with the onset of his love for Anna Barker, to whom he shortly became engaged and who was staying with Fuller when her relationship with Ward ended. Ward's rejection produced an almost ecstatic outpouring of selfless passion on behalf of Barker and toward her most intimate friend in this period, Caroline Sturgis. The Conversations began a month later, in the aftermath of "nights of talk and days of agitation" (LMF II 93).

[24]Ellen Moers, *Literary Women* (New York: Oxford University Press, 1976), chap. 9, "Performing Heroism: The Myth of Corinne."

inne's power to fascinate arises out of sacrifice, the renunciation of love. Her heroic stature and her inspiriting voice gain their signifying force from the purgatorial experience of loss—loss in advance of the actual love affair in which she loses the man all over again. Coleridge reverses Corinne's gender in order to assume, in "The Improvisatore," the interpretive centrality of the unloved lover. But unlike Corinne and in a quite different fashion than Coleridge, Fuller periodically conflates the understanding produced by mental suffering with the capacity for abstract thought.

The dynamics of Fuller's idealism involve more than the prophetic quest for principles in the hearts of individuals, however. The other aspects of law, according to her view of it, extend to the domain of analysis and argument. "A Short Essay On Critics" shows how closely classification is bound up for her with the exercise of critical—or, as she argues in that essay, precritical—strength. Her "ambition" in the Conversations, as she formulates it in her initial proposal, is "to pass in review the departments of thought and knowledge and endeavor to place them in due relation to one another in our minds." Women will be trained up to rationality and then to reflection. They will be taught "to systematize thought" and to acquire the "precision in which our sex are so deficient" (lacking as they do "inducements to test and classify what they receive"). But even in the midst of such a program, a feminine adaptation intervenes in which behavior and desire take priority over method. Fuller also hopes "to ascertain what pursuits are best suited to us in our time and state of society, and how we may make best use of our means for building up the life of thought upon the life of action" (LMF II 87). Education in the skills of criticism, passing in review "the departments of thought and knowledge," opens up a more urgent interpretive drama.[25]

The interpreter will supply "a point of union to well-educated and thinking women" and "a place where they could state their doubts and difficulties with hope of gaining aid from the experience or aspirations of others."[26] Fuller challenges the class "to lay aside the shelter of

[25]For a discussion of Fuller's Conversations as an educational project, see Charles Capper, "Margaret Fuller as Cultural Reformer: The Conversations in Boston," *American Quarterly* 37, 4 (1985): 509–28.

[26]Clearly, Fuller regarded herself as speaking to an exclusively middle-class membership. Dall remembered that Fuller's Conversations were priced unusually high for the time, running two dollars a session, twenty dollars for a series of ten. (By comparison, a season membership in the average New England lyceum cost about one and a half dollars.) Dall also mentions Fuller's "great need of money" at this time, which rein-

vague generalities, the cant of coterei criticism and the delicate disdains of good society," implying that the venture into mind entails a degree of resistance to bourgeois social assumptions. The real heroism of such an enterprise lies not in the encounter with society, however, but in the need to "fearless meet the light although it flow from the sun of truth." The sun is identical, in its centrality, to the "interpreter" of "many-languaged eyes" and to Fuller's own position in the group. Speaking on behalf of the principle of illumination, Fuller issues a call for the "generous courage" to tackle the "great questions. . . . What were we born to do? How shall we do it?" To inquirers ready for the undertaking, she somewhat ironically promises a drawing-room variety of unmediated vision: the "vigor which may enable them to see their friends undefended by rouge or candlelight" (LMF II 86–88).

Our own vision of the Conversations is anything but unmediated. The best sources of commentary we have on them are Fuller's own letters, the notes kept by Elizabeth Palmer Peabody, and Caroline Dall's accounts of the sessions of 1841, the one series open to men. These dubiously accurate records concur in two important ways: first, as testimonials to the performance of mutually devoted friendship so crucial to the Conversations' economy (and resistant, as Dall notes, to the person who refuses to engage in this exchange); and second, in their characterizations of the Conversations' prevailing intellectual style, the translation of post-Kantian and Neoplatonic mythopoeia into allegories of the Conversations themselves. This figurative strategy itself (and not simply the feminine archetypes that, as Steele demonstrates, it tends to promote) replaces the effort to train women in masculine mental skills with practices that reinforce a sense of feminine difference.[27]

At the first meeting Fuller again argued that women's need to "reproduce" their learning in action implicitly defines conversation as the moral equivalent of such action. To "take subjects on which we know words, and have vague impressions, and compel ourselves to define those words," to make "a simple and earnest effort for expression," itself constitutes use or reproduction.

Women are now taught, at school, all that men are; they run over, superficially, even *more* studies, without being really taught anything.

---

forces my argument that the Conversations operate according to an economy of exchange (CHD 9).

[27]Steele, *The Representation of the Self in the American Renaissance,* 114–21.

When they come to the business of life, they find themselves inferior, and all their studies have not given them that practical good sense, and mother wisdom and wit, which grew up with our grandmothers at the spinning-wheel. But, with this difference; men are called on from a very early period, to reproduce all that they learn. Their college exercises, their political duties, their professional studies, the first actions of life in any direction, call on them to put to use what they have learned. But women learn without any attempt to reproduce. Their only reproduction is for purposes of display. (MMF I 329)

"Reproduction," therefore, occurs through the interpreter, whose claim to representativeness enables others to be changed by encounters with her more potent subjectivity. The Conversations offer a training ground in applying myths of freedom to the business of female intimacy, for the purpose, as we shall see, of launching the self in a trajectory of romantic aspiration.

Peabody's notes on the second series of Conversations (1840) give us a sense of Fuller's quest for liberating abstraction:

The question of the day was, What is life?

Let us define, each in turn, our idea of living. Margaret did not believe we had, any of us, a distinct idea of life.

A. S. thought so great a question ought to be given for a written definition. "No," said Margaret, "that is of no use. When we go away to think of anything, we never do think. We all talk of life. We all have some thought now. Let us tell it. C——, what is life?

C—— replied,—"It is to laugh, or cry, according to our organization."

"Good," said Margaret, "but not grave enough. Come, what is life? I know what I think; I want to find out what you think."

Miss P. replied,—"Life is division from one's principle of life in order to a conscious reorganization. We are cut up by time and circumstance, in order to feel our reproduction of the eternal law."

Mrs. E.,—"We live by the will of God, and the object of life is to submit," and went on into Calvinism.

Then came up all the antagonisms of Fate and Freedom.

Mrs. H. said,—"God created us in order to have a perfect sympathy from us as free beings."

Mrs. A. B. said she thought the object of life was to attain absolute freedom. At this Margaret immediately and visibly kindled.

C. S. said,—"God creates from the fulness of life, and cannot but create; he created us to overflow, without being exhausted, because what he created, necessitated new creation. It is not to make us happy, but creation is his happiness and ours."

Margaret was then pressed to say what she considered life to be.

Her answer was so full, clear, and concise, at once, that it cannot but be marred by being drawn through the scattering medium of my memory. But here are some fragments of her satisfying statement.

She began with God as Spirit, Life, so full as to create and love eternally, yet capable of pause. Love and creativeness are dynamic forces, out of which we . . . go forth bearing his image, that is, having within our being the same dynamic forces, by which we also add constantly to the total sum of existence, and shaking off ignorance, and its effects, and by becoming more ourselves, *i.e.* more divine;—destroying sin in its principle, we attain to absolute freedom . . . we return to God, conscious like himself, and, as his friends, giving, as well as receiving, felicity forevermore. In short, we become gods, and able to give the life which we now feel ourselves able to receive.

On Saturday morning, Mrs. L. C. and Mrs. E. H. were present, and begged Margaret to repeat the statement concerning life, with which she closed the last conversation. Margaret said she had forgotten every word she said. She must have been inspired by a good genius, to have so satisfied everybody,—but the good genius had left her. She would try, however, to say what she thought, and trusted it would resemble what she had said already. She then went into the matter, and, true enough, she did not use a single word she used before. (MMF I 345–47)

Assuming that this account is circumstantial enough to be accurate about the thematic content of the Conversation, we can see that Fuller's own definition of "Life" conveys exactly her motives for idealism. The "dynamic forces" that reside "within our being" constitute the idea or self that she has striven to realize in friendship. The connection between self-realization and friendship is dramatized on a divine plane. "By becoming more ourselves," we acquire the "absolute freedom" of the properly 'reproductive' subject, and from this position of strength, we enter into a relationship of friendly equality with God, "as his friends, able to give the life" which we now only receive.[28]

The whole curriculum of the Conversations is based on analogical transpositions of the kind that slide easily from analysis to fable in so much romantic prose. In her plan for the first series, Fuller gives "Poetry" as an example of a possible topic, "Poetry as expressed in / External Nature / The Life of man / Literature / The Fine Arts / a

---

[28]Lawrence Buell remarks on the extent of "premeditation" apparent in the "carefully calculated" definitions of each speaker and suggests that this and the "frequent cross-allegations of personal coldness" in Transcendentalist relationships demonstrate a pervasive inhibition. *Literary Transcendentalism* (Ithaca: Cornell University Press, 1973), 88–89.

History of a nation to be Studied in / Its religious and Civil institutions / Its literature and arts, / the characters of its great men" (LMF II 88).[29] This plan bears a close resemblance to the structure of contemporary lecture series. Emerson's lectures on "Human Life" in 1838–40 included "Doctrine of the Soul," "Home," "The School," "Love," "Genius," "The Protest," "Tragedy," "Comedy," "Duty," "Demonology."[30] In Fuller's Conversations and Emerson's lectures the topic is neither analyzed nor defined but exemplified and shown in its manifold embodiments, an idea within the personalities of history and culture, as the self is an idea within the friend. "Interpretation," in this context, is the narration of a principle as it is "reproduced" in its multiple characters.

The first series of the Conversations, in fact, was devoted not to poetry, but to Greek mythology. Mythology gave Fuller a subject matter that would conduct her pupils pleasurably between its "tangible" imagery and abstract ideas. As such, it provided her with a familiar romantic demonstration of figurative thinking as the basis of culture: "forms of the mythology . . . are great instincts, or ideas, or facts of the internal constitution, separated and personified" (MMF I 330). "Margaret said that a fable was more than a mere word," reports Dall of the 1841 Conversations, also devoted to Mythology. "It was a word of the purest kind, rather, the passing of thought into form" (CHD 45). The Greek gods pass through the transforming fluid of the late-eighteenth-century view that mythology is the original language of philosophy, psychology, theology, and natural science, and come out like this, in Fuller's account: "the will (Jupiter); the Understanding, (Mercury). . . . the celestial inspiration of genius, perception and transmission of divine law (Apollo)[;] the terrine inspiration the impassioned abandonment of Genius (Bacchus)[;] of the thunderbolt, the Caduceus, the ray, and the grape having disposed of as well as might be, we came to the wave, and the seashell it moulds; to Beauty, and Love, her parent, her child" (LMF II 102). Here is the point at which the critic and the interpreter become indistinguishable. The romantic critic free to indulge in idiosyncratic relativism merges with the interpreter whose authority is earned through the display of such substitutions.

[29]The topics of other Conversation series given by Fuller included "Fine Arts" (or "enacted poesy"), "Ethics," "Education," and one miscellaneous series (MMF I 327–51, esp. 350–51).

[30]*The Early Lectures of Ralph Waldo Emerson, 1833–1842,* ed. Stephen E. Whicher, Robert E. Spiller, and Wallace E. Williams (Cambridge: Belknap Press of Harvard University Press, 1959–72), vol. 3.

To what extent and in what fashion is this mode of critical figuration gendered? The topical organization of Emerson's lecture series during the same five-year period shows the same repetitive translations of moments from the history of culture into the phenomenology of idealism. It is not the realm of spirit that gratifies Emerson's imagination, but figurative variation itself and the repeated surge upward toward the "prospective" point of view, to echo the final chapter of *Nature*.[31] Metaphors of empowerment in the language of Fuller's Conversations offer similar pleasures. In the Conversations, however, mythology is embedded in a context of female intimacy which alters the meaning of allegorical exercises. Part of that context is the intricate relationship of figuration to pain. The link between the performance of understanding and the experience of pain—associated with Rousseau, Coleridge, and Corinne, but in each case marked as sentimental or womanly—is part of what gives the discourse of the Conversations their specifically feminine character. Fuller's accounts of the Conversations to her friends are pervaded by the topic of her ill health, especially her recurring headaches. She treats sickness as both the cause and the trope of discouragement; if energy signifies ambition, headache signifies failure. "My constant ill-health makes me daily more inadequate to my desires, and my life now seems but a fragment," she writes. "My health is frail . . . I am little better than an aspiration" (LMF II 126, 187).

The references to Fuller's emotional and physical distress make it clear that she regards the Conversations as both debilitating and therapeutic. The dynamics of comfort that support Fuller are part of what is understood within the circle to be its structuring drama: the performance of communion. An emotional economy is acted out through gesture, facial expression, tone of voice, confidences, nursing, and gift-giving. Affection and money (as its material proof) are exchanged for interpretation and the atmosphere of self-discovery:

> Anna sat beside me, all glowing, and the moment I had finished she began to speak. She told me afterwards she was all kindled, and none there could be strangers to her more.
>
> I was really delighted by the enthusiasm of Mrs. Farrar. I did not expect it; all her best self seemed called up, and she feels that these meetings will be her highest pleasure.
>
> Ellen Hooper too was most beautiful.

---

[31]See my *Emerson's Romantic Style*, chap. 9, "Figurative Language," for a detailed analysis of the critical position implied by Emerson's metaphoric structures.

The exertion of this class made Fuller ill, a recurring reaction that produces further exchanges of care and transcendence: "I went home with Mrs Farrar and had a long attack of nervous headach. She attended anxiously on me, and asked would it be so all winter. I said if it were I did not care, and truly I feel now such an entire separation from pain . . . such a calm consciousness of another life . . . that pain has no effect except to steal some of my time" (LMF II 183–84).

Fuller, like the "genius" whom she had imagined as "interpreter" to a circle of "many-languaged eyes," understands the gaze of others on herself to represent the means by which their need for comprehension is fulfilled—but also feels it as offering the affection she needs in her prophetic or queenly position. "You joke about my Gods and Goddesses," she wrote to a friend in Providence, "but really my class in Boston is very pleasant." The comfort of "real society" gives priority to the mutual revelation of "thoughts" over the examination of "topics": "There I have real society, which I have not before looked for out of the pale of intimacy. We have time, patience, mutual reverence and fearlessness eno' to get at one another's thoughts. Of course our treatment of topics is superficial but good, I think as far as it goes" (LMF II 118).

In thinking over the participants, she notes that one "came out in a way that surprized me," having "shaken off a wonderful number of films" to exhibit "pure vision, sweet sincerity, and much talent"; as a whole, the gathering was "intent," and afterward many "said words of faith and cheer." The acting out of affection, in the form of "glistening eyes," "glowing" faces, "melted" hearts, and anxious nursing, stimulated Fuller's interaction with the other women in the group, including the pleasure of 'trumping' their definitions with a more splendid one. Her pleasure then feeds back into the group in the form of "satisfaction": "I was so fortunate as to rouse at once the tone of simple earnestness which can scarcely, when once awakened, cease to vibrate. All seem in a glow and quite as receptive as I wish. They question and examine, yet follow leadings; and thoughts (not opinions) have been trumps every time" (LMF II 101).

Fuller's emphasis on the attitudes of receptivity assumed by her pupils is consistent with her claim that the classes did not challenge her intellectually. "I am never driven home for ammunition; never put to any expense, never truly called out," she observed after the first meeting, contrasting her easy dominance to the willingness of others to "follow" her "leadings." This striking chain of metaphors, contrasting the lesser efforts required by the Conversations to the extremities of warfare, extravagance, and ecstasy, suggests that the pragmatics of an intimate tone strengthen Fuller herself (LMF II 97). Affection conveyed by the bodily semiotics of feminine emotion reinforces her own sense and the collective sense of her superiority.

The claim made by all the participants in the Conversations whose views are known (including the ambivalent Caroline Dall) concerning the cultivated atmosphere of tenderness, inspiration, and mutual caregiving brings us to the question of sentimentality. The question is not so much whether the Conversations operated according to a sentimental ethos, which I think is evident. The difficulties arise, rather, with the implications of this statement and, above all, with the meanings we ascribe to the term "sentimental." Eve Kosofsky Sedgwick, meditating on the "conscious rehabilitation of the category of 'the sentimental'" by feminist critics, investigates the term's negative meanings, which provoked the project of feminist transvaluation in the first place. She is not willing either to discredit the feminist exposure of how the charge of sentimentality has been used against women's writing or to relinquish the power of the word to make visible "figures of concealment, obliquity, vicariousness," forms of desire and bad faith. In urging the critic who deploys the term "sentimental" to engage in a dialectical specificity of reading, Sedgwick reiterates the extent to which interpretation is itself a sentimental endeavor: "'Sentimental' with its quiverful of subcategories—morbid, prurient, snobbish, etc.—don't they work less as static grids of analysis against which texts can be flatly mapped than as projectiles whose bearing depends utterly on the angle and impetus of their discharge?"[32]

Thus framed, of course, the Conversations stand before us as a spectacle of sentimental interpretation and as a spectacle we are tempted to be sentimental about. Fuller's expositions of mythology give rise to strongly wishful interpretations, particularly of female figures. Her interpretation of the tone of the Conversations is a sentimental one, insofar as it names as "affection" the more ambivalent fantasy of—what else?—interpretive centrality. The temptation for the feminist critic to assimilate the Conversations into "the female world of love and ritual" provides an opening for yet another sentimental interpretation or relationship of vicarious desire.[33] Sentimentality is an appropri-

[32]Eve Kosofsky Sedgwick, "Epistemology of the Closet (I)," *Raritan: A Quarterly Review* 7(4): 65–67.

[33]Carroll Smith-Rosenberg, "The Female World of Love and Ritual: Relations between Women in Nineteenth-Century America," in *A Heritage of Her Own*, ed. Nancy F. Cott and Elizabeth H. Peck (New York: Simon & Schuster, 1979), 311–42.

ate name for the tendency to describe the Conversations as governed by a nonconflictual ethic that transposes a scenario of inequality into the language of intimacy and exchange.

Philip Fisher, in exploring the development of American "social space," historically locates the sentimental aspects of a wide range of scenarios structurally resembling the Conversations. While he focuses on a later period, his sense of the way "performer, act or product, and public, all come into existence by a process of mutual conferring of reality" illuminates the relationship between theater and subjectivity in Fuller's classes for women. Although Verena, in *The Bostonians,* is much more explicitly commodified than Fuller, Fisher's description of the way she exemplifies this whole field of meanings is clearly pertinent to the Conversations. "If we ask what the intimate power of Verena consists in," Fisher remarks, "it lies in the fact that she is herself both the speaker of the ideas and a personal allegory of them. She is the enactment of the yearning for freedom, including the paradoxes of freedom: . . . that she is bought and sold, managed and produced for the public . . . that she is hidden away and then displayed with tickets sold. . . . She is the iconography of her ideas. . . . The ideas take visual form in the materials of personality." Fisher's performative model, in which intimacy and display are mutually constituted and in which the economic or use value of the scene is functionally related to its sentimental mood, clarifies what the celebration of affection conceals in the records of Fuller's Conversations.[34]

The extent to which sentimentality is sought after (indeed, is promoted as a contractual relationship between Fuller and the women who attended the Conversations) emerges in her account of one of the most memorable classes, the first session of the 1840 series. Fuller opened by narrating her "conversion" of recent weeks, a confession that brings her into a new relationship to the group, "a much more satisfactory communication than before." What she announces is, in some sense, the decision to be self-centered, but the confessional aspect of the scene transforms it in a sentimental fashion into the basis for a

[34]Philip Fisher, "Appearing and Disappearing in Public: Social Space in Late-Nineteenth-Century Literature and Culture," in *Reconstructing American Literary History,* ed. Sacvan Bercovitch (Cambridge: Harvard University Press, 1986), 162, 166, 183. Fisher also speculates on the emphasis on the metaphor of personal magnetism or "electricity" so prevalent in Fuller's descriptions of herself: "The performed self is at so great a distance from the intimate self that hypnotism, dream, trance, the memorization of a role by an actress are all needed to make the distance and the moral peculiarity felt" (182).

shared faith in closeness within the circle: "Wednesday I opened with my class. It was a noble meeting. I told them the great changes in my mind, and that I could not be sure they would be satisfied with me now, as they were when I was in deliberate possession of myself. I tried to convey the truth, and though I did not arrive at any full expression of it, they all with glistening eyes seemed melted into one love.—Our relation is now perfectly true" (LMF II 182). Fuller's changed relationship to herself requires a new contract with the participants in the Conversations. Characteristically, she frames the question as one of their 'satisfaction' with her, as though the loss of "deliberate [self-]possession" might be perceived as undermining the interpreter's reproductive efficacy. The very loss of subjective certainty, however, brings about an expressive effort that produces the desired response, the "true" relation authenticated by tears.

The language Fuller used in trying to "convey the truth" of "the great changes" in her mind almost certainly echoed the metaphoric hyperbole that fills the key letter about her "conversion" written to Caroline Sturgis in October 1840 (of which I quote a very small portion). She temporarily renounces heroic identities and assumes a virginal persona, though it should be noted that her retreat lands her precisely where her fantasy of the interpreter-genius had ended—at the point of central meaning, or "undreamed of diamond":

> I was stern and fearless. I am soft and of most delicate tenderness. I rushed into the melee an Amazon of breast undefended save by its inward glow. Shrouded in a white veil I would now kneel at the secretest shrines and pace the dimmest cloisters—I rushed out like the great sea, burst against all rocks . . . I feared no rebuff, I shrunk from no publicity, I could not pause yet ever I sobbed and wailed over my endless motion and foamed angrily to meet the storm-winds which kept me pure—I would now steal away over golden sands, through silent flowery meadows farther still through darkest forests . . . into the very heart of the untrodden mountain where the carbuncle has lit the way to veins of yet undreamed of diamond. (LMF II 168)

What are the implications of the change characterized in these terms? In transforming herself from an Amazon (though of undefended breast) into Wordsworth's "white doe," the primary goal is, again, "the tone of simple earnestness" (LMF II 169). The transaction with other women binds all in one "perfectly true" communication as divinatory understanding surpasses what "full expression" could accomplish. The shift from combative associations to allegories of the feminine alters the ethics of self-reliance. Fuller's letters reveal that she understood her "conversion" to require adjustments in the Conversations. But it could be, too, that the dynamics of the Conversations, in which the attributes of receptivity and tenderness among women were paramount, became for a time the model for her whole emotional life. At any rate, Fuller's need to sentimentalize herself as the recipient of care, though a recurring trope in her writings, is by no means the single or even the controlling figure and never again attains the intensity it acquires during the early years of the Conversations. To be more precise about the aversion to conflict inherent in this moment, we need to look at the way Fuller articulates the character of the critic, as opposed to that of the interpreter.

"A Short Essay on Critics": Law, Strength, and Subjectivity

In "A Short Essay on Critics" (1840) Fuller sets forth the critical program of the *Dial* by offering a taxonomy of the species. Her role as practicing critic and the theme of criticism combine to generate a greater tolerance for aggressive judgment than was permissible in the discourse of the Conversations. She launches at once into classifications that sharply impose negative values and rigidly sequester positive ones. By invoking "law," the standard of eternity, she justifies an unflinching aggressiveness at the outset of the essay (which marks the outset of the *Dial* itself). But "law" is a term that shifts among several meanings. Within the seven pages of Fuller's article these variations correspond to the complexities of critical ethics. For if "law" is imposed with considerable moral ferocity as the "absolute, invariable principle" that discriminates what is worthy, it is also the source of "the full tone of truth," the "earnest voice" of tentative individuality. As in "The Great Lawsuit: Man vs. Men, Woman vs. Women," law expresses both the element of personal longing in idealism and the opposition generated by idealism in the service of social values.

In light of these texts of the same period the ethical configuration of the Conversations looks particularly deliberate. For the link between subjectivity and the realm of law had been established in the Conversation classes without producing idealistic aggression, a result of the particular ethical economy of women's talk. What was suppressed in the Conversations, however, was not inhibited in print. This was especially the case in the arena of periodical criticism, strongly associated with the tradition of nasty reviews established by the *Edinburgh Review* early in the century and the equally venerable attacks on such practices.

The first paragraph of "A Short Essay on Critics," though it invokes both "the laws of criticism as a science" and the interior law of subjectivity ("the only law is, 'Speak the best word that is in thee'"), is mostly concerned with the uncertain status of law as a set of cultural norms in the "republic of letters":

> though this age be emphatically critical, the writer would still find it necessary to investigate the laws of criticism as a science, to settle its conditions as an art. Essays entitled critical are epistles addressed to the public through which the mind of the recluse relieves itself of its impressions. Of these the only law is, "Speak the best word that is in thee." Or they are . . . got up to order by the literary hack writer, for the literary mart, and the only law is to make them plausible. There is not yet deliberate recognition of a standard of criticism, though we hope the always strengthening league of the republic of letters must ere long settle laws on which its Amphictyonic council may act. (SEC 51)

The obsessions of an "emphatically critical" age, Fuller implies, arise from the unsettled social and cultural status of "essays entitled critical." The *Dial* will operate in the gulf between essays as "epistles" from "the mind of the recluse" and essays as pure commodities produced in conformity with the economic "law" of plausibility.

Fuller appears to shift the responsibility for drafting a cultural constitution to the vague collectivity of the "league of the republic of letters." The task of "classifying the critics" ("let us not venture to write on criticism, but by classifying the critics imply our hopes, and thereby our thoughts") emerges as a way of avoiding the legislative responsibility implied in writing "on criticism" itself. It is already clear, however, and quickly becomes even more so, that the shift from product (criticism) to agent (critic) does not arise from any queasiness about setting a "standard of criticism" or even dictating its "laws." Indeed, if anything, Fuller's gesture of classification itself, quite apart from the phenomena that are being classified, gives her the strength of judgment that she attributes to her own "comprehensive" critic: "Sustained by a principle . . . he can walk around the work, he can stand above it, he can uplift it and try its weight. Finally he is worthy to judge it" (SEC 53).

The shift to persons moves us into the figurative habits of Fuller,

Emerson, Carlyle, and Coleridge: the romantic typology of character in which the laws of personality, the laws of the marketplace, and the eternal laws governing "the analogies of the universe" are expressed through exemplary lives (SEC 53). The advantage of this kind of classification, I suspect, is the way character implies topographies of class, gender, economy, and morality, along with a full range of personal qualities. To prefer critics to criticism is to prefer narratives in which the opposition between "the mind of the recluse" and the "literary mart" has already begun to dissolve.

The scale of value according to which Fuller's three classes of critics are judged is measured in degrees of subjective development. The "subjective class" of critics is somewhat misnamed, since it is characterized by the absence of self-consciousness. Subjective critics are not "driven to consider . . . that they are deliberately giving their thoughts an independent existence"; they experience "no agonies of conscientious research, no timidities of self-respect," and "see no Ideal beyond the present hour." In the catalog of what such critics lack, the absence of feeling—"agonies," "timidities"—is as important as the deficiency of intellect and philosophy. These pre-Kantian critics, who assume "that their present position commands the universe," are therefore the pure products of society, "nation . . . church . . . family." They lack the simultaneously inner- and outer-directed idealism that produces both selfhood and universality: "He [the subjective critic] has never attempted . . . to find a law or raise a standard above all circumstances, permanent against influence. He is content to be the creature of his place" (SEC 52).

Predictably, other types of critics, the "apprehensive" and "comprehensive," are characterized by increasing degrees of self-consciousness. The "apprehensive" reader can "enter fully into a foreign existence" in the spirit of "the genial sympathies of nature," with "the ready grace of love" and with "the dignity of . . . friendship." The "comprehensive" critic surpasses this only in the ability to "estimate" the "relations" of the literary work to the universe at large (SEC 52). The highest form of critical art and science is classification in the light of eternal ideas—the project Fuller herself takes on in "A Short Essay."

She states with perfect clarity the relationship between idealism and negativity. "We detach the part from the whole, lest it stand between us and the whole." While she disavows any intention to "degrade" in the procedures of classification, she accepts its hurtful character: "the moment we look for a principle, we feel the need of a criterion, of a standard; and then we say what the work is *not*, as well as what it *is*;

and this is as healthy though not as grateful and gracious an operation of the mind as the other. We do not seek to degrade but to classify an object by stating what it is not" (SEC 54). Raising the issue of the ethics of analysis in this methodological way leads directly into Fuller's most scornful paragraph. She translates idealistic criteria at once into social caricatures. This transition exemplifies one of the most characteristic gestures of association in the Anglo-American critical tradition—a gesture strikingly repeated in the deliberately idiosyncratic context of the *Dial*. Nor is the passage typical of Fuller, whose satire tends to be more closely linked to personal observation. She has been defending the critic's authority but turns on the stock character of the anonymous periodical reviewer: "Wo [*sic*] to that coterie where some critic sits despotic, intrenched behind the infallible 'We.'" Such an "oracle" has "infused . . . soft sleepiness" and "a gentle dulness into his atmosphere" in his attempts at "dictatorship," and his readers have lapsed into "indolent acquiescence." In her caricature of bourgeois readers Fuller echoes the portraits disseminated by Coleridge and other periodical writers of the first quarter of the century: "the public, grown lazy and helpless . . . can now scarce brace itself even to get through a magazine article, but reads in the daily paper laid beside the breakfast plate a short notice of the last number of the long established and popular review, and thereupon passes its judgment and is content" (SEC 55).

This prefabricated paragraph moves Fuller into what she is really interested in saying, which is that the excessively homogenized voice generated by class or party must be abandoned. Idealism, which has induced her to treat modern readers as a class of persons devoid of individuality, now provides the basis for her call for personality. The reading audience "perceives that the voice is modulated to coax, to persuade." The public rejects "the judicious man of the world" in favor of "some earnest voice," which, with the stuttering that is so frequently the mark of Transcendentalist sincerity, "is uttering thoughts crude, rash, ill-arranged it may be, but true to one human breast." The philosophical critic who will speak in such tones bears a striking resemblance, in his relationship to his readers, to the "interpreter" who provided the characterological basis for the Conversations. "We would converse with him, secure that he will tell us all his thought," writes Fuller in her peroration. In a striking reversal of a Coleridgean trope the critic will teach by a healthful "contagion," not by direction; he will be "our companion and friend." This figure addresses the specific needs of literary criticism in terms familiar from Coleridge, however.

The philosophical critic personifies the ethical dilemma of the romantic reader, whose virtue consists mainly in the differential expertise that avoids either excesses or deficiencies of aggression: "Such an one will not disturb us . . . with sectarian prejudices, or an undue vehemence in favor of petty plans or temporary objects. Neither will he disgust us by . . . an inexpressive, lifeless gentleness. . . . He will teach us to love wisely what we before loved well, for he knows the difference between censoriousness and discernment, infatuation and reverence" (SEC 55–57).

In *Woman in the Nineteenth Century* Fuller's attention shifts from critics to the conditions that need to be criticized. This shift signals the participation of the feminist critic in what she describes. The later and vastly more involved text incorporates both Fuller's interpreter and her critic while it draws, for its complex range of styles and voices, on the heterogeneous style of her correspondence. The facile, if feisty, hierarchy of "An Essay on Critics" disappears. In its place arises a different standard of proof and a psychology, as well as a morality, of the anger produced by social facts.

CHAPTER 8

The Ethics of
Feminist Discourse

"The aspect of offence"

Woman in the Nineteenth Century (1845) is a book preoccupied with its own status as a feminist document. This means that the relationship between reform and literature, invoked allusively and critically, is fundamental to its way of unfolding. Literary and social facts function as equally valid forms of evidence and of history. Furthermore, the ethical connection between politics and reading is established through the way violent feelings surface in both. Since both critical reading and the call for political change bring with them the problem of aggression, exacerbated by the question of gender, it is hardly surprising that Fuller's text is hypersensitive to the antagonistic position of nineteenth-century feminism. As she develops her exposé of patriarchy and her argument for a temporarily intellectual rather than an intuitive feminist response, she also invents a feminist manner.

Fuller's feminist critic repeatedly shifts the responsibility for conflict onto social institutions, presumably to assuage anxiety about women's aggression. Anger becomes a symptom of cruel social limitations that will disappear under more fluid circumstances. Everything that is threatening in George Sand, Mary Wollstonecraft, and Fuller herself is also epiphenomenal and transient. But it can be restrained only through prolonged self-limitation. The violence of uncontrolled rebellion against

261

unfair conditions is transposed into the dynamics of costly internal restraint.

Fuller dramatizes these conflicts in the poetic fable of storming the castle that closes *Woman in the Nineteenth Century*. The battle call of the high-minded feminist reformer defies the irrational hostility of the "rabble rout":

> Then fear not thou to wind the horn,
> Though elf and gnome thy courage scorn;
> Ask for the Castle's King and Queen;
> Though rabble rout may rush between,
> Beat thee senseless to the ground,
> In the dark beset thee round;
> Persist to ask and it will come,
> Seek not for rest in humbler home;
> So shalt thou see what few have seen,
> The palace home of King and Queen.
>
> (WNC 208)

In this monarchist vignette, consistent with the feudal idiom of Fuller's youthful fantasies of authority, the woman warrior strives to move toward the "palace home of King and Queen." The union of the quester and her goal—the "home" of public and familial power—is blocked by a grotesque mob linked with the dehumanized "elf and gnome." The mob represents both internal and external resistance; its chthonic energy, which threatens unconsciousness, dark confusion, and claustrophobia, conveys the psychological as well as the social price of blowing one's own horn. The need for a strongly defended "palace home" suggests that feminist ambition desires refuge as much as glory.

The mob is clearly Jacobin, seen from the point of view of, say, Edmund Burke. Elsewhere, however, Fuller is quite clear about the careless way in which the term "Jacobin" had been bandied about, almost fifty years after the French Revolution and an ocean away. The abolitionist movement, she writes ironically, "makes, just now, the warmest appeal in behalf of women," but its members are "coldly regarded" by "society at large" as "the Jacobins of their day." Why, then, does Fuller seem genuinely repelled by the "rabble" in her closing poem and why is she so anxious, a few pages earlier, to claim for women a partially innate nonviolence that freedom cannot disturb?

Were this freedom to come suddenly, I have no fear of the consequences. Individuals might commit excesses, but there is not only in the sex a reverence for decorums and limits inherited and enhanced from generation to generation, which many years of other life could not efface, but a native love, in woman as woman, of proportion, of "the simple art of not too much," a Greek moderation, which would create immediately a restraining party, the natural legislators and instructors of the rest, and would gradually establish such rules as are needed to guard, without impeding, life. (WNC 94, 204)

This moderate ethos hovers between enforcement and instinct. On the one hand, it is culturally produced, "enhanced from generation to generation"; on the other, it is "native" to "woman as woman." But its natural inevitability clearly does not suffice to control the potential "excesses" of the liberated woman. A "restraining party" is needed, a parliamentary estate that will intervene with stabilizing "rules" between the monarchs and the "rabble rout." The legislative function turns out to be an interior one, and the risk of excess turns out to be a present fact rather than a future possibility.

Fuller's anxiety about the personal costs of feminism is most palpable when she writes about the women who are her immediate precursors as authors of feminist texts and, perhaps more significantly, of unconventional lives. She takes up Mary Wollstonecraft in an oblique and surprising fashion, beginning her ambivalent comments with unqualified praise of William Godwin. In the section of *Woman in the Nineteenth Century* on exemplary marriages of various degrees of spirituality, it is Godwin, as author of Wollstonecraft's biography, who emerges as the feminist hero: "This man had courage to love and honor this woman in the face of the world's sentence, and of all that was repulsive in her own past history. He believed he saw of what soul she was, and that the impulses she had struggled to act out were noble, though the opinions to which they had led might not be thoroughly weighed." Mary Wollstonecraft herself enters as the confused object on which Godwin and now Fuller exercise their clarity. Her "existence better proved the need of some new interpretation of woman's rights," Fuller asserts, "than any thing she wrote": "Such beings as these, rich in genius, of most tender sympathies, capable of high virtue and a chastened harmony, ought not to find themselves, by birth, in a place so narrow, that, in breaking bonds, they become outlaws" (WNC 130, 160).

Under "petrified and oppressive institutions," Fuller generalizes, the guiding principles of independent women "have made them warlike, paradoxical, and in some sense, Pariahs": "If they found stone ready in the quarry, they took it peaceably, other wise they alarmed the country by pulling down old towers to get materials." They wear "the aspect of offence" and feel "obliged to run their heads against any wall." The women of the eighteenth and nineteenth centuries in this respect resemble their foremothers, Fuller's Renaissance queens. Elizabeth, for example, "put on her virtues as armor" when, "half-emancipated and jealous of her freedom," she assumed a "combative attitude" (WNC 133–34, 122).

George Sand likewise exemplifies the development of radicalism, a process that begins with "the assault upon bad institutions, and external ills," moves through the maturing "experience of comparative freedom," and ends in the necessary faith in "individual character." If Godwin provides the moderating "interpretation" of Wollstonecraft, Elizabeth Barrett does the same for Sand, according to Fuller. Barrett "is such a woman, so unblemished in character, so high in aim, and pure in soul, that should address this other [Sand], as noble in nature, but clouded by error, and struggling with circumstance." Barrett's two remarkable sonnets to Sand, quoted in their entirety by Fuller, characterize her as the hero and victim of the effort to "deny / Thy woman's nature with a manly scorn." Barrett recognizes the survival of feminine difference in the woman who, "amid the lions / Of thy tumultuous senses moans defiance, / And answers roar for roar":

> Ah, vain denial! that revolted cry
> Is sobbed in by a woman's voice forlorn:
> —Thy woman's hair, my sister, all unshorn,
> Floats back dishevelled strength in agony[.]
>   (WNC 131, 130)

The need for a sisterly or brotherly figure to negotiate between overt rebellion and society's demand for conventional forms of "purity" recurs throughout Fuller's writings. If we look back at the figure of the teacher who taught Mariana to survive at the price of sacrificing her brilliantly antiauthoritarian performances, and at the role of Ellen Kilshaw, Susan Prescott, and Eliza Farrar in instructing Fuller's own adaptations, we can infer the powerful connection between her characterizations of Sand and Wollstonecraft and her own fabulous selves.

The theme of protest never enters into Fuller's writing without the insistence on self-restraint, the acceptance of existing social judgments. Fuller's sympathy extends to rebels, but she regards them (like Hawthorne in *The Scarlet Letter*) as being incapable of founding a new era: "the mind of the age struggles confusedly . . . better discerning as yet the ill it can no longer bear, than the good by which it may supersede it. But women, like Sand, will speak now and cannot be silenced. . . . But though such forbode [a new era], not such shall be the parents of it."[1] Reformers must be intensely self-controlled—"severe law-givers to themselves"—so that the charge of violence may be directed entirely against the circumstances they seek to change. They must eschew "wild impulse" and "passionate error": "Their liberty must be the liberty of law and knowledge." Fuller protests on behalf of those, like Eloisa and Abelard, who commit "the transgressions against custom which have caused such an outcry against those of noble intention." But with one of the characteristic swerves away from extremism which show romanticism in its full difficulty, she also defensively credits the point of view of those who are outraged: "society has a right to outlaw them till she has revised her law; and this she must be taught to do, by one who speaks with authority, not in anger or haste" (WNC 132–33).

This middle figure, whose authority derives from the power of virtue so self-evident that it need not be asserted against public opinion, coincides with the ethical position of the "interpreter" as Fuller imagined it in the Conversations and of the "critic" as she developed it

---

[1]Hawthorne could well have based this passage in the Conclusion to *The Scarlet Letter* on Fuller's views: "She assured them . . . of her firm belief, that, at some brighter period, when the world should have grown ripe for it, in Heaven's own time, a new truth would be revealed, in order to establish the whole relation between man and woman on a surer ground of mutual happiness. Earlier in life, Hester had vainly imagined that she herself might be the destined prophetess, but had long since recognized the impossibility that any mission of divine and mysterious truth should be confided to a woman stained with sin, bowed down with shame, or even burdened with a lifelong sorrow. The angel of the coming revelation must be a woman, indeed, but lofty, pure, and beautiful; and wise, moreover, not through dusky grief, but the ethereal medium of joy" (*The Scarlet Letter* [New York: Signet, 1959], 245). The theme of the mutually exclusive character of feminist efficacy and anger, sin, shame, or sorrow is intriguing in its recurrences, particularly since it does not seem to apply to other kinds of radicalism. It is precisely his suffering as a slave, for example, which qualifies Frederick Douglass for leadership; it is the suffering of women at the hands of alcoholic husbands which is produced as the basis for the temperance movement. Nonetheless, there is a discernible tendency, after the French Revolution, to find political protest on the part of victims suspect on the grounds that it will lead to irrational retaliatory violence.

in "A Short Essay on Critics."[2] In *Woman in the Nineteenth Century* the iconic force of Emily Plater, the Polish fighter, or of Abby Kelley, the women's rights activist, derives from the moral beauty of their presence, as opposed to the absence or lack that motivates conflict. "She acted like a gentle hero," Fuller quotes from a description of Kelley, "with her mild decision and womanly calmness. All heroism is mild and quiet and gentle, for it is life and possession, and combativeness and firmness show a want of actualness" (WNC 132–33, 106–7, 158).

Fuller's sense that activism makes women suffer arises from her view of mid-nineteenth-century gender politics as produced by the interaction of woman's temperamental difference and historical process. She is acutely aware—presciently so, in the light of recent writings on feminist theory—of the need to apprehend subjectivity and ideology simultaneously. This emerges, for example, in her synthetic handling of the way one representative dualism—Goethe and Fourier—stands for the claims of consciousness and institutions, respectively, and in her appreciation of Sand's movement from society to character, which concludes with the call for "a parallel movement in these two branches of life" (WNC 168, 132). If we look closely at her theory of sexual difference as it is revealed in these difficult negotiations between interior and historical life, we quickly find that it rests on the assumption of women's psycho-moral uniqueness—a uniqueness defined, circularly, as the gift of perceiving psychomoral nuance.

When Fuller ventures "to retrace, once more, the scope of my design" at the end of *Woman in the Nineteenth Century,* she summarizes her theory of sexual character in a myth of symmetrical binarisms, a spatial figure rapidly complicated by the "undulated course" of sexual relations in "the order of time." "The growth of man is two-fold, masculine and feminine," she begins, "two methods" distinguished as "Energy and Harmony / Power and Beauty / Intellect and Love." "Or," she adds, "some such rude classification." Then she proceeds to call her stereotypical contrasts into question. The two sides are evident "in man and woman" only "as the more and less, for the faculties have not been given pure to either." In addition to the mixed proportions of masculine and feminine within each individual, there are "exceptions in great number" to every rule.[3] In "the order of time," to which she

---

[2]See WNC 130, 147, 148, and 186 for Fuller's use of "interpret" and "interpreter."

[3]Fuller also refers to the structurally similar notion of the androgynous soul, the idea "that, in the metamorphosis of the life, the soul assumes the form, first of man, then of woman." Taking on the voice of an interlocutor, she queries, "Why, then . . . lay such emphasis on the rights of woman?" She replies, "That makes no difference. It is not

next turns, "Man . . . was developed first. . . . Woman was therefore under his care as an elder." But temporal models are as skewed as spatial ones: "as human nature goes not straight forward, but by excessive action and then reaction in an undulated course, he misunderstood and abused his advantages, and became her temporal master instead of her spiritual sire" (WNC 200–202)

The tendency for Fuller's symmetrical allegories of sexual/moral difference to make several arguments at once, arguments that are frequently irreconcilable, is nowhere more visible than in the chiasmic pair of quotations at the beginning of the volume. Echoing the title of the *Dial* essay—"The Great Lawsuit: Man vs. Men; Woman vs. Women"—Fuller juxtaposes the debased condition of each sex against its ideal longings. The first line, of course, is from *Hamlet;* the second is almost certainly by Fuller herself:

"Frailty, thy name is WOMAN."

"The Earth waits for her Queen."

The connection between these quotations may not be obvious, but it is strict. Yet would any contradict us, if we made them applicable to the other side, and began also

Frailty, they [*sic*] name is MAN.

The Earth waits for its King.

As the frailties and powers of each sex are contrasted, so the paradoxical situation of woman is symmetrically compared—and, by virtue of this symmetry, implicitly likened—to that of man. But the meanings and, in small ways, the language of the two pairs of quotations are not identical. The quotation marks around the first set accentuate the derivation of the line from *Hamlet*. As the epigraph for a book about women, the framing of this theatrical charge of inferiority sets Fuller's critical irony in motion. This line is ironic in a distinctly different way from its counterpart, "Frailty, [thy] name is MAN," the source of which is Fuller's revisionary (if not retaliatory) intent. The transition to the

---

woman, but the law of right, the law of growth, that speaks in use, and demands the perfection of each being in its kind, apple as apple, woman as woman. Without adopting your theory I know that I, a daughter, live through the life of man; but what concerns me now is, that my life be . . . a complete life in its kind" (WNC 207).

second half of each pair, referring to the desired apotheosis of woman or man as Queen or King, produces the "gulf of death" that yawns between "mental faith" and "practice" throughout *Woman in the Nineteenth Century*. The earth's change of gender—from "her Queen" to "its King"—conveys in miniature the asymmetrical relation of masculine and feminine styles of power which, in this book at least, unsettles Fuller's attempts to situate feminism in universal human renovation (WNC 84, 126).

The most passionate claim for the essential difference of woman's nature comes immediately after Fuller's defense of the "spiritual dignity" of "old maids." This passage modulates from a strongly pragmatic grasp of the fact that "the business of society . . . could now scarcely be carried on without . . . these despised auxiliaries" to more ideal claims. Such a woman, Fuller writes, "at once a priestly servant, and a loving muse," may become "the intellectual interpreter of the varied life she sees; the Urania of a half-formed world's twilight." Sexual difference reveals woman's ability to mediate between binary oppositions, which gives the feminine its particular ethical quality. If the "spiritual tendency" is feminine, "the intellect, cold, is ever more masculine" until, "warmed by emotion, it rushes towards mother earth and puts on the forms of beauty." Divination has a double role, therefore, as the opposite of masculine analysis and as the aesthetic process of joining intellect and emotion. Elsewhere in *Woman* Fuller identifies the area between genders as one of Emersonian transition belonging to neither: "Male and female represent the two sides of the great radical dualism. But, in fact, they are perpetually passing into one another. Fluid hardens to solid, solid rushes to fluid. There is no wholly masculine man, no purely feminine woman" (WNC 147–52, 161). Fuller claims these metamorphic energies for woman but also thinks of them as the state in which we are released from the claims of gender altogether. She depicts the phenomenological effect of this structural redundancy as more productive of suffering than pleasure.

The divinatory potential of women makes them most unhappy. Fuller makes this point in two steps, the first of which is a classic description of feminine interpretive gifts:

> The electrical, the magnetic element in woman has not been fairly brought out at any period. Every thing might be expected from it; she has far more of it than man. This is commonly expressed by saying that her intuitions are more rapid and more correct. You will often see men of high intellect absolutely stupid in regard to the atmospheric changes, the

fine invisible links which connect the forms of life around them, while common women, if pure and modest, so that a vulgar self do not over-shadow the mental eye, will seize and delineate these with unerring discrimination.

The "common" sense that bypasses and outruns intellect may not lead "common" women to misery, but those "who combine this organiza-tion with creative genius, are very commonly unhappy at present" (WNC 152). This second step of Fuller's argument relates gender dif-ference to the psychology of genius. As Coleridge had done in his chapter controverting "The irritability of Men of Genius," Fuller looks for historically specific manifestations of an essential difference.

If Coleridge's poet was less cantankerous than other men, Fuller's female genius is more tormented than other women. Gifted men and women both "see too much to act in conformity with those around them," Fuller observes. But because women are more generally ex-pected to display "an obvious order and self-restraining decorum," deviations by women of "an impassioned sensibility" are punished more harshly and felt more deeply: "The world repels them more rudely, and they are of weaker bodily frame." Physiological or "ner-vous" weakness, however, is a sign (as all readers of romantic literature know) of mental dominance. It is hardly surprising that the women "who seem overladen with electricity frighten those around them." Fuller seems to want to say that feminine genius is not necessarily negative in its effects, that genius and negativity are separable in wom-en's experience. But although in a liberal milieu "the electric fluid will be found to invigorate and embellish, not destroy life" (especially in the performances of "actresses" and "songsters"), there is "something tragic" in the air of the muses and Sibyls from the time of the Greeks on down. They are *over*-flowed with thought": "The eye is over-full of expression, dilated and lustrous; it seems to have drawn the whole being into it" (WNC 152–53). Whatever the power of woman's elec-tromagnetism to flood the theater of performance, it has a wasting effect on her other faculties.

The apparent excess of intuition in nineteenth-century women gives rise to Fuller's short-term feminist program. After characterizing the fem-inine as having more in common with "the Muse" than "Minerva," she calls for an emphasis on critical intellect to protect women from their own sensibilities. The "Muse," or the "especial genius of wom-an," she sums up, is "electrical in movement, intuitive in function, spiritual in tendency. She excels not so easily in classification, or re-creation, as in an instinctive seizure of causes, and a simple breathing out of what she receives that has the singleness of life, rather than the selecting and energizing of art." But the pain of creative women in-spired by such a muse leads Fuller to impose a check on essential fem-inine tendencies. She welcomes "every thing that tends to strengthen the fibre and develop the nature on more sides," so that "the intellect and affections" may be "in harmony." "If it has been the tendency of these remarks to call woman rather to the Minerva side," she explains, "if I . . . have spoken from society no less than the soul," it is out of "love for many incarcerated souls, that might be freed, could the idea of religious self-dependence be established in them, could the weak-ening habit of dependence on others be broken up" (WNC 161, 163).

Intellectual discipline, experiential verification, causal reasoning, along with self-consciousness in a more diffuse sense, are the discriminating mental acts comprising self-reliance. When the expressive power of intuition entangles woman too deeply with others, she must be "cured by a time of isolation" or "celibacy" devoted to such thinking: "It is . . . only in the present crisis that the preference is given to Minerva. The power of continence must establish the legitimacy of freedom, the power of self-poise the perfection of motion." Having called for "the armor and the javelin" of Minerva and for meditation in "virgin loneli-ness," Fuller finally does not construct a rational boundary to feminine intuition but throws women back on intuition. She begins by counter-ing "Femality" with the demand for self-discipline and intellectual clarity; then the theme of self-reliance leads her to celebrate a visionary state of feminine being.[4] In their armed solitude women can "retire within themselves, and explore the groundwork of life until they find their own peculiar secret," after which they will come forth "renovated and baptized." The apotheosis of sexual difference endows woman with a fully ethical power, purged of all negative aspects: "It is not the transient breath of poetic incense. . . . It is not life-long sway. . . . It is not money, nor notoriety, nor the badges of authority that men have appropriated to themselves. . . . It is for that which at once includes these and precludes them. . . . the intelligent freedom of the universe, to use its means; to learn its secret . . . with God alone for their guide and their judge" (WNC 160, 165, 120). As intuition is both the op-posite of masculinity and the means of changing it into something less

---

[4]For the source of the term "Femality," as it appeared in the *Pathfinder* of 18 March 1843, see WNC 160n.

monolithic, so intellectual Minerva is both the opposite of the feminine Muse and the source of its independent strength.

These theoretical surpluses—for that is really what they are, rather than contradictions or paradoxes—justify Fuller's "both/and" policies with regard to her contemporaries. She wants women both to discover their special powers as women and, in her "let them be sea-captains" mood, to claim equal opportunities with men. She oscillates, therefore, between honoring divination, which proceeds out of the natural law of sexual difference, and celebrating the manifold exceptions to gender typologies: "Nature provides exceptions to every rule. She sends women to battle, and sets Hercules spinning; she enables women to bear immense burdens, cold, and frost; she enables the man, who feels maternal love, to nourish his infant like a mother. . . . Presently she will make a female Newton, and a male Syren." Turning on her own myths, she sings out, "Woman the heart, man the head! Such divisions are only important when they are never to be transcended. . . . Nature seems to delight in varying the arrangements, as if to show that she will be fettered by no rule, and we must admit the same varieties that she admits" (WNC 204, 161–62, 135).

Not surprisingly, Fuller's theories of sexual difference and gender multiplicity lead to a mixture of attitudes toward masculine behavior and toward texts by men. She validates the longing for the feminine and the divinatory in men's writing. And she directs a range of indignant, aggressive, and accusatory opinion against the way men talk to and about women. If Fuller's women shift between withdrawal from and engagement with masculine roles, her men veer between desire and obduracy toward feminine and feminist articulations. As an ethical strategy this has the advantage of setting in play a shared orientation to the maternal which is natural to women and internalized by some men as a form of idealism. In dramatizing the disjunction between the spiritual possibilities of men and their present actions, Fuller assuages the fear of feminist anger while retaining the force of righteous indignation.

Several lengthy portions of *Woman in the Nineteenth Century* are given over to the subject of the rare masculine sympathy for the feminine spirit. Fuller seeks to demonstrate that this affinity has been kept alive and, in the romantic period, strengthened by a small elite of intellectuals and artists. The ability to express longing for the maternal coincides with the prophetic temperament of the genius, who intuits the moral direction of the future. The male artist's ethical imagination endows him with feminine visionary potential.

In tracing male fantasies of the maternal, Fuller indulges pathos until it becomes of symptom of high principle. The psychological effect of the mother recurs in the lives of adult men as intuitions of the feminine; it enters into cultural history by way of art, literature, and religion. "Man is of woman born," Fuller begins, "and her face bends over him in infancy with an expression he can never quite forget." While acknowledging that these sentiments may be "hacknied," as they certainly were, Fuller nevertheless relies on the elevating power of nostalgia:

> Some gleams of the same expression which shone down upon his infancy, angelically pure and benign, visit man again with hopes of pure love, of a holy marriage. Or, if not before, in the eyes of the mother of his child they again are seen, and dim fancies pass before his mind, that woman may not have been born for him alone, but have come from heaven, a commissioned soul, a messenger of truth and love[.] (WNC 110)

The associative leap from the image of the mother to the idea of an independent womanly spirit liberates Fuller's representative male just at the point where his fantasy seems most self-serving. The tenuous reality of the maternal impression—in "gleams, in dim fancies"—means that it is more available to creative than to "careless men." Its truths "shine with radiant clearness" into the minds "of the poet, the priest, and the artist" and henceforth become culturally available in systems of belief and iconography.

Long sequences of *Woman in the Nineteenth Century* are built out of commentary on "the idea of woman" as it is "nobly manifested" in the "mythologies and poems" of one civilization after another. Fuller presents myths of the feminine as empowering images while using a different kind of historical speculation to criticize the absence or belittling of female figures. In Greece, "Ceres and Proserpine, significantly termed 'the great goddesses,' were seen seated, side by side. They needed not to rise for any worshipper or any change; they were prepared for all things. . . . More obvious is the meaning of these three forms, the Diana, Minerva, and Vesta. Unlike in the expression of their beauty, but alike in this,—that each was self-sufficing." But when confronted by the "neglect of woman" in Roman culture, Fuller shifts to a more anthropological approach, suggesting that this "was a reaction on the manners of Etruria, where the priestess Queen, warrior Queen, would seem to have been so usual a character" (WNC 111–12).

She is troubled by the discrepancy between mythical content and the historical realities of the cultures that produced it. Elsewhere she acknowledges the gap between "the vulgar Greek sentiment" that women are of negligible civic value and the Greek philosophical capacity to imagine "the ideal man" and "the ideal woman" as a balanced pair—ideality being, for Fuller, often inseparable from symmetry. She postpones the contradiction, again swerving away from material debasement in favor of the products of what she judges to be desire: "whatever were the facts of daily life, I cannot complain, of the age and nation, which represents its thought by such a symbol as I see before me at this moment"—the zodiac with paired busts of gods and goddesses. Having elided the question of fact, she continues on her associative path. "Coming nearer our own time," she finds "religion and poetry no less true in their revelations," chiefly through the Christian compensation for the Old Testament "disgrace" of woman. Fuller's summary shows again the curious mixture of realism and allegory in her readings of culture: "Nor, however imperfect may be the action, in our day, of the faith thus expressed, and though we can scarcely think it nearer this ideal, than that of India or Greece was near their ideal, is it in vain that the truth has been recognized . . . that women are in themselves possessors of and possessed by immortal souls" (WNC 115).

Fuller takes up the evidential display of texts once more, blending history and literature, as she launches into an overview of the feudal literatures of Europe. But she does so without pretending that there is anything but "a gulf of death" between culture's "broad intellectual effulgence" and "the practice of the world." The "gulf" yawns greatest in Fuller's own era. She detects a "throng of symptoms" in the "unison of . . . male minds" on the subject of women, minds that "take rank as the prophets of the coming age, while their histories and labors are rooted in the past." Among the "prophets" who set forth a mature "idea of woman" are the "late Dr. Channing," Alexander Kinmont, and Shelley, along with the Continental triumvirate of Swedenborg, Fourier, and finally Goethe, who towers above the rest in Fuller's regard.[5] The function of their writings is to "[educate] the age to a better consciousness of what man needs, what man can be"—"man" signifying "humanity." It is only after an essay on the types of virtue and "free development" embodied in Goethe's female characters that Fuller turns briefly to the "hints" thrown out by women writers, much

[5]Kinmont (1799–1838) was author of *Twelve Lectures on the Natural History of Man, and the Rise and Progress of Philosophy* (1839) (WNC 78n, 160).

as her approach to Mary Wollstonecraft was preceded by more enthusiastic comments on Godwin (WNC 126, 158–59, 165–72).

The turn from the prophetic use of literature to the critical use of social fact precipitates a sharp alteration in Fuller's stance. This change corresponds to a shift in subject matter from the male artist to "the legislator and man of the world," "the *citizen*" of the commercial metropolis. The ethical difference between art and life which has been implicit all along becomes obvious as Fuller's tone moves from appreciation to aggression. The distance between the feminine as idealized in high culture and the realities of nineteenth-century sexual economies suddenly produces a fiery voice when Fuller arrives at the subject of prostitution.[6]

The sociocultural regions for the expression of antagonism are rather strictly delimited and are carefully prepared in *Woman in the Nineteenth Century*. Within the range of topics "on which she neither can nor will restrain the indignation of a full heart," Fuller has few qualms about ferocity. She parodies the way men rationalize the inevitability of prostitution: "I refer to . . . the daring with which the legislator and man of the world lifts his head beneath the heavens and says 'this must be; it cannot be helped; it is a necessary accompaniment of *civilization.*'" Her caricature of the middle-class businessman operates over against the language of feminist principle: "So speaks the *citizen*. Man born of woman, the father of daughters, declares that he will and must buy the comforts and commercial advantages of his London, Vienna, Paris, New-York, by conniving at the moral death, the damnation, so far as the action of society can insure it, of thousands of women for each splendid metropolis." Fuller's irony, one of her principal weapons in similar passages throughout the book, gives way at this point to the high pitch of what might be termed a feminist jeremiad: "Your forms degraded and your eyes clouded by secret sin; natural harmony broken and fineness of perception destroyed in your mental and bodily organization; God and love shut out from your hearts by the foul visitants you have permitted there; incapable of pure marriage; incapable of pure parentage; incapable of worship; oh wretched men, your sin is its own punishment!" Abandoning men, she addresses herself "to you, women, American women," although her sarcastic survey of male

[6]Fuller's discussion of prostitution begins with her defense of the publicly expressed opinions of the British writer Anna Brownell Jameson. Jameson was best known as the author of *Shakespeare's Heroines*, reviewed by Fuller, as were Jameson's memoirs and letters (WNC 173).

deception continues in her exhortations to her own sex. She demands confirmation and recognition: "You know how it was in the Oriental clime. . . . You know how it was with the natives of this continent. . . . Now pass to the countries where marriage is between one and one." In high dudgeon Fuller turns on women who are beyond the reach of idealism: "I ask of you, young girls—I do not mean *you,* whose heart is that of an old coxcomb. . . . Not of you whose whole character is tainted with vanity. . . . To such I do not speak. But to thee, maiden, who, if not so fair, art yet of that unpolluted nature which Milton saw when he dreamed of Comus and the Paradise" (WNC 173–76).

Such passages show that Fuller's literary romanticism cannot be separated from her feminist commitments. For even as she is engaged in setting forth the dynamics of sexual exploitation, the standards she invokes derive, in the course of a few pages, from Greek mythology, Canova, Beethoven, Michelangelo, Sidney, Milton, and pindarics by Fuller herself (WNC 173–79). Her divorce of the economic and the imaginative allows her to use culture against itself in the interests of women's self-reliance—and in the interests of romanticism. For there is no question but that the heterotextual discourse of *Woman in the Nineteenth Century* generates an idiosyncratic but recognizably romantic canon that operates in the subject as a stimulus for fantasies of power. Romantic or romanticized texts are treated as bearers of a desirable contagion that women can catch. Yet their aura conveys the extent to which such quotations stand apart from their feminist uses.

Internalized "laws" also provide the basis for the analogical motives that link blacks, women, Jews, Indians, and the subjects of European monarchies in an idealistic alliance based on "a natural following out of principle." Fuller's most complete exposition of the relation between women and slaves begins and ends with "the principle of liberty." Her account of the French Revolution, "that strangely disguised angel," condemns its lack of spiritual content and "mere outward" emphasis The absence of ideas resulted in the rape of the "Gooddess [*sic*] of Liberty," despite the fact that women were granted some degree of equality, reflected in the title of "citoyenne." In retrospect, however, the Revolution provides a crucial text for present reform. "Europe is conning a valued lesson from the blood-stained page"—a theme soon confirmed by a spate of European revolutions—and the same interpretive "tendencies, farther unfolded, will bear good fruit in this country" (WNC 90–91).

Turning to the United States, then, she attacks the contradiction between an ostensible Christian mission and the facts of slavery and genocide, "what has been done towards the red man, the black man." Fuller's critique of the way religion and economy collaborate in oppression is grounded in the "moral law," which, in turn, is grounded in the subject. The "gain of creation consists always in the growth of individual minds," in which "the continual development of . . . the thought of human destiny" takes place; still, the "great moral law" of America is given "to eternity," not to present individuals, "to express."[7] The efficacy of quotation lies in perpetuating "the verbal statement" of principle so that it can again be internalized as aspiration and desire. Proclamation, even in bad faith, has historical force: "it is not in vain, that the verbal statement has been made, 'All men are born free and equal.' There it stands, a golden certainty wherewith to encourage the good, to shame the bad. . . . That which has once been clearly conceived in the intelligence cannot fail sooner or later to be acted out." "It has become a law," Fuller asserts, and since "law" carries with it a principle of expression, as such it "cannot fail of universal recognition" (WNC 92–93).

Here we have the basis for the method of *Woman in the Nineteenth Century,* the cycle of "law" articulated as belief or historical action, then reinternalized through reading to be felt as the subjective aspiration that gives rise to new action. At this juncture, Fuller tries not to depend on sexual difference (although since both understanding and hope are deeply gendered capabilities, sexual difference has not disappeared from the text). Such views, in which pragmatic social reform and emotional impulse are linked by the passage of both through the written record, underlie Fuller's commitment to the Italian Revolution, as well as her later perspectives on women. In her letters from Europe in the late 1840s Fuller does not move from romanticism to feminism and from feminism to socialism. Rather, she recontextualizes feminism in such a way that it becomes less dependent on the ethical

---

[7]A more specific occurrence of the same themes is found toward the end of *Woman in the Nineteenth Century*. Encouraged by efforts to aid Jews in their return to Palestine and the release of the Irish political agitator Daniel O'Connell, she is simultaneously revolted by the annexation of Texas, which "threatens to rivet the chains of slavery and the leprosy of sin permanently on this nation." She continues, "Ah! if this should take place, who will dare again to feel the throb of heavenly hope, as to the destiny of this country? The noble thought that gave unity to all our knowledge, harmony to all our designs . . . flutters as if about to leave the breast, which, deprived of it, will have no more a nation, no more a home on earth." The thought that one's "home on earth" is established through a popular commitment to freedom comes to the fore in Fuller's Italian writings.

and divinatory characteristics of women. Eventually, divination, passion, and their "electro-magnetic" aura migrate to the Italians, simplifying Fuller's theoretical predicaments as a feminist while complicating her revolutionary identity.

"A Crowd of Books to Sigh Over": Fuller's Method

The recurring clash of social experience and textual representations of the feminine takes us some way into the discursive structure of *Woman in the Nineteenth Century*. When we observe the whole range of allusive and intertextual events that constitute the book, however, their meanings alter somewhat. The energy of quotation, the urgency of manifold forms of cultural reference, and the unstoppable cataloging—*as signs*—of "signs of the times" produce writing as a "stream which is ever flowing from the heights of my thought," as Fuller describes it, a flood of cultural associations which descends on the present. Or, in a moment of understandable fatigue, not a flood, but the somewhat depressing prospect of an urban crowd, a "crowd of books." As she makes a transition "from the future to the present," she effects the less exhilarating descent from myth to book review. "It would seem as if this time [of transformation] were not very near to one fresh from books, such as I have of late been—" and here she interrupts herself to revise her phrasing—"no: *not* reading, but sighing over." From the number of books sent to her "since my friends knew me to be engaged in this way," she concludes "that almost all that is extant of formal precept has come under my eye." Her reaction is characteristic. "Among these I select as a favorable specimen, the book I have already quoted" and which she goes on to quote some more: "'The Study of the Life of Woman, by Madame Necker de Saussure, of Geneva, translated from the French'" (WNC 200, 192).

Fuller's repetitive, accumulating, and associative style is hardly unique among romantic authors. Emerson's essays are constructed in a similar way, although their recurring episodes of transformation and collapse are quite different from Fuller's movement between allegorical allusions and multivocal performances. The status of philosophical discourse in Coleridge's prose, set against the anxiety-inducing materials of journalism and novels and the compensatory references to domestic sensation, again differs in its specific economy but is alike in the close link between its mania for quotation and its ambivalent drive for idealization. The difference is that whereas the male romantics situate the feminine over against the reading of philosophy, Fuller performs reading that generates feminism and does it in the name of philosophy or the ideal. For Coleridge, Sara Hutchinson is the emotion that abstruse research has blocked; for Fuller, abstruse research reveals the desire for the feminine soul in the founding texts of Western culture. In *Woman in the Nineteenth Century* reading opposes not feeling but masculinity. Insofar as Fuller makes oppressive masculine practices speak only in idioms that are not aesthetic or literary—if anything in this highly referential book can be called "not literary"—she relegates codes of habitual behavior and speech to the enemy while appropriating the aesthetic for woman.

The character of Fuller's protagonist, the romantic essayist who marshals such diverse materials and argues their meanings, is unusually active and self-referential. The persistent reference to her emotional imperatives as both reader and writer—in addition to the allusive redundancy such emotion generates—gives *Woman in the Nineteenth Century* its tone of urgency. The vocalized energy of association and transition, Fuller hovers on the edge of her interpolated dramas as producer, interpreter, and alter ego of the figures populating the book. As the one who brings the stories before us, she cannily declines the role of heroine. Yet as metanarrative strategist, she draws attention to her own overburdened feelings of pain and pleasure and the necessary demonstrativeness to which they lead:

> Such instances count up by scores within my own memory.

> I said, we will not speak of this now, yet I have spoken, for the subject makes me feel too much.

> We must insert in this connection the most beautiful picture presented by ancient literature of wedded love. . . .

> I must quote two more short passages from Xenophon, for he is a writer who pleases me well.

> I could swell the catalogue of instances far beyond the reader's patience.
> (WNC 97, 138, 143, 119)

Fuller speaks as the device that turns the images stored up through reading and social witness into texts to be witnessed by others. Quantity signifies both politically and authorially. She chooses her anecdotes from a crowd of instances and calls attention to the feeling of pressure behind and within her allusions, arguing as one for whom the sublime of multiplying references is proof of her sincerity. Retold stories thus acquire the status of evidence that proves the legitimacy of the feminist critique.

Fundamental to Fuller's discourse both as an explanation for the serial construction of *Woman* and as an outlet for its semiotic excess— its surplus of examples—is the logic of "the signs of the times":

> Under these circumstances, without attaching importance, in them-selves, to the changes demanded by the champions of women, we hail them as signs of the times.
>
> Another sign of the times is furnished by the triumphs of female authorship.
>
> All these motions of the time, tides that betoken a waxing moon, overflow upon our land.
>
> Among the throng of symptoms which denote the present tendency to a crisis in the life of woman . . . I have attempted to select a few. (WNC 100, 144, 155, 165)

The basis for resemblance among such signs is an underlying law or principle that turns the whole field of culture and events into a collection of allegories all meaning roughly the same thing. Heterogeneous assemblages prove historical laws. By virtue of their capacity to appear as a "throng," such signifiers can be apprehended only en masse; like all nineteenth-century crowds, they can only "denote the . . . tendency to crisis." But if the books, deeds, or utterances enumerated after such statements as I have just quoted function as quantity or mass, they also make possible other stylistic attributes. Within such a structure, for example, Fuller is bound neither by chronological sequence nor by syllogistic logic. She moves among "signs" and "symptoms" in a loosely associative way, and in these associative openings her loyalties and antipathies surface.

Fuller's most complex entry into her own discourse takes place when Miranda arrives in the text of *Woman* as Fuller's half-fictive, half-autobiographical description of what feminism looks like. Miranda is thereby related to the series of personae related to Margaret—Mariana, Minerva, the Muse—defined by their status as representations of female resistance and suffering. But she alone is given a voice in which to instruct the essayist in the grounds for pessimism about women's condition. And finally, it is "from the papers of Miranda" that Fuller has "borrowed" the material in Appendix G on "characters of women drawn by the Greek dramatists" (WNC 224). Postponing the question of the appendix for the moment, we can trace, in the account of Miranda, Fuller's tendency to approach and to avoid her master signs. In the course of a few pages she is Miranda's biographer, interlocutor, and double—and eventually her critic.

The paragraph preceding the Miranda episode concludes, "Let us consider what obstructions impede this good era, and what signs give reason to hope that it draws near." Miranda then materializes in two roles: as Fuller's collaborator in interpreting signs and as herself a sign of hope that turns out to be cause for pessimism as well. A brief biography sets forth the reasons why Fuller "had always thought [of Miranda] as an example": specifically, an example "that the restraints upon the sex were insuperable only to those who think them so, or who noisily strive to break them" (WNC 101–2).

What are the conditions, then, that enable Miranda to "speak without heat and bitterness of the position of her sex?" That produce the ethic of nonoppositional independence for which she stands? There are three: the apparent absence of a mother, who is never mentioned; a father who treated his daughter as "a living mind" and "child of the spirit"; and an intensely feminine or "electric" temperament in which sexuality is nonetheless muted. Miranda never possessed "those charms which might have drawn to her bewildering flatteries." Despite the fact that her personal magnetism attracts both men and women, she is "affectionate without passion, intellectual without coldness." In other words, Fuller gives Miranda an idealized version of her own paternal education and characteristic "electricity," without the fault of alternating "passion" and "coldness." At this point, then, Miranda crystallizes as "an example" of the feminist way, the precariousness of which emerges in Fuller's balanced phrasing: "She had taken a course of her own, and no man stood in her way. Many of her acts had been unusual but excited no uproar. Few helped, but none checked her, and the many men, who knew her mind and her life, showed to her confidence as to a brother, gentleness as to a sister. And not only refined, but very coarse men approved and aided." Independence without opposition, unconventionality without "uproar," self-reliance without check, brotherly and sisterly love: Miranda receives all of the benefits of feminism without any of the costs. But it is she who articulates fundamental doubts about the growth of self-reliance in women and respect for women in men. "I talked with her upon these matters, and . . . said very much what I have written," Fuller interjects. She enters as a participant to resist Miranda's pessimism (WNC 101–2).

Miranda is fully conscious of the paradoxical nature of her position. "This self dependence, which was honored in me, is deprecated as a fault in most women," she asserts. "This is the fault of man." Because she was able to take her stand on "self-reliance" at a very young age, she was not subjected to the "precepts" of male "guardians." Most girls, their minds "impeded by doubts . . . lose their chance of fair free proportions." Miranda has arrived at her current bleak outlook after a period of hopefulness: "Once I thought that men would help to forward this state of things more than I do now." But, she says, "early I perceived that men never, in any extreme of despair, wished to be women." Male conversation, in which "any sign of weakness" is mocked as feminine and any form of power is honored as manly, is the basis for her revised conclusions about the "rooted skepticism" of men on the subject of female equality. Miranda concludes her explanation by quoting Jonson's "On Lucy, Countess of Bedford," that "learned and . . . *manly* soul." Fuller has already quoted this passage at the head of her Preface. When she argues with Miranda here, it almost initiates a critique of her own loyalty to men's praise of women: " 'Methinks,' said I, 'you are too fastidious in objecting to this. Jonson in using the word "manly" only meant to heighten the picture of this, the true, the intelligent fate, with one of the deeper colors.' " " 'And yet,' said she," zeroing in on Fuller's vague argument about "deeper colors," "so invariable is the use of this word where a heroic quality is to be described, and I feel so sure that persistence and courage are the most womanly no less than the most manly qualities, that I would exchange these words for others of a larger sense at the risk of marring the fine tissue of the verse. Read, 'a heavenward and instructed soul,' and I should be satisfied" (WNC 104).

The Miranda episode comes to an end as Fuller shuffles between giving men the benefit of the doubt and concurring with Miranda's dim view of relations between the sexes. Whenever a woman has "nobly shone forth in any form of excellence," men have praised her. But here Fuller shifts into satire, for men's "encomiums" are "mortifying; they show too much surprise. Can this be you? he cries to the transfigured Cinderella; well I should never have thought it, but I am very glad. WE will tell every one that you have '*surpassed your sex.*' " Fuller's impatience now lights even on Schiller, in whose poem "Dignity of Woman" she finds "only a great boy to be softened and restrained by the influence of girls." And if "Poets, the elder brothers of their race," are incapable of better, "what can you expect of every-day men?" Even Richter just wanted a wife who would "cook him something good." At this point Fuller unites with Miranda on the "delicate subject" of cooking, defending "in behalf of Miranda and myself" women who keep house (WNC 105).

In the story of Miranda, then, two unresolved issues in Fuller's writing come together: first, the possibility that women whose behavior is ethically ideal cannot bring about, by nonantagonistic means, a general change in male perceptions; and second, the possibility that alluding favorably to men's celebrations of women merely perpetuates inequality based on gender. Avoiding conflict in the name of self-sufficiency or literary tradition, Miranda implies, accomplishes nothing in either the social or the textual domain. Such an ethic makes a difference to the individual woman who lives it, but not to others.

Fuller continues to regret clashes between feminists and society and to use texts by men as incentives for women for the rest of her book's considerable length. She even makes Miranda the agent of allusion in one of the eight appendices that add thirty pages to the volume in a climactic series of extracts. Appendix G is a loosely structured critical essay cum appreciation devoted mostly to the female characters of Euripides and Sophocles, but also touching on Tennyson, James Fenimore Cooper, and Joseph Haydn. Fuller accounts for its inclusion on educational and practical grounds: since she has made "many allusions . . . in the foregoing pages to characters of women drawn by the Greek dramatists, which may not be familiar to the majority of readers," she has "borrowed from the papers of Miranda, some notes upon them." Exposure to these materials offers, she endlessly hopes, "a mental standard, as to what man and woman should be." Allusions, then, are supplemented by further allusions and by commentary on key moments of "pathos" in Greek tragedy that is *less* skeptical than Fuller's writing elsewhere in *Woman.* It is so enthusiastic, in fact, that Fuller attributes it to Miranda's juvenilia: "I trust the girlish tone of apostrophizing rapture may be excused. Miranda was very young at the time of writing, compared with her present mental age. *Now,* she would express the same feelings, but in a worthier garb—if she expressed them at all" (WNC 238, 224–25). If we are to understand why the arguments vested in Miranda do not impede Fuller's habit of quotation and are even subsumed by it, why allusion does not simply represent subservience, and why Fuller is able, in fact, to write the very antagonisms she deplores, we need to go more deeply into the problem of quotation. Quotation and allusion constitute the mature public style of the heterogeneous subject whom we first encountered in Fuller's letters. The tactics of quotation both accentuate cultural differences and create a feeling of sameness as diversity is blurred by the identical textual status of discursive bits.

As in the letters of Fuller's early adulthood, heterogeneity refers not to a random mixture of styles, but to a structured movement among certain discourses and the cultural positions associated with them. The tension between the *effect* of quotation or allusion, which makes the most ordinary utterance into a literary event, and Fuller's often strenuous reference to the literal exacerbates all the questions we have confronted previously about the politics of romantic feminism. On the surface Fuller appears to play off the glamor of literary tradition against the gritty facts of nineteenth-century behavior. But insofar as it is the *speech* of her contemporaries which she most notices, even the realistic portions of the book become theatrical as Fuller finds the legitimate style of aggression.

Fuller breaks out of the pathos of literary reference and into the realm of social satire most sharply when she focuses on the ordinary speech of Americans, especially American males, as they casually exhibit their prejudices about woman's sphere. As an example of men "under the slavery of habit" she introduces a representative anecdote:

> Once two fine figures stood before me, thus. The father of very intellectual aspect, his falcon eye softened by affection as he looked down on his fair child, she the image of himself, only more graceful and brilliant in expression. I was reminded of Southey's Kehama, when lo, the dream was rudely broken. They were talking of education, and he said,
>
> "I shall not have Maria brought too forward. If she knows too much, she will never find a husband; superior women hardly ever can."
>
> "Surely," said his wife, with a blush, "you wish Maria to be as good and wise as she can, whether it will help her to marriage or not."
>
> "No," he persisted, "I want her to have a sphere and a home, and some one to protect her when I am gone." (WNC 165)

Fuller, always moved by closeness between fathers and daughters, characteristically starts to assimilate the pair to an ennobling and colorful poetic context (Southey's "Kehama"), but this impulse receives its comeuppance here. The confident banality of the father's spoken words breaks the "spell" cast by his physiognomy. The "blush" of the mother—who was not mentioned and perhaps not seen until now—enters as the mark of awareness, signifying the contradiction between the father's "intellectual aspect" and his spoken policy.

Fragments of men's derogatory but everyday comments provide Miranda with the grounds for pessimism. She is "above her sex," they say; she "makes the best she can of it"; she is "a manly woman." In her angry attack on the sexual double standard built into the marital economy, Fuller seizes the stock phrases of masculine self-justification in the pincers of feminist paraphrase:[8]

> "You," say the men, "must frown upon vice . . . you must not submit to the will of your husband when it seems to you unworthy, but give the laws in marriage, and redeem it from its present sensual and mental pollutions."
>
>   . . . it has been inculcated on women for centuries, that men have not only stronger passions than they, but of a sort that it would be shameful for them to share or even understand. That, therefore, they must "confide in their husbands," i.e., submit implicitly to their will. . . .
>
>   Accordingly a great part of women look upon men as a kind of wild beasts, but "suppose they are all alike" . . . assured by the married that, "if they knew men as they do . . . they would not expect continence or self-government from them."[9] (WNC 187)

Fuller's elementary but effective translation of mystification into fact is contained in that "i.e.": "they must 'confide in their husbands,' i.e., submit implicitly to their will." The social rules of mutual misunderstanding, according to which women accept both the fact that they should not understand male sexuality and the fact that they themselves cannot be understood by men, are shattered by the descendental vo-

---

[8]The only literary framework for these colloquial moments is the novel, which receives its share of excoriation as a behavioral influence that "give[s] the tone to the manners of some circles." "I do not believe," Fuller interjects, "there ever was put upon record more depravation of man, and more despicable frivolity of thought and aim in woman, than in the novels which purport to give the picture of English fashionable life" (WNC 179). The effect of novels is the precise opposite, therefore, of citations that elevate the nineteenth-century mind above its social contexts.

[9]One example, it is worth noting, inverts the image of Coleridge's patriarch, who censors his children's acquaintance but not their promiscuous reading. Fuller's head of household bans books but sells his daughter into corruption. "'It is indelicate,' says the father or husband, 'to inquire into the private character of such an one. It is sufficient that I do not think him unfit to visit you.' And so, this man, who would not tolerate these pages in his house, 'unfit for family reading,' because they speak plainly, introduces there a man whose shame is written on his brow. . . . The mother affects ignorance, 'supposing he is no worse than most men.' The daughter *is* ignorant; . . . she supposes it is 'woman's lot' not to be perfectly happy in her affections; she has always heard, 'men could not understand women'" (WNC 187–89).

cabulary of "i.e.," the much-repeated "suppose," "inculcate," and so on.

These little satires are structurally and thematically distinct from the literary materials that form the basis for the "mental standard" by which Fuller judges contemporary conversation. In a ten-page catalog of admirable marriages, all derived from literary or historical writings, conversation between exemplary spouses is retold by the appreciative nineteenth-century reader (WNC 136–45). The love of Count Zinzeldorf for his wife is followed by the Indian legend of Flying Pigeon (a paragon of Victorian womanhood, lovingly remembered by her son); this, in turn, is superseded by a veritable binge of quotations from Xenophon on the marriage of Panthea and Abradatus, plus "two more short passages . . . for he is a writer who pleases me well." The unifying "thread" of Fuller's subject, spiritual marriage, produces a selective insensibility to cultural difference and historical specificity which is reflected in her refusal to break down these writings into their constituent phrases, as she does with American speech. The tendency to lengthen quotations and to string them together reflects an inspirational urgency intimately related to the dynamics of sublimity, which in certain modes requires repetition, extension, and velocity of feeling. This is why Fuller's quotations are voluminous when she is favorable but fragmentary when she is hostile.[10]

At the end of *Woman in the Nineteenth Century* Fuller momentarily renounces pathos for the intense clarity of realism and the enjoyment of immediacy: "I stand in the sunny noon of life. Objects no longer glitter in the dews of morning, neither are yet softened by the shadows of evening. Every spot is seen, every chasm revealed." But it is quickly apparent that this moment of poise has not taken Fuller beyond longing. The landscape of the real becomes symbolic of the way past cultures still resonate even in the uncompromising "experience" of the

---

[10]The texts Fuller invariably quotes in their entirety are her own poems, of which she includes four in *Woman in the Nineteenth Century* without identifying herself as the author: "Each Orpheus must to the depths descend" (89); "The temple round" (177–78); "For the Power to whom we bow" (208); and "The Sacred Marriage" (238–39). The first is a psychological retelling of the Orpheus myth; the second, an awkward attempt at pindarics; the third contains the fable of storming the "palace home of King and Queen" and marks the end of the main body of the book; and the fourth, a description of marriage founded on a shared spiritual project, comprises the final appendix. The climactic positioning of these poems indicates that Fuller, like most of her contemporaries, regards poetry as generically privileged when it comes to resounding conclusions.

literary historian sighing over her books: "Climbing the dusty hill, some fair effigies that once stood for symbols of human destiny have been broken; those I still have with me, show defects in this broad light. Yet enough is left, even by experience, to point distinctly to the glories of that destiny; faint, but not to be mistaken streaks of the future day" (WNC 207). The "glitter" and the "softened" lights of prophecy and allusion reenter in the visual effects of the "streaks of . . . day" and the "dusty" effigies. The very style of allegory that Fuller cannot resist despite its anachronism is represented as almost having outlived its inspirational power. Yet, committed to reality, she feels even *within* experience the motions of divinatory witness.

Woman in the Nineteenth Century is the product of exactly such shifts between accuracy and desire, or between idealistic pluralism and feminine psychological difference. Fuller never writes in just this way again. To trace all the changes among this book, her myriad writings for the *Tribune* while she was living in New York between 1844 and 1846, the accounts sent back during her European tour, and her published letters from Rome, not to mention her private correspondence, is impractical here and, I hope, unnecessary. My goal in the final section of this chapter is to demonstrate the complicated differences between *Woman in the Nineteenth Century,* which I regard as a thoroughly if variably romantic work, and the no less romantic texts she produces during the Roman uprising of 1848–49. The effect of these changes is principally to remove sexual difference from its privileged ethical and interpretive position, without abandoning the conviction that the subjective internalization of spiritual law is the basis for social reform.

If woman is displaced as the center of divinatory insight after 1844, however, this does not mean that gender is any less operative in Fuller's discourse. Rather, feminine qualities are attached to the Italian people (particularly Italian men) and, at times, to the city of Rome itself, which becomes Fuller's "home." She embraces the identity of historian as though it, too, were a home. It offers a vocational choice that allows her to experience the "spectacle" of Italian demonstrativeness without feeling that expressive performance inhabits a separate culture from political action. All of this is by way of arguing against the opinion that "Margaret Fuller's career before the period of social and political activity" is best characterized as a "long detour" through romanticism. Fuller's radicalism is inconceivable without its transcendental (not necessarily Transcendentalist) basis and never reaches the point at which "no patriotic idealism veil[s] reality, and she confront[s] class division in all its nakedness."[11] Her idealism never was especially patriotic and, though her sense of class conflict does become sophisticated, it does not derive from a materialist theory.

Fuller in Rome:
"Let it not end in a mere cry of sentiment"

In one of her letters to the New York *Tribune* written in December 1847, Fuller testifies to the clarifying effect, for an educated American, of European travel: "What was but picture to us becomes reality; remote allusions and derivations trouble no more: we see the pattern of the stuff and understand the whole tapestry. There is a gradual clearing up on many points, and many baseless notions and crude fancies are dropped" (NYT Jan 1 1848). This observation can be taken as a comment on Fuller's style as well as on her material. Comparing *Woman in the Nineteenth Century* to Fuller's newspaper pieces, readers have repeatedly testified to the impression that they are moving from "picture" to "reality," from "allusions and derivations" to the "stuff" of experience, from "baseless notions and crude fancies" to an easy sense of "pattern." Instead of finding classical texts to verify the workings of mind over time, Fuller locates intimations of spirituality in present needs, crises, and attempts at reform and in recent books. In her Italian experience, allusion and reference are no longer distinguishable. This is precisely what she means when she says that "remote allusions . . . trouble no more": all "allusion" invokes something remote and alienated, but by living among one's sources, the cultural past becomes domesticated. Particularly in the dramatic circumstances of 1848 and 1849, Rome could become the locale of an entirely pragmatic romanticism, in which journalism did not have to give up prophetic sensations in its account of the obvious. Fuller is relieved from strenuous movement between the aestheticized past and the literal present. In her letters to the *Tribune* these tensions are transposed into the relation

[11]Although I disagree with Chevigny on the interpretation of Fuller's political development, I find entirely persuasive her account of the dynamics of Fuller's sexual involvements, her relationship with her husband or lover, Ossoli, and her feelings about the child she had with him. Chevigny is particularly astute in identifying the ways in which Fuller negotiated these familial attachments so as to gratify needs associated with her childhood as well as the need for resistance and autonomy. Her suggestion that Fuller identified Ossoli and her mother with the same kind of affection is especially striking. Bell Gale Chevigny, *The Woman and the Myth: Margaret Fuller's Life and Writings* (Old Westbury: Feminist Press, 1976), 282–83, 294, 366–97.

between her descriptions of the painterly effects of Rome and her chronicle of events there.

If allusion is 'cleared up' or domesticated and a romantic reading of history no longer needs to be sustained by an elaborate mythic apparatus, what happens to Fuller's anxiety about the aggressiveness of radical statement? Her emphasis in *Woman* on the nonconflictual character of feminism was supported by the logic of moral differences between the sexes, which guaranteed woman's capacity for ethical mediation. Does sexual difference in the realm of ethical interpretation become less necessary as Fuller, faced with armed conflict, worries less about the perceived violence of protest literature? And if, as I think they do, Fuller's unique claims for the feminine greatly diminish in these years, where does she then locate the qualities of divination, feeling, and expressiveness she had formerly associated with feminine subjectivity, and what are the political implications of this revision?

In the first stage of her European travels in England, as in her journalistic period in New York, Fuller focuses persistently on the status of women but has almost nothing to say about the idea of woman. She seeks out the unglamorous and innovative instance, not as though the argument about women's position were settled, but as though exemplification were an adequate form of polemic. Her marvelous description of "an establishment for washing clothes" in London rivals her defense of old maids in *Woman in the Nineteenth Century* in its insight into the human costs of keeping house. "Especially the drying closets," she writes, "I contemplated with great satisfaction." Fuller finds the renowned Reform Club only "*stupidly* comfortable," lacking "that elegant arrangement and vivacious atmosphere which only women can inspire." The all-male kitchen staff meets with her approval, however. "I was not sorry," she notes, "to see men predominant in the cooking department, as I hope to see that and washing transferred to their care in the progress of things" (NYT Mar 3 1847, Feb 19 1847).

Of her authorial relationship to London out of season, she writes, "with my way of viewing things," it offers "an inexhaustible studio." As artist, witness, and interpreter, "I would live there for years obscure in some corner," issuing forth "to watch unobserved the vast stream of life, or to decipher the hieroglyphics which ages have been inscribing on the walls of this vast palace," an edifice reared for "human culture" but never yet "used efficaciously." Her reports on women, such as the account of her visit to Joanna Baillie and the praise of women painters which follows, belong to her observations on the "stream of life" and far less to the "hieroglyphics" of the past. In London the retrospective sense of the "ages" comes through powerfully in the almost mournful tone that colors her response to "that pomp . . . of . . . luxury in contrast with the misery, squalid, agonizing, ruffianly, which stares one in the face in every street of London, and hoots at the gates of her palaces more ominous a note than ever was that of owl or raven in the portentous times when empires and races have crumbled . . . from inward decay" (NYT Feb 2 1847, Jan 26 1849).

If Fuller's later residence in Rome "sharpened my perception as to the ills of woman's condition and remedies that must be applied," the feminist cause confronts her there also, as part of a more multifarious "battle with giant wrongs." It becomes part of Fuller's sense of her radical vocation to articulate the waste and violence of history, the economy of suffering in which the class divisions of modern Europe form the latest episode. Writing from Paris, she registers a "prayer, daily more fervent," for "peaceful revolution," uttered in a mood of pity. Her pity, itself a gesture of class reconciliation, extends to the poor; to the "English noble" with his "Sad" dilemma of possessing "that for which so many thousands are perishing"; and to the middle classes, who, like herself, see "too close . . . the evils they cannot obviate, the sorrows they cannot relieve." Reflecting a year later, from Rome, on the position of the "thinking American" abroad, she describes in more sweeping terms the pressure of loss that both causes and inhibits political change:

> The history of our planet in some moments seems so painfully mean and little, such terrible bafflings and failures to compensate some brilliant successes . . . above all, so little achieved for Humanity as a whole, such tides of war and pestilence intervening to blot out the traces of each triumph, that no wonder if the strongest soul sometimes pauses aghast. . . .
>
> . . . see this hollow England . . . see this poor France . . . which could not escape from a false position with all its baptism of blood; see that lost Poland, and this Italy bound down by treacherous hands in all the force of genius; see Russia with its brutal Czar and innumerable slaves; see Austria and its royalty that represents nothing and its people, who, as people, are and have nothing! If we consider the amount of truth that has really been spoken out in the world . . . the public failure seems amazing, seems monstrous. (NYT Feb 2 1847, Jan 1 1848)

The amazement of the chronicler who stands "aghast" but who also calls others to "see . . . see" grows out of the dynamics of what we might call the postimperial sublime. Fuller's catalogs are similar in kind to the passages in which she linked the cause of American women with the battle against slavery and the defense of Indian rights in *Woman in the Nineteenth Century,* though far wider in extent and more emotional in tone. In *Woman* the feminine capacity for divinatory insight and "impassioned sensibility" resulted in the tendency to suffer from the condition of being *"over-*flowed with thought" (WNC 152–53). In Fuller's European writings this empathetic potential belongs to the involved historian, but her pain (speaking now from the point of view of the authorial subject) is relieved of its neurotic or self-destructive quality because it emerges in response to the generalized suffering of humanity. Fuller avoids the double bind of the feminist who, angry at injustice, is held to a special moral standard of peaceableness and goodwill. At the same time, she enters into a vision of inclusive belonging which feeds into the sense of coming "home" to Rome.

The home-like quality of Rome arises from the intimacy of one's relation to it, from the way in which knowledge depends on love. On the spectrum marked out in *Woman* by the Muse and Minerva, Rome is undoubtedly the Muse: "Yet I find that it is quite out of the question to know Italy; to say anything of her that is full and sweet, so as to convey any idea of her spirit, without long residence . . . and without an intimacy of feeling, an abandonment to the spirit of the place, impossible to most Americans." "Abandonment" takes on a different meaning in a passage written almost two years later, on Fuller's return to Rome after the birth of her son. Here, Rome is at once a fascinating woman of electromagnetic appeal, seducing Fuller, and a maternal sanctuary of "repose":

> Rome so beautiful, so great; her presence stupefies, and one has to withdraw to prize the treasures she has given. City of the Soul! yes, it is *that;* the very dust magnetizes you, and thousand spells have been chaining you in every careless, every murmuring moment. Yes! Rome, however seen, thou must be still adored; and every hour of absence or presence must deepen love with one who has known what it is to repose in thy arms.

The passionate intimacy with a city that "reveals herself day by day" and "tells me some of her life" conforms to the ethics of the "dialogue of love" which has recurred throughout this study as a trope for nonexploitative understanding. The antithesis of "the scorch and dust of foreign invasion (the invasion of the *dilettanti* I mean)," this divinatory and feminine exchange is Fuller's way of dissociating herself from cultural imperialism (particularly that of the British, "the most unseeing of all possible animals") (NYT Aug 5 1847, Jan 26 1849, Jan 26 1848).[12]

Fuller's romance with Rome is complicated by her strong feelings of identification with Italians. She characterizes Italians in stereotypical terms as passionate, intuitive, expressive, naturally artistic and theatrical, and instinctively restrained when appropriate: precisely those qualities that were defined as feminine in *Woman in the Nineteenth Century*. But the aura Fuller bestows on the Italians derives from the fact that she sees their passion as unencumbered by the painful self-consciousness that afflicts the women of industrialized nations.[13] In the eyes of Mazzini's pupils in England, "that Italian fire that has done so much to warm the world glows out." She sees, in her first encounter with Italians, the "capacity for pure, exalting passion" in their faces and exclaims, "The fulfillment of a hope!" The Roman crowd displays a "natural eloquence and . . . lively sensibility to what is great and beautiful," and the wounded fighters Fuller nurses embody for her the capacity for "childlike radiant" inspiration (NYT Feb 19 1847, May 29 1847, June 13 1848, July 23 1849).

Partly because Fuller defines them as wholly passional and rarely critical, Italians as she sees them do not suffer from the conflict between expression and analysis. Their struggle for self-reliance is not individual, but collective; the mental costs of opposing a foreign enemy are minimal compared to those incurred by the individual feminist. Surrounded by such a population, Fuller no longer feels that she represents an alienated intensity. As in her apprehension of humanity's universal suffering, she tends to disperse qualities that were gendered in *Woman in the Nineteenth Century* among groups defined by race, class, or political status.

Fuller's plan to write the history of the Italian Revolution flows from her choice of the historian's identity; this identity derives, in turn, from

[12]For an account of Fuller's activities during her residence in Rome, see Joseph Jay Deiss, *The Roman Years of Margaret Fuller* (New York: T. Y. Crowell, 1969).

[13]Fuller comments more on Italian men than Italian women, but she extends the talent for unconstrained expressiveness and feeling to the latter as well, who thus do not exhibit the conflicts felt by American and Northern European women. Fuller's perceptions of Italian women are determined by their Mediterranean character rather than by their sex, except when she is focusing specifically on sexual oppression (NYT Jan 26 1849).

the ethos of response that structures her relation to Italy. "Of this great drama I have much to write," she announces in December 1848. "The materials are over-rich. I have bought my right in them by much sympathetic suffering." The richness of Fuller's "materials" corresponds to the richness of her sympathy, a justification of the historian's task which subsumes the criteria of expertise and research Fuller always honored. As "Ambassador" and "sister," her relation to the rebellion is defined by the vicarious logic that structures all her accounts of Italy: "I suffer to see these temples of the soul thus broken . . . but I would not, for much, have missed seeing it all." The relationship among suffering, "spectacles," and consolation emerges clearly in the next sentence, as she anticipates how the "memory of it will console amid the spectacles of meanness, selfishness, and faithlessness which life may yet have in store" (NYT Jan 19 1849, Jan 26 1849, Aug 11 1849).

Fuller's chronicle derives its authority from its status as an eyewitness account, but the act of observation is inseparable from the reflex of feeling, which in turn depends on the construction of narrative in terms of spectacle:

> I passed into the Ripetta, and entered the Church of *San Luigi dei Francesi*. The Republican flag was flying at the door. . . . I looked at the monument Chateaubriand erected when here. . . . and gazed anew on those magnificent representations of . . . St. Cecilia. . . . I love to think of those angel visits. . . .
>
> Leaving the church, I passed along toward the *Piazza del Popolo*. . . . I heard the drums beating. . . .
>
> I climbed the Pincian to see better. There is no place so fine for anything of this kind as the Piazza del Popolo, it is so full of light, so fair and grand, the obelisk and fountain make so fine a center to all kinds of groups.
>
> I returned to the house, which is very near the Quirinal. . . . Presently I saw the carriage of Prince Barberini drive hurriedly into his court-yard gate. (NYT Jan 26 1849)

Political action is aestheticized not only because it is staged by the picturesque Italians, but because the historian is an artist, seeking out the vantage points from which to be moved and stirred. Rome's status as a living museum incorporates the performative rituals of revolution as one more series of masterpieces. For all of Fuller's efforts to avoid being one of the "dilettanti," one of the sensation-seeking northerners who devour Italy's picturesque views, she comes very close to doing the same thing herself, and not simply in the pages of the *Tribune*. Indeed, it is her nervousness about the resemblance between her narratives and conventional tourism which makes the demonstration of family sympathies necessary. For Fuller, aesthetic pleasure has to be earned by the ability to read correctly the power relations represented in the scene before her.

When a circular is published granting "a sort of representative council," for example, the brilliantly choreographed torchlight procession signifies the fact that this "limited . . . improvement" was nonetheless "a great measure for Rome."[14] The interdependence of political spectacle, sympathetic witness, aesthetic sensation, and ideological understanding is spelled out explicitly in Fuller's account of another crowd scene:

> Between each of these expressive sentences the speaker paused; the great bell of the Capitol gave forth its solemn melodies; the cannon answered; while the crowd shouted, *Viva la Republica! Viva Italia!*
>
> The imposing grandeur of the spectacle to me gave new force to the emotion that already swelled my heart; my nerves thrilled; and I longed to see in some answering glance . . . a little of that soul which made my country what she is. The American at my side remained impassive. Receiving all his birthright from a triumph of Democracy, he was quite indifferent to this manifestation on this consecrated spot. Passing the winter in Rome to study Art, he was insensible to the artistic beauty of the scene—insensible to this new life of that spirit from which all the forms he gazes at in galleries emanated. He "did not see the *use* of these popular demonstrations."
>
> . . . . He said, "*The people* seem only to be looking on; they take no part."
>
> "What people?" said I.
>
> "Why, these round us; there is no other people."
>
> There are a few beggars, errand-boys, and nurse-maids.
>
> "The others are only soldiers."
>
> "Soldiers! The Civic Guard! all the decent men in Rome."

14"I saw them first assembled in the Piazza del Popolo, forming around its fountain a great circle of fire.—Then, as a river of fire, they streamed slowly through the Corso, on their way to the Quirinal to thank the Pope, upbearing a banner on which the edict was printed. The stream of fire advanced slowly with a perpetual surge-like sound of voices; the torches flashed on the animated Italian faces. I have never seen anything finer. Ascending the Quirinal they made it a mound of light. Bengal fires were thrown up, which cast their red and white light on the noble Greek figures of men and horses that reign over it. The Pope appeared on his balcony; the crowd shouted three vivas; he extended his arms; the crowd fell on their knees and received his benediction; he retired, and the torches were extinguished, and the multitude dispersed in an instant" (NYT Aug 5 1847).

The failure to see "soldiers" as "the people"—a failure based on a lack of detailed political information—makes Fuller's representative American unable to perceive the link between "spirit" and "forms" and thus incapable of responding to her desire for an "answering glance" of emotion. It "requires much acquaintance, much thought, much reference to books," she writes elsewhere, for Americans to realize that phenomena which look like "a senseless mass of juggleries to the uninformed eye" are in fact "growths of the human spirit struggling to develop its life, and full of instruction for those who learn to understand them" (NYT April 4 1849, Jan 26 1848). Spectacle, speaking to the informed eye, mediates between subjectivity and public life for Fuller. As verbal performance fulfilled the 'interpretive' function of externalizing the private experience of women in Fuller's Conversations, and as allusion called attention to the mutual influence of text and social vision in *Woman in the Nineteenth Century,* so the crowd scenes of the Roman Revolution transform public events into the observer's private emotion even as they provide a social medium for the feelings of the participants.

The climax of Fuller's writing in this mode, and, indeed, the visual and rhetorical climax of her whole series of letters on the Revolution, comes at the moment of defeat when French troops are about to enter the city. "I went into the Corso with some friends," she begins. And suddenly, "the lancers of Garibaldi galloped along in full career." The novelistic sheen of this costume drama is not lost on Fuller, who immediately invokes the master of historical fiction: "I longed for Sir Walter Scott to be on earth again, and see them" in their erotic glory, "light, athletic, resolute figures . . . the finest manly beauty of the South, all sparkling with its genius and ennobled by the resolute spirit, ready to dare, to do, to die." In the absence of Scott, Fuller herself depicts the union of beauty, pain, and ideological integrity in the ensuing tableau in the piazza of St. John Lateran:

Never have I seen a sight so beautiful, so romantic, and so sad. Whoever knows Rome knows the peculiar solemn grandeur of that piazza . . . the obelisk standing fairest of any of those most imposing monuments of Rome, the view through the gates of the Campagna, on that side so richly strewn with ruins. The sun was setting, the crescent moon rising, the flower of the Italian youth were marshalling in that solemn place. . . . They must now go or remain prisoners and slaves. . . . They had all put on the beautiful dress of the Garibaldi legion, the tunic of bright red cloth, the Greek cap, or else round hat with Puritan plume, their long hair was blown back from resolute faces; all looked full of courage. They had counted the cost before they entered on this perilous struggle; they had weighed life and all its material advantages against liberty, and made their election. . . . [Garibaldi] himself was distinguished by the white bour-nouse [tunic]; his look was entirely that of a hero of the middle ages, his face still young, for the excitements of his life, though so many, have all been youthful, and there is no fatigue upon his brow or cheek. . . . Hard was the heart . . . that had no tear for that moment. Go, fated, gallant band! . . . And Rome, anew the Niobe! (NYT 11 Aug 1849)

The role of spectator in relation to these masculine glories is intrinsically feminine in Fuller's construction of the scene. Her own emotion joins with the maternal tears of the suffering city to make violence in an idealistic cause legitimate.

Framing warfare in scenes like these contributes to the apparently nonproblematic status of violence in Fuller's Roman writings. The violence of woman's temperament and rhetoric was the source of her deepest anxieties for many years. Bearing witness to history as the panorama of suffering inflicted by the violent is a major concern of the *Tribune* letters from Rome. But revolutionary violence seems to strike her as a foregone and wholly justifiable conclusion. There is perhaps an element of relief for Fuller in seeing violence externalized rather than felt as a savage personal impulse, as there was in seeing passion and suffering played out visibly before her. Fuller's own passional life was so powerfully shaped by fantasies of heroism, including military hero-ism, that a degree of vicarious wish fulfillment may also be at work. The question of violence continues to operate in terms of gender, therefore, even though Fuller's feminist critique is in abeyance.[15]

---

[15]In a remarkable letter to her New York Quaker friends Marcus and Rebecca Spring, Fuller wrestles with her position on revolutionary violence, shifting between the memory of recent bloodshed and projected scenes of righteous self-defense. She concludes that she is "consistent no way" but cannot imagine a Christ who was not consoled, at his death, by a "prophetic" vision of the crusades: "What you say is deeply true about the peace way being the best. If any one see clearly how to work in that way, let him in God's name. . . . Meanwhile I am not sure that I can keep my hands free from blood. I doubt I have not the strength. . . . You, Marcus, could you let a Croat insult Rebecca, carry off Eddie to be an Austrian serf; and leave little Marcus bleeding in the dust? Yet it is true that while Moses slew the Egyptian, Christ stood to be spit upon. . . . You have the truth, you have the right, but could you act it, Marcus in all circumstances? Stifled under the Roman priesthood would you not have thrown it off with all your force? . . . If so, you are a Christian; you know I never pretended to be except in dabs and sparkles here and there. Yet the agonies of that baptism of blood I felt Oh how deeply in the golden June days of Rome. Consistent no way I felt I should have shrunk back. I could not have had it shed. Christ did not have to see his dear ones pass the dark river; he could go alone; however, in prophetic spirit no doubt, he

If making war and dying in it are masculine pursuits, mourning and history writing—a significant conjunction of the epitaphic and the radical—are feminine ones in Fuller's texts of the late 1840s. The effect of violence on women is displaced onto the body of Rome as the revolution's theater becomes its retrospective voice:

> A Contadini showed me where thirty-seven braves are buried beneath a heap of wall that fell upon them in the shock of one cannonade. A marble nymph, with broken arm, looked sadly that way from her sun-dried fountain; some roses were blooming still, some red oleanders, amid the ruin. The sun was casting its last light on the mountains on the tranquil, sad Campagna, that sees one leaf more turned in the book of woe. . . . I then entered the French ground, all mapped and hollowed like a honeycomb. A pair of skeleton legs protruded from a bank of one barricade; lower a dog had scratched away its light covering of earth from the body of a man, and discovered it lying face upward all dressed; the dog stood gazing on it with an air of stupid amazement. (NYT 11 Aug 1849)

The thirty-seven buried soldiers and the exposed limbs and face of two more seem to have their female counterpart in the nymph with the broken arm. But her position is significantly different. She embodies the look of sadness that Rome casts over itself and that Fuller casts over Rome. In the conjunction of the marble nymph, the oleander, and the corpse Fuller joins in a powerful vignette the imperial past, picturesque nature, and the bare immediacy of death. In this passage it is the last that seems to govern.

The dog's expression of "stupid amazement" instantly produces, "at that moment" and in Fuller's letter, the thought of America. Whether the dog's shock is what Americans should be feeling and are not, or whether the dog's stupidity reminds Fuller of her ineffectual compatriots, she launches at once into a diatribe stimulated by "recalling some letters received": "O men and women of America, spared these frightful sights, these sudden wrecks of every hope, what angel of heaven do you suppose has time to listen to your tales of morbid woe?" Whatever specific reference is contained in the tales of woe, their politi-

---

foresaw the crusades" (LMF V 295–96). Fuller treats her susceptibility to the glories of resistance as a temptation, a lack of "strength" that she feels most strongly when confronted with the 'stifling' effects of oppressive authority. She oscillates between arousal and horror, each emotion linked to a particular scenic effect: resistance to the Austrians, the recent "baptism of blood," and the crucifixion, in which the two impulses compete.

cal meaning quickly becomes clear: "I see you have meetings, where you speak of the Italians, the Hungarians. I pray you *do something;* let it not end in a mere cry of sentiment. . . . Send . . . money, send cheer—acknowledge as the legitimate leaders and rulers those men who represent the people, who understand its wants, who are ready to die or to live for their good" (NYT Aug 11 1849).

Fuller has already, and more than once, celebrated Rome itself as the embodiment of a "cry of sentiment." In a passage that comes close to the preoccupations of a remarkable letter to Marcus and Rebecca Spring (see note 15), the ruin of Rome induces more emotional writing than either the social degradations of war or the sensations of the wounded. "War near at hand seems to me even more dreadful than I had fancied it," she admits. Despite its capacity to inspire, "it breeds . . . drunkenness, mental dissipation," family separations, and economic waste.

> And the ruin that ensues, how terrible. Let those who have ever passed happy days in Rome grieve to hear that the beautiful plantations of *Villa Borghese*—that chief delight and refreshment of citizens, foreigners, and little children—are laid low, as far as the obelisk. The fountain, singing alone amid the fallen groves, cannot be seen and heard without tears; it seems like some innocent infant calling and crowing amid dead bodies on a field which battle has strewn with the bodies of those who once cherished it. . . . Rome is shorn of the locks which lent grace to her venerable brow. She looks desolate, profaned. I feel what I never expected to, as if I might by and by be willing to leave Rome.

The next paragraph begins, "Then I have, for the first time, seen what wounded men suffer," but quickly turns to an indignant account of French falsehood (NYT June 23 1849). The fountain, which calls forth the tears of the listener, is the "cry of sentiment" that constitutes the aftermath of violence. The maternal pathos induced by the image of the orphaned child among the bodies resembles the sad gaze of the marble nymph amid exposed corpses. Sentiment has all along been fundamental to Fuller's radicalism, and these images of the failed revolution do not undermine, but rather reinforce, the power of feminized emotion to fill in with commemorative voices the times between military and political engagements. It was Fuller, after all, who in an earlier and more sanguine phase of the rebellion suggested that an appropriate expression of American support would be a cannon. It would be used, of course, in spectacles, but its literal deployment as a weapon is left in doubt: "It would please me much to see a cannon here bought by the contributions of Americans . . . to be used by the Guard for salutes on festive occasions, if they should be so happy as to have no more serious need" (NYT Nov 27 1847). The cannon would provide a cry of sentiment that, by a rapid shift of context, could become a "serious" or literal attack. Its gratifying symbolic expressiveness and ambiguous military potential make it an appropriate image for Fuller's fascination with the ethical status of women's voices in a radical setting.

It is irresistible but also appropriate to follow the link between cannons and canons. Fuller's ceremonial artillery emerges from the same sense of discursive politics which led her to write, in 1844, "it is not in vain that the verbal statement has been made, 'All men are born free and equal.'" In her reflections on the meaning of the French Revolution, she had stressed its continuing power as historical text: "Europe is conning a valued lesson from the blood-stained page." If "truth was prophesied in the ravings of that hideous fever," the truth can continue to operate beyond the appalling violence caused by the reaction to "long ignorance and abuse." American readers should make themselves susceptible to the prophecy, for the "same tendencies, farther unfolded, will bear good fruit in this country" (WNC 90–92).

By implication, both the events of the Roman rebellion and Fuller's writings about them enter into the canon of works capable of generating new motions of change. As entities that are produced by violence and that point forward to the chance of future combat, such histories take on the virtual status of Fuller's cannon. The gun, which, she suggests, should even be named ("the AMERIGO, the COLUMBO, or the WASHINGTON"), is the gift of American *readers*—those whose principal access to European events comes through newspapers (NYT Nov 27 1847). Political activity is part of a spectrum or cycle of signifying practices which moves from reform or military measures through historical text and memory, through the process of reading and interpretation, through the returning gift of weapons to be deployed both symbolically and literally. The same logic governs Fuller's development of a feminist tradition in which many of the prophetic texts are feminist not in intent or context, but in their later interpretations. The double entendre of cannons and canon applies best of all, perhaps, to the status of Fuller's writings in feminist criticism of the late twentieth century. For it is here that the contested romantic equation of allusion, subjectivity, and radical action continues to operate, within a skeptical view of romanticism itself.

Index

Library of Congress Cataloging-in-Publication Data

Ellison, Julie
  Delicate subjects : romanticism, gender, and the ethics of understanding / Julie Ellison.
    p. cm.
  Includes bibliographical references.
  ISBN 0-8014-2378-3 (alk. paper)
  1. English literature—19th century—History and criticism—Theory, etc.
2. Romanticism. 3. Sex roles in literature. 4. Feminism and literature. 5. Ethics in
literature. 6. Schleiermacher, Friedrich, 1768–1834—Criticism and interpretation.
7. Coleridge, Samuel Taylor, 1772–1834—Criticism and interpretation. 8. Fuller,
Margaret, 1810–1850—Criticism and interpretation. I. Title.
PR457.E5 1990
820.9'145—dc20   89-45979